THE
DISCIPLINE
OF POWER

THE
DISCIPLINE
OF POWER

Essentials of a Modern World Structure

by George W. Ball

An Atlantic Monthly Press Book

LITTLE, BROWN AND COMPANY · BOSTON · TORONTO

LIBRARY OF CONGRESS CATALOG CARD NO. 67-28228

FIRST EDITION

The lines quoted on page 155 are from W. H. Auden's
poem "September 1, 1939," which appears in his *Collected
Poetry;* and are reprinted here by kind permission of Random House, Inc., and Faber & Faber Ltd.

ATLANTIC-LITTLE, BROWN BOOKS
ARE PUBLISHED BY
LITTLE, BROWN AND COMPANY
IN ASSOCIATION WITH
THE ATLANTIC MONTHLY PRESS

*Published simultaneously in Canada
by Little, Brown & Company (Canada) Limited*

PRINTED IN THE UNITED STATES OF AMERICA

To R.M.B.

with love

Acknowledgments

I AM indebted to many people for the ideas that have gone into this book. Several of my friends have read all or bits of it at various stages of its parturition but I shall not mention their names, since, even with the customary disclaimer, they might feel compromised by some of its heresies.

I do owe particular thanks to my son Douglas B. Ball, who by embarrassing me with facts has deprived the world of some startling historical insights, as well as to that redoubtable fellow, John F. Campbell, who, in spite of his training as a professional diplomat — and a good one at that — can still look a simple declarative sentence in the eye without blanching.

And finally my gratitude to Joan McCarthy and Aimee Allen. It has been their special privilege to transcribe any number of dictaphone tapes recorded over the roar of jet engines and to bear with my whims and humors during a period when I was trying to do far too many things at one time.

G. W. B.

Contents

THE
DISCIPLINE
OF POWER

Introduction

THIS book reflects my personal experience covering more than three decades near the center and on the periphery of foreign policy on both sides of the Atlantic. It stems more immediately from nearly six years' service in the Department of State under Presidents Kennedy and Johnson.

Yet this is not a memoir. It reveals no state secrets. It discloses no personal confidences. It is instead a book of argument — an attempt to illuminate the central problem that has absorbed my interest in and out of government for thirty-five years: how free men can organize their power in a rational way. In other words, how can we, under the brooding omnipresence of weapons of mass death and brutish nihilism, stay civilized and get on with the world's pressing business of ending poverty and injustice and securing peace?

For a variety of reasons — call them historical accidents if you will — the answers to this question must be principally provided by a handful of highly industrialized Western nations that by their action, or inaction, will go far to shape the future. That is why this book is addressed as much to Europeans as to Americans, for it is the peoples of those two continents who command the lion's share of world power, possess the most advanced technology, and enjoy in common a humane tradition that asserts for man an unprecedented degree of dignity and liberty and rationality. This book is about them and about how they must modify their obsolete political structures and nostalgic habits of thought if the world is to be spared further calamity and if mankind is to prevail over accident and cynicism and blind compulsion.

As ambitious as this may seem, there are large omissions in the pages that follow. One will find nothing in this book about "world peace through world law," noble as that sentiment may sound. There are only a few references to the United Nations in spite of its essential value as an instrument of peace (as I found through direct experience with crises in Cyprus and the Congo and other troubled parts of the world). Nor have I suggested any novel solution to the Vietnam conflict, although I fully recognize the stakes at risk for all of us.

For none of these subjects could be adequately treated in a few pages or paragraphs. Their omission involves more than a desire for symmetry and stylistic unity; I have not thought it wise to make large digressions from the central theme of the book. The argument is, I think, reasonably self-contained and I hope that the reader will assess it within its own terms of reference.

Although this is not a memoir, I have drawn on my personal recollection of events to illustrate an occasional point. My years in the Department of State left me with rich experiences, warm friendships and deep loyalties shared with Secretary Rusk and my other colleagues as well as with two strong and able Presidents. I feel an obligation to them as well as to myself to continue, in private life, the discussion of those critical issues of foreign policy that we undertook together as a high public responsibility — and from a selfish point of view the process of systematically setting down my thoughts (or prejudices) has been useful as a discipline and catharsis.

In these days there is a great deal of talking and writing about foreign policy, but there can never be too much, since there is an insatiable need for fresh insights and new appraisals. And in a time when men try to build the future with a political architecture that depends on the precarious balance of giant forces, we Americans and Europeans, in and out of chancelleries, must all continually search for an answer to the question posed by Faust's servitor:

"How shall our counsel serve to lead mankind?"

I

The Need for Reassessment

D URING the long millennia of history when time seemed to stand still, men spent their lives in speculation as to their ultimate fate. Now in the last third of the twentieth century, caught in a whirlwind of accelerating change, we are so bedeviled by the demands of a shifting environment that we rarely ponder where events may lead us even a decade hence.

Consider some of the things that have occurred in the brief time span of a generation. Famous empires have been dismantled piece by piece. New states have been created by the carload lot — more than sixty of them. Nuclear science has given a handful of men on opposite sides of an argument the power to blow up a large part of the human race, while jets and satellites and television cameras and computers have revised our concepts of time and space.

In the new politics as in the new technology the only constant is change. In a time of troubles, a period of scattered but persistent violence, the threat of a general world conflict haunts homes as well as foreign offices, but it is not nuclear death alone that threatens and preoccupies us. Ever since 1945, the year of the bomb, we have found no better word than "explosion" to describe much that has occurred in widely separated areas — an explosion in population and productivity, an explosion in the power of armies and scientists, an explosion in the hopes and demands of poor nations and the thirst for justice of the disadvantaged.

To cope with such cataclysmic events men have turned largely to government. But now the pace of change — social and scientific and political — is taxing our political capacities. Not only the atomic peril but crowding and confusion and conflict in great and small nations — more people breathing dirtier air and wasting a finite source of clean water and hydro power, more men shooting at each other in the Middle East and Mississippi and the rain forests of Southeast Asia for the same old reasons of avarice, or racial or tribal contempt, or lust for power — all these things threaten civilized mankind with a reversion to the primitive, the time when "Whirl was King."

No one can be sure what we are witnessing — whether the dawn of a new age of reason and progress, or a gigantic "back to nature" movement on a world scale — because this is an interval when men are caught up in revolutions they neither fully comprehend nor control, revolutions that may be only a prelude to further cycles of violence. New tyrannies threaten to overtake us as we discard old forms of oppression; social disorganization tears at the fragile fabric of civil government. Whether man with his large brain will be able to transmute the crass stuff of natural force into something better and safer for himself and his fellows — in short, whether "civilization" is possible — is a question no easier to answer today than at the first spawning of the species.

This book deals with only one aspect, but a most important aspect, of human civilization that is now under stress, the political side of the larger social prism: the systems and structures by which nations and governments conduct their affairs and live together amid the shifting forces and strains of modern life. At the moment, such structures are in desperate need of rethinking, and of rethinking with a purpose, for the shattering changes of the past two decades, in a climate of persistent danger, compel necessary if unpleasant decisions. Mankind must adjust to the modern world or be destroyed by it. Politicians must take account of its requirements. Each major nation must reassess its own national interest and redefine its role. And, particularly in the United States, it is essential that men ponder and puzzle — as I tried to do in nearly six years of public life — how the leading nations can effectively employ the vast but finite power that is their peculiar blessing and burden.

To reassess the national interest in the terms I have suggested is damnably difficult, requiring tough-mindedness and the avoidance of moralistic mush. It is no job for the starry-eyed and even less for the stodgy, nor can one expect much from those political leaders who survive by milking the clichés of the past. So I do not find it astonishing that in the fast-changing world of the last twenty years no state has successfully redefined its role — nor even completed the self-analysis at home that must precede an effective reassessment abroad. It may be too much to expect complete rationality in appraising all that has happened since 1945, but this does not excuse us from making the effort, since, as Hamilton pointed out, if we fail to follow the path of "reflection and choice," we will be "forever destined to depend . . . on accident and force."

In the course of this book I shall try to give some shape and substance to a workable concept of national interest while taking full account of the political realities, since a clear identification of our own national interest subsumes the essence of what this book is all about. I recognize, however, that no matter how thoughtfully defined, even the national interest is not a fixed point of reference, not something precise and immutable; the most one can hope to achieve is a kind of navigational fix for a nation buffeted by winds of change that have been blowing with gale force on anybody's Beaufort scale.

These winds have tended to foreshorten time. In no more than two decades, the span of a generation, they have, in an accelerating sequence, blown down old structures and blown in new ones, unleashing a series of events that, in terms of all earlier experience, could have occurred only over centuries. It is hardly surprising that these events have called into doubt many of the institutional arrangements by which we live, since it is to mankind's eternal embarrassment that human institutions have never kept pace with human requirements. Today, however, the gap that separates the two is large, ominous and ever widening, for at a time when old political forms are crumbling there has also been a quantum-jump in the rate of social change. Instead of a rational mold to contain and give meaning to the new wants and capacities of an evolving human society there have been voids and vacuums as the old political containers crack and decay.

Few will quarrel with the immensity of the shifts and movements that have defined our new environment or the explosive character of the events that have brought them about. And I am willing to wager that, though there may be argument as to the relative and absolute significance of those events, there will be little dispute as to the identity of the main changes of the last decades.

One begins of necessity with the cold war since the division of the world into two competing parts has left its mark on almost everything else that has occurred. It has led to an ugly and interminable arms race, brought about the creation of the Western alliance, provided cement for European unity, drained from the United Nations much of the purpose for which it was created, pushed the United States into two troublesome shooting wars, cluttered up our democratic society with compulsory military service, hastened the dismantling of the great colonial systems, and made the less developed nations of the world a battleground for competing ideological and power plays. We have lived so intensely with the cold war that it would be hard for us to comprehend a world in which it did not distort the relations among countries and peoples.

As late as 1941 many Americans still believed that isolationism was an acceptable way of life and that our country might cultivate its own garden without concern for the drought and blight and grassfires in the other gardens around us. But awakened by the World War and alarmed by the cold war that followed, we became deeply absorbed in what other people were doing. In our anxiety to prevent the Communist nations from extending their dominion, we worked with an alerted Europe to build a dike against Soviet expansion, and later undertook — perhaps unwisely — to enlist other allies in the construction of an elaborate *cordon sanitaire* around the whole outer limits of Communist power. We deployed our men and resources to trouble spots in the far reaches of the world.

Under the conditions of even a quarter-century ago we could have accepted the ordeal of a continuing struggle with a remote adversary like Russia without serious fear for our homeland. But the advent of nuclear weapons has brought us face to face with a new reality that has undercut the confident and optimistic view which has been the distinctive heritage of America. The bomb has injected an additional and ominous unknown into the already complex equation of our international relations — the vivid symbol of mankind's ancient preoccupation: the concept of last things, finality, the end of the world. It has been this force, this fact with all its awful implications, the existence of weapons controlled by a small group of men capable of ultimate destruction, that has surcharged the world's business with incertitude, with corrosive doubt as to the solidity of all that has come before; that has compelled men to end all confident assertions with a question mark, implicitly echoing Winston Churchill's sad speculation that "The Stone Age may return on the gleaming wings of science."

We Americans, with faith in our own achievements and unquestioning devotion to the idea of progress, have been shocked more than most by this new sense of the precarious. Unlike the peoples of Europe, we have not been conditioned by history to regard war and devastation as things that go and come with the seasons, and even the Europeans have been forced to recognize that atomic weaponry is a new political fact vitally transforming old power relationships. Yet no one yet knows how to read that new fact with any certainty, since the meaning of nuclear weapons in the conundrum of peace is yet to be tested.

Men can read it either way — in a sanguine or somber mood. If we search for a rose among the nettles, we can take some comfort from the idea that nuclear arms may have created a power stalemate, a "balance of terror," in Churchill's phrase, on the happy assumption that both the United States and the Soviet Union will try, within undefined limits, to avoid any head-on clash that might lead to a nuclear exchange. In this inverted sense the optimists among us can regard atomic bombs as a new factor for restraint, a new force for prudence. But that is as far as anyone can safely go; we had better be on guard and not overindulge our national failing for wishful thinking, since only the pathologically optimistic would count on the nuclear standoff as foreclosing the possibility of war.

Already there is evidence on this point. Although both great powers have been led to exercise caution in the heart of Europe where even a minor clash of arms might flare into nuclear conflict, awareness of the atom's capacity for destruction has not prevented the threat or use of force within the dominant power spheres of one nation or the other or in disputes in peripheral parts of the world.

Thus wherever one side has had the overwhelming interest and military advantage, it has acted with strength and confidence. The Soviet Union sent its tanks into Budapest, while we threatened violence to enforce the Cuban blockade. Nor has either side hesitated to use force in the no-man's-land that lies to the south of the industrial power centers, so that today places with oddly spelled names on the periphery of power are the new battlefields — just as the Balkans and parts of Africa served as theaters of combat in the late nineteenth century. Thus the United States has intervened with some confidence in Southeast Asia where the Soviet interest is marginal, while the Soviets have supported North Korea's attack on South Korea and Hanoi's guerrilla warfare against South Vietnam, because both great powers have been reasonably sure that these actions would not challenge the other's most vital interest and thus trigger a nuclear response.

In the past few years some scientists have indulged in remorseful breast-beating because of their part in developing the atom as an instrument of destruction. But they did not create nuclear power; they simply disclosed it and made it available to mankind. Thus, if the world blows itself up, neither science nor the scientists will be to blame — only man's pathetic inability to order his affairs in a rational manner. Science, after all, is morally indifferent, something for the world to use for good or evil. And although in the advanced industrialized countries man has made nuclear bombs he has also employed the new technology for a great many useful things — including the achievement of a new conception of living standards for himself and his neighbors.

This then has been another of the great postwar innovations — the wide acceptance of the revolutionary idea that a high level of economic growth in the advanced industrial economies can and must be sustained — and it has been proved in practice. For the last sixteen or seventeen years Americans and Western Europeans alike have enjoyed an economic growth rate of four or five percent a year while Japan has been growing almost twice as fast. And we have begun to take it for granted that this is the normal order of affairs, forgetting that the multiplication of industrial output, with constantly rising living standards is a totally new concept bringing a fresh element to world politics.

Not until the industrial revolution in the late eighteenth and early nineteenth centuries did Europe's previously static economy begin to expand by about two percent annually, and even in the most dynamic states, Britain and Germany, it did not, prior to the First World War, exceed annual increments of two and a half to three percent. Even so, war and depression jeopardized hard-won advancements in living standards. Recovery after 1918 was agonizingly slow. Germany, by 1925, had recovered only to the per capita income level of 1891, and by 1936 Frenchmen had barely regained a pre–World War I standard of living. For the industrialized countries of Western Europe the average annual growth rate between 1913 and 1950 was little better than one percent. Even in our own rich country it took us more than ten years after the depression of the thirties to recover to the 1929 level, and as recently as 1949 our economy was failing to grow.

It is hardly surprising that this new concept — that the industrialized nations can double their output every twenty years — has affected peoples in different ways. In America it has increased the appetite of the consumer, while at the same time troubling our social conscience by bringing into sharp relief the wide gaps that separate different income groups. In Europe it has made possible a new social mobility and has eroded social structures built on privilege and class. Yet, impressive though this accomplishment has been, its scope and ultimate meaning have been limited because Europe's new economic vigor and resilience have not been matched by a comparable degree of political progress, and this lack of phasing lies at the heart of many of our problems.

To be sure, Europeans have taken the first steps toward building an integrated economy — and that is a remarkable achievement — but they have made almost no progress toward the modernization of their political structure, so that today it is more archaic and creaky than it seems. Papered over by prosperity, internal divisions and instabilities lie just below the surface, weakening the political will and the capacity of national governments to make hard decisions, with the result that, while democracy survives, it does not flourish. Twelve of the sixteen states of Western Europe have coalition governments, which means that there is not a sufficient consensus among the people to give any party an absolute majority. Of the remaining four, where governments do have absolute majorities, one nation, France, lives with an unassimilated Revolution and an unresolved succession problem, with parliament suspended and a beleaguered and splintered opposition seeking to maintain its democratic virginity while making electoral deals with the Communists. Two of the remaining three, Spain and Portugal, are unabashed dictatorships; Britain alone has a majority government constrained by a united opposition.

Europe's political weakness has many causes. Not the least is the discovery by the European peoples that prosperity at home cannot be translated into power status on the world scene so long as it is achieved within political structures that are too small for present world requirements. The result is a disquieting paradox, since Europe's newfound sense of economic strength and well-being has been accompanied by the shrinking of political horizons.

And this brings us to one of the central challenges of our time — the problems that derive from the most far-reaching of all the postwar changes, the collapse of empire and all that has flowed from it. There is nothing in history to equal in scale or significance the perilous passage of more than a billion people from colonial status to at least juridical independence, compressed within the period of two decades. It has had profound and profoundly differing consequences for most of mankind.

For the metropolitan nations of Western Europe, it has meant the relinquishment of ancient dreams of world importance, compelling them to recognize that, measured by the present-day standards of world politics, they are after all only medium-sized powers. Although varying in degree from country to country, the impact of this recognition has tended to narrow the European vision to the point where today, as never before in modern times, the people of Europe look inward, concentrating their energies on their own small cape of the Eurasian land mass.

For the vast populations liberated from colonial dependence, the experience has been both sweet and bitter, exhilarating and disappointing, encouraging and frustrating. Out of the shards and wreckage of the old colonial systems, they have created a disparate collection of roughly sixty new nations, varying in physical size from the half billion people of India to the ninety thousand citizens of the Maldive Islands. The differences among these nations, giant lands and mini-states alike, are great; their common qualities few but critical. All have been born weak and poor, many born prematurely. Each seeks self-respect, world recognition, and a better standard of living for its people. Thirty-nine, or two-thirds, of the new states have come to independence since 1960, and almost every one of them from Gambia to Singapore has a seat in the United Nations General Assembly.

For the United States the demise of colonialism has meant not the interruption but the beginning of world involvement. Under pressure of the cold war we have been propelled into the power vacuums created by the withdrawal of Europe, and, while making querulous noises, we have enjoyed it. Foregoing the luxury of introspection we have walked, without blinking our eyes too much, into the full glare of the klieg lights — amid, of course, both hisses and applause. We have moved center stage so quickly, it is no wonder that we have occasionally behaved more exuberantly than the part has required, with the breathless energy of the understudy called suddenly to perform when fame and whiskey have finally done in the old star.

But on the whole we have, as a nation, shown a measure of wisdom and prudence. Not that it has been easy, for the scope and complexity of our diplomacy have abruptly widened. Instead of conducting our business with the world through a handful of embassies in the European capitals, we have found it necessary to send men and women to remote corners of the earth to engage in activities a Talleyrand or even a Benjamin Franklin would never have recognized. Someone must provide the emerging states with the kind of help and protection they formerly derived from their colonial masters. Elected to the job by a unanimous silent vote, we have involved ourselves deeply in their economic and military problems.

Our selection for this task has occurred not only through the default of others but because we are the only Western nation competent to take up the burden — a fact that puts in clear relief a final aspect of the great mutation that has taken place in the structure of world power. This is the emergence of two "superstates," the United States and the Soviet Union, both commanding the resources of continents and, for the first time, possessing the internal cohesion and unified political will to deploy those resources around the world. Both superstates embrace extensive geographical areas and have vast populations that enable them to realize the economies of scale with great and growing internal markets that were always the implicit promise of the new technology. To these advantages must be added the fact that both possess enormous arsenals of nuclear weapons, which do not — as some have foolishly argued — tend to equalize the power of great and small nations, but on the contrary have quite the opposite effect. For the logic of the bomb accentuates the special position of the superstates that alone command the technology and industrial plant required to produce one generation after another of increasingly sophisticated weapons, each with the life span of a June bug. Possessing the scope and power commensurate with today's requirements and possibilities, only the superstates can marshal that surplus of resources that nations must have to play big power politics around the world.

It is against the background of these changes, occurring so rapidly and on so vast a scale, that we must reassess the structure of world power and the play and press of national interests. This is irksome business but it is not to be put off. We must look closely at the allocation of both resources and burdens among the Western countries and do so promptly, lest it be done for us irrationally under the blind pressure of events we cannot control. For the imperative is clear; the world today has grown far too complicated and dangerous for the United States to mold and manage world affairs without the active help of others who share our humane political heritage and aspirations and our security requirements. These are great common tasks and they are not easy. If they are to be performed adequately, if the rational, civilized ideals of Jefferson and Montesquieu and Goethe are to have any relevance in this changed world, ways and means must be found to reshape the structure of power to permit a more effective sharing of world responsibilities.

That is the subject of this book.

I I

The Larger Implications of the
Changed World Power Structure

POWER and responsibility in the lives of nations are not abstractions. Each has changing concrete meaning defined
by the configurations of history, the special conditions and
requirements of a particular time and place. One begins quite
naturally with the nature of a nation's resources, which are not
confined to factories or armies or bombs, but extend also to culture, political ideas, and education, all of which play their part in
that elusive definition of power that man will always seek in vain.
But, as a generalization, the few modern states that can make
large contributions to the physical security and economic welfare
and even the cultural advancement of all the world's peoples are
those that possess in abundance the physical and intellectual resources of modern technology. The Romans showed us long ago
that the spread of a nation's culture followed the expansion of
its physical power, not the converse. This implied no moral virtue; it was simply an historical fact.

We have seen this principle in operation for the last twenty
years. While the United States has been deploying enormous resources throughout the world, the English language has become
the *lingua franca* of nations and peoples extending in the Southern Zone from Barbados to Bangkok and in Europe all the way
from the Atlantic to the Carpathians, and in recent years even

beyond to the Urals. Thais and Indonesians and Ethopians com-
municate among one another and with foreign governments in
English. The French African governments invite the Peace Corps
in to teach English, while this tongue — or more frequently its
American variant — has, in Europe, become in less than twenty
years the second language for educated French, Germans, Slavs
and Italians. Earlier generations of the South American elite sent
their sons to Paris for higher education; now they are packed
off to New York or Boston or Boulder, Colorado. American universities are bursting as never before with foreign students —
eighty-seven thousand in 1966. There are twenty thousand more
of them in the United States than the combined total in France,
Britain and the Soviet Union.

The fact that Ho Chi Minh smokes Salems rather than Gau-
loises, or that Middle Eastern potentates sip Coca-Cola rather
than ginger beer, may be a fatuous measure of American prestige. But perhaps even the trivial cultural nationalism of cigarettes and soda pop and comic strips is a ritual representation of
a deeper reality: the passion of non-Western leaders for power
and modernity and their psychological association of those qualities with all things American. To state the proposition in more
generalized terms one can say that the possession of surplus
resources and the political will to use them are what gives any
nation the ability and authority to exert a decisive influence on
world tastes and cultural values, as well as on world politics.

This is not to suggest that the world-power position of a state
can be measured by a simple statistic. Many elements must be
ground into the formula — the size of its population, the scale
and efficiency of its industry, the strength and integrity of its
institutions, the character and vigor of its people, and its internal
stability and cohesion — for these are the components which together permit its political leaders to marshal and use its resources
of men and ideas and material for a common set of objectives.
The elusive equation of modern world power can thus be described in a kind of mathematical shorthand: continent-wide
resources and population plus a high degree of internal stability
and cohesiveness plus strong leadership with an ability to define,
and a will to act on, the common purposes of the society.

The formula was not always thus, for the magnitude of resources and the degree of internal unity and political will required for great power status have varied with different periods of history. Effective size is a relative requirement, dependent on the magnitude of competing political units as well as on the nature of the tasks to be performed.

Every age has its own scale. Alexander conquered much of the known world with only forty thousand armed men. Two and one-half million Romans commanded an empire of fifty million that extended from the North Sea to the Arabian Desert. Sixteenth-century Spain controlled most of Western Europe and the New World with a population of seven million, and two hundred years later a France of twenty-five million was the largest and most aggressive nation on the Continent. As late as 1939, Germany with seventy million people could still make a bid for global power and scare civilized man half to death in the process.

What distinguishes the present from the past is not merely that the requirements of world power have become greater and more demanding but that, since 1945, they have been given a quantum jump by the vast changes that have occurred during the period. Today the game is played by new yet definable rules: only a cohesive society with a population approaching two hundred million and a national income of at least $300 billion can claim a commanding position of world power. The day is past when a nation like Germany, with a population a third as large and a national income (allowing for inflation) only a quarter as great, could — even for a brief time — dominate Europe and threaten the world. For the quantitative requirements of world power have increased three- or four-fold in twenty years, an unprecedented leap for so short a time span. A new concept of scale thus makes it necessary for nations in the 1960's to command very large resources indeed if they are to play influential world roles.

The concepts, even the terminology of past years that distinguished "great" from "small" powers, require revision, since our descriptive vocabulary has not kept pace with events. In 1945, we still spoke of the Big Five — the United States, the Soviet Union, Britain, France and China — who received permanent seats on the United Nations Security Council because they were all presumably "great powers." (The inclusion of China in the club was, of course, never realistic, but a self-conscious conceit of Franklin Roosevelt's, stemming in large part from his desire to give a symbolic place in the counsels to a nonwhite nation.) But today even the "Big Four" has little reality, for, since the 1940's, the crucial elements of power have been heavily concentrated in the United States and the Soviet Union, and the resources of Britain and France are in no way comparable. Each of the superpowers is organized to comprehend the territory and population of a continent; each commands enormous physical resources and highly skilled manpower to put them to work. Each possesses, largely by virtue of its size and scale, a highly advanced technology and a weaponry that includes sophisticated and effective nuclear armament — and, what is most important, the ability to stay the course when it mounts upward at a sixty degree gradient. Each has the internal cohesion and political will to employ its resources around the world. Each is a global power.

Thus, instead of a concert of great powers in the nineteenth-century sense, we have two competing global powers, with enough domestic resources to obviate the physical need for overseas empires. Because the industrial heartland of Europe lies between those superstates, world economic and military power is largely confined to the Northern Hemisphere and, more narrowly, to the temperate zone extending over three parts of three continents; for it is North America, Europe, the Soviet Union and Japan that together produce eighty percent of the world's goods, as well as most of its helicopters and bazookas and political ideas. As a result of the cold war the largest nations in this area are great armed camps; but by the same token, because of their wealth and power, they have special relationships and responsibilities toward the less prosperous and politically less organized nations to the south. If my analysis, therefore, directs itself largely to the industrialized North, it is only because that is where the power is. If, narrowing the lens further, my focus fixes largely on Europe, it is because that is where most of the danger is.

That has been the danger zone for a long while; it was Europe that spawned the two destructive wars of modern times — and it can do so again if we have learned nothing from that experience. Today, as for many decades, any serious clash at the sensitive center of world power could unleash forces of incalculable destruction. The European nations have got us all into trouble before, and they have a special responsibility for staying out of trouble again, but to do so they must take counsel from a bloody history and put aside the corrosive national rivalries of the past. This, as I shall point out later, means more than a change of heart. It requires the institutionalizing of that change of heart through a modern political structure.

Such a structure is essential if the European peoples are to play the role in world affairs that is their heritage, since the dismantling of the colonial systems has made the wielding of influence on the world scene immensely more complicated — and particularly difficult for states with Western democratic traditions since they do not have the same unfettered options as the Communist nations. De Tocqueville pointed out long ago that a democracy is incapable of acting in foreign affairs with the secrecy and dispatch of an autocracy — and he was speaking in a day when reporters did not crowd close to green baize tables or television cameras peer through chancellery windows.

Nor is secrecy the only advantage foreclosed; democracies suffer from two further inhibitions. The first is that they must, if they are true to themselves, use raw power sparingly; and the second is that they can no longer, within the sanctions of the new morality, assert direct political control over subject peoples. They must proceed with deference to the self-respect of new nations, abjuring the use of physical force and employing instead a full complement of political, economic, and moral resources while conducting their affairs under the constant pressure of a competing power system. For they are dealing with nations deeply suspicious — and not without good historical reasons — of superior power, nations determined to stay disengaged from the global struggle between East and West. Thus, while democracies must have gunboats at their command, they can use them only at high political cost; they must avoid, so far as possible, resort to force, while maintaining constant vigilance to prevent the nations hostile to democracy from using weapons under circumstances that might set off a major conflagration.

To have any lasting effect on the world at large, democratic countries must also be at home what they are abroad. A policy that presses for racial equality in Africa will seem hollow cant if it is not accompanied by progressive racial equality at home. Improvement in domestic welfare must be related to any attack on foreign poverty. The elusive and indefinable sense of purpose and hope that a people expresses and demonstrates in its domestic affairs has a telling effect on how that people appears to others, because the respect a nation stimulates among foreigners reflects not so much what tune is trumpeted by its propagandists but who its citizens are, how they comport themselves and what they achieve. One can even make some rules about it, for, just as I have observed — from participating in interminable international conferences — that the size of a nation's territorial demands tend to vary inversely with its ability to manage its own affairs, so I am convinced that nations that boast too stridently of their virtues or pose too piously as peace-lovers are more likely than not betraying deep doubts about the strength and integrity of their own societies and resentment at their own military impotence.

Thus foreign policy for a large modern democracy is a game played in a tough league. The epic events I have enumerated in the previous chapter make global diplomacy both difficult and costly, requiring not only immense resources but the will to employ them. This keeps the Western European powers, as they are presently organized, largely off the playing field, since the fact that they cannot individually command such resources debilitates their will. And the frustration that stems from the unhappy realization that they no longer have the size required for a global role leads to a dead-end — hollow assertion without constructive action or else retreat into the womb of isolationism.

The Western European nations, in short, are enduring the agony of trying to find a new place in a mutated world. It is even hard for them to determine where their interests lie, for the dismantling of the colonial systems not only removed the leverage of small European nations over great populations, but it also blurred the once clearly identified geographic interests of the metropole in specific pieces of real estate. By destroying the incentives of privileged commerce and imperial pride it changed the rules of the game for the colonial powers, which, while they quarreled among themselves over the possession of bits and pieces of territory, were all prepared to devote both men and money to protect — and often develop — areas over which they individually exercised dominion.

Thus Belgium, a nation whose population throughout the nineteenth century never exceeded 6.7 million, had no doubt of its clearly defined interest in the Congo (or, at an earlier point, of its sovereign's interest), just as the Netherlands, with a population of six million, sixty years ago saw its world interests largely in terms of the Dutch East Indies. France had an empire which it continued to build as late as 1919, and the British spent vast sums on the defense and development of that one-fifth of mankind once ruled by the British Crown. The motive was not so much economic gain as the satisfactions of power. Some few colonies — such as the Congo, the Dutch East Indies, and Malaya — paid handsome profits to the colonizing power, but most others were probably what Adam Smith called them two hundred years ago: wasting ventures pursued at great cost and economic loss to the metropole as "a sort of splendid and showy equipage of Empire." A European leader like President de Gaulle thus found it possible to rationalize France's loss of colonies as ending an economic drain on the mother country, reduced by events in relative world importance, when he stated quite frankly in 1961: "It seemed to me contrary to France's present interests and new ambition to remain bound by obligations and burdens which are no longer in keeping with the requirements of her strength and influence."

The United States, commanding a continent and needing no colonies, recovered from an hallucinatory bout of colonial fever soon after the turn of the century. It required no exceptional moral insight for us to concede without pain (though not without piety) that colonialism was marked for the dustbin, but most metropolitan peoples came to that conviction less easily. Yet all but the bitter-enders had known in their hearts for a long while that the institution of colonialism, like royalty and slave-holding and snuff-taking, was near the end of its life span and that the colonial wars of the last twenty years were rearguard actions, though no less expensive or frustrating or traumatic for being fought without real hope. These struggles produced serious internal shocks: Algeria wrecked the Fourth Republic; Suez jolted Britain; Indonesia, Holland; the Congo, Belgium; and Goa, Portugal. More serious and disturbing than even the financial drain of these conflicts was the sense of political capital lost, the humiliation of military defeat and withdrawal, the moral chastisement of a vociferous "world opinion" channeled through the General Assembly of the United Nations and all too frequently expressed as sanctimonious outrage by nations that had nothing at stake.

For the major colonial powers, France and Britain, the debacle of Suez had its own special nightmare quality. It was the European version of the American Bay of Pigs, the Western European counterpart of the Soviet capitulation in the Cuban missile crisis. Yet it was different in one fundamental aspect and that difference was apparent to all the world: unlike the United States or the Soviet Union, France and Britain were not global powers, and the world did not treat their public backdown as the acknowledgment of an aberrant mistake, the admission of a transient miscalculation, but as the disclosure of a basic impuissance. And added to the gall of revealed impotence was the censure by an American Secretary of State, whose responsibility for creating the conditions that led to the affair might well have disqualified a more sensitive man from casting the first stone. Anthony Eden and Guy Mollet appeared before their countrymen wearing the Emperor's new clothes. As Jacques Freymond wrote not long after the event (*Western Europe Since the War*, p. 125), "the failure of the Suez expedition showed to all the world the limits of French and British power and the degree of their dependence on the United States." Or, as Professor Hugh Thomas has written more vividly (*The Suez Affair*, p. 164), "the spectacle of over one hundred thousand men setting off for a war which lasted barely a day and then returning has few parallels in the long gallery of military imbecility. The 'grand old Duke of York' at least got to the top of the hill."

Suez was a major turning point not only in colonial policy but in Atlantic relations and the balance of Western influence in the Middle East. Whatever the merits of the narrow issue — Nasser's nationalization of the canal — they paled in significance before events that the world saw as a plot to preserve and even restore old empire and colonial relationships. The Anglo-French failure at Suez accelerated the tempo of decolonization in Africa and Asia by tearing away for European electorates, as well as for the world, the flimsy façade of power to reveal the relative political weakness and dependence underneath.

The Europeans drew most of the necessary inferences and proceeded to complete their withdrawal from Africa and Asia in the next five years. The overseas springs of empire were running dry. As de Gaulle asked in 1961, "Why should we cling to costly, bloody and fruitless domination when our country has to undergo complete renovation . . . ?"

With the substantial liquidation of overseas empires, the European place on the larger world stage was no longer chalked out in specific territorial terms, and, since no nation of fifty million people has resources to disperse widely throughout the globe, the Western European nations have been progressively withdrawing from world responsibility. They have receded into an isolationism not unlike that of the United States before the world wars, preferring, as we did then, to criticize the players from the spectator stands while staying out of the game. Today, sometimes as umpire and other times as competitor, America is on the receiving end of the Bronx cheer, and this has made many of us not only unhappy but baffled and indignant. Why should the world no longer love us when we have been trying only to do our duty? And why should the European nations continue to pull back from far outposts when their economic resources are growing at such a rapid pace, while we are itching and scratching from an unfamiliar (and hitherto foreign) ailment called a balance of payments deficit?

The question, in more precise and less self-righteous terms, can be phrased in this form: Why should North America go on expending its power in support of general principles of social justice and independence for the new nations while Europe's industrialized states are contracting their commitments with the disappearance of special territorial interests? It is a fair question, and there is another. Just as Western Europe is reducing its participation in essential tasks around the world because its individual nations are no longer able to define interests related to specific territories outside Europe, is it not possible that we Americans are diffusing our power and employing it with too little discrimination because we have not fixed clearly defined limits to our world interests and responsibilities?

This latter question goes to the heart of a proper American policy and we cannot allow it to stand unanswered. We urgently need a satisfactory rationale for the use of American power and resources, or we may find ourselves increasingly involved in ambiguous quarrels far distant from our shores while the Europeans content themselves with carping from the sidelines. Such a development would prove intolerable at some point down the line, and it could do great damage. It could lead to an isolationist atavism in America that would be dangerous for the common principles and ideals of a humane Western civilization.

Thus, we must find an answer that is plausible not only to the American people but to the rest of mankind, who tend to regard much that we are doing today with troubled skepticism. Of course, it is natural that Europeans, who ruled most of the world until after 1945, should take it for granted that we Americans have inherited their own colonial motives and ambitions. It is inevitable that many should even suspect that our strong assault on colonialism was consciously or subconsciously motivated by a wish to push the European powers out of positions we coveted for ourselves. Throughout his war memoirs, General de Gaulle expresses exactly this suspicion about Presidents Roosevelt and Truman. He suggests that, in pressing for France's withdrawal from the Levant and independence for Syria and Lebanon, they were hatching Anglo-American plots to supplant the French. But, no matter how far-fetched, is this, after all, surprising? Is it not natural that — against the background of their own experience — many Europeans should believe that our employment of power and resources in remote and unfamiliar areas, where we justify our interest only in terms of a diffusely formulated general principle, reflects little more than the traditional tendency of a nation with power to use it?

That we have hurt feelings about this does less credit to our objectivity than to our evangelical tradition. It is to our credit that we Americans believe in ourselves. By and large we have always tended to think of our nation as moved by the highest motives and a kind of missionary purpose. Our greatest spokesmen and leaders from Cotton Mather to Woodrow Wilson have described America as a pristine land in a corrupt world, God's instrument on earth for leading an oppressed and benighted humanity out of the darkness. Jefferson complained in a letter to Dr. Priestley of March 21, 1801, of the "disorders" and "contagions" of that "great Mad House," the monarchical Old World. We could, he wrote, no longer say that there was nothing new under the sun, for this "whole chapter in the history of man" was new. Before America, "nothing was known to history but the man of the old world, crowded within limits either small or overcharged, and steeped in the vices" generated by that situation.

Such a self-righteous perspective is too cloying a brew for any people intimately involved with the problems and peoples of six continents in the exercise of global power, and most of us find it, if not embarrassing, at least not very relevant to today's situation. We have learned that it is unwise, if not impolite, to wear a halo in the conference room, and for all our size and strength we do not have a monopoly of power, or anything approaching it. The great strength we do have must, therefore, be committed with care and prudence — and, as Jefferson wrote (albeit in a different context), "with a decent respect for the opinion of mankind." This means, in operational terms, that we should relate the expenditure of our resources and the exertions and sacrifices of our people to principles and purposes and objects that a great many foreign nations, as well as we Americans, consent to, approve of and consider beneficent. For, not only have we no monopoly of power, we are like every other nation in lacking a monopoly of wisdom. Intelligence and vision are commodities fairly evenly distributed among a diversely endowed humanity and we have not cornered the market — nor will we ever. Large numbers of us began to learn this truth when the Second World War brought more citizens of the New World in contact with more foreign peoples than ever before, but, although since 1945 we have moved far from the old concepts of parochialism, the process is still anything but complete. The United States has not fully learned that the political advice or criticism of less powerful friends who share a common heritage does not necessarily denote hostility or envy or malice — or even bad judgment.

Particularly as the menace of Moscow has begun to appear less intense — although the menace of Peking may seem to many to be growing — the doubts expressed by Europeans are finding their way into the American dialogue as well. Are we always using our power in pursuit of purposes directly related to definable American interests? Why should we have to do so much by ourselves? How can we persuade the other competent industrial powers — principally those in Western Europe — to participate with us in a common effort?

These are difficult questions. They compel us to look hard at the underlying nature of today's world, since I am convinced that the fundamental problem is structural. If we find the key to the puzzle, it will come only from fully understanding to what extent the political organization of power has failed to keep pace with the changing requirements of a world in rapid evolution. At the same time we must develop a clear view as to how we would like to see world power organized in order best to protect our own security without assuming more of the world's burdens than we can competently carry. Finally, we must pursue policies that will encourage the achievement of that structure of power which best serves our interests.

This is a formidable assignment, imposing the need for perception and discipline. It means not only that we need to construct a coherent concept of the kind of arrangements that are good for us (and for General Motors and the world) but also that, in making from day to day the individual decisions that guide American policy, we must resolutely reject measures that offer short-term advantages while prejudicing long-range objectives. This is not easy; indeed, one of the most formidable tasks confronting a government and a foreign office is to pursue a consistent line of policy, resisting temptations to go down attractive byways for transient benefits.

I stress this point heavily, for there has been a recent tendency to scoff at the utility of conceptual thinking in foreign policy in favor of a pragmatism that masquerades as a commendable hospitality to fresh ideas. Without doubt rigidity as such can be a serious fault. But a foreign policy conducted without some well-developed conceptions as to desirable structures of power is not a foreign policy at all but simply a series of unrelated improvisations. It is because of my feeling on this point that I have been disturbed over the years at the extent to which many — but by no means all — of my academic friends, inspired, no doubt, by the yeasty air of the Potomac, have been so seduced by the challenge of operational problems as to renounce any attempt at conceptual thinking as "theology," and, in aid of their own abstractions, have erected a specious dichotomy between "theologians" and "pragmatists."

This is not an anti-intellectual observation, since I have deep respect for the universities — in fact, some of my best friends are professors — but I record it as an item of curiosa and a source of some concern at what seems to me a dangerous intellectual fad. For I was clearly impressed by the comment made to me recently by a wise European that "If America ever dies it will be from a surfeit of pragmatism," and I very much fear that, in the matter of guiding a great nation's relations with the rest of the world, the negation of what some call "theology" may well be nihilism. No major nation has ever conducted a successful foreign policy without a clear idea as to when, how and where it should use its power and how that power could be related to, and organized with or against, the power of others in a way that would enhance the national interest. And no nation ever will.

But to form a clear idea as to how we should order our power we must first be quite sure that we know the framework of competing and supplementary power within which we operate. We need to have, in other words, some well-defined sense of the existing or potential arrangements if we are intelligently to answer the question: What kind of a power structure should we try to erect within the four walls of the possible? And how should we go about erecting it?

The first step toward answering this question is to take a close look at the key networks of relations that dominate world affairs: the relations among the nations and peoples of Western Europe; the relations between the two sides of the North Atlantic and particularly between the United Kingdom and ourselves; our relations with the Far East and those between the rich nations of the North and the poor nations of the South; and finally the so-called East-West relationship between the Communist world and the world of diversity. This is the necessary point of departure; for only when we are clear as to the nature and potential of other peoples' power and responsibilities and how they are likely to employ them can we arrange to fit ourselves effectively into a world scheme.

Let us begin then with Western Europe and let us start back a few years, since it is essential to recall the past if we are to understand where Europe is now and especially why some of its history-haunted figures, particularly General de Gaulle, behave as they do.

I I I

The Failure of the European System

G ENERAL Douglas MacArthur believed in 1944: "We made the same old mistake of intervening in European quarrels, which we can't hope to solve because they are insoluble. . . . Europe is a dying system. It is worn out and run down" (Koen, *The China Lobby in American Politics,* p. 12).

His description of Europe was one shared by a good many Europeans at the time and it is accepted by a few Americans even today. Three years after the General's diatribe, Winston Churchill looked out on the bleak and devastated continent of mid-1947. "What is Europe now?" he asked. "It is a rubble heap, a charnel house, a breeding-ground of pestilence and hate." Yet the shattered cities and empty, bomb-blackened factories of 1947 were not the beginning and perhaps not the end but only one more Goya painting of the agony of Europe, a continent that has been for three and a half centuries a battlefield of clashing dynastic and national ambitions, a theater of conflict in which first one and then another of her rival states has claimed a transient dominance.

It has been a bloody era during which primacy in Europe has passed from hand to hand (from Spain to France to Britain to Germany), a period of incessant warfare (except for a brief respite in the nineteenth century), which has seen six men (two Spanish Habsburg Kings, two Frenchmen and Two Germans) come close to unifying all of Europe under their sway. Come close but yet not succeed because each of these men — Charles V and Philip II, Louis XIV and Napoleon, William II and Hitler — consolidated enough power against himself to defeat his ambitious designs. Each bled his country white in the process, exhausting the economic reservoirs of Spain and France and Germany.

The tempo of modern technology accelerated the rise and decline of empire, shortening the life span of ascendancy. Spain held predominant place on the Continent for about a hundred and fifty years, as did France who followed her. Britain enjoyed a century of supremacy, while the latecomer Germany had only half as long in which to bid twice for dominance. In retrospect it seems clear that the fleeting primacy of a particular state largely reflected its superior population and economic resources. In the Spanish wars of the sixteenth and seventeenth centuries the treasure of the Aztecs and Incas swelled the gold and silver coinage of Europe eight times over, financing the weapons to devastate and terrorize the Continent. Passing from the Spanish government to soldiers and moneylenders to merchants of Flanders and Augsburg and Genoa, it laid the foundations for an evolving mercantile economy that would revive shattered finances in the North and provide the financial sinews to be exploited by new rulers for new wars.

Superiority of resources was also the key to success for the next bidder, France, which by the seventeenth century had become the largest nation in Europe. Her twenty million people were one-fifth of Europe's total population. There were three times as many Frenchmen as Englishmen, and more Frenchmen than Germans and Italians combined. Given these resources of population, together with the wealth of a large and bountiful land, Louis XIV and his Bourbon successors sent booty-hungry French armies all the way to the Danube, until Britain, protected by the channel and supplied by an overseas empire, manipulated the diplomatic engine of the defensive alliance to overcome the heavy advantage of French manpower.

But the foreign wars that impoverished France did not end her hegemonic ambitions. To be sure, they changed her society forever by helping to produce the crisis that brought about the convocation of the Estates General in 1789 and ultimately the Revolution, but that Revolution spawned Napoleon and a new era of even greater bloodshed. Impelled by revolutionary fervor, France introduced Europe to nationalism as a popular ideology and a proselytizing doctrine. The armies of the empire brought France a twelve-year mastery of the Continent and a lingering nostalgia for something called "grandeur" — which meant the plunder of armies and elegant pageantry and being top dog. But at appalling cost. For, though Bonaparte aimed his "continental system" at destroying England's economy by a protective blockade against British trade, he succeeded only in stulifying the Continent — depriving it for a generation of the new and still carefully guarded ideas and techniques of an emerging industrial revolution that was in the end to prove even more significant than the convulsion of 1789.

Nationalism begets nationalism, and popular uprisings in the Iberian Peninsula, subsidized with British gold, steadily thinned the ranks of the Grande Armée, until, when midnight struck, it was England's sixteen million island people, controlling the far seas and a remote two hundred million Asian subjects, who brought down the Bonapartist rule. Before the end of the decade that saw Napoleon's retreat from Moscow, the artificial frontier he had built from Hamburg in the north to Rome in the south had crumbled to dust. When the accounts were totaled at the end of the day, they showed that Napoleon, like other would-be world conquerors before and since, had left his country smaller than he had found it. Never again after 1815 would France be the greatest state of Europe.

With the collapse of Napoleon and the Congress of Vienna the nineteenth century became clearly the age of the *Pax Britannica*. It was a time of turbulent domestic change and frantic industrialization, but on the whole it secured for the world a breathing spell of peace and relative stability. To be sure there were small wars in the corners of Europe and colonial wars on the periphery of power, but the balance established at Vienna was not disturbed in a major way until 1871. Then, the ministers of a lesser Napoleon, in a vain attempt to reestablish the grandeur of France (tarnished by the Mexican fiasco and the political consequences of Sadowa), declared war on Prussia and exposed the pretensions of the Tuilleries as a tinsel façade. Intended to regain for France not only her "honor" but also her "natural" frontiers, the contest led, within two months, to the debacle of Sedan and the downfall of France's second Bonapartist Empire. In confirmation of Hegel's maxim, it was true that the "facts and personages of great importance in world history" did in fact occur twice, but, as Karl Marx observed in *The 18th Brumaire of Louis Bonaparte* (p. 15), "the first time [was] tragedy, the second [was] farce."

What happened to France in the nineteenth century was not that her wealth accumulated and her men decayed, but that her wealth and population suffered in relation to her neighbors'. France had lost her place even as the largest nation in Western Europe, since by 1850 the German states with thirty-six million people had already surpassed her, although across the sea a United States with twenty-three million was still behind. But from then on the ratios changed every week, for, with the impact of industrialization, both Germany and America leaped forward at a fantastic pace. In each country a war for national unification was followed in the latter 1870's by a burst of economic vitality. Between 1870 and 1913 the United States had an annual economic growth rate of 4.3 percent — the highest the world had known until then — while Germany grew by 2.9 percent in the same period. By 1900 Germany's economic strength challenged and overtook Britain's. Within another ten years she was producing twice as much steel as England and five times more than France, and beginning, in a formidable way, to compete with Britain for trade and maritime power. As Lord Keynes wrote in *The Economic Consequences of the Peace* (p. 40), "the German empire was built more truly on coal and iron than on blood and iron."

Germany emerged suddenly — too suddenly for the peace of the world — as the giant of the Continent. She was Europe's first parvenu power; Walter Rathenau referred in 1911 to "the insolence of our wealth gone mad." But whatever her gaucherie or bombast or arrogant nationalism, most historians agree that Wilhelmian Germany did not embark on a conscious policy of domination through war. With her growing economic strength, she had much more to gain by another half generation of peace. What began in August 1914 was not a *planned* war; on the contrary, it was the classically unique case of a tragic conflict caused by muddle and miscalculation. In hastily committing the full prestige of his empire to the punitive settlement of another Balkan post-assassination squabble, Kaiser Wilhelm made two egregious errors. First, he elevated a bilateral *affaire* into a wide-ranging international crisis totally incommensurate with the original cause of the dispute or the consequences that might follow from it. Second, he pledged support for a war on the periphery of power without regard to the German national interest and in the full knowledge that his only important ally could disintegrate under the strain of extended hostilities. This was asininity beyond history's tolerance; while these blunders were bad enough in themselves, they were magnified by coming on top of a series of other German blunders: confused leadership after Bismarck's retirement in 1890, a generation of blustering and incredibly stupid diplomacy, a military "blank check" extended to Austria-Hungary, a senseless naval armaments race with England, constant interference in the colonial disputes of others, and the tortuously slow evolution of parliamentary government in Berlin. All these factors, as well as the bombast of parvenu power, contributed to the mistake and misfortune of Germany's plunge into chaos in 1914.

It was a catastrophe with few equals in history for ever since that tragic summer, nothing has been the same again. The established order could not survive that much killing; institutions proved impotent to justify themselves, and the carnage undermined the physical and moral premises of a whole world system. One result — little noted at the time — was economic stagnation for a generation. Average annual growth in Europe from 1913 until 1950 approximated only two percent and living standards hardly rose at all. During the same period we Americans — even taking into account the Great Depression of the 1930's — multiplied the wealth of our economy six times. But the greatest costs to Europe could not be measured in economic terms. Strewn on the battlefields of the Marne, the Somme,

Verdun, were the bodies of the best of her youth — a generation destined to die and not create; and until Nazi crimes twenty years later brought to an already brutalized world a new dimension of horror and new maps of Hell, the First World War was distinguished as the costliest slaughter in history.

Nor was this the end of it. Beyond even physical facts of death and destruction, the conflict brought moral exhaustion and cultural malaise, the intangible loss of vitality and purpose that Paul Valéry captured in the title of an essay, "*La crise de l'esprit,*" which has haunted European intellectual life ever since. His brooding, famous first line, "Nous autres, civilizations, nous savons maintenant que nous sommes mortelles," evoked an even deeper shock of self-recognition for sensitive Europeans in 1945 than when written in 1919. "Elam, Ninevah, Babylon," he wrote,

> were very vague and beautiful names, and the total ruin of these worlds had as little meaning for us as their very existence. But France, England and Russia — these will also be beautiful names. Lusitania is also a pretty name. . . . We see now that the abyss of history is large enough for everyone. We sense now that a civilization is just as fragile as a life. (Valéry, *Oeuvres,* I, 988)

This sense of decline and decadence, this crisis of the European spirit, opened a void that twenty years later would be filled with new prodigies of nihilism.

Taken together, the two great world wars can be regarded, as Paul Valéry, Desmond Donnelly and later Dean Acheson have pointed out, as successive chapters in the European Civil War. In a speech delivered in 1963, Acheson remarked, with his customary perception, that these conflicts brought changes "of a magnitude unequalled since the collapse of the Roman Empire." "This Civil War," he said, "destroyed the six great empires which, by their concert and balance, gave order and system to human affairs throughout the world — the British, French, German, Austro-Hungarian, Ottoman and Russian empires." And, he added, "This collapse set off the Russian and Chinese revolutions."

Bloody and catastrophic as it was, however, this European Civil War — in its two beastly episodes — was not a self-contained

drama but one more episode in a dramatic cycle of rivalry between European nation-states that had been playing at the same
stand for four hundred years. What distinguished these two modern episodes was their scope and violence, both of which were of
a new order. Coming only two decades apart, they shattered the
political and social fabric of Europe as the Thirty Years' War
had shattered the political and social fabric of Bohemia and
Germany three centuries before. They challenged men's confidence in established institutions, leading many Europeans to
conclude that existing political structures were no longer tenable. Western Europe had not been so internally weak — or felt
so internally weak — so completely at the mercy of outside
forces, since the Moors had seized the Iberian Peninsula and
penetrated France as far north as Tours in the eighth century or
since the Mongol hordes had crumbled the Eastern frontiers five
hundred years later.

A troubled and confused Continent sought some fresh alternative to the discredited prewar system. Men reacted, as always,
according to their individual tempers. Some sought a total escape
from politics and the nation. They turned to the inner personal
experience of religion, as did the German philosopher Karl Jaspers, who saw no hope for the future except through "uplift by
illumination and growing transparency — love of man," or the
historian Friedrich Meinecke, who wrote, "anxieties of the very
darkest sort press upon us. . . . Everything, yes everything, depends on an intensified development of our inner existence. . . .
We must go back beyond the ruins to seek out the ways of
Goethe's era."

A second group sought another kind of total escape. By voting
Communist, one out of every three or four Frenchmen and Italians expressed their hopeless disillusion with the European political order, hoping to smash the existing state apparatus and
submerge national aspirations in homage to a New Rome — the
Moscow International. Communism promised a decisive break
with the past; it offered an activist alternative to the discredited
politics of the thirties. The ground was already well prepared.
Communists had played prominent roles in most of the wartime
Resistance movements, which almost everyone believed would

be the nucleus on which to build a New Europe. Yet, while the European political mood was a mood of the Left, it did not bring Communists to power. In Britain the Labour Party was given charge after 1945. In France and Italy Communists participated in Popular Front coalition governments until May 1947, and the experts were convinced that the April 1948 Italian elections would mean success for the Communists, allied with left-wing Socialists. But, as has happened before and since — even in this computer age — the tealeaves and goat's entrails bore false witness; when the votes were tallied a nervous world discovered that Alcide de Gasperi's Christian Democrats had gained an absolute majority, and he was to hold power for eight crucial years.

The same story was repeated elsewhere. In the Western Zones of Germany the Communists were overshadowed by the German Social Democrats, then far to the left of Fabian Socialism in doctrine but avidly anti-Communist. It was widely thought that, when Germany held its first elections in 1949, Kurt Schumacher's Socialists, and not Konrad Adenauer's Christian Democrats, would win — but the experts again were wrong. In France a renowned war leader, Charles de Gaulle, headed a coalition that included Communists, until he resigned in January 1946, piqued that mere "parties" should challenge his military budget. By winning twenty-nine percent of the total vote in the November 1946 elections, the Communists gained the largest bloc of votes in the National Assembly. But, though a disruptive force, they were never in position to enact Leninism into law. They never gained control, and they have not come that close again.

The personalism of philosophers like Jaspers and the apocalyptic vision of the Communists were avenues of retreat from politics — expressions of despair and disillusion. But many Europeans chose not to retreat; they foresaw a third course of action. They read the lessons of the past tragic years as meaning not that all politics were evil and should be either shunned or smashed, but that the political arrangements under which they lived were inadequate and obsolete. They proposed to tackle the problem frontally by building a common "Europe." They sought progressive social change at home within a gradually evolving political unity; they rejected defeatism for a creative optimism they regarded as the only decent working hypothesis of rational man.

In public-opinion polls from the end of the war to the present day the majority of Europeans have consistently expressed a desire for this third course which is vaguely referred to as "European unification." This term has shadings of different meaning for different people but it has meant for all the hope for a larger, more inclusive, more generous, structure than the national states of the prewar era. Since 1945, every European leader — even a passionate nationalist like General de Gaulle — has had to pay at least lip service to this deeply felt aspiration for something better than the old divisive structures of national power, the source of much enduring achievement over centuries, but also the cause of so much collective catastrophe and personal heartbreak in recent history.

Unity has, however, been consistently and totally opposed from the far left and far right, and for very good reasons. It spoils the Communist case by offering Europe a navigable path from present weakness to future strength, a means of synthesizing the human traditions of her past with the technological possibilities of today and tomorrow. It provides an attractive alternative to the Communist insistence on wrecking the present structure and starting a "new order" from scratch. And, by a quite different logic — because "unity" implies a threat to the familiar form of the nation-state — it has also been opposed by traditionalists and nationalists whose narrow perspectives of allegiance and habits of thought cannot comprehend something larger than the customary; for among the motive forces of the human mind surely one of the most potent is nostalgia, man's desire to recapture and relive vicariously a world he never knew. Every political party arrives at its own definition of the "Golden Age," and for European nationalists that age is the nineteenth century; for French nationalists it is particularly the first decade and a half of that century. But in the ashes of 1945 a politic of nostalgia was no longer tenable; Europeans preferred to build on the future and not on the past.

The new politic that reflected the desire for a unified Europe — the diffuse wish for some new, more inclusive structure than

the system of rival nations that had wrecked the Continent —
had its urgent focal point in France. The French experience had
been one of special travail. Defeat and liberation had brought
long-festering political hatreds and corrosive divisions of social
classes to the surface of national life. The old arguments were
heard again; the differences that had troubled the nation since
the Ninth Thermidor were rekindled. The atmosphere was anything but healthy. Yet the months after V–E Day were not
merely a time for paying off old scores but also for rethinking
the future.

Frenchmen accepted this task as their proper role. It was to
them that Europe looked for leadership toward a new kind of
union to be achieved not by forcible conquest but by intelligent
agreement. France, after all, was Europe's natural home, a land
whose sons had contributed richly to the common political heritage and civilization. Only a generation before, it had been a
French Prime Minister, Aristide Briand, who advocated European federal union at the League of Nations. A century earlier,
Victor Hugo had claimed for the "Party of civilization" the same
goal. And now again French leaders were the first to give confident institutional substance to the generalized hopes of postwar Europeans. Modest, painstaking architects, they began to
raise the economic girders and mix the political cement of a new
structure built on old historic foundations.

In Paris, during the years after the War, I watched these men
clear away the rubble of nationalism and begin to build a united
Europe — and with what talents I had I worked by their side.

I V

The Drive for Unity

I FIRST met Jean Monnet in Washington during the War when he had been co-opted to be vice chairman of the British Purchasing Commission and I was working with Edward Stettinius on lend-lease matters. Later, when I returned from an assignment in Europe in the fall of 1945, I served as his lawyer and adviser while he reorganized the French purchasing services to meet the new and pressing needs of reconstruction.

During the years that followed, Monnet devoted his superb talents of imagination, practical good sense, persuasion and encouragement to a succession of major enterprises. First, as chairman of the French Planning Commission, he drafted a practical blueprint — based on effective cooperation among all elements in the industrial society — for the rehabilitation of France. Then, as deputy head of the CEEC (the group of European leaders called together in response to General Marshall's historic speech at Harvard), he worked with Oliver Franks in drawing up a balance sheet of Europe's needs. Later he played a role in guiding negotiations that led to the creation of the OEEC, the permanent organization through which Europeans sought more effective working relationships in managing their common economy.

Jean Monnet's finest hour came, however, when he persuaded Robert Schuman to give his name and support to the creation of a Coal and Steel Community. The negotiation that followed was a model of its kind. It took place in an eighteenth-century building on the rue Martignac on the Left Bank which was the headquarters of the French Plan, and during a year of intense effort Europeans worked together in common purpose, each seeking, as one said to me with awe and astonishment, to find ways to make progress, not to block it. Monnet became the first president of the European Coal and Steel Community based in Luxembourg. He remained there for three years, during the period of the formative decisions, then founded the Action Committee for a United States of Europe through which he played a major role in the shaping of Euratom and the Common Market.

For me these were yeasty years during which — from time to time, for long or short periods — I worked with Monnet officially and unofficially, professionally or simply as a friend, in connection with all of these enterprises. When in Paris I usually occupied a small office down the hall or under the stairs, but our most fruitful hours together were quite as likely to occur during the night or over the weekend at his country house in Les Bazoches as in his office during the day. I was one of Monnet's dialectical punching bags. My normal assignment was to try to express on paper his evolving conceptions, for he is a man who thinks by a process of refining successive formulations of an idea. Thus it was a rare paper of any importance that did not go through at least seventeen or eighteen drafts, for we thought together as we wrote together.

This was sustained and concentrated effort, since Jean Monnet on the trail of an idea is indefatigable. Small, compact, wiry and resilient, he looks, as has often been remarked, like a shrewd French peasant. (It is a comment that pleases him.) But, in contrast to his physical stature, he is, in the idiom of intellect and spirit, one of the towering figures of the age. A great part of what has been done to build unity in Europe today — and the Common Market alone is a monumental achievement — results from the genius and persuasive qualities of this one individual. What exists of Europe's unity today is, to a large extent, a Monnet tour de force.

For those who know him well it is clear why Jean Monnet has become "Mr. Europe." He is preeminently a modern man. More deeply than any of us he has perceived a major dilemma of our complex time — the discord between our technology, on the one hand, with its rapid pace of advance and its requirements of scope and scale, and, on the other, the institutional arrangements under which we live, so slow to change and so often parochial in character. The consequences of this discord are familiar enough. They are evident in the problems we deal with every day — the problems of our cities, of our schools, of our transportation systems, and even of the air we breathe. But they find their most significant expression in the relations among the peoples of the Atlantic world, where defense is indivisible, where economic life is interdependent, and where the major political decisions must of necessity be taken in concert if the full potential of free men is to be effectively mobilized.

Yet the fact that Jean Monnet is a modern man does not mean that he is unaware or disdainful of the past. He is no scholar, yet he has, I think, a profound sense of the meaning of history and of the deep forces it has generated. He has had the insight to recognize that history is not static, not the constant replaying of old themes, but a flow of events which, if man is to survive, must be channeled in directions that meet the requirements of an evolving new age. He has, therefore, never been tempted into the unhappy error — induced by an atavistic longing for a world that never was — of seeking to recapture the past. He has not sought to unfurl ancient banners, reinstate old forms, revive the vanished symbols that beglamored (and debauched) the centuries gone by. Instead he has pursued the more relevant purpose of bending men's efforts toward a nobler future.

It is because Jean Monnet so clearly perceives the nature of the great tidal forces at work in the world that he is sturdily immune to transient disappointments. I have been with him on more than one occasion when the progress of a new design has seemed to many of us irrevocably halted by the abrupt intrusion of obsolete — yet fiercely held — ideas that echoed a distant and earlier age. Invariably — and sometimes almost alone — Jean Monnet has remained undismayed. At such moments of crisis his reaction is always the same. "What has happened, has happened," he is inclined to say, "but it does not affect anything fundamental. The important point is for us not to be deflected, not to lose momentum. We must go forward. We may alter our tactics but never our main objectives."

It is due to this apparent imperturbability that Jean Monnet is known — to the admiration of his friends and the exasperation of his opponents — as an incorrigible optimist. This attitude of mind does not stem from any Panglossian idea that all is for the best in the best of all possible worlds, but rather from a dauntless faith in the logic of events and the essential rationality of man — a faith in the ineluctable direction of deeply moving forces. Jean Monnet is an optimist because he is a practical man with a passionate desire to get things done.

As a practical man he pursues his purpose in a way that is peculiarly his own. Mr. Walter Lippmann once spoke of him as a man who can "induce and cajole men to work together for their own good." To say it in other words, Jean Monnet is the supreme practitioner of the art of personal diplomacy. And he practices that art with unfailing perception of the loci of power and with an extraordinary single-mindedness. Optimism works for him because he accepts opponents but not defeat. I still remember a book he once gave me — the story of an Arab prince who, in a time of troubles, went out to the desert to find the wisdom of the ages. The prince returned from his sojourn with this motto:

> *May God bless even my enemies.*
> *For they too are a means to my end.*

It is by the vital force of his deep convictions, in short, that Jean Monnet has become the keeper of the conscience of a continent. And he has demonstrated anew the ancient adage that one resolute man, plus the truth, can become a majority.

The fact that Monnet has perceived the dangers and limitations of traditional nationalism does not mean that he is without feeling for his land and its people. He is a dedicated European because he loves France. He is deeply convinced that Frenchmen and other Europeans have priceless energies and ideas to contribute to the world but that they will be able to make their proper contribution only if they are unified. This is the conviction of a man who is at the same time both practical and philosophic, a conviction springing from a deep desire to create the conditions in which Europe can fulfill itself.

Monnet recognizes frankly that Germans and Frenchmen are not cut from the same mold, but, he is fond of pointing out, neither are any two Frenchmen. One of his favorite stories illustrates this point. Following the Gold Rush in the middle of the last century someone brought vineroots from California to see if they would grow well in French soil. To everyone's dismay, those roots carried a plant lice known as the phylloxera, which, over a period of three or four years, devastated the vines of France and of a large area of Western Europe. In spite of the efforts of Pasteur to find a cure, the pest was not arrested until someone — recognizing that the California roots were themselves immune — hit on the stratagem of grafting French vines onto California roots. As a result the present-day wines of France are genealogically traceable to vine roots brought from California.

Monnet sees in this incident an explanation of the diversity of the French character. After all, he is fond of pointing out, one can go seven hundred miles up and down the coast of California and clearly identify only a dozen different kinds of grapes, but "in the Grand Champagne area where I was born, which is no more than twenty kilometers by thirty kilometers, there are more than a hundred distinct species of grapes."

"If the same roots in America can produce only a dozen types of grapes while a few acres in France can produce a hundred types, isn't it clear why the French people are such extreme individualists? With a soil so varied, how can the people be anything but diverse?"

This homely story, which he tells with sly whimsy, was transformed by Monnet and his colleagues into a philosophy. They saw in Europe the result of a stable association between man and nature. Like Valéry, they argued that the source of Europe's prodigious achievements over the centuries was her diversity — the fact that every possibility of man could exist from the Mediterranean to the North Sea. The variety and genius of these European peoples made it miraculously possible for their civilization to create substitutes for nature as no other civilization had ever done. To survive as they grew in numbers they found ways to conserve the soil and to multiply the productive force of man. They evolved an optimistic concept of man based on his liberty and dignity as an individual. And they invented machines which in one century had done more to liberate man than all the revolutions and wars since the beginning of humanity.

But, Monnet felt, Europe did not know how to control what it had created. It did not experience the psychological revolution that should have accompanied the industrial revolution; along with eighteenth-century boundaries it maintained a fragmentary conception of politics and economics no longer in accord with the system of production. It clove to a rigid national framework in which the full potential of modern technology was frustrated.

War, pursued to expand one nation's territory and productive scope, ended only in impoverishing everybody. Europe had created a new world of reality that outstripped her imagination. Her fundamental problem was moral: the European spirit had ceased to dominate Europe. But to solve this crisis of the spirit, Europe had less need of a spiritual "mental health" campaign than a reinforced material foundation. She needed to produce a higher standard of living for her people to reawaken their genius, and this implied concerted plans for larger economic and political structures, for European unity. The tasks of the philosopher and of the politician were thus one and the same in postwar Europe.

Monnet, although a preeminently practical man, has been, like every Frenchman, touched by the Cartesian discipline, and this has been even more true of some of the men around him. In our long arguments about Europe, Monnet and his French colleagues came out at the same point as I did, though they were inclined more than I to begin with universal first principles. They reasoned, like Aquinas or Hegel, from matter to spirit to matter. Educated in what General de Gaulle would call the "Anglo-Saxon" tradition, I tended to reason, like Hobbes and Hume, from effect to cause to effect. But, regardless of the fact that we followed different roads, we all arrived at the conclusion that the logic of European unity was inescapable.

For it seemed clear to us that only unity could assure peace and security by ending once and for all the foolish and destructive rivalries of European nation-states that have produced two frightful wars in modern times. Only within the framework of a united Europe could there be a settlement of the major unfinished business left over from the Second World War — the division of the German people — on terms that Europeans would be prepared to accept. Of course, it is one thing to favor a united Europe. It is quite another to define that hopeful and elusive phrase in institutional terms and then try to achieve in action one's definition in principle. Human nature makes us all creatures of habit and conservators of tradition. All societies resist change, and unity means a fundamental change in the traditional structure of Europe.

We Americans, like Europeans, have, by fits and starts, moved forward to dismiss illusions and accept and act on the implications of change. But the evolution of America to world power is different in nature from the evolution of Europe away from world power and, eventually, back to it again through a transcendence of old forms. The "transvaluation of values," which a modern Nietzsche would see implicit for Europe — the attack on the very *raison d'être* of her oldest nation-states — means that unity will at every step encounter opposition. This is not to say, however, that it will fail of achievement. On the contrary, I am confident that sooner or later Europe will unite. Admittedly there is no precedent for so profound a transformation; but neither is there any precedent for the vast shifts and upheavals in the power structure that are bringing it about.

For if the proof of the pudding is really in the eating, the most hopeful augury for the future is what has been done so far, since Europe, in spite of all opposition, has gone much farther and faster toward unity than most of us believed possible two decades ago. In those dark and confused days we were not dealing with a prosperous and complacent Europe but with a scared and uncertain Europe, and the problems seemed immense. Four questions dominated European politics to the exclusion of almost everything else — four negative questions that were so all-consuming that the positive case for uniting the Continent intruded on them only by the back door. They were: (1) physical and economic devastation bordering in some countries on social collapse: and what to do about it, how to start recon-

struction; (2) political weakness: how to build a strong government and how to wrest hard decisions from fragile coalitions,
in a milieu without strong national parties or leaders; how to
restore democracy and deal with large Communist parties; (3)
what to do about Germany; and (4) how to conduct the cold
war and resist the threat from the East.

In 1945 economic survival took precedence over all else; a
government's first concern was whether or not it could feed its
people. In Central Europe a flood of refugees — liberated from
Nazi labor camps, expelled from the German territories annexed
by Poland, or fleeing the Red Army — filled the Western Zones.
I watched them myself in Germany throughout the early months
and summer of 1945, clogging the roads in a frenzied effort to
move west beyond reach of the Red Army.

In Britain, wartime food rationing stayed in effect through
1948, meat rationing until 1954. Bomb damage everywhere made
decent housing a luxury, rail and road transport difficult, communications uncertain. In Germany barter replaced a dubious
currency. In Italy inflation pushed the cost of living index by
October 1947 to fifty-three times prewar levels.

Clearing away the rubble and opening the roads and factories
and electric power plants and sewage systems were the first tasks
of governments in those bleak years. Only the Europeans could
solve European problems, yet the margin of resources from
America was the necessary catalyst. The Marshall Plan, prepared
in June 1947 and in effect by April 1948, pumped, over five years'
time, nearly $18 billion (more than France's GNP in 1948) into
the European economy. No money was ever better spent, for it
produced both goods and confidence. The recipients cooperated
in creating a new body, the Organization for European Economic
Cooperation (OEEC), to determine priorities and divide up the
Marshall aid. As director of France's economic plan from 1947 to
1952, Monnet, together with the brilliant French economist
Robert Marjolin, sought to give the OEEC a measure of supranational authority as a beginning toward integrating Europe's
economy. Great Britain, unprepared to concede even a scintilla
of sovereignty to a European institution, vetoed the plan.

Amid the confused alarms, in an atmosphere of economic despair, patchwork coalitions of weak parties with hairbreadth margins of parliamentary support tried to govern Europe. The Communist parties, highly organized states-within-the-state, were active and militant as the smell of power filled their nostrils. They did their best to take over in Europe, while at the same time other comrades were attacking Europe's "soft underbelly of Greece and Turkey" — and with some hope of success. Abruptly in March 1947 both the Communist insurgency in Greece and Soviet pressure in Turkey became American problems, when Britain, faced with a financial crisis, advised Washington that it would have to withdraw its support from those countries. The result was the Truman Doctrine, which committed the United States to the support of free peoples against aggression. In February of the following year the brutal coup in Prague, by making clear beyond argument not only the reality of the danger but the weakness of Western defenses, precipitated the decisions leading to the North Atlantic Treaty, which was signed in April 1949.

It was in an atmosphere of anxiety that in May of the following year Monnet induced Foreign Minister Robert Schuman to launch the initiative for a Coal and Steel Community. Schuman's declaration of May 9, 1950, is a document which even today remains a stirring manifesto for European unity. "Europe will not be made all at once, or according to a single general plan," it asserted. First there must be concrete achievements to create a *de facto* solidarity. It was the failure to achieve a united Europe in the past that had made war possible, and if there were ever to be a stable peace there must be a gathering together of the nations of Europe which would eliminate the age-old rivalry of France and Germany. By pooling basic production and creating a new higher authority whose decisions would be binding on governments, the European peoples would, Schuman declared, create the first concrete foundations for the European Federation that was "indispensable to the preservation of peace."

Within less than a year four European states had joined with France and Germany in a treaty that transformed Schuman's manifesto into a living institution. "Good Europeans," as they came to be called, all recognized that this was only the first step. They privately admitted that the Coal and Steel Community by itself made little sense, since one could not isolate and merge only one sector of economy. But they were convinced that the taking of an essentially irrational step would compel rationality. This meant, as they saw it, that Europe would inevitably move toward a fully integrated economy; for they felt certain that over time the concept of supranationality would gradually be accepted as essential, as different sectors of the separate national economies were merged and confidence developed bit by bit in common political bodies to which greater degrees of sovereign authority could be delegated. This was a self-conscious strategy. The time was not yet ripe for a large-scale assault on the citadel of national power, and experience had shown that an effort to move frontally toward some kind of new political organization was likely to lead only to watered-down arrangements for international consultation. It was better, therefore, to make a decisive breakthrough at a narrow point than to undertake an assault on a wide front against entrenched concepts of sovereignty.

Washington responded quickly and affirmatively to Schuman's initiative. American support for European unity has never — as some critics suggest — stemmed merely from a simple-minded belief that Europe can, or should, slavishly repeat our American experience of federalism. Anyone who makes much of the resemblance between the fragmented American states of the 1780's and Europe in the 1960's discloses his own ignorance of history and innocence of the world today. We had better reasons than a bogus historical analogy for supporting Europe's brave move toward unity — not just good will or piety but compelling considerations of national interest. We were firmly convinced that a united Europe would be stronger and less dangerously unstable and no longer a seedbed of war. Combining the strength and talent of a great body of peoples, she could take onto her own shoulders some of the burden of her own defense and well-being otherwise carried at great cost by the United States.

The proposal for the Coal and Steel Community widened the angle of European vision. As the negotiations got under way, it encouraged men to think more broadly about steps that could translate unity from a concept into a functioning reality; and, long before the treaty was finally ratified, Jean Monnet and the

small circle around him were laying plans for a move toward a
political Europe — the creation of institutions that could decide
hard political questions in common. Such was the luck of the
game, however, that the immediate carrying out of this intention
was to be frustrated by an event none of us had anticipated.

On Sunday, June 25, 1950, I had gone to Monnet's thatched-
roof country house sixty kilometers from Paris for a day of work
in connection with the Schuman negotiations. Three or four
Europeans from other delegations had assembled during the
course of the afternoon, when someone brought the word that
the North Korean army had invaded South Korea. Monnet was,
I recall, quick to see the implications. The Americans, he was sure,
would not permit the Communists to get away with a naked
aggression of this kind, since it could mean the beginning of the
erosion of the lines drawn with such difficulty during the postwar
years. Yet an American intervention would not only jeopardize
the Schuman Plan, it would create serious problems for European unity. It might well stir up an atmosphere of panic in Europe
while increasing American insistence on a larger role for Germany
in the defense of the West.

This last point was of special importance.

The United States had quickly got over the insanity of the
Morgenthau Plan, which would have turned the German landscape into a pastoral painting by Millet; and, although the idea
of keeping Germany down had greater survival value in Europe,
pressures for an unstable and punitive settlement did not prevail.
As the war receded, statesmen, first in America and then in Europe, saw the necessity for avoiding the mistakes of 1919. This
time the defeated people would be brought back, cautiously at
first, into the family of Western civilization, encouraged rather
than undercut in their first experiments with democracy, and
integrated into a larger Europe. The Berlin blockade in the
autumn and winter of 1948–1949 pushed the issue to the fore.
It made it necessary to rethink earlier conclusions about German
disarmament and to speed up the timetable for ending the occupation and reestablishing German control of their own affairs.
But it was not easy for Europeans to adjust their thinking to a new
arrangement that would ultimately lead to a reversal of wartime

alliances. France and the Benelux countries still bore the visible wounds of Nazi brutality; Coventry was still in ruins; and only five years had passed since the macabre funeral pyre outside the Führerbunker in Berlin.

Saved from the searing scars of invasion and occupation, we Americans found it easy to take a more flexible line. We foresaw the first glimmerings of a workable German democracy. Moreover, we had special responsibilities as Europe's banker and policeman. Our occupation costs were immense, our Marshall aid substantial, and our world responsibilities were large and growing larger. If Germans were capable of making a financial and military contribution to lighten the burden, why not? Why should they enjoy the privilege of security without contributing to it?

This difference of power and interest and perspective and psychology was to create the first really divisive issue between America and Europe after the war. With the shock of the Korean invasion it was to come to a head very quickly.

The United States first moved to rearm Germany at a conference in the Waldorf-Astoria Towers on September 12, 1950. At that time a fledgling NATO, whose unified command still existed only on paper, had fourteen divisions in Western Europe, facing 175 Soviet divisions in the East. Nonetheless, the European allies found it hard to accept a German participation in European defense that evoked the specter of a new Wehrmacht. After some hesitation, the British Foreign Secretary, Ernest Bevin, agreed to a united defense force, including Germans. But the French representatives remained adamantly opposed, contending that the National Assembly and the French people could not psychologically accept a new German army so quickly after 1945. Agreement of the French government in principle was finally obtained only after assurances were given by General Marshall and the American side that substantial United States forces would be stationed in Europe and the French army would be given financial support. But this was an unpalatable decision for France to make, and Frenchmen did not like it. A month later the French Premier René Pleven proposed to the National

Assembly that the rearmament of Germany be undertaken in a "safe" framework — a fully integrated European army.

I think it almost certain that, had the Korean War not occurred and the Waldorf-Astoria proposals not been made, the European leaders — on Monnet's initiative — would soon have considered the creation of a political community. This was the proper order of events. Monnet knew as well as the next man that there would be a great deal of emotional and irrational resistance to the integration of military forces, given the special sentiments and loyalties involved, particularly in France, and that this was not a soft point in the line for an early attack. All other things being equal, he would have preferred to postpone the effort until a unified framework of political institutions could be erected, since the orderly way to proceed was first to create a political authority and then establish the integrated military force and economic institutions which that authority would control. But all other things were not equal. The American insistence on German rearmament had forced the issue and Monnet feared that, if events were let alone, the creation of a German national army would evoke bitter and frightened responses that would deal a serious blow to the cause of unity.

As drafted, the proposal for a European Defense Community (which came to be known as the EDC) contemplated a European army under a single European executive with all elements in that army wearing a common European uniform, receiving common pay, training under a common system and serving under an integrated command — in the beginning at the army corps level. Germany would be asked to raise twelve divisions. On the political side there would be a Commissariat, which would in effect be Europe's Defense Ministry with authority to form, recruit and train the European army, determine common rates of pay and rules of recruitment and play a major part, in cooperation with the national parliaments, in determining military budgets. In the detailed EDC Treaty finally negotiated and signed by France, Germany, Italy, and the Low Countries on May 25, 1952, Article 38 also committed the signatories to work toward a full federal union. An additional protocol of agreement negotiated by the Six with London in April 1953 committed Britain to keeping four divisions and a fighter air force on the Continent indefinitely.

This imaginative plan was at first viewed skeptically in Washington, particularly by the Pentagon, but Truman and Acheson were won over by the end of 1951 and thereafter the United States gave the idea strong diplomatic support. Europe generally received the proposal with favor, although in France, it was recognized, there would be a vocal and not inconsiderable opposition. Nevertheless Premier Edgar Faure, who headed the fourth of eight French coalition governments in the four years that spanned the birth and death of EDC, was able to obtain Assembly approval *en principe* before attending a NATO meeting at Lisbon in early 1952. The vote, however, was disturbingly close: 327 to 287.

The main opposition votes came from 101 Communists and 114 Gaullists. These two groups of the far Left and Right shared no common philosophy, but they habitually united to oppose all moves toward European unity. In December of 1951, when the Assembly ratified the Coal and Steel Community Treaty by a vote of 376 to 240, all 101 Communists and all 116 Gaullists cast negative ballots. Though Charles de Gaulle had "retired" from active politics, he had called for a "Rally of the French People" (RPF) to express his ideals in political life. In national elections in 1951 the new Gaullist party won 4.3 million votes — second only to the Communists' 4.9 million — and the largest number of seats (120) in the Assembly. The General would later complain of the impotent "regime of parties" under the Fourth Republic, yet his own party contributed in good measure to French parliamentary negativism.

To Communists, the EDC was treason against Moscow and a wicked plot to arm an unreconstructed and still Nazi Germany. To Gaullists the EDC meant treason against France because it involved delegating French sovereignty to a supranational entity and merging the French army, which, to the General, embodied the highest traditions of the French nation. "When I joined the Army," he wrote reverentially (*Complete War Memoirs*, p. 4), "it was one of the greatest things in the world."

In a ferocious propaganda attack on the EDC, the Gaullists and Communists enlisted other allies from among the many Frenchmen worried by a supposed new "German threat." Declared the General in 1952:

> Pell-mell with the two vanquished nations, Germany and Italy, France has to give manpower, arms and money to a stateless melting pot. This humiliation is imposed on her in the name of equality of rights, so that Germany can be considered as not rearmed while rebuilding her military strength. (Lerner and Aron, *France Defeats EDC*, pp. 134–35)

The Communist newspaper *L'Humanité* declared: "We are ready to agree with everybody in order to oppose German rearmament." EDC, it argued, was the cover for a vengeful Wehrmacht that would reconquer East Prussia and annex Alsace-Lorraine. In the press and in the Assembly Left and Right joined in shouting, "The treaty means the end of the French nation." "The European army is nothing more or less than . . . Hitler's Europe without Hitler." "A European S.S. Corps." "Germany," cried a passionate parliamentarian, "is a kind of poisoned cake."

Raymond Aron in *France Defeats EDC* has described the four-year fight over the issue as "the greatest ideological and political debate France has known since the Dreyfus affair." The country was confused, agitated, and unsure of its own views. At the time the Assembly finally voted, public opinion polls showed slightly more than one-third of the nation favoring EDC, slightly less than one-third opposing it and the remaining one-third undecided. A major cause of the defeat and of the deep divisions it opened in France was that its vociferous opponents of the Left and Right focused the debate entirely on the question of Germany, and tried with some success to distort the vote into a referendum on German militarism.

Conducted in a passionate atmosphere that aroused bitter wartime memories and a strong chauvinism, the debate largely ignored the political, economic and military issues of EDC or its meaning as a vehicle for Franco-German rapprochement and European stability through unity. André Philip, a Socialist deputy and a strong advocate of the European Army, summed up the climate of nationalist opinion:

> The main passion which . . . influenced public opinion was *fear*. The glorious era of imperialism when France would assert her power to rule inferior native populations was gone. . . . The nationalism which prevailed against EDC was a peevish and whimpering nationalism which affirmed France's inferiority and her incapacity to adapt to the modern world, by assuming that in a fair competition other countries inevitably would win because of their inherent technical superiority and organization. (Lerner and Aron, *France Defeats EDC*, p. 27)

France in 1954 was a country with public neuroses. It was then, as again today, deeply preoccupied with its own problems and sensitivities. French opposition to the treaty was parochial and particularized, for the treaty was after all a French initiative. Certainly the opposition did not reflect the general color of opinion in Europe, which generally favored the treaty as the breaking of an old cake of custom. The parliaments of four out of the six signatory nations had ratified it prior to 1954 and the Italian parliament was clearly prepared to ratify but was waiting for France to act first. Belgium and Holland had amended their national constitutions to permit the Defense Community. Yet in the end the treaty failed from French constitutional weakness — a casualty of the Fourth Republic's politics of the absurd.

Years later it became fashionable in some American circles to regard the European Defense Community as a jerry-built contraption which never had a chance of success. From time to time I have heard it referred to as though it were an American idea which failed from excessive American zeal. To anyone who watched the situation at first hand, this is, of course, nonsense. It reflects an ignorance of the facts, an insensitivity to the tides and currents of the time, and the fatuous habit of blaming American impetuosity for all the world's blunders.

Pressure from our government was not the reason for the plan's failure; on the contrary it was American support that enabled its proponents to come so near to success. The primary cause of failure was the unwillingness of any of a succession of French governments over a period of four years to risk putting the plan to the parliamentary test. As we Americans were to find out later in connection with our own proposal for a multilateral nuclear force, nothing undermines a good idea more than the indecision and inaction of the nation that puts it forward. But there were other factors as well: virulent Gaullist opposition, the parliamentary weakness of France's eight successive governments (there was no government for over a month in mid-1953 after the fall of René Mayer), rising national frustrations as colonial wars dragged on (Dien Bien Phu fell in May and the Geneva settlement came in July of 1954), Britain's refusal to merge its troops into the "continental" army, and finally the political problems of Mendès-France, whose cabinet included Gaullists.

The failure of ratification of the treaty was, in the light of subsequent history, a tragic event. Had an integrated European army come into being the battalions of retrograde nationalism would have suffered a sharp defeat, fears of rearmed Germany would have been allayed, the momentum toward unity would have been sustained, the Franco-German rapprochement would have been advanced within a congenial framework, and General de Gaulle would have found it almost impossible to try to pull apart the NATO Alliance as he did twelve years later.

Two months after the failure of the EDC, the German Federal Republic became a member of the Alliance. French fear of German rearmament — exploited by politicians of both the Left and the Right — had ironically created a German national army which many Europeans saw as the beginning of the revival of German nationalism. In both Europe and America, editorial writers interpreted the demise of EDC as the end of the drive toward unity in Europe. Some columnists even displayed a kind of masochistic glee in reporting the permanent disappearance of "supranationalism," as though it were a dirty word.

Yet, as has repeatedly happened over the years, the gravediggers had misjudged the vitality of the alleged corpse. A deep strong tide of unity was running and it could not be stopped by the Communists or by the frightened or by Achilles in his tent at Colombey. Ten months after the French Assembly rejected an integrated European army, representatives of the Six met at Messina to "relaunch" the movement toward unity by proposing a revolutionary plan to merge national economies in a European Economic Community.

The projects begun at Messina proceeded more successfully than most experts on either side of the Atlantic believed possible. In Rome on March 25, 1957, the Six signed treaties establishing both the European Atomic Energy Community and the Common Market. In those treaties they declared their determination "to establish the foundations of an even closer union among the European peoples" and called upon "the other peoples of Europe who share their ideal to join in their efforts." In ten years they have taken the first long strides toward merging their national economies in a single European economy, creating a mass market in which goods and capital can move freely across boundaries. No one can say with precision how fully the Common Market is responsible for the spectacular increase in Europe's standard of living in the past decade, but I would challenge anyone to deny that it has been the single most significant factor.

Today Europe is enjoying the benefits and suffering the frustrations of a task half done. By creating a vast mass market it has greatly increased its standard of living and is exploiting the economies of scale, but it is far from achieving full economic integration, primarily because it has not made parallel progress on the political front — and that remains a very big piece of unfinished business.

V

European Unity
and the Atlantic Partnership

THE phrase "European political unity" has always meant different things to different men. Like other abstract and spacious terms that cloud our political discourse — "special relationship," "détente," and even "peace" and "aggression" — it often suggests a swampland of semantic confusion. To the empirical British, all a priori definitions of European unity are suspect; thus Harold Macmillan argued that "We British will certainly be prepared to accept the merger of sovereignty in practice if not in principle." To the Gallic mind, more attuned to conceptual thought, the term can mean several different things — depending on the philosophy of the speaker and sometimes on his convenience.

General de Gaulle, who regards the word "Europe" as synonymous with "France," employs the expression "European unity" in two quite different ways. When he uses it with approbation he refers to a kind of Latin-Teutonic confederation of "the Rhine, the Alps and the Pyrenees," presumably run from Paris, or "a Europe from the Atlantic to the Urals," presumably run by a Franco-Soviet directorate. When he employs the term in a denigratory manner it is usually to condemn the functional approach of the Rome Treaty. That approach, in the General's view (expressed at a press conference on May 15, 1962), would result in "some kind of integrated Esperanto or Volapuk . . . ruled by some technocratic, stateless and irresponsible Areopagus."

To find a single and reasonably well-articulated definition one must turn to the "founding fathers" of the Coal and Steel Community and the Common Market. They have a clearly formed conception of what European unity means and how it should evolve. Their central thesis is that, even though human nature may not change, human conduct and responsibility can be molded by institutions. The first step in unifying Europe, therefore, is to create common institutions capable of administering common rules of conduct. With increasing experience these institutions can be given additional shape and content and made progressively more responsible to the will of the people. In the end the enforcement of common rules through these evolving institutions and the adjustment of human behavior to such rules will lead the peoples of Europe inexorably away from smaller allegiances to nation-states, toward a common adherence and larger loyalty to a single European political entity — a full-fledged federation.

These European activists have never lost their way in abstract argument over political philosophy. There is little in their speeches and writings reminiscent of the eighteenth-century *philosophes* or even the *Federalist* papers, although they certainly have the intellectual equipment for such speculation, and constitutional controversies may well become more relevant as institutional evolution proceeds. The preeminently practical approach of men like Schuman and Monnet has reflected not only their personal temper; it has no doubt also been a reaction to the long and not very happy French experience with constitution-making. But whatever the reasons for abjuring the codifying habits of the civil lawyers, the so-called "good Europeans" are in agreement on two fundamental theses.

The first is that substantial progress is unlikely to be made merely by formal arrangements for consultation among governments, which the British had insisted upon, for example, in drafting the final acts of the OEEC. The futility of such arrangements has been proven again and again. Intergovernmental debating societies are simply not good enough.

The second thesis is equally demonstrable. To make sound progress toward unity, Europeans should, at an early period, get on with the creation of a common parliament directly elected by the European people and not just a body of representatives from national legislatures. The limited utility of this latter device has been demonstrated by the Council of Europe and even by the Common Assembly created under the treaties of Rome and Paris.

Given these views, it was no accident that the perceptive drafters of the Rome Treaty in 1957 included a provision that proposals should be made for the future convocation of a directly elected European parliament. The creation of such a parliament would serve many purposes. It would give unchallenged legitimacy to the Brussels institutions. By providing for the direct involvement of the electorate in the choice of representatives to a common European legislative body, it would influence people to see issues through a European and not merely a national focus. It would, over the years, build up a body of European statesmen by inducing politicians to seek careers for themselves in a larger political arena. Finally, it should bring about the development of a party structure on European rather than national lines.

In addition, of course, a common parliament would tend to expand its own powers since it is in the nature of legislative bodies to regard themselves as the authentic repositories of the popular will. When the King's messenger ordered the States-General to disband on a fateful July day in 1789, Mirabeau responded, "Tell your master that we are here by the will of the people, and shall not leave except under the force of bayonets." The "will of the people" is the title deed of legitimacy and legislators invariably feel its authority. The House of Commons was only the first of many parliaments to demonstrate the kinetic dynamism of legislative assemblies in accumulating political power.

Our country has, ever since the war, supported the goal of a united Western Europe of the kind contemplated by Monnet and Schuman. Congress expressed its endorsement of European unity consistently in successive enactments of legislation to give effect to the Marshall Plan. General Eisenhower's famous speech at the Guild Hall in London in 1945 was a brillant and eloquent endorsement of the idea by an American leader whose experience gave his views a ring of special authority. To be sure, American formulations of the goal have shifted in emphasis as Europe has regained her economic health and vitality. In the 1940's, when Europe was under acute military pressure from the East and was still absorbed in rebuilding her cities and industries, Americans looked on European unity primarily as a measure to speed recovery and underpin military security. But as the European economies grew stronger, while at the same time America was expanding her world responsibilities, the United States began to feel the need for a unified Europe that could carry her fair share of the common burden and act as our "equal partner." This idea was explicitly enunciated by President Kennedy in one of his greatest speeches — his address at Independence Hall in Philadelphia on July 4, 1962. There he said:

> We believe that a united Europe will be capable of playing a greater role in the common defense, of responding more generously to the needs of poor nations. . . . We see in such a Europe a partner with whom we can deal on a basis of full equality in all the great and burdensome tasks of building and defending a community of free nations.

A year later and only five months before his death, Kennedy made a triumphant tour of Europe. At the Paulskirche in Frankfurt, where professors and parliamentarians had drafted the first German Constitution in 1849, he amplified the concept further:

> . . . we have and now look forward to a Europe united and strong — speaking with a common voice — acting with a common will — a world power capable of meeting world problems as a full and equal partner. . . . The great present task of construction is here on this continent where the effort for a unified free Europe is under way. It is not for Americans to prescribe to Europeans how this effort should be carried forward. . . . Yet the reunion of Europe, as Europeans shape it — bringing a permanent end to the civil wars that have repeatedly wracked the world — will continue to have the determined support of the

United States. For that reunion is a necessary step in strengthening the community of freedom.

As an objective, the duality of European unity and Atlantic partnership seems to me beyond cavil. Yet it is possible that the habitual linking of these two concepts in American official statements has not been altogether wise. It may have tended to create false conceptions both at home and abroad.

The confusion at home is one of emphasis. Some Americans have been tempted to believe that partnership with the United States is more important than the unity of Europe, disregarding the fact that such unity is an essential prerequisite to the development of strong Atlantic ties. I find this kind of thinking thoroughly wrongheaded, for, until Europe knows the reality of roughly equivalent power, Europeans will never risk the full acceptance of a partnership relation. They are quite aware that a junior partner has little to say about the affairs of a firm, and unless they feel equal in fact they will be likely to regard "partnership" as a Yankee device designed to induce them to serve as bush-beaters and gun-bearers in support of United States policies — including policies of which they are skeptical and in the making of which they have had little voice.

There is nothing odd or reprehensible about such an attitude. Europeans, by and large, were inclined to follow America during the postwar period when they saw their own interests directly engaged, as in the case of the defense of Western Europe. In the immediate postwar period, there were, to be sure, collisions with European views and interests largely over colonial issues, but these tended to be submerged in Europe's preoccupation with affairs at home and forgotten as prosperity increased. For the most part, Europeans were inclined to let us Americans go our own way when we occupied ourselves with activities in faraway countries that did not seem to concern them directly.

More recently, our preoccupation with our expanding obligations has led us to nag European governments to participate in projects which, no matter how commendable in abstract terms, did not appear to them as particularly relevant to, or within the scope of, their immediate interests. During the early days of the Kennedy Administration, for example, we regularly "dunned" our European allies to provide supplementary gifts of foreign aid to specific African and Asian countries, including a fund for the stabilization of the Laotian kip. Since both France and Britain were providing assistance to their former colonies, we directed our Community Chest drives most persistently at the German Federal Republic, which, having no vestigial colonial territories, was only just beginning to think about foriegn aid — the self-respecting twentieth-century equivalent of the burden of empire. The Germans were polite but confused; they found the urgency of our importunings hard to understand. With no well-developed national tradition of philanthrophy they viewed the whole enterprise with doubt, since, though they were making notable economic progress at home, they felt no responsibility for the areas overseas to which America was beseeching them to give money. The result was predictable. In the course of time, as American demands became more routine and cumulatively more irksome, Germany gradually built up not only resistance but an unhappy — though not very well-founded — sense of being put upon. And Americans have not always been sufficiently aware of the truism that the law of diminishing returns applies just as much in diplomacy as it does in economics.

Apart from soliciting funds and demanding that other nations do their share, the American government has, I fear, often tended to take it for granted that its European friends should support its world policies. We have, we hope, outgrown the expressions once frequently heard in political speeches. "What's the matter with those Europeans? Why don't they help us in Laos or support us in Cuba or Zanzibar or the Dominican Republic? After all, think of all the Marshall Plan money we gave them." But we still tend to feel sorry for ourselves for carrying too great a share of the burden of the world's troubles without recognizing that our assumption of some of this burden was not automatic but the result of a careful or careless decision. Moreover it was a decision that could in the individual case be right or wrong, since, while we may feel reasonably comfortable about the purity of our motives, we cannot be certain of the infallibility of our wisdom. Yet I have never known us to concede that other nations might be right in suggesting that we have gotten into certain messy situations through an excess of zeal or evangelical purpose. Nor have we American very often acknowledged even to ourselves that Europeans are unlikely to see their interests in the same global terms in which we see ours because of the structural factor — the disparity in size and resources.

These remarks are not intended to diminish either the motives or effectiveness of our efforts around the world throughout this convulsive postwar period. I think on the whole that we have done reasonably well and that there is no historical precedent for the generosity of our policy. But that does not mean that other peoples completely share our own appraisal of our own motives or our own effectiveness. Most fair-minded Europeans would agree that we have no discernible selfish motive for much of our involvement in far places, although this sometimes leads more to suspicion and incredulity than to admiration. What is most important to them is that we have become involved because of a decision made in Washington in which they and their governments had little or no part. They feel themselves spectators rather than players, and no amount of sanctimonious exhortation is going to change their psychology. One cannot induce the fans onto the playing field by a sheer act of will, any more than the fact of equality can be created by a mere act of grace.

Thus, so long as there remain those structural differences — the disparity of size and resources — that lead to quite different definitions of national interest and hence of national involvement, there will be an awkwardness in the relationship across the Atlantic. And this awkwardness will only be exacerbated by attempts to bridge the gap through slogans that ignore the realities. I am convinced, therefore, that there can be no truly easy and effective partnership between America and Europe until there is a Europe in the political sense. Meanwhile, good working relationships across the Atlantic will be limited to those areas where there is a substantial identity of interest between the United States and the individual small or medium-sized European nations.

There are, I recognize, many confirmed and dedicated "Atlanticists" who would not agree with these views. They would ask us to concentrate our efforts on the creation of Atlantic committees and parliamentary assemblies and they argue that our problems with Europe would be resolved if we would only engage in greater consultation with our European neighbors. But I know of no one experienced in peacetime transatlantic consultation who honestly believes this. My own experience has certainly been to the contrary. Disturbed by the growing gulf of Atlantic misunderstanding, particularly with regard to Vietnam, I proposed to President Johnson in the autumn of 1964 that we try to establish procedures for high-level, systematic consultations among the NATO members on important problems arising outside of Western Europe. Having previously tried out the idea on NATO's Secretary General, Manlio Brosio, who gave it his blessing, I argued that the fifteen NATO nations should add four extra meetings annually, at the level of Deputy Foreign Ministers or above, to their existing schedule. These would concern themselves with questions beyond the geographic limits of the Alliance, such as Cyprus and the Congo and China. They would supplement the two existing annual NATO Foreign Ministers' meetings. In this way a top-level NATO consultation lasting three days would occur once every two months. The agenda of the meetings would be "open," so that any NATO member could raise and discuss any topic of particular interest to his government. Between formal meetings of the Fifteen there would be time for more limited, informal talks among smaller groups bilaterally and multilaterally.

With the approval of President Johnson, I discussed the plan with a number of European Foreign Ministers, and at the December 1964 ministerial meeting in Paris it was agreed to hold a few meetings on an *ad hoc* basis to try out the efficacy of the idea. Three such NATO meetings were, in fact, held in early 1965, one at the request of Belgium and two at the request of the United States. Agendas were organized and any member government was permitted to table any subject it wished. I represented the United States at two of the sessions on March 31 and July 13, 1965, and found a number of the conferees, including Belgium's Foreign Minister, Paul-Henri Spaak, and the veteran Dutch Foreign Minister, Joseph Luns, enthusiastic participants. Yet these consultations on world problems rarely advanced beyond the *pro forma* stage of expressing known positions. They failed to stimulate much lively discussion about alternative policies or to become a serious vehicle of coordination among the foreign offices of Europe and America.

In spite of efforts to give meaning and reality to these discussions, the impression persisted that this was merely another American-made gadget designed to corral European approval for United States policies. Most governments shied away from the expression of any but the most formal views, emphasizing that their interests outside of Europe were marginal, and that each problem discussed was basically one for the United States to deal with as it saw best. There was some criticism of American policies but no suggestions of constructive alternatives. France, which had sought in 1958 to create a World Directorate (composed of the United States, France and the United Kingdom) to develop strategy and concert policy around the globe, refused to participate in the discussions at all. Under instructions from his government, the French representative read a statement expressing the view that NATO was not an appropriate forum for considering problems that occurred outside the geographic limits defined by the North Atlantic Treaty.

Quite possibly, the French aversion to the use of NATO to discuss problems in Africa, Latin America and the Middle East derived in part from a sense of politesse — or if you will, *snobisme*. It was beneath the dignity of the important powers like Britain, France and the United States to discuss serious world problems in the presence of their smaller allies, such as the Benelux countries, Norway, Denmark, Portugal and Greece. Yet it was not the disparity in size between France and Belgium that impeded effective consultation on matters outside the European area; it was the disparity between the individual nations of Europe, on the one hand, and the United States on the other. There was a crucial difference, in other words, between a nation having the means and will needed to assume world responsibilities and nations disabled from doing so by their limited national resources. My conclusion from this experience is that equality is a political fact measured by the possession of power. It cannot be achieved simply by improving arrangements for international consultation. It is not a question of diplomatic manners, but of the realities of resources and the national will to use them. Thus, it seems to me that European feelings of vexation in relations with America are bound to increase so long as Europe, because of her anachronistic structure, is unable to translate her economic strength and prosperity into political terms giving her a single effective voice in world affairs.

I come, therefore, to a very simple point: it does not make sense to build more comprehensive institutions for European-American cooperation until the Europeans themselves progress toward unity. This will be regarded as heresy in some circles in my own country. In fact, there is a vocal body of American opinion that believes we should actively discourage efforts to modernize the structure of Europe because a unified Europe might not in all instances support United States policy. In my view this is arrant nonsense. It is based on a disregard both of European opinion and the realities of transatlantic cooperation, for, unpleasant as the thought may be to many Americans, there is little resonance in Europe for closer Atlantic ties. Europeans are, of course, anxious that we continue to provide an effective nuclear defense for the West and by and large they wish us well. They are prepared to cooperate with us on monetary policies and matters of trade and on other specific problems within the Atlantic area, but except in a very narrow circle the Atlantic idea speeds few heartbeats. Politicians on both sides of the water speak grandiosely about an Atlantic Community but the term is abstract and remote from everyday experience, though it is clearly more real than the patent rhetorical artificiality of the "Pacific Community," which some have tried recently to call up out of the deep. For, rhetoric aside, there is a fear among Europeans that if they get too close to us we will absorb and smother them by the preponderance of our own size and weight and energy — and we may even get them into trouble through an excess of zeal.

I think we should recognize, therefore, that so long as Europe remains in its present fragmented state Europeans will shy away from a wholehearted participation in efforts to make decisions through Atlantic institutions — particularly decisions that relate to matters outside the Atlantic area. Washington, they fear, will dominate every council and impose its will on every issue, making the Europeans simple ancillaries of American policy. I find little reason to regard this fear as well founded, since existing Atlantic institutions like the OECD, far from being efficient instruments of American policy, have not been able to do very much at all; and that would be the fate of any other Atlantic institutions established before progress is made toward the reorganization and rationalization of European political power on a modern basis.

I would, therefore, say to the more Atlantic-minded of my American friends that the road they advocate is not likely to lead far at the present time. And I think that some of them are being very foolish when they conjure up the specter of a united Europe that would constitute a "third force" and thus, by their definition, a dangerous element in world affairs. There is, of course, nothing new about such a fear and it has not been limited to America. Hugh Gaitskell argued in 1962 that "a new powerful European state may seek to become a 'third force.' . . . It is possible that . . . it would prove a most unstable influence on world affairs. I do not pretend to be sure, but we cannot ignore these possibilities" (Cook, *Floodtide in Europe*, p. 263). I thought it curious at the time that the leader of the British opposition should be frightened by the vision of an emergent third global power that might play a balance of power role, the traditional policy of his own country; and, on any premise, I considered his alarm quite ill founded.

The united Europe I posit would include the British as an integral and active component, and would thus be a political amalgam of the most historically creative and civilized peoples of the West, tied together not merely by a common geography but by the commitment to a common civilization. Such a Europe would undoubtedly see certain issues from a point of vantage differing from ours on the Western side of the Northern Ocean.

But would this be a bad thing? I do not think so. It seems to me that we Americans have been handicapped by our lonely power position in the West and that we have missed a great deal by having to shape policy without the active intellectual and power contribution of a Europe *engagé*. I would, therefore, like to see a strong assertive Europe, expressing its independent views and its own personality. I have little fear that over the years such a Europe would disagree with the United States on many great issues; by and large, we would see things in the same general terms and react with the same humane impulses. Moreover, we would, I think, find ourselves working closely together not so much because of institutional arrangements bridging the Atlantic but because we could regard one another for the first time with full mutual respect, recognizing that equality was now a fact and no longer a stylized figure of speech, which deceived no one — least of all the participants.

V I

The Special Problem of the
United Kingdom

F IVE years ago on a chilly December day a former Secretary
of State journeyed to West Point, New York, to address a
student conference. Halfway through his address Mr. Dean
Acheson said:

> Great Britain has lost an empire and has not yet found a role.
> The attempt to play a separate power role — that is, a role apart
> from Europe, a role based on a "special relationship" with the
> United States, a role based on being the head of a "common-
> wealth" which has no political structure, or unity, or strength and
> enjoys a fragile and precarious economic relationship by means
> of the Sterling area and preferences in the British market — this
> role is about played out.

Flashed across the Atlantic on news agency wires, these words
caused a noisy flap in London press rooms and government offices, not to mention clubs and countinghouses. There were cries
of outrage and wounded dignity; the Beaverbrook press referred
to an American "stab in the back" of her British ally. Even the
Prime Minister felt compelled to get into the act. Mr. Acheson,
said Prime Minister Macmillan, had underestimated the British,
thus falling into an error "whch has been made by quite a lot of
people in the course of the last four hundred years, including

69

Philip of Spain, Louis the Fourteenth, Napoleon, the Kaiser and Hitler" (Cook, *Floodtide in Europe*, p. 266).

Today Mr. Acheson's formulation is part of the conventional wisdom and no one would think of listing him in such curious company. In the press, in trade unions, at Oxford and Cambridge, on both sides of the House of Commons, much starker terms than his are used to describe the decline in Britain's power. An English journalist writes that "Britain and America have exchanged roles. Britain has inherited America's self-righteous isolationism. . . . There would be something comic, if it were not also tragic, in this remarkable transposition" (Mander, *Great Britain or Little England?*, p. 30). A Labour Member of Parliament cribs from Acheson when he says "Britain has given up an Empire. She has not yet found a new national purpose. . . . Her national petulance is often preposterous. . . . I see symptoms of the same kind of malaise in Britain that afflicted France in the 1930's." A sardonic generation of young Englishmen refers to its state as "mini-Britain" and suggests with mock seriousness that it is evolving into an insular version of Austria or Sweden. In five years Britain has gone a long way to, in the words of Adam Smith, "accommodate her future views and designs to the real mediocrity of her circumstances." From the stage of John Osborne to the hemlines of Mary Quant to the pop culture of the Beatles, Englishmen have expressed an irreverence for past and passing forms — a recognition that Kipling died at Dunkirk.

This adjustment has not occurred without tears, and it is easy to understand why. A century ago the United Kingdom was the richest and most powerful nation in the world. Victoria ruled over one-fifth of all mankind. The imperial sun had not finally set even when her grandchildren reigned. The standard of living of the British elite was the envy of the world. The City of London was everybody's banker. British bottoms carried most of the world's commerce. With the British fleet and merchant marine the largest in the world, "Britannia Rules the Waves" was a geopolitical truism as well as a patriotic song.

The 1914–1918 War destroyed the furniture if not the façade. It struck down a gifted and gallant generation that would otherwise have led the country during the 1920's and 1930's. (I know no one who even now can read the posthumous World War poetry of British youth without a choke in the throat, a sense of ineffable waste and loss and poignancy.) It made England debtor, no longer creditor, to the New World. It set in motion social forces and economic dislocations that brought critical changes after 1945. The black years of the 1920's and early 1930's seared the British soul and made Englishmen as sensitive to unemployment as are Germans to inflation.

Britain had been the first nation to experience the industrial revolution. Yet from the flower of success obtruded a nettle of danger, for early industrialization and a long-dominant position in world trade produced an enervating complacency that was disturbed but not destroyed by the Second World War. Britain's position as banker and as manufacturer was increasingly challenged by nations organized with the great internal mass markets that Britain lacked. As a small island engaged in transforming raw materials into industrial products, the United Kingdom depended on trade; but now trade was shrinking, endangering the pattern, and protectionism could do no more than alleviate the symptoms while reinforcing the disease. Thus, turning the Empire into a closed trading system through the Ottawa Preferences of 1932 proved only a short-term expedient; perhaps it helped the United Kingdom weather the depression of the 1930's and the first postwar years, but it was costly in the long run, since it enabled the British to postpone hard decisions about the structure of their economy in relation to Europe. Nor did it prevent British trade with the Commonwealth from decreasing after the war, as newly created member nations raised their tariffs and built their own steel mills, turning the old preferential system into a series of levies on the mother country rather than a supporting crutch for her economy.

The Second World War accelerated a process that was already far advanced. Even German bombs did not force needed modernization. The Luftwaffe wreaked urban destruction, but nothing like the wholesale industrial havoc that Allied bombers imposed on the Ruhr — destruction that, in the end, made necessary the replacement of much of Germany's industrial plant with up-to-date factories. For this reason and many others Britain failed to match continental growth rates. Throughout the 1950's Germany's economy grew three times faster than that of the United Kingdom, Italy's more than two times faster, and France's one and one-half times more quickly than the sluggish British economy. So far in the 1960's the British growth rate still lags behind the others.

Weakened by the First World War, the Empire bled to death after the Second, but this did not keep the British entrepreneurial class from living on accumulated wealth and following traditional policies and habits. Nominally the United Kingdom headed a World Commonwealth. But, swollen by the addition of newly independent Afro-Asians, it lost most of the clubby, Anglo-Saxon character of the old prewar Commonwealth. It changed, as one disappointed Australian once told me, from Boodles to the Royal Automobile Club. Each new addition saw the collective political meaning of the Commonwealth wither to little more than a congeries of bilateral arrangements between the Motherland and the ex-colonies.

There was, of course, unfairness in all this and some British felt it. England in a real sense had been penalized by her own valor. Staying bloody but unbowed had impaired her ability to adjust to a new world. Unlike the continental nations that were conquered and occupied, her political fabric had remained intact. The British were not compelled by failure and defeat to challenge the competence or question the adequacy of their political institutions; the "victory" of 1945 reinforced the illusion that Britain was still a great power. Alongside the United States and the Soviet Union, she was automatically the third member at every parley; in the postwar world she could take for granted a seat in every world council.

Yet the contrast between her accepted position and the power she could command injected ambiguity into British policy. Every postwar government from Attlee's to Harold Wilson's has been unsure of England's real place in the world. What was Great Britain in the mid-twentieth century? Was she: (1) the industrial third "great power," (2) the leader of the Commonwealth, (3) a major European nation, (4) America's special partner, or (5) the West's "honest broker" with Moscow? Some of these roles were mutually contradictory, yet governments were tempted to try to play them all at the same time — and as a result they often stumbled over their own feet.

Each successive British leader has, to some degree, pursued what Anthony Eden called the policy of the "three-legged stool," the concept that British policy rests on three equally important and complementary "legs": the Commonwealth, Europe and America. In a similar figure of speech Churchill told Adenauer that British policy saw America, the Commonwealth and Europe as three distinct circles that touched each other.

But the script has been rewritten again and again and the role has become much more exacting. In the early years after the war most of the British believed that they could still go home again to the world of 1939. Certainly no one could deny that England remained a great, if declining, colonial power. Even six years after the war she still controlled a hundred million colonial peoples and her soldiers manned a string of strategic bases that girdled the globe, with seventy-five thousand troops in Egypt alone. The Union Jack still flew in Suez and Singapore, Khartoum and Zanzibar. The economic belt-tightening at home, it was thought, was only temporary; Britain was better off than the Continent, which in 1948 was still suffering an ordeal of deprivation. In 1945, the Empire seemed more powerful than all of Western Europe — and the British believed it was. Thus when Britain could have had the leadership of Europe for the asking, she saw no reason to ask.

Five years earlier, Winston Churchill had seized upon a plan developed by Jean Monnet to merge France and Britain in a single state, with common citizenship and with a single parliament and cabinet. It was the anxious moment when France was falling and the Reynaud government in Bordeaux was debating whether to capitulate to the Germans or continue the fight by moving the government to North Africa and bringing along the still intact French navy and as much of the army as could be speedily evacuated. The Forty-nine-year-old Under Secretary of War, Charles de Gaulle, advocated this latter course. In the midst of defeat and exhaustion, de Gaulle saw in Monnet's bold proposal for union a tactical move that could stiffen the will to resist of a divided French cabinet. It was one of the few occasions when de Gaulle and Monnet saw eye to eye on anything.

Churchill recognized the same possibilities and sold the Monnet proposal to his cabinet. De Gaulle, in London, flashed the word to Bordeaux. All this happened on June 16, 1940 — a few days or hours too late. The Reynaud government had already decided to resign, paving the way for Pétain's succession and a humiliating armistice with Hitler less than forty-eight hours later. It was a moment of weariness and cynicism and disenchantment, a time of hysteria and the death of idealism, and there is little wonder that, peering through the distorted lenses of their own despair, the last tired leaders of the Third Republic viewed Churchill's offer without hope or comprehension. They saw it merely as an improvised "gadget" — which in part it was — rather than a bold stroke of political vision — which it also was. Schooled in the petty politics of Anglo-French diplomacy in the interwar years, they discerned nothing more than a "plot" by Britannia Militant to gobble up the French Empire at its moment of maximum weakness.

This was a historic moment lost — but not irretrievably. After the war Churchill took up the theme of Anglo-French cooperation in rebuilding a common Europe. As opposition leader from 1945 to 1951, he became the chief apostle of European unification. In a speech at the University of Zurich in September 1946, he argued for Franco-German reconciliation as the first step toward "a kind of United States of Europe"; and four years later, at Strasbourg in August 1950, he proposed "immediate creation of a European Army under a unified command in which we should all bear a working and honorable part." In the same election year the seventy-six-year-old opposition leader gave one of his most memorable speeches in the House of Commons, a plea for building a united Europe on the three pillars of Britain, France and Germany. Forgetting "ancient feuds and the horrible deeds and tragedies of the past," said Churchill, Frenchmen and Englishmen should raise Germans "to an equal rank and to a lasting association with them." These three peoples could then "make the core on the nucleus upon which all the other civilized democracies of Europe . . . can rally and combine." In the mid-twentieth century, "the grand design of Charlemagne must be readapted to modern conditions." There were, of course, difficulties, but "How easy it is to mar large unities, how hard to make them." Yet, he concluded, "It takes too poor a view of man's mission here on earth to suppose that he is not capable of rising . . . far above his day-to-day surroundings," to surmount ancient national rivalries and submerge them in a better unity.

This was intoxicating rhetoric, but it was not embodied in a new British policy when Churchill returned to power in 1951; for Sir Winston never cleared up the ambiguity in his own mind between the claims of an empire he had served all his life and the demands of a very different future for Britain. His government still avoided entangling ties with the Continent; it continued to try to "keep all the options open" seeking to pursue a wide variety and complexity of foreign roles.

In this the Conservative government of Winston Churchill was doing nothing different from the Labour government that had preceded it. In 1947 and 1948, Ernest Bevin had stoutly resisted French argument for a supranational OEEC to administer Marshall aid. In 1949, Sir Stafford Cripps had vetoed Monnet's ambitious plan for a merger of the French and British economies. In the same year, when the Council of Europe was born in Strasbourg, Britain had joined halfheartedly but had torpedoed attempts to make it the effective nucleus of a true "European Parliament."

Monnet had made a heroic effort — in a series of secret meetings in London — to bring Britain into the Coal and Steel Community in 1950, but he had been answered with a flat "no." "A political federation, limited to Western Europe," the Labour government had said, "is not compatible either with our Commonwealth ties, our obligations as a member of the wider Atlantic community, or as a world power" (Stanley, *NATO in Transition*, p. 42). This sentiment was echoed by opposition politicians like Harold Macmillan who declared, "We will allow no supranational authority to put large masses of our people out of work in Durham, in the Midlands, in South Wales, or in Scotland," while David Eccles conjured up the vision of "a cartel made into an honest woman of colossal proportions."

Thus when Churchill came to power it would have been surprising had he translated his high-flown European vision into British policy. As it was, his government did nothing original; it simply continued well-established policies of frustration and noncooperation. London stayed clear of the very European army scheme that Churchill himself had first proposed, with his Foreign Secretary, Anthony Eden, expressing the prevailing outlook in a speech at Columbia University on January 11, 1952. Referring to "the frequent suggestions that the United Kingdom should join a federation of the continent of Europe," Eden said, "This is something which we know, in our bones, we cannot do." The reasons were ones of deep tradition and sentiment, combined with the mysterious and potent springs of an ancient sea power. "Britain's story and her interests," Eden argued, "lie far beyond the continent of Europe. Our thoughts move across the seas to the many communities in which our people play their part, in every corner of the world. These are our family ties. That is our life: without it we should be no more than some millions of people living on an island off the coast of Europe, in which nobody wants to take any particular interest."

The Eden and Macmillan governments rejected invitations to join the continental nations in building a Common Market. They contented themselves with a series of weak counterproposals involving no derogation of national sovereignty. To France and her five partners this was simply not good enough. The Six went their own way toward a revolutionary pooling of national economies. Then came Suez in 1956, which shattered some old illusions and undercut at least three of the five independent roles British governments had sought to play since the war. After November 6, 1956, Britain looked less and less like an independent "great power"; the "special relationship" with America turned out to be not so special after all; and the Commonwealth came close to fragmentation under strain. Subsequent events, including the Berlin and Cuban missile crises and the Rhodesian problem, continued the trend toward weakening those old roles, pushing Britain each time a little closer to the realization that she was no longer, as Professor Andre Siegfried had once called her, "a ship moored in European waters" but an integral part of the European mainland separated from the rest of Europe by a channel that technology had shrunk to the width of a canal. The one attractive but still untried role was to seek her destiny in a larger arena by joining in the building of a united Europe.

From the vantage point of 1967 I think it sad that the British did not come to this realization twenty years ago. From the same Olympian but not very helpful perspective I find it very bad luck that their latter-day conversion to the European cause should have occurred only after a domineering nationalist leader had come to power in France. A critical deficiency of history is that events are so rarely in phase; yet in international affairs progress quite frequently depends on the simultaneous existence of like-minded governments. The Schuman Plan got under way because the leaders of France and Germany and Italy were all Christian Democrats who shared a common world view and saw eye to eye on the European politics of the day. But the Christian Democrats were not in power in the United Kingdom; Britain's Ernest Bevin and even Clement Attlee were men cut from a different cloth, worlds apart in outlook and temperament. To many British Socialists, both in the trade unions and in Fabian circles, there was something suspect, something popish and reactionary, about "Christian Democracy," with its subtle shadings of the black and the red. A Bevin and a Schuman just did not speak the same political language. Preoccupied at home with nationalizing transport and fuel and steel, a Labour government was not apt to risk the dreams it had cherished during years in the wilderness by a hazardous venture with Europeans — who, everybody knew, were not very trustworthy.

Across the Channel, suspicions ran the other way. Many "good Europeans" were products of a nineteenth-century continental tradition that saw Britain aloof and apart and "different" from the rest of Europe. Men like the late Konrad Adenauer were ill-at-ease in the presence both of Britain and "Socialism" and quite prepared to go it alone without either; in fact, "der Alte" betrayed this parochial sense of suspicion and superior virtue in an interview not long before he died, when he said:

. . . the British . . . have no particular urge to work. After they were thrown out of Northern France, they turned to trading and colonizing, and acquired an easy way of life — different from the hard work that is the style on the Continent. They are still at it.

Europe, as I wrote to President Kennedy early in his administration, was "still bemused by the conflicting prejudices of Lord Vansittart and Major Thompson."

By 1961, however, eleven years had passed since the Schuman Plan, and the Common Market was already an unchallengeable success. With their instinctive ability to recognize a *fait accompli* when they saw one, the British were gradually adjusting their view to the new reality. I was brought face to face with this in London a little more than two months after the inauguration of President Kennedy when, on March 30, I called on the Lord Privy Seal, Mr. Edward Heath, at his request. Present at the meeting were several British civil servants, including Sir Frank Lee, an old friend from wartime days, who was then Joint Permanent Secretary of the Treasury.

Mr. Heath launched immediately into the purpose of the meeting, which was to discuss Britain's evolving approach toward European integration. He advised me of recent but preliminary British conversations with certain members of the Six. As our discussion continued it was made clear that the British government wished to ascertain how the United States — and particularly the new administration — would react if Britain were to apply for accession to the Rome Treaty.

I had to confess that I had never had occasion to discuss the specific question with President Kennedy. Thus, I said, I could not state definitely whether I was making United States policy or interpreting it, but, in any event, I would give an unambiguous answer which I was confident the President would support. I reviewed at some length the reasons why the United States had consistently encouraged efforts toward unity in Europe, putting great emphasis on the need for Franco-German rapprochement and the necessity of tying Germany firmly to the West. There were, I noted, latent dangers in the continuance of a divided Europe and specifically a divided Germany. I underlined our regret that the United Kingdom had never been prepared to accept fully the commitments of the Treaty of Rome, since we had always felt that British membership was an indispensable element of European stability.

"If," I concluded, "Britain is now prepared to recognize that the Rome Treaty is not a static document but a process that could eventually lead to an evolving European community — something in the nature of a European federation — and if Britain can make the great national decision to join Europe on those terms, I am confident that my government will regard this as a major contribution to Western solidarity and the stability of the free world. So long as Britain remains outside the European Community, she is a force for division rather than cohesion, since she is like a giant lodestone drawing with unequal degrees of force on each member state. But if Great Britain now decides to participate in the formidable efforts to unite Europe, she can, and I am sure will, apply her unique political genius — in which we have great confidence — toward the creation of a unity that can transform the Western world."

I left the meeting with a sense that something historic might have happened, although my elation was not fully shared by all my colleagues. One of the economic experts in our Embassy — a man of first-rate competence and perception — felt that I had given the British government too much encouragement and had thus undermined the position the United States had consistently taken regarding a merger of the Six and Seven.

The dubiety of my colleague was based on the past few years of experience with British efforts to have its economic cake and eat it too. At the time they first stood aside from the Common Market negotiation, the British had apparently been convinced that the scheme had little chance of adoption. As soon as it became reasonably certain that the Treaty of Rome would be signed and ratified, they countered with a proposal — put forward in June 1956 — that the European Economic Community become a part of a broader but looser Free Trade Area which would include virtually all the other countries of Western Europe. The idea was to create, in essence, a commercial trading bloc that would be discriminatory against the United States and the rest of the world yet offer the West none of the political benefits of true European integration. This British proposal was widely, and I think correctly, interpreted by the Six as an attempt to provide a watered-down substitute for the Common Market, and after a year and a half of technical negotiations the proposal failed — primarily in the face of opposition from France.

Thereafter, almost as a conditioned reflex of balance of power politics — reasoning that in the face of a continental alliance Britain should automatically organize the rest of Europe against it — the United Kingdom put together a loose commercial arrangement of the so-called Outer Seven countries — Britain, Switzerland, Sweden, Norway, Denmark, Austria and Portugal — with the apparent hope that they could thereafter merge the Six and Seven, thus achieving their original purpose of creating a large, loose, a-political trading bloc. Since these successive tactical maneuvers were, it appeared to us, essentially efforts to dilute the Common Market and drain out its political content, the United States had greeted them with considerable chilliness.

I was, of course, thoroughly familiar with all these considerations since I had been close to the problem for many years. But I detected in the atmosphere of the Heath meeting the glimmerings of something quite new. It was clear to me that Edward Heath, Sir Frank Lee and their colleagues had quite sincerely decided that Britain's interest was no longer in merely gaining a European beachhead from which she could frustrate efforts to build economic and political unity. They were now willing — and had said so at the meeting — to do a number of things they had up till then rejected: to embrace the idea of a common external tariff, to agree that joining the Common Market would include accepting its political institutions "as a full member," to agree to all treaty provisions including those having nothing to do with tariffs, and to harmonize British agriculture with the general agricultural policy of the Community. I was convinced, therefore, that the representatives I had talked to honestly saw the need for Britain to participate wholeheartedly in building political unity. They identified her future with that of Europe.

Heath's meeting with me at the end of March 1961 was arranged in anticipation of Prime Minister Macmillan's projected visit to

Washington early in May. On the first day of that visit, when we had gathered around the table in the cabinet room, the Prime Minister lost little time in repeating Mr. Heath's question: How would we react to British entry? President Kennedy turned to me, and, at his request, I answered in the same terms I had used in London five weeks before. The Prime Minister then made it clear that Britain would try "very soon to go into Europe." We dined the following night at the British Embassy. Twice during the evening Macmillan drew me aside to repeat that he was determined to sign the Rome Treaty. "We are going to need some help from you in getting in but we are going in. Yesterday was one of the greatest days of my life."

The sequel to these events is well known. Britain made formal application for membership in October 1961. Edward Heath was appointed chief negotiator on the British side. Thereafter, through days and nights of haggling, the attempt was made to reconcile the competing interests of Great Britain, its farmers, the Outer Seven and the Commonwealth with the provisions of the Rome Treaty and the steps that the Six had already taken under it. It was a gallant and indefatigable effort but inevitably mired in technicalities. During the ensuing debate the British purpose became obscure; the political momentum was lost in niggling bargaining.

Even five years later one can only guess at the precise complex of motives that caused de Gaulle to torpedo Macmillan's bid in his historic press conference of January 14, 1963. The General emphasized, among other things, the "Anglo-Saxon" Nassau Agreement, but that was by no means the whole explanation. It may well be that General de Gaulle and Prime Minister Macmillan had not fully understood each other when they met at Rambouillet in October 1962. There is evidence that de Gaulle sought the cooperation of Britain in developing his nuclear *force de frappe* and felt he had made clear at least by nuance that France would react badly to any new nuclear arrangements between Britain and the United States. In part the misunderstanding may have been a linguistic one since the two principals insisted on conducting their most sensitive conversations outside the presence of interpreters.

The Nassau meeting occurred in late December 1962, and when

I arrived in Paris during the second week of January 1963, there were already premonitions that Zeus was on his way up Olympus with a thunderbolt under his arm. A French newspaperman gave me an oral précis of the position the General would presumably announce on the following Monday, based, I was told, on a background briefing given by the Elysées Palace to a handful of French correspondents. On Friday, January 11, three days before the General's press conference, I repeated what I had heard to the French Foreign Minister. M. Couve de Murville answered reassuringly. I should not, he said, pay attention to rumors emanating from newspaper sources, since "there are no such ideas in this house."

That night Edward Heath and I had dinner à deux in a private dining room in the Hotel Plaza Athenée. In ebullient good spirits, Heath detailed his conversations with various members of the French government. He had received assurances similar to the one given me. While some serious obstacles remained, he seemed reasonably confident that the British application was in no serious trouble. Over that weekend I flew to Bonn and, on the Monday morning of President de Gaulle's press conference, met with Chancellor Adenauer to discuss the then pending proposal for the creation of a multilateral nuclear force (which later came to be known as the MLF). It was clear from our conversation that the Chancellor had no advance information about the General's press conference; in fact, he asked me at lunch what I thought the General would say.

Our morning talks had begun in an atmosphere of restraint and suspicion on the German side. The Chancellor told me later that he had had a bad dream the night before. "I dreamed," he said, "that I was going to have a big fight with Mr. Ball about the nuclear fleet. I didn't like the idea of it at all. But I have listened to you all morning and you have cleared away my anxieties one after another. I am now convinced that the nuclear fleet has great merit, and after lunch I am going to announce that the Federal Republic will give it full support."

My pleasure at this evidence of tangible progress was, however, not long lived. Toward the end of the afternoon — during a cocktail party at the American Embassy — we learned not only what the General had said in Paris but the brutality with which he had said it, and the climate in Bonn was heavy with dismay. This does not mean, of course, that all Germans had looked forward to British entry into the European Community with un- qualified enthusiasm. Only a few months earlier Chancellor Adenauer had remarked to me, "Mr. Ball, you don't think for a minute that Harold Macmillan is really ready for Europe, do you? You don't think he is ready to get on the European bus?" This had struck me at the time as a particularly infelicitous re- mark since missing buses was associated in the political vocabu- lary with Neville Chamberlain's fatuous comment that Hitler had "missed the bus" at the time of the Trondheim landing. Some years later I was to say half seriously and half in jest to the new British Foreign Secretary, George Brown, that I felt Brit- ish postwar foreign policy had never kept pace with events: "You have missed every bus," I observed, "except the ones you sold to Cuba."

Chancellor Adenauer's suspicions of British intentions were not, I believe, widely shared by members of his government who, for the most part, were enthusiastic at the prospects of British entry. Nevertheless, there was worry even among "good Europeans," including some members of the Commission of the Economic Community in Brussels, that Britain's entry might slow rather than speed political unity. The Commission was preoccupied with its own troubles. It had been making slow but steady progress toward a solution of the highly complex prob- lems involved in full economic integration. Yet the members saw formidable obstacles ahead, particularly the difficulties of agreeing on a common agricultural policy. Might not the addi- tion of a new member nation with special interests and concerns retard this process further?

One can never give categorical answers to the "ifs" of history. But I had faith at the time that Britain's accession to the Rome Treaty would add a new and hopeful dimension to European unity. I felt confident then — and in retrospect I am sure I was right — that once Britain joined Europe it would play a vigor- ous and constructive role. This conviction was founded in part on what I felt to be the basic motivation of Prime Minister Macmillan and others in his government. Quite clearly their objectives — which they were often reluctant to disclose — were more political than economic. They had arrived by a different path at the same conclusion as Schuman, Monnet, Spaak and other "good Europeans" on the Continent, that the world could no longer risk a recurrence of catastrophes such as had occurred twice in a generation and thus there must be an end to the old divisive national rivalries.

Prime Minister Macmillan made this point eloquently during private conversations at the Nassau Conference which I attended with President Kennedy in December 1962. "During the First World War," he told us, "most of my comrades and my closest school-friends were killed. I saw my Guards battalion destroyed at Loos in 1915 and on the Somme a year later." He and his older brother, Daniel Macmillan, were "invalided out of the war" with severe wounds in five engagements. He had known the desolation of the battlefield and the futility of war. He was haunted by the slaughter of 1914–1918 and did not believe the world could stand a continuation of the vicious national rivalries of Europe. He said all this to us at Nassau, and was to repeat much of it in the first volume of his memoirs published three years later. Writing of his war experience (*Winds of Change*, p. 98), he said:

> I brooded over these dire events . . . few of the survivors of my own age felt able to shake off the memory of these years. We were haunted by them. We almost began to feel a sense of guilt for not having shared the fate of our friends and comrades. We certainly felt an obligation to make some decent use of the life that had been spared to us.

His major motivation for trying to lead Britain into Europe, the Prime Minister assured us, was political and not economic. He wanted Britain to participate in building something better than the self-destructive system of the past. Yet when the debate began he held back from putting the issue to the British people in these frank political terms. Domestic opposition was intense and the government had a hard row to hoe. The imperialist wing of the Tory party, the Beaverbrook Press, and a considerable segment of Labour opinion were making it clear that many Englishmen were still intellectually and morally unprepared to join Europe. Moreover, the government had its hostages. There was the Commonwealth and then again a hostage of its own making, the European Free Trade Association (EFTA).

As a result, Macmillan put his case to the country almost entirely in terms of commercial and economic expediency. British industry, he said, needed the "cold douche" of competition in a great market, but this was not an argument to stir men's hearts or inspire their imagination, and the government made little effort to educate public opinion on the larger issues. There were strong, favorable voices in the Conservative party, but the vocal Old Guard of Labour continued to affirm with doctrinal finality that democracy ended at the Channel and wickedness began on the other side, that the Germans were a danger, and the French were wogs. And it is not over yet. Even in 1967 that quaint and venerable ornament of Labour militancy, Emanuel Shinwell, was quoted in the Washington *Post* on February 21 as saying of the Germans, "I think they are as tricky as a bag of monkeys."

To Labour in 1962 economic collaboration with Europe appeared to pose a danger to its social objectives on the home front. The head of the Labour party, Hugh Gaitskell, my friend over many years, was a man of brilliance, but by training an economics don, and, in his approach to Europe, he seemed unable to see outside the blinders of his discipline. For him the Common Market was little more than a commercial device, and on balance he thought it not good for England. In December 1962, Gaitskell sent President Kennedy a carefully written brief, expounding the Labour party's reason for taking a negative view. The document came while I was with the President at the Nassau meeting, and Kennedy gave it to me to prepare a reply, but I sadly record the fact that the reply was never sent, because Hugh died tragically in January a few days after de Gaulle's press conference.

Given these cacophonous voices it is quite clear that Macmillan could not have found the path to Europe a boulevard strewn with flowers. The walls of Continental Europe, he knew, could not be cast down merely with trumpets of rams' horns; and, being much more a tactician than a strategist, he foreswore a frontal assault, preferring to try to move in sidewise like a crab. He had long doubted that his people were ready for an explicit national decision; that was not their habit. "Britain might be united [with Europe]," he once said, "in a fit of absence of mind or by a series of improvisations, which would be particularly gratifying to my countrymen" (Beloff, *The General Says No*, p. 59). But other Europeans were not eager to gratify his countrymen by indulging their reluctance to face hard issues. They thought of European unity as a serious affair which Britain could no longer pass off as a minor commercial arrangement to be embraced in a mood of abstraction — and, besides, there had already been too many improvisations. Shadow-acting of this kind was out of tune with the time; it appeared to the world as evidence of a lack of conviction, and the tactical complexity of Britain's position damaged her case with the Continent.

Many important events have occurred since Harold Macmillan extended his hand across the Dover Straits and Charles de Gaulle one January afternoon put a dead fish into it. A British Labour government today is again exploring the road to Europe. It clearly has more room for maneuver than did Prime Minister Macmillan five years ago. The government has the full support of the Conservative opposition, of the Liberal party and of public opinion. Britain no longer needs to negotiate under the suspicious eyes of her EFTA partners, who have now given their blessing. Nor is the Commonwealth any longer an obstacle, since the advantages of Britain in Europe are today widely understood. Finally, the Community's common agricultural policy has now been defined so that its costs to Britain can be clearly ascertained.

Most important of all, the present British government seems determined to get on with the job with a minimum of haggling. By January 1963, negotiations had dragged on for fifteen months and lost the vital qualities of scope and momentum; they had soured in the mouths of all the participants. Endless hours had been consumed in arid debate over desiccated coconut, kangaroo meat and cricket bats. Today the Wilson government seems clearly to have learned the lesson of that experience. It appears to have recognized the strategic reality that Britain's position as an applicant to membership may not be strong enough to support demands for special treatment; but her bargaining position once she is a member of the Community should enable her, in collaboration with other members, to shape the application of the treaty to meet her most urgent interests.

So long as the present French government remains in power, there is a strong chance that at the end of the road it will resist Britain's entry on purely political grounds — as the General may have intended to do in his press conference of May 16, 1967. While this would be an act of caprice quite foreign to the spirit of the treaty, it would by no means be the end of the story. The Wilson government is clearly determined to wait the General out, while the Conservative leadership has long seen British salvation in European terms.

The more relevant part of the May 16 press conference was President de Gaulle's suggestion that France might rest her strongest objections to Britain's admission on the unsatisfactory position of sterling. Support for such an attitude could be found in the fact that the Treaty of Rome provides for mutual assistance if any member should get into monetary difficulties; thus the other members were entitled to assure themselves that the entry of Britain into Europe would not expose them to undue burdens and risks.

Like most Americans who followed European developments closely, I had long assumed that a limited devaluation would be one of the adjustments that would be made at the time of British entry. In fact, once in 1966, following a speech at Chatham House, I had almost gotten into trouble by expressing this view in a private conversation with a gentleman whom I failed to identify as a leading member of the London financial press. There was precedent for a devaluation at the time of entry, the French government had adjusted the value of the franc when the Rome Treaty first came into effect; and, had the devaluation of sterling occurred as a step taken in connection with Britain's accession to the Rome Treaty, the world would almost certainly have regarded it as a constructive measure. Unfortunately the closing of the Suez Canal, a protracted dock strike, high interest rates in the United States, and the overtime operation of the Paris rumor mills forced premature action.

Nonetheless, the devaluation will have served its purpose if British goods do in fact become more competitive in world markets ånd her balance of payments moves towards equilibrium. This will depend, of course, primarily on the ability of the British government to enforce an incomes policy, the willingness of British labor to restrain its wage demands and the determination of British management to cut costs. We can only hope that this will occur, for it is clearly in the interest of a stable and peaceful world that the British application to accede to the Rome Treaty be granted as soon as possible.

Britain's application to accede to the Rome Treaty is epic in its implications. I have long been convinced that British initiative and leadership could spark a renascence of the European idea at a time when dark shadows of nationalism have begun to fall on the Continent, for Europe has sore need of British political maturity, just as Britain needs a dose of continental vitality. With the passing of the Fourth Republic and the temporary ineffectiveness of its "good Europeans," the Continent has been showing the cracks and fissures that warn of disunity. Italy is still too weak, the Benelux countries too small. Britain is the only state that could provide a third strong pillar for the European edifice along with Germany and France, because she has a special political heritage to offer. For three hundred years Britain has been a stranger to revolution, while France has endured absolutism, two empires, five republics, two constitutional monarchies and two dictatorships. In the ninety-five years since it became a nation, Germany has averaged one violent change of government every twenty-four years. The Weimar Republic and the Fourth Republic each saw twenty-two governments during their brief life spans, while, in contrast, during the last twenty-two years Britain has had only six governments. Intimate British participation in the affairs of the Continent could provide the necessary element of strength and solidity;

it could moderate these latent instabilities and provide a permanent balance, securing democracy in Europe.

Englishmen reared on the heady heritage of exotic empire are more apt to feel negative pressures and not these positive possibilities from Europe — but the result could well be the same. Whatever Anthony Eden might have "felt in his bones" ten years ago, Britons know now they have to go into Europe because there is no place else left for them to go. As Dean Acheson noted, the other roles are "about played out." They could go the way of Sweden if they chose, but that is certainly a path they would never choose. To the political genius of the British that is just not good enough.

VII

The Disadvantages of the Special Relationship

F Atlanticism as a concept strikes few fires on the Continent, a special and limited kind of Atlanticism has an ardent body of adherents both in the United Kingdom and America. Many in Washington regard Britain as our natural ally and collaborator in far-ranging enterprises. Many in London look on the United States as Britain's strong and affluent friend, propping up her world interests and giving her entree to that most exclusive club, "the Summit." This is the psychological underpinning of the "special relationship." Yet the "hands across the sea" psychology is something relatively new, for our dealings with Britain were not always easy.

In the early days of the Republic pro-British and pro-French factions were the principal antagonists in our domestic politics. This phase ended early in the nineteenth century, and for a hundred years we were non-aligned neutralists. Busy with the conquest of a continent, we posed no threat to Britain's imperial interests. To be sure, there was friction with France over the Second Empire's ambitions in Mexico and with Britain over Canada and British Guiana, but for the most part we enjoyed the benefit of Britain's power and prosperity. The merchant banks of the City provided the capital to build our railroads and the British navy kept us secure from foreign attack. But the impact of two world wars reversed the balance of dependence. The *Pax Britannica* was shattered in 1914, and after 1917 we leaned less and less on a Britain who herself depended more and more on us. As empire faded and the British became aware of the relative weakness of their new position, they placed a correspondingly greater emphasis on cultivating their overgrown American cousin, at a time when we were passing from adolescence to maturity.

Britain's wooing of America did not go unrequited. Burgeoning wealth and power brought with it sobering responsibilities, while the clamant Anglophobia of late-arriving immigrant groups was drowned in the gurgle of the melting pot. Forty years ago when I was a boy in Illinois, a mayor of Chicago could assure himself reelection by threatening to "punch King George in the snoot," but that is no longer good politics. And, while that dusty relic of Middle Western xenophobia, the *Chicago Tribune*, still makes faces at the British lion, the zest went out of the act with the passing of Colonel McCormick.

On the objective facts, there is every reason why Great Britain and America should have a "special relationship," since to an exceptional degree we look out on the world through similarly refracted mental spectacles. We speak variant patois of Shakespeare and Norman Mailer, our institutions spring from the same instincts and traditions, and we share the same heritage of law and custom, philosophy and pragmatic *Weltanschauung*. More often than not, British and American diplomats tend to like each other (though the bitter Eden-Dulles relationship showed there is nothing absolute about this). Starting from similar premises in the same intellectual tradition, we recognize common allusions, share many common prejudices, and can commune on a basis of confidence. There is, in this sense, some foundation in fact behind General de Gaulle's use of the generic term "les Anglo-Saxons."

But the full flowering of the relationship is little more than a generation old. It is largely since 1940 that historical circumstances have made *les Anglo-Saxons* increasingly intimate. While the lights were out on the Continent, Americans and British learned to work closely together, and, years later, some forgotten journalist coined the phrase "special relationship" to describe that growing intimacy. As an unvanquished nation that, unlike France, emerged from the war politically intact, Britain has had no trouble claiming a seat at the High Table beside the United States and the Soviet Union. And, being shrewd and experienced, she has recognized the importance of her ties with us in a dozen ways; not the least is the fact that she consistently sends to Washington her ablest diplomats with the most attractive wives. We reciprocate on our side by sending effective citizens to London, including distinguished Americans such as the present Ambassador, David Bruce (also with a lovely wife), recognizing full well that the American Ambassador to the Court of St. James's occupies a place of special respect, as Philip Guedalla, in his *Supers and Supermen* (p. 46–47), pointed out forty years ago:

> His language, when he says something in public, can be understood. His hearers cheer, and even laugh in the right places. He does not speak in that broken English, which is the language of diplomacy; and reporters are in a position to misrepresent him almost as though he were a native statesman. It is nothing that his idioms are misunderstood; it is less than nothing that the point of his raciest, most republican anecdote is always exquisitely missed. The proud fact remains that, while sub-editors relegate all foreign diplomats to the Court Circular, the American Ambassador is News.

These then are the components of the "special relationship." Added together they have made a leavened loaf pleasant to both sides. Yet the savor should not lead one to confuse its chemistry, for it is more the product of sociological affinity than of political agreement, and the recipe does not always work. It has not prevented either side from going its own way in secrecy in pursuit of what it deemed its national interest — as Britain did at Suez and we did when we found missiles in Cuba.

For most British leaders the value of the "special relationship" stems from the knowledge that, beginning with lend-lease and the Truman Doctrine, America has progressively taken over burdens Britain could no longer carry. It consists further in the conviction — documented by experience — that Washington will bail out sterling in any crisis. Finally — and this is perhaps most important — British and American foreign offices share the comforting knowledge that each knows a great deal about the other's problems and will take them into account. Neither will go out of its way to be beastly to the other — with the notable exception of Suez, which involved two-way aberrations. The British and the Americans have, therefore, a considerable reservoir of mutual confidence, a valuable asset for each country that should not be underestimated. The British know that we Americans will, in our relations with them, normally act with sympathy and generosity. And we know that Britain's firmly based democracy is something solid and enduring, an anchor of certainty in the turbulent seas of world politics.

To the extent that the "special relationship" merely reflects those natural bonds of affinity between the two countries and their governments, it would seem not only harmless to others but in fact a stabilizing force in an unstable world. Unfortunately, however, there has been a tendency on each side to exploit the "special relationship" for short-term advantages at the expense of long-term objectives. By indulging British weakness we have all too often encouraged the United Kingdom to act in a manner that was not in its own larger interest nor in the West's. At the same time we have sometimes demanded that, in support of our policies, Britain take actions she could clearly not afford.

In the postwar years, Britain has confronted two major decisions that vitally affect her future place in the world. The first is how to put her economic house in order, which must include fundamental changes in the attitudes of labor and management so that the British economy can adjust to the standards of efficiency of the present day. The second — a not unrelated problem — is how to play an effective role in a uniting Europe. Our government, as a matter of policy, has recognized the importance of both these objectives. Yet we have frequently yielded to the temptation — either because of the subtle seductions of the "special relationship" or for reasons of our own short-term convenience (or often from a confusion of the two) — to assist Britain to avoid actions, or to induce Britain to take actions, that have directly conflicted with the long-range goal of an economically healthy Britain playing a role of leadership in Europe. Mutual indulgence can sometimes lead to costly mistakes.

One can start with Britain's economic and financial problems.

We have, of course, been the United Kingdom's best financial friend ever since the Lend-Lease Act, the $3.75 billion British Loan of 1945 and the Marshall Plan. But our continued willingness to bail out sterling whenever there was trouble — and the confident assurance of every British government that we would do so — encouraged Britain over a long period of years to temporize with her economic and financial problems when she should have faced up to them.

Then again there is the widely debated question of a continued British role east of Suez, where Britain over the past five years has maintained something in excess of fifty-five thousand troops, mostly in Malaysia. Until recently this deployment was justified by the need for a deterrent to prevent Indonesian forces from overrunning Malaysia in pursuance of Sukarno's grotesque policy of "confrontation." Today, however, Sukarno's time has run out, and Indonesia no longer threatens its neighbors. At the same time, Britain, economically hard pressed, has been forced to pare down the budgetary and foreign exchange costs of flying the Union Jack overseas. It is no secret that the decision of the Wilson government to continue to station troops east of Suez at a cost of $1.6 billion has reflected to a large extent the wishes of the United States. Absorbed by a particularly frustrating and open-ended war in Southeast Asia, we simply do not want to be alone in the Pacific. Not only for purposes of domestic politics but also for our general world posture we wish it to be clear that our Western allies are concerned about Pacific problems and that we are not isolated. We are not yet fully accustomed to the loneliness of power.

Yet, in spite of these short-term advantages for American policy, I think it is a mistake for us to press the British government to maintain a significant presence east of Suez; that is, under any circumstances, a wasting asset, since the realities of Britain's limited power and declining interests will sooner or later force her withdrawal. Britain is not likely to remain in Singapore for a long time; her political interests are fading and she wants out. Instead, therefore, of pressing Britain to undertake things which she frankly cannot afford — and for which she will naturally expect a substantial *quid pro quo* in American concessions to her own short-term interests — I think we should recognize that we are doing harm to both Britain and ourselves by insisting that she perpetuate the pattern of an imperial past.

Psychologically, we would like to have Western companionship in the areas east of Suez, but, from the point of view of our long-range interests, it is a costly luxury, for our first priority should be to bring about a politically united Europe that can someday assume serious and continuing world responsibilities. If Britain can be persuaded to concentrate on the central objective of playing a major European role, the United States can well afford to forego the evanescent advantages of a benign British presence in the Far East.

Here it seems to me is a test of how wise we really are. Pragmatists would argue that we should concentrate on keeping the British in Singapore and Malaysia in order to gain comfort and sanction for our own efforts in South Vietnam, but, if we are seeking a stable and rational organization of world power, we must stop trying to prop up the obsolescent and ephemeral and concentrate on bringing about arrangements that can endure. I can think of no better test of this issue than the question of British deployment, since it is inevitable that Britain should view the issue as a choice of priorities — whether to maintain a substantial presence east of Suez or maintain the full strength of the British army on the Rhine. To my mind, the answer should be clear and unequivocal. Britain's future lies in playing an effective role in Europe, and a British decision to reduce her forces in Germany, while maintaining her presence in the Far East, would be widely regarded as getting things in the wrong order. Here is the case, it seems to me, where we Americans should use whatever influence we have not to deflect Britain from important objectives for the sake of a dubious short-term advantage, but to encourage Britain to maintain her position in Europe even though that may mean the reduction of her military commitments in Asia.

The indulgence of sterling and Britain's vestigial role of empire illustrate the principal vice of the "special relationship" — that it leads each party to indulge its short-term interests at the expense of the long-term interests of the other party or even of itself. But an even better example of how this has worked in practice is to be found in the series of arrangements between Britain and the United States with regard to nuclear weapons. These arrangements and how they came about are worth examining as a case study, since, under the spur of the "special relationship," the United States has enabled Britain to maintain a dubious status as a nuclear power at substantial cost to the long-range interests of both ourselves and the United Kingdom.

From the beginning Great Britain had an honorable claim to a national nuclear capability, since the original unleashing of the atom was a joint wartime enterprise of ourselves, the United Kingdom and Canada. Work proceded simultaneously in Britain and America until Churchill and Roosevelt made the decision to concentrate the development of a bomb in the United States because of the greater resources available and the immunity from wartime hostilities. It seemed more sensible to bring British technicians to America to assist in the development work than to send American scientists to a crowded little isle, vulnerable to enemy assault; and, although British scientists played a significant role, they were, on balance, clearly junior partners in the common enterprise.

After the war Prime Minister Attlee apparently took it for granted that Britain would reap the full benefits of this wartime cooperation. The British had decided as early as October 1941 to produce a nuclear weapon, and only after we entered the war did they submerge national considerations in the joint allied effort; so the Prime Minister was understandably miffed when President Truman wrote him on April 20, 1946:

> As to our entering at this time into an arrangement to assist the United Kingdom in building an atomic energy plant, I think it would be exceedingly unwise from the standpoint of the United Kingdom as well as the United States. . . .
>
> I would not want to have it said that on the morning following the issuance of our declaration to bring about international control we entered into a new agreement, the purpose of which was to have the United States furnish the information as to construction and operation of plants which would enable the United Kingdom to construct another atomic energy plant.

After an acid exchange of letters in which Attlee sought, and

Truman denied, passage of full atomic information to Britain, the MacMahon Act was passed on August 1, 1946, formally forbidding such exchange.

Harsh as this decision may have seemed to the British, President Truman was, it seems to me, entirely correct in refusing them nuclear assistance. Not only our own long-range interests but those of the whole world called for limiting the number of nuclear powers to the absolute minimum. Ideally, we had hoped to bring about international control of the atom, but that failing, we would have liked to maintain our original nuclear monopoly. However, when that proved impossible, it was to everyone's advantage that the possession of nuclear weapons not be extended beyond the two superpowers, since, for reasons that will be pointed out in chapter XI, the possession of nuclear weapons by any nation less than a superpower was bound to create strong pressures for the general proliferation of nuclear capabilities. Thus, there were compelling reasons for us to hold fast to the policy established by President Truman of refusing assistance to the United Kingdom.

To be sure President Truman's negative attitude did not stop the British from going forward on their own, since they were at the time in a nationalistic mood. As Prime Minister Attlee put it (with a logic not unlike the later rationale of General de Gaulle): "We had to hold up our position vis-à-vis the Americans. We couldn't allow ourselves to be wholly in their hands, and their position wasn't awfully clear always" (*A Prime Minister Remembers*, p. 118). No one doubted Britain's ability to go it alone through the early stages of a nuclear program, but in the absence of American help she was bound to become an involuntary dropout from the nuclear race somewhere down the course, since nuclear weapons systems become progressively more expensive as nations move toward increasingly sophisticated delivery vehicles. Yet she did not want to resign even her junior membership in the nuclear club since her renunciation of a national nuclear deterrent was one more step in facing up to the unhappy reality of her diminished world position. The considerations that dictated our American policy were, however, quite different, and from the point of view of larger world interests we should have doggedly pursued the clear objective of keeping the number of nuclear nations at the lowest possible figure, which meant that we should have seized every opportunity to recreate the duopoly of the two superpowers, since this would have eased the problem of making nuclear power manageable.

Unfortunately, we did not keep this basic objective clearly in mind; on the contrary, under President Eisenhower, we made the mistake of helping the British not once but twice to stay in the nuclear race, and, under President Kennedy, we made the same mistake a third time.

The Initial Mistake — The 1958 Amendments to the MacMahon Act

The MacMahon Act was amended in 1954 to permit a limited degree of cooperation between the United States and other NATO nations in the area of trading and operation, but that was of small importance. Not until four years later did we take a step that reversed the position President Truman had wisely established. By that time the British were having serious trouble with their atomic weapons program and mounting costs were raising doubts as to its continuance. Had we merely held our hand — had we done nothing to assist them — they would, in due course, of necessity, have phased out of the nuclear weapons business altogether.

The villain again was the "special relationship," which once more got in the way of a sensible United States policy. Three weeks after the appearance of the Soviet Sputnik in October 1957 — and no doubt somewhat rattled by the shattering disclosure of an unsuspected Soviet lead in the space race — President Eisenhower promised Prime Minister Macmillan that he would seek amendments to the MacMahon Act to make possible the resumption of a close nuclear partnership between Britain and the United States. Those amendments, as finally passed in June 1958, were couched in anything but subtle language; and they fooled no one. By authorizing the transfer of information and nuclear materials and nonnuclear parts of atomic weapons to any nation that had made "substantial progress" in the development of an atomic weapons capability, the amendments obviously were addressed to the special case of Great Britain, since the United Kingdom was the only allied nation that could then meet this standard.* On the other hand, the literal phrasing of the amendments was grotesquely at variance with our own obvious interest, since, read as written, they encouraged proliferation by offering the carrot of assistance to any nation that would make "substantial progress" toward creating its own national deterrent.

I regard the 1958 amendments to the MacMahon Act as a major blunder in American policy. Among other unhappy effects, by flaunting the "special relationship" while at the same time implying a promise of help down the road, they almost certainly played a role in stimulating the French to build a nuclear weapons system, for I doubt it was a coincidence that the French decision was announced on April 11, 1958, only a few weeks after President Eisenhower had decided to seek amendments to the MacMahon Act. Fifty days later, General de Gaulle was back in the driver's seat from his long exile as the hermit sage of Columbey-les-Deux-Eglises, and one of his first decisions was to open up the throttle on the French nuclear program.

Cruel as history sometimes seems, it does not always deny stumblers a second chance, and only three years later we were given the opportunity to undo some of the damage we had done; for by April 1960 the British were once more in trouble with their nuclear program. Such trouble was inevitable since it stemmed from the increasing sophistication of nuclear delivery systems and air defenses. Building a nuclear weapons system is a breathless race against obsolescence, and, as the vehicle for delivering weapons shifted from the manned bomber to the ballistic missile, costs rose enormously.

Faced with the problem of trying to stay in the race, Britain had earlier undertaken the development of a delivery vehicle known as Blue Streak, an intermediate-range ballistic missile to which, during several years, she devoted substantial manpower and resources. But because of technical problems and competing economic demands she reluctantly decided in 1960 that the Blue Streak program should be abandoned. She was thus left in a

*Immediately after the passage of the act we saved Britain $400 million by transferring enriched uranium.

position where, as soon as her fleet of 180 V-bombers became obsolete in the face of improved Soviet defenses, she would be phased out of the nuclear deterrent business.

The Second Mistake — Skybolt

Here, therefore, was another golden chance for the United States — simply by doing nothing — to reduce the number of nuclear powers and thus diminish the pressure toward proliferation. But again the lesson was not heeded. During a meeting with Prime Minister Macmillan at Camp David in 1960 President Eisenhower found a new way to help the British stay in the nuclear club by offering to provide Skybolt missiles under a financial arrangement extremely favorable to the United Kingdom. As conceived by American scientists Skybolt would be an air-to-surface missile with a limited range of only one thousand nautical miles, but it would substantially extend the useful life of Britain's V-bomber force. Every improvement in Soviet air defenses made it more difficult for manned bombers to penetrate to key targets, but with Skybolt, the RAF hoped that its bombers could stand outside defense perimeters and still reach the targets with nuclear rockets. Thus their V-bomber fleet — then on the verge of obsolescence — could keep Britain a nuclear military power into the 1970's.

Almost from the beginning, however, the Skybolt program was ill-starred. The first five test launches were abortive. Development costs doubled in three years and the predicted operational date was pushed back from 1965 to 1967. The technical problems of launching a rocket from a fast-moving and unstable platform were proving greater than had been foreseen; development was costing too much; and the results were uncertain. When in the fall of 1962 the Secretary of Defense decided that the project should be canceled, about $400 million had already been spent, of which the British share was only $30 million.

The decision to cancel had been foreshadowed in casual conversations with the British for the past two years, although Secretary McNamara did not explicitly warn the British Ambassador or threaten cancellation until November 8. From the American point of view the scrubbing of Skybolt would cause pain to the air force but no damage to our total deterrent strength. When Skybolt was begun in 1960, no one could be certain that other programs would be developed quickly and successfully, but, by 1963, we were beginning to deploy Minute Man intercontinental missiles in protected silos, while at the same time building a fleet of Polaris submarines with a high degree of invulnerability to enemy attack; thus Skybolt had become for us a marginal, not an essential, part of our deterrent arsenal. Not so for the British, and herein lay the problem, for a point had been reached where our requirements and those of Great Britain diverged. The Skybolt was for us an unneeded supplement to already adequate existing programs; for Great Britain it was her only means to keep an independent nuclear capability.

All of us in Washington were aware that the cancellation of Skybolt would stir up a noisy political reaction in Britain, and that, if the United States took the initiative in canceling the program, many Englishmen would hold us responsible for blackballing Britain out of the nuclear club. We had been warned that London would argue that we owed her the chance to keep her membership, and that, since we were unilaterally fracturing existing arrangements, it was up to us to provide a substitute weapons system. Obviously the impact of this kind of contention was heavily influenced by the sentimental bias of the "special relationship," for tested by objective logic it would not wash. If the British no longer had the resources to stay in a race of mounting costs, then why should we feel obligated to keep them in it?

In retrospect, I think that the responsible officials of the United States government — and I include myself — should have quite calmly and dispassionately asked themselves certain pertinent questions.

(1) Did we really have any obligation to continue a development program in which we were paying over ninety percent of the costs for a weapon of doubtful efficiency that we no longer needed?

(2) Did we have any obligation to keep Great Britain in the nuclear club? Would it not be better to assist her to phase out her nuclear deterrent?

(3) What would be the reaction of the French Government to a new and far-reaching nuclear deal between the United States and Great Britain and what effect would this have on Britain's pending negotiations for entry into the Common Market?

The Third Mistake — Nassau

The answers to these questions were needed from the point of view of a fully informed United States policy. But unfortunately the questions were not asked in those terms, and thus — under the spell of the "special relationship" — we threw away the third chance to move the management of nuclear power in the direction of greater rationality and thus slow down the trend toward proliferation.

I attended the Nassau Conference and — though perhaps less clearly than some of my colleagues in the State Department — I foresaw the dangers of giving Britain a new and relatively long-term lease on nuclear life and argued against it; yet I failed as an advocate, and whatever I write about the conference is *mea culpa*. Perhaps because I did not see then the issues as clearly as I do now with the benefit of hindsight, I did not make the dangers and disadvantages sufficiently stark and vivid. Hence I could not prevail against the general desire to go ahead in spite of the warnings of those of us who wanted at the least to buy time.

We believed that instead of offering Britain Polaris submarines to form part of their national deterrent we should try to settle for the time-honored diplomatic formula of a bilateral committee to examine the problem at leisure and report its recommendation a month later. That would give a chance to deal with the problem more rationally, and besides there were compelling reasons why the timing was bad for an affirmative decision — among other reasons being the possibility, as certain of our experts foresaw more clearly than I, that a Polaris deal might shipwreck Britain's application for entry to the Common Market.

But if the experts were concerned at what was likely to happen, why did we go ahead? It was another case, I think, where the emotional baggage of the "special relationship" got in the way of cooler judgment. From the distance of more than five years, I can see two things quite wrong with the American position at Nassau. First, we had painted ourselves into a corner, for we had, even before the Nassau Conference, made clear to the world that we thought the Skybolt project was a failure, an announcement which the London press interpreted as an act of bad faith for which we had to make amends. Second, we did not recognize that the problem was ninety percent political and only marginally military. In our anxiety not to sully the sacred principles of cost effectiveness we ended by extending the life of the British deterrent far longer than we would have done had Skybolt succeeded.

The first point is of particular interest since it illustrates the unavoidable inequality that is concealed by the phrase "special relationship." Whenever the United States and the United Kingdom join together in a common enterprise, decisions are distorted by the disparity in the resources that each nation can command. Thus, when the Skybolt program got into trouble, we felt we could not cancel it and let it go at that, as the British had themselves canceled Blue Streak, even though we no longer needed the Skybolt missile for our own uses. Implicit in the relationship — as we saw it at Nassau — was an obligation to come up with a substitute for the British.

But such an analysis tells only part of the story. Above and beyond the logic of the situation was the atmosphere of the Nassau Conference itself, the overwhelming circumstance that the participants liked one another. President Kennedy was fond of Prime Minister Macmillan and he had a relationship of extraordinary confidence and intimacy with the able British Ambassador David Ormsby-Gore, now Lord Harlech. The two had been young men together in London many years before, and Lord Harlech is a man everyone likes and respects.

So we Americans approached the conference determined not to create unnecessary problems for our friends. The Macmillan government was in political trouble because we had decided to cancel Skybolt. They were nice people and we should try, if we could, to help them out. For there is one international distress signal recognized by politicians all over the world, and that is the cry of another politician in trouble. The efficacy of this signal is, in fact, not even limited to relations among democratic states-men. Chairman Khrushchev felt free to talk to American political leaders about his own internal difficulties with some expectation that they would be understood. He expressed himself in turn as prepared to modify his actions to accommodate the pressing prob-lems of an American President.

I think our desire to help Macmillan at Nassau was a natural and healthy thing. There was nothing conspiratorial about it. Certainly it did not mean that President Kennedy was working for the continuance of a Conservative government in power in Britain; as a matter of fact there was greater rapport between the Kennedy Administration and many of the personalities in the Labour opposition. But there is a sense of special reciprocity between the political leaders of Great Britain and the United States. Each can appreciate the domestic problems of the other, and each wants to avoid situations that exacerbate those prob-lems. I saw those same principles at work later in the relation-ship between President Johnson and Prime Minister Harold Wilson.

The difficulty at Nassau, however, was that this decent desire to be mutually helpful became — in the atmosphere of the "special relationship" — the central rather than the subsidiary element in shaping a political decision with far-reaching conse-quences. Most of us who were there — and I was among them — had a sense of participation in an historic tradition. It was Prime Minister Macmillan's sixth meeting with President Kennedy, another in the long series of meetings of British and American leaders that had begun with Churchill and Roosevelt twenty-two years before. There is a time when a sense of history can obtrude itself in awkward ways, bemusing the normally hardheaded, and getting in the way of cool judgment.

If we had handled the Skybolt more adroitly we need not have offered Polaris submarines to the British. Even though we our-selves no longer needed the Skybolt missile, the British did need it, and their own technicians were by no means persuaded that Skybolt was a failure. It seemed to me at the time, therefore, that our obligation to the British could be fully discharged by an offer to turn over the developmental work already done with a "Godspeed" to the British to carry on, accompanied if need be by some financial assistance.

Unfortunately, however, we destroyed this option even before the conference. The attitude on the American side was dominated by the Pentagon's quite commendable distaste for the inefficient use of resources, and by insisting on informing the British public that we thought Skybolt a failure, we greatly limited the negotiating terrain. By forcing Her Majesty's government to insist on something different from Skybolt or risk discredit with their own public, it encouraged the British military experts — with their expectations heightened by events — to press for Polaris submarines. The public outcry in Britain that followed our assertion that the Skybolt missile was no good set the tone for the Nassau Conference.

Although I think it more than likely that General de Gaulle would have vetoed British entry into the Common Market even if Nassau and the Skybolt crisis had never occurred, yet we knew we were stirring up possible trouble with the General and we tried to think of ways to make the result less offensive. It was President Kennedy himself, as I recall, who suggested that he write the General, offering the same deal to France that we were making with Britain. Some of us at Nassau believed that a letter to General de Gaulle would be more likely to annoy than appease him, but we had nothing better to suggest.

We were all prisoners of the situation that the "special relationship" had brought about. Since we were dealing with the British differently from any other nation, a personal letter from the President would tend to place in sharp relief the fact of our favoritism, even more than the intended benefit. It would thus emphasize the very element of discrimination that other nations — and particularly France — would find most obnoxious.

Concern about a possible adverse French reaction was not, as I recall it, shared with the same intensity by the British, even though they had the most to lose if the French shut them out of Europe. It is one of the corrosive aspects of a particularly intimate relationship between nations of unequal size that the less powerful tends to take pride and comfort from favors and privileges it receives on a discriminatory basis, even though the fact of that discrimination may spoil its relations with others.

In any event, the letter sent to General de Gaulle, while well intended, did not temper the violence of the General's reactions. There were several reasons for this. For one thing, France had been building its own nuclear force without help from the United States. She had already invested in that enterprise more resources than she could afford. For the United States, this late in the day, to offer her Polaris submarines was not likely to be taken as a gracious gesture. It would be interpreted instead as an after-thought of a government that felt it had been a little churlish in its earlier behavior, and de Gaulle's answer might well echo the rebuke of Doctor Johnson to Lord Chesterfield: "The notice which you have been pleased to take of my labors, had it been early, had been kind; but it has been delayed until I am indiffer-ent and cannot enjoy it. . . ."

Nor could de Gaulle reasonably be expected to relish the role of grateful beneficiary of a meeting to which he had not been invited. Given the General's known resentment at the exclusion of France from the wartime Big Three conferences, a pointed reminder that Britain and the United States were having a clubby talk about nuclear matters without including "the third nuclear power of the West" was almost certain to infuriate him; it had too much the flavor of a compassionate letter from a honeymooning couple to a jilted suitor: "Having a fine time, etc."

Yet even had the circumstances of the meeting been more in tune with the General's sensitivities, even had the atmospherics been right, the arrangement proposed was bound to be substan-tively offensive. An agreement that the Polarises provided by America would be assigned to NATO and that the British would consider sympathetically the creation of a mixed-manned multi-lateral nuclear force was hardly likely to attract a leader who had already withdrawn units of the French fleet from NATO. Could anyone reasonably believe that a fervent French nationalist would wish to buy Polaris submarines for the purpose of turning them over to NATO command, with the right to take them back only in the event that "supreme national interests" were at stake?

Such a proposal would cut directly across the General's distaste for "integration."

I have dealt at length with the Nassau Conference because it has already done perceptible havoc and we shall have to live with its consequences for a long time and because it showed in especially vivid light the unhappy effects of the "special relationship."

First, it perpetuated the discriminatory nuclear relations between the United States and the United Kingdom foreshadowed in the Atomic Energy Act amendments of 1954 and institutionalized in the amendments of 1958.

Second, it encouraged Britain in the belief that she could, by her own efforts — so long as she maintained a specially favored position with the United States — play an independent great power role, and thus it deflected her from coming to terms with her European destiny.

Third, it made it possible for Britain to continue to maintain a luxury that is beyond her means and that even today is a severe drain on her limited resources and balance of payments position.

Fourth, by underlining the very fact that Britain was enjoying a favored transatlantic position and had special ties with the United States, the Nassau Conference provided the occasion, if not the cause, for General de Gaulle four weeks later to veto Britain's entry into the Common Market. It thus contributed to a destructive action that checked the momentum toward unity in Europe and relit old flames of nationalism.

Fifth, through the agreement to extend the useful life of the British deterrent indefinitely into the future, Nassau passed up the opportunity for Britain, by gradually phasing out her deterrent, to set an example that would ease the pressure for nuclear proliferation. I shall have more to say about this in chapter X. For the moment I need note only that, by pressing Polaris submarines on the British, we made possible the unedifying spectacle of a Britain that clings to a nuclear deterrent which she cannot afford, which, by itself, has no realistic military value, and which has got in the way of her entry into Europe. At the same time we and the British continue to press the other nations of the world not to do as we do but to do as we say. They should not, we argue, challenge the present nuclear oligopoly; rather they should pledge that they will themselves stay out of the business.

Will We Make the Same Mistake a Fourth Time?

If we are serious about checking nuclear proliferation — as I am certain we are — then we should be extremely careful not to make for the fourth time the mistake of taking affirmative action to keep Britain in the nuclear weapons business. Fortunately, we shall in the normal order of things have a fourth chance, for our two existing agreements with the British for nuclear cooperation contain termination provisions. Our agreement for the exchange of nuclear information continues by its terms for an additional five years unless denounced by December 1968. Our agreement for the exchange of nuclear materials expires unless renewed before December 1969.

These options should not be dealt with in a routine manner. We can, if we choose, let both agreements run on or denounce both agreements, or let the information agreement run on, since its denunciation would involve a positive act on our part, while permitting the materials agreement to expire simply by taking no action to renew it.

I do not know whether the continuance of the materials agreement is essential to the carrying out of Britain's Polaris program, but if it is, then I believe we should use this occasion to talk with the British seriously about the discontinuance or relinquishment of the Polaris submarines and, if necessary, take over those already completed (I shall have more to say about this in chapter XI). But whether or not we take action to denounce the information agreement or let the materials agreement lapse through inaction, it may well be that the British will, by their own volition, phase out their nuclear weapons program. Nuclear submarines are no more effective than the weapons they fire and, armed only with the present Polaris missiles, they will become obsolete and relatively useless as we and the Soviet Union complete even a "thin" anti-ballistic missile deployment. As I understand it, we are still trying to persuade the Soviet Union to agree with us not to go down this road, since it can lead only to a new phase of costly and futile nuclear competition; but, while no one should prejudge the outcome — and I hope I am wrong — the chances seem to me very slight that an effective agreement can be worked out.

Yet the consequences if this negotiation fails will be tremendous, because once anti-ballistic missiles are deployed no presently operational offensive weapons system will be of much value, since only weapons with multiple warheads will be able to penetrate Soviet defenses. It is for that and other reasons that on our own nuclear submarines we are going to replace the present Polarises with the new generation of Poseidon missiles which have multiple warheads. Prime Minister Wilson, however, has already stated that Britain will not follow us down this path and that his government has no intention of acquiring Poseidons for the submarines it is now building — which, literally interpreted, could mean only that Britain must either herself develop a multiple warhead missile (possibly with the French) or resign from the nuclear club. It may be, of course, that the Prime Minister's statement was intended merely to stake out a tactical position in connection with Britain's efforts to join the European Community and to make clear that there would be no Nassau this time to poison the negotiations. But I would prefer to think that it reflected a decision not to go further in the nuclear race. Such certainly is the more hopeful hypothesis, since the independent development of multiple warhead missiles would be a fantastic waste of resources, and both London and Paris should embrace this new occasion for escape as an opportunity rather than a disaster.

Thus a fourth chance is presented for the British to strike a blow for nonproliferation by setting a brave example for the world, while at the same time discouraging the French from continuing to cling to a shadowy symbol of status which — because they can never keep up in the nuclear race once the superpowers have installed anti-ballistic missiles — will increasingly be revealed as a futility.

Certainly the United States should do nothing affirmative to keep Britain in the club under these circumstances. We have made three mistakes already and we need not make a fourth. We have let the "special relationship" distort our judgment as to what is best for our own interests and those of Britain. It is time for a fresh reassessment of how our two countries can live together in the long-range interests of both.

Unquestionably, it is important to the United States that Britain flourish and that her talents and political genius be brought to the aid of a world in trouble; and the question in my mind has never been whether but how this can be done. Thus if, in challenging the "special relationship" as it now operates, I appear as indifferent to British interests, nothing could be farther from the truth. As the son of a native of Devon, submerged in my childhood in English history and literature, I have a deep affection for Britain and the British people and a strong desire that Britain play a world role worthy of her traditions. If I see that role within a uniting Europe, it is because I am convinced that it offers the only feasible course that will enable the British, for the benefit of the world, to fulfill their remarkable talents within a political and economic framework which can provide the necessary scope.

It is, of course, not surprising that in the last year or two many thoughtful writers and political leaders have sought alternative ways in which this might be accomplished. Discouraged with the narrow and petty policies of the French government that have frustrated British efforts to join Europe, they have proposed that a new role be found for British talents, not by curtailing or limiting the "special relationship," but by giving it institutional form through the creation of an Anglo-American economic or political union. Obviously there is nothing astonishing about the thought of reversing the American revolution. Ideas of this kind have been peddled for years, but in the context of the present day, they hold a fresh attraction and should by no means be rejected out of hand.

It was for this reason that, at a particularly discouraging point in Anglo-European relations in the latter part of 1965, I asked my personal staff in the State Department to draw up, for purposes of analysis and discussion, a contingency plan for what might be called quite infelicitously a political English-speaking union. Although they worked hard at a proposal, I never submitted it either to the Secretary of State or the President, since it would, I concluded, create more problems than it would solve. Yet the idea should not go unmentioned, for similar proposals have been suggested in both the British press and the American press, and until Britain joins Europe these possibilities will continue to hold attractions.

In general terms proposals of this kind have been made along one of two lines: one narrow, one broad. The narrow projects are strictly limited to commercial policy; they envisage the establishment of some kind of free trade area that would presumably comprise at least Britain, the United States and Canada, if not Australia and New Zealand. The others, more ambitious and more realistic, contemplate the creation of an Anglo-Saxon political confederation that might over the years transform itself into a federation.

I have no difficulty in rejecting the first group of proposals. We Americans for more than thirty years have been faithful to the principle of nondiscrimination in our commercial relations. To be sure, a good argument can be made for a free trade area limited to ourselves and Canada, since our two economies are so integrally intertwined, but a free trade area that would include the United Kingdom and perhaps Australia and New Zealand as well would clearly be inconsistent with our position as a world leader. After all, a free trade area is by definition a discriminatory arrangement among the member states and against the rest of the world; and for the United States to undertake a purely commercial arrangement offering free access to our market to Britain and the other members of an Anglo-Saxon free trade bloc, while continuing to exact relatively high tariffs from producers in the rest of the world, would generate anti-American resentment everywhere.

The same consequences would not result — or at least would not result to the same degree — if we were to form a real political confederation with other Anglo-Saxon countries. In that case we would be pouring political content into a new and significant relationship, with incidental commercial consequences. And, while this would create many problems — particularly in Europe —

most of the world would see it as a political move of high importance and judge it sympathetically or antagonistically on that basis.

A plausible case can be made for a proposal of this kind. If one assumes that Britain is to be penalized for the "special relationship" by being permanently excluded from Europe, then why should we not together turn the "special relationship" into a new political arrangement? Since the peoples of the Anglo-Saxon countries are united by common bonds of language and institutions and history, the building of Anglo-Saxon political unity ought to be far easier than the construction of a political Europe. America could benefit from British political maturity and experience; Britain would have free access to a great market and her economy would be revitalized by an enormous infusion of American capital and know-how.

I do not deny the attractions of such a proposal. The "special relationship" in its present form embodies discrimination without political unity. It offends other nations and gives us the worst of both possible worlds. On the other hand, the forthright movement toward a full-fledged political confederation with Britain could offer definite advantages. Nor, if they continue to exclude Britain from Europe, could the Continental nations have any right to object to such an arrangement. They would have asked for it by their own small-mindedness.

When I gave the problem to my staff two years ago, I fixed as the terms of reference of the study something larger than an arrangement between the United Kingdom and the United States: I asked that the study be addressed to the possibilities of a full-fledged Anglo-Saxon state, including not only the two major components but also Canada, Australia and New Zealand. Such an area would comprise nearly three hundred million people and would have a total gross product of close to a trillion dollars. I decided to include these other countries in the study only after considerable thought. First, it seemed to me that the union of merely the United Kingdom and the United States would give the remaining members of the Old Commonwealth a sense of isolation and exclusion that would not be healthy. Second, examining the position of each, I came to the conclusion that the broadening of the concept was entirely feasible.

Canada, I have long believed, is fighting a rearguard action against the inevitable. Living next to our nation, with a population ten times as large as theirs and a gross national product fourteen times as great, the Canadians recognize their need for United States capital; but at the same time they are determined to maintain their economic and political independence. Their position is understandable, and the desire to maintain their national integrity is a worthy objective. But the Canadians pay heavily for it and, over the years, I do not believe they will succeed in reconciling the intrinsic contradiction of their position. I wonder, for example, if the Canadian people will be prepared indefinitely to accept, for the psychic satisfaction of maintaining a separate national and political identity, a per capita income less than three-fourths of ours. The struggle is bound to be a difficult one — and I suspect, over the years, a losing one. Meanwhile there is danger that the efforts of successive Canadian governments to prevent United States economic domination will drive them toward increasingly restrictive nationalistic measures that are good neither for Canada nor for the health of the whole trading world.

Thus, while I can understand the motivating assumptions of the Canadian position, I cannot predict a long life expectancy for her present policies. The great land mass to the south exerts an enormous gravitational attraction while at the same time tending to repel, and even without the divisive element of a second culture in Quebec, the resultant strains and pressures are hard to endure. Sooner or later, commercial imperatives will bring about free movement of all goods back and forth across our long border; and when that occurs, or even before it does, it will become unmistakably clear that countries with economies so inextricably intertwined must also have free movement of the other vital factors of production — capital, services and labor. The result will inevitably be substantial economic integration, which will require for its full realization a progesssively expanding area of common political decision.

Canada has for a long time struggled against the implications of this logic, seeking to strengthen her position toward the United States by developing her Commonwealth ties with Great Britain. But as the vitality of the Commonwealth has diminished, this exercise has lost much of its meaning, and if Britain joined Europe it would mean even less. Yet the very fact of the struggle underlines the possible value of an arrangement for a political confederation that could reconcile Canada's nostalgic ties to Britain with her insistent economic ties to the United States. Thus, while I have no doubt that the majority of Canadians would — at least for the foreseeable future — balk at a confederation that would leave them alone with the United States, they would feel much more relaxed about joining a confederal system in which not only Britain but Australia and New Zealand were members. One can argue, in fact, that such an arrangement may offer the best solution for neutralizing the conflicting pushes and pulls in Canadian life.

Australia and New Zealand are, of course, in positions quite different from that of Canada. Australia, particularly, has undergone a significant change of attitude in the years since the war. She can no longer depend on Britain for her security, and she knows it. As a nation vast in size but meager in population — a Western island in a Far Eastern sea — she cannot ignore the ferment of Asia or the diminished authority of the West in that boiling continent. Australians look to us increasingly for defense. They feel at home with us and like us, and by and large the feeling is reciprocated, since we have much in common. We are both immigrant peoples who have conquered a continent, and we tend to see in Australians a reflection of ourselves as we must have looked some decades ago when the last frontier was won.

Quite clearly, American strength in conjunction with the geographical loneliness of both Australia and New Zealand is bound to bring us together in close working relations, even if we do not involve ourselves in other Asian wars. Australia's dependence on Britain, even in commercial matters, is far less than in the past; only about half of her foreign trade now is with the United Kingdom. As in the case of Canada, participation of both the United States and Britain in a common political arrangement would save Australia and New Zealand from the embarrassment of competing loyalties, and, on balance, I think they might show considerable enthusiasm for some form of political confederation.

As I saw the situation in 1965, however, it did not call for heroic action. We did not need a "dramatic new initiative," as the journalists would write it, and the kind of confederation I posited for purposes of study was a relatively modest affair that contemplated only limited relinquishment of sovereignty to central institutions. I suggested, by way of example, that there might be regular Council of Ministers meetings with permanent sub-groups to concert policy with regard to political, military, monetary and trade matters. There would be a merging of the dollar and sterling areas, with common monetary reserves, complete freedom in the movement of goods and people throughout the area, and free movement of capital as soon as the situation permitted.

There would be a provisional legislative body in which, during the initial stages at least, members would be selected from the national parliaments of the member states. But the British government and the British parliament would survive as the governing bodies of Britain just as the United States government would continue to govern our country. In other words, there would be no yielding of sovereignty in domestic affairs, unless the Council of Ministers agreed unanimously.

The study made by my staff indicated that the scheme I had outlined might, in the event that Britain found herself prevented over a long period from entering the Common Market, become acceptable to the parties involved, provided it were carefully prepared and presented and a substantial program of education undertaken. On the surface, at least, it seemed to have plausibility. Yet, was it realistic to believe that the British people would opt for it, once its full implications were apparent? Britain is capable of playing a leading role in Europe, but merging with a giant would mean the effective assimilation of England and the Old Dominions into an American mold.

Mr. Desmond Donnelly has suggested that it would result in "some kind of larger and more complicated 'Puerto Rico' status for Britain," but this is the wrong analogy, since Britain would have an independent vote in any such arrangement, which Puerto Rico with its Commonwealth status does not have. I think it more likely that Britain would, during a long period of experiment and transition, settle in as a kind of junior partner of the United States — a minority stockholder in the firm. Perhaps in the end, as the pressure for unity became more intense, she might become a larger Scotland. But this is scarcely a vision to inspire the British people and, as Mr. Donnelly points out, they would be likely to regard it as a defeatist retreat rather than a bold adventure.

Viewed in the narrower terms of economics, the proposal was not unattractive. Our study showed, for example, that, as the confederation moved toward internal free trade, the aggregate balance of payments position of the members would be strengthened by import diversion in the rough magnitude of $1.5 billion a year. British producers might suffer an initial shock from increased American competition, but the effect would be selective and the overall consequence would be to force the structural changes British industry sorely needs. Thus, while there might be some initial unemployment, there would be a long-range tendency for the British standard of living to rise until it approached approximately the level of America's industrial states. (At the moment, per capita income in Britain is half of $3,700, the American figure.) America meanwhile would benefit greatly from fresh ideas and attitudes and the inclusion of a superbly talented people in her national life. The final meaning would be the fusion of those Western peoples that have the strongest and most uninterrupted democratic tradition.

The argument for such a project is, therefore, not all one way. Should we, after all, be too sentimental about sovereignty and history when the logic of world peace argues strongly for the gradual merger of nation-states into larger units with the consequent reduction in national rivalries? And, in any event, what is wrong with reversing a stupid eighteenth-century political blunder? Very likely the peoples of Britain and Canada and the United States would still be united if the policies of George III and Lord North had been more soundly conceived and been executed with greater sensitivity for the feelings of the colonies.

I pondered all this. I examined these arguments with care, but I could not bring myself to put the proposal to my seniors. Certainly the scheme, as I envisaged it, would be costly to the national values of the British people. It would almost surely mean the ultimate absorption of much of their culture and identity in a very much larger United States. But what deterred me from promoting the scheme was the insistent thought that it would exacerbate, rather than solve, the problems of Europe.

As a participant in a uniting Europe Britain could play a leading political role, but that role hardly would be possible vis-à-vis giant America. And, as I shall argue at length in the course of this book, I can find no solution to the problem of Europe without Britain. Only her participation can dilute the intense interplay of forces between France and Germany, and, by helping offset the weight of German population and power, make possible the ultimate incorporation of the East German people into Europe on a basis acceptable to their neighbors. On the other hand, for Britain and the United States to join a political confederation would cut Germany adrift. It would leave her alone in Europe with, on the one side, a vindictive Soviet Union, and on the other, a France still frightened of German power. And that, as I see it, would be a certain way to pile up trouble.

There is, therefore, every reason for us to stick to our policy of encouraging the building of Europe and not to be deflected toward doubtful options no matter how seductive. The wisest course — for both countries and for Western civilization — is not to expand Britain's dependence on the United States but rather to contract it, while at the same time encouraging her to play a vital role in constructing a political Europe. Should that role be denied her — should Paris continue even after the passing of General de Gaulle to operate a kind of reverse continental blockade — then, and only then, might it be wise to consider the less attractive alternative of an Anglo-Saxon construction.

But I do not think that day will come. I hope not.

VIII

The Political Consequences of
General de Gaulle

RANCE is a country diverse enough to produce a Jean
Monnet and a Charles de Gaulle. Her politics are
various enough to have given continental Europe its
first experience of popular democracy and its first taste of
Bonapartism. She spawned in an intellectually rich nineteenth
century the reactionary sermons of De Maistre and the utopian
visions of Saint-Simon; she balanced Auguste Conte against
Henri Bergson, and for every Emile Zola there was a General
Boulanger. Modern-day theatergoers are reminded of an even
odder juxtaposition: that of Jean Paul Marat with the Marquis de
Sade.

A nation rich enough in genius to produce such exquisite
diversity is great by any standard, and one obvious measure of
France's greatness is her impact on the world. Beyond her own
borders she is — and has long been — regarded with affection or
irritation — frequently with both — but never with indifference.
As one who knows France from more than casual experience, I
have found among her people rare insights and perceptions as
well as warm and loyal friendships. Yet she is a land with an unparalleled capacity for paradox. In the hundred and fifty years
that have seen two Napoleons and five republics, France has been
alternately Europe's inspiration and Europe's troublemaker, and

these contradictions continue to fascinate the Western world today.

How could a nation that had launched and nurtured the "European idea" in 1950 abruptly check the trend toward a larger unity in January 1963, less than thirteen years later? Or was there a subtle internal twist? Was General de Gaulle really, after all, just as much a "good European" as Robert Schuman?

However one answers these questions, there can be no doubt that the policy of France in the 1960's has been, more than in any other Western democracy, the policy of a single strong-willed man, a leader who has demonstrated to all but the most fanatical believers in economic determinism that the influence of the "hero" — in Carlyle's terminology — can be decisive, even in this most mass-produced of all centuries. By force of character and personality, extraordinary single-mindedness, a flair for the flamboyant dramatic effect, and an ability to say striking and unpredictable things in elegant French, General de Gaulle has made sure that his statements and actions are never ignored.

As the last member of the galaxy of World War II statesmen still to hold power, he is a commanding figure, a blinding flash of color against the drab background of contemporary world politics. Over a sustained period he has played with panache a repertory of historic roles beyond the competence of lesser men. During the grim days of the war and occupation, he was the symbol and the rallying point for the French people. Out of the disparate and violently competing elements that had emerged in France during the war, he forged a workable government. Again summoned like Cincinnatus at a time of crisis, he commanded the popular support, ruthlessness and political dexterity to put down three army insurrections and lance the festering carbuncle of Algeria.

I have seen General de Gaulle at various times over the last nine years, sometimes briefly, sometimes for discussions lasting an hour and a half or more. Invariably he has been polite, warm and forthright. Nor has he ever let his historic personality obtrude. No one as old as I can meet the General without recalling the long chronicle of his accomplishments. Here is a man who twice bound up the wounds of a nation at war with itself, who found a country with its eyes cast down and restored its self-respect and confidence. No one can ever diminish this achievement.

Yet while he has served France brilliantly during a time of troubles, he has been one of the destructive elements in the larger chemistry of the West. This is not only a personal misfortune, for I am convinced that history will give him bad marks for what he has done to Europe, but it is a tragedy for the European people. It is a tragedy not only because of the breakage caused, but — what is even more poignant — because of the opportunity missed; of all the postwar leaders he has been the only one with the necessary authority to head a Europe that desperately wanted his leadership.

Why then has he failed to comprehend and to act as the age and hour required?

Mr. Walter Lippmann, one of President de Gaulle's most eloquent admirers, has, I think, provided the answer quite inadvertently. In a 1965 television interview, Mr. Lippmann remarked,

> De Gaulle is like a man who can't see very clearly what's right in front of him, who sees pretty well what's across the room, or halfway down the street, but who sees absolutely perfectly what's in the distance. He has the farthest vision, he can see further, than any man in our time. (*Conversations with Walter Lippmann,* pp. 213-14)

Put in this manner, Mr. Lippmann's observation can provoke little dissent. Most students of de Gaulle's prose and conduct would certainly agree that he looks out over the centuries. The relevant question, however, is whether he is gazing forward or backward.

That question must be answered if we are to make intelligent judgments about the diplomatic pulling and tugging now going on in the West. My own view is quite clear and I have made it known before. The General's vision of France's role in Europe and the world derives not from the future but from the past. He is facing backward, seeking by a politic of nostalgia to conjure up in this century something that is beyond the competence of even the greatest magician — a time three hundred years ago when France was indeed the largest and richest nation of the West. De Gaulle would "call spirits from the vasty deep," but they will come not for him nor any man.

For the strength and the weakness of this great leader is that he is, to the exclusion of everything else, an intense French patriot — a word of honor, which he deserves, but which, when it becomes a dominating life force, can also be translated "nationalist." France — idealized and idolized — is the consuming passion of his life. To grasp that fact is to understand what he has done and what he is likely to do, and what unfortunately he can never do. But to ignore the fact, or be unaware of it, is to open the door to endless confusion.

One source of misunderstanding is the fact that the patriotism of a Frenchman expresses itself in quite different terms from those which we Americans normally employ. It is compound of history and agony and pride and shame and anger; it owes much to French education and perhaps even more to the Church, for it is no accident that de Gaulle is both a devout Catholic and a devout Frenchman. "All my life," he writes at the beginning of his *Memoirs*, "I have thought of France in a certain way." This, according to the General,

> is inspired by sentiment as much as by reason. The emotional side of me tends to imagine France, like the princess in the fairy stories or the Madonna in the frescoes, as dedicated to an exalted and exceptional destiny. Instinctively, I have the feeling that Providence has created her either for complete successes or for exemplary misfortunes. If, in spite of this, mediocrity shows in her acts and deeds, it strikes me as an absurd anomaly, to be imputed to the faults of Frenchmen, not to the genius of the land. But the positive side of my mind also assures me that France is not really herself unless in the front rank; that only vast enterprises are capable of counterbalancing the ferments of dispersal which are inherent in her people; that our country, as it is, surrounded by the others, as they are, must aim high and hold itself straight, on pain of mortal danger. In short, to my mind, France cannot be France without greatness. . . .
>
> As a young native of Lille living in Paris, nothing struck me more than the symbols of our glories: night falling over Notre Dame, the majesty of evening at Versailles, the Arc de Triomphe

in the sun, conquered colors shuddering in the vault of the In-
valides. Nothing affected me more than the evidence of our
national successes: popular enthusiasm when the Tsar of Russia
passed through, a review at Longchamps, the marvels of the
Exhibition, the first flights of our aviators. Nothing saddened me
more profoundly than our weaknesses and our mistakes, as revealed to my childhood gaze by the way people looked and by
things they said: the surrender of Fashoda, the Dreyfus Case,
social conflicts, religious strife. (*Mémoires de Guerre, L'Appel*,
pp. 1-2).

One cannot help but admire the moving and simple sincerity
of de Gaulle's attachment to his country. It is a deep and personal
faith. To be a Frenchman is, for him, a lyrical experience. It is
to be an actor in a passion play presented on a great stage —
and the General has had no doubt as to his membership in the
cast. He has expressed this with candor. To the people of France
he has written (in his *Complete War Memoirs*, p. 995), there was
"something primordial, permanent and necessary which he [de
Gaulle] incarnated in history and which the regime of parties
could not represent." He is "a kind of capital of sovereignty" em-
bodying the nation. His entire career has been dedicated to a
single purpose: the restoration of France to the role of major
power and the establishment of its hegemony in Western Europe.

In *Le Salut*, published in 1959 as the final volume of his wartime reminiscences, de Gaulle recalled his vision of the French
role in the world (pp. 730 ff.): "This role was to be that of one
of the greatest states." He had told the National Assembly years
before, "we must reinstate the power of France! This, henceforth,
is our great cause!"

Implied in much of what the General has said is regret that he
was born at the wrong time in history, and demography is against
him, though he would change it if he could. In a televised address
to the nation he has summoned forth the image of a future state
of "100 million Frenchmen," the hopeful solution to his demographic lament:

At the beginning of the last century — quite recently, in historical terms — our country was the most populous in Europe, the
strongest and richest in the world, and her influence unequalled.

But disastrous causes had combined to drive her from this dominant position and to start her down a slope where each generation saw her stumble lower. Mutilated of the territories nature intended her to have, grotesquely costumed in artificial frontiers, separated from a third of the population springing from her stock, France had been living for a hundred and thirty years in a chronic state of infirmity, insecurity and acrimony. . . .

To wish to establish France on a par with the global powers despite the implacable facts of population and resources is to deny the realities of the twentieth century, and I am certain that General de Gaulle knows it. Taken literally his expressed ambitions for France would have been realistic in the time of Louis XIV, when she was indeed the largest and richest nation of Europe. But, in terms of material resources, she is overshadowed today even by other nations in the Western part of the Continent. Her gross national product is $92 billion, $7 billion less than that of Britain and $20 billion below West Germany (rump of a country that it is). In terms of population she is only the fifth largest of the NATO countries. For France, acting alone as a single nation-state, to seek recognition as a power of equal importance to the two superpowers, the Soviet Union and the United States, is an ambition that transcends the possible, since what Raymond Aron says of Europe (*Peace and War*, pp. 318-19) applies with special force to France:

The obsolescence of [European] nations assumes, in our period, the appearance of an irrevocable destiny. The approximate proportionality between force and resources, between resources and the number of men and the amount of raw materials, between mobilizable force and power, does not permit any hope that the leader's genius or the people's virtue might reverse the verdict of number.

President de Gaulle has never accepted Professor Aron's view and never will. He has never conceded that a "leader's genius," when combined with "the people's virtue," could not "reverse the verdict of number." By the concentration of personality and will he has tried to overcome a perverse reality and make France a superpower in spite of herself. It is a task beyond the competence of even a man with his extraordinary qualities and like King Lear the General must in the end be reduced to complaining to the heavens — rebelling self-destructively at the deaf neutrality of impersonal forces. As Carlyle said of Napoleon, he "has words in him which are like Austerlitz battles." For the tragedy of de Gaulle is that the extraordinary gifts and exceptional devotion which have made him a great leader of France have largely disabled him from leading Europe.

Over the years, I have watched the supple tactics of the General with fascination and have tried to understand what his next move might be. But I have been educated in the humanities and the law and am thus ill-equipped for the task. All successful political leaders must combine the talents of the theater and the battlefield, and it is the essence of the General's effectiveness that he excels in both métiers. He is not only a superb actor, but one of the great captains.

As an actor, he has played France in four distinct masks: (1) France as spokesman and natural leader for all "Gauls, Latins and Teutons"; (2) France as an independent "great power" claiming equal rights for herself in a global Western directorate, organized as a Washington-London-Paris axis, which would give Paris a veto over American nuclear plans and American policy around the world; (3) France as arbiter with Moscow for Europe and the West and protector of nationalism "from the Atlantic to the Urals"; and (4) France as moral spokesman for "the thought of more than two billion human beings who think as she does" in the underdeveloped countries, or what the General chooses to call the "Third World."

None of these roles has won more than mixed critical notices. Each is, in the end, impossible for France and uncomfortable for other countries.

To dwell too heavily on the theatrical analogy can, however, be misleading and unfair to General de Gaulle, who is preeminently a military man. He attended Saint Cyr at a time when, he tells us, to be in the French army was "one of the greatest things in the world." His first colonel was Pétain. The First World War was not long in coming, and French reverses were a searing experience for the young subaltern from Lille. They left a deep imprint on his thoughts about the elemental worth of his country, weakened by unworthy governments. The war was for him a frightening melodrama with narrow escapes for France in every scene, but with a glorious last act. As he himself wrote the synopsis of the plot (*Complete War Memoirs*, p. 5), one could

> see France, though deprived of part of her necessary means of defense by an insufficient birth rate, by hollow ideologies, and by the negligence of the authorities, extract from herself an incredible effort, make up by measureless sacrifices for all she lacked, and bring the trial to an end in victory.

Unlike the young Harold Macmillan, also a lieutenant, who, steeped in the classics, saw the conflict as Europe's Peloponnesian War and the beginning of the end of old empire, the young Charles de Gaulle was aware only of the glory of his country and future greatness for France. His youthful mind was formed by the nationalistic histories and political writings of Michelet and Péguy. In the 1920's he was momentarily attracted by the bilious rantings of Charles Maurras, a kind of latter-day French and crypto-fascist embodiment of Thomas Carlyle; but there is no evidence that this was more than a passing interest.

Never for a moment did he doubt his ultimate mission: to gain power and hegemony for France; nor has he ever since doubted it. Brilliant tactician that he is, he has sought that objective by a mastery of movement. His political maneuvers have reflected tactical perceptions not unlike those of the mechanized tank and air warfare he recommended to General Weygand in the 1930's. He has played Machiavelli's "lion and fox," accommodating his tactics to changing circumstances, but never deviating from a lifelong objective — to make France one of the world's first powers.

Even in 1945, his strategic plan was quite well developed. He wrote then in his *Memoirs* (pp. 872–73):

> It seemed likely that the new period would permit me to achieve the great plan I had conceived for my country.
> I intended to assure France primacy in western Europe by preventing the rise of a new Reich that might again threaten

its safety; to co-operate with East and West and, if need be, contract the necessary alliances on one side or the other without ever accepting any kind of dependency; . . . to persuade the states along the Rhine, the Alps, and the Pyrenees to form a political, economic and strategic bloc; to establish this organization as one of the three world powers and, should it become necessary, as the arbiter between the Soviet and Anglo-American camps. Since 1940, my every word and act had been dedicated to establishing these possibilities; now that France was on her feet again, I would try to realize them.

When I first began to deal officially with French policy I memorized these words and used to quote them to my disapproving colleagues. Here was a major political leader who had clearly set forth his intentions and had thereafter pursued them with implacable consistency. But it has been General de Gaulle's fate or fortune that, as a prophet, he has never been taken fully at his word even in foreign countries. I can only conclude that many who write, if they read at all, continue to embrace their own individual brand of wishful thinking. For there is a remarkable congruence between the de Gaulle of words in his *Memoirs* and speeches and the de Gaulle of action as a political leader. Both as literateur and as tribune, he attacks the problem at hand as a brilliantly resourceful field commander. One does not need the insight of a Liddell Hart to identify the successive and clearly differentiated tactical campaigns that the General has pursued since the war.

First, to prevent "the rise of a new Reich" he initially sought to bring about the dismemberment of Germany and the extension of French political control to the Rhine.

Second, he sought agreement from the United States to accept France as the third member of a great power directorate that would, among other things, give the French a vote on American foreign policy and a veto on nuclear strategy everywhere in the world.

Third, failing to achieve his purpose by obtaining the agreement of America, he endeavored to establish France as the only nuclear power on the continent of Western Europe and to protect that exclusive position by preventing other Western continental powers from having any role in nuclear management and by keeping Britain out of Europe.

Fourth, he sought "to persuade the states along the Rhine, the Alps, and the Pyrenees to form a political, economic and strategic bloc" and "to establish this organization," under French hegemony, "as one of the three world powers."

Fifth, he sought to gain strength through alliances "without ever accepting any kind of dependency"; the negative side of this tactic was to gain full freedom of diplomatic and political maneuver for France by freeing her of any alliances contracted by earlier French governments that might involve "any kind of dependency."

And, sixth, he sought to "cooperate with East and West" and "should it become necessary" to become "the arbiter between the Soviet and Anglo-American camps" — or in other words, to play "one great hegemony" off against the other.

Careful consideration of how he has attempted to carry out each of these separate tactics since the war can, I think, go far toward explaining the mainsprings of French policy. It can also suggest what new tactical feints and deployments we may expect in the future.

First Tactic — The Dismemberment of Germany

In 1945 General de Gaulle argued with the Allies that there should be, as he himself tells us:

> . . . no further sovereignty of the central German state on the left bank of the Rhine; the territories thus separated retaining their German character but receiving their autonomy and con- sistency, economically speaking, from the Western zone; the Ruhr placed under international control; the Eastern German frontier marked by the Oder and the Neisse.

Seeking to "assure France primacy in Western Europe" once and for all, he wished to redraw the contours of Napoleon's Empire at Germany's expense. He remarked in his *Memoirs* that "action on the Continent" was "the age-old destiny of France!" He argued for "replacing the Reich by a confederation of states . . . trans- formation of the Palatinate, Hesse and the Rhineland into

autonomous states . . .;" and added, "we can countenance a
settlement only if it assures us the elemental security which
nature has defined by the Rhine."

Every nationalistic French leader since Richelieu has wished
to see Germany broken up and diminished in territory, and the
American government had its moments of aberration with the
Morgenthau Plan. But experience argued the opposing case,
since efforts to bring about this result have, over the centuries,
been uniformly disastrous. The first Napoleon succeeded so well
in annexing Germans that he provoked a reaction — and the first
genuine stirrings of a unified nationalism in Germany in 1813.
His nephew, Napoleon III, played the same game, but with tragic
ineptitude, losing Alsace and Lorraine, provoking the Paris Commune and revolution in 1870. After 1918 it was Poincaré's insistence on economically detaching the Ruhr and the Saar —
more than any single act — that brought about economic disaster
and political discredit for the Weimar democrats, paving the way
for Hitler.

Fortunately for world stability, the Allies rejected the madness
of a vengeful solution to the German problem. Meanwhile de
Gaulle retired to the war room of Colombey, preparing himself
during twelve years in mufti for the future tactical moves of his
grand battle plan.

*Second Tactic — Effort to Achieve Great Power Status Through
the Establishment of a Directorate*

During the war de Gaulle had sought vainly to persuade
President Roosevelt to include France at the High Table with
Great Britain as one of the three great powers of the West. But
if this tactic failed with Roosevelt — whose chemistry did not
mix well with the General's — it might still succeed with Eisenhower, a general like himself and thus capable of appreciating
the need for coordinated strategic planning on a world basis. It
was to this end that he launched a campaign shortly after coming
to power in June 1958, by informing an American official that
France wished to play a central role in the development of Western strategy around the world and that she was unhappy that a
German general had been selected for NATO's central European

command. A month later Secretary of State Dulles made a special trip to Paris to learn what the French President had in mind. De Gaulle told him that unless France felt she were a "world power" she would degenerate internally. Problems of global security and nuclear deterrence, he argued, required collaboration at the highest level among France, Britain and the United States. NATO, restricted in competence to Europe and North America, should be extended to cover the Sahara and the Middle East, where France had vital interests. Germany was not yet a major Western power and should be kept out of the trilateral directorate.

Dulles replied that if France wished to achieve "great power" status she must first build up her society at home. A formalized "world directorate" was unrealistic and would be resented by other Western and nonaligned countries, although, of course, the three Western allies would continue to consult each other informally on problems of common interest and try wherever possible to concert their policies. Lebanon, Dulles mentioned, was in the midst of crisis and it might be necessary for the United States to intervene. De Gaulle asked that France be allowed to participate in any Western intervention, but Dulles argued that the intervention of France, the ex-colonial power in the Levant, would hardly be welcomed by the Lebanese.

In a now famous letter to President Eisenhower in September of the same year, de Gaulle made his *"directoire"* proposal more explicit. He said France had direct interests in the Middle East and Africa and the Indian Ocean and the Pacific. He proposed a new organization with Britain, France and America as the sole members to make joint decisions on political questions affecting security around the world and to arrive at strategic plans for the use of nuclear weapons (France at the time was a year and a half away from even exploding her first nuclear device). He envisaged a possible organization or division of the world into specific "theaters" or spheres of interest, and implied that a failure to do so would jeopardize continued French cooperation in NATO. He hoped that talks among the three countries could begin in Washington to discuss his plan.

This proposal had been foreshadowed years earlier. After entering the war in December 1941 the United States had asked routinely for air landing rights in New Caledonia, which was controlled by the Free French. De Gaulle answered that he would be glad to consider this question in the framework of overall joint planning that would give France an equal voice with America in determining allied strategy in the Pacific. Again in 1950 he had declared, "There must be a system of common European defense, the plans of which should normally be drawn up by France, and whose chief should be appointed by France, just as in the Pacific this predominant role should be played by the United States and in the Middle East by England." In 1953 he believed that France must have a key role in the West "not only as a European power, but as an African, Asiatic and Oceanic power which we are and which we want to remain." It was, in essence, the claim of a nation of less than fifty million to be recognized as the full equal of Washington and Moscow.

Soon after de Gaulle's letter to Eisenhower, European chancelleries were buzzing with partially accurate versions of the "directorate" proposal, and Germans, Italians and Belgians made their displeasure known to Washington. Over the years partial and often distorted versions of the plan have appeared in the press. The British were at first ambiguous — the "directorate" meant enhanced power for them, and a Franco-British veto on the American nuclear force was intriguing — but Britain felt, rightly or wrongly, that she had a special political relationship with America and did not need to formalize it with the French invited along.

The unrealistic nature of the de Gaulle proposal was evident to Washington and to most other NATO capitals, but it was not rejected out of hand. After all, it might be regarded as merely an extreme and not wholly serious expression of a natural French desire for an enhanced position in Western councils. President Eisenhower's reply to de Gaulle's letter suggested, with diplomatic politesse, that formal global arrangements were not really necessary but that tripartite talks to discuss the plan and try to concert Western policy were certainly possible. In December a series of talks began in Washington among the British and French ambassadors and Deputy Under Secretary of State Murphy for the United States. But these were not at all what the French had in mind, and they soon lost interest.

The General revived the idea with President Kennedy at their first meeting in Paris in June 1961. Again he received a negative response. Since that time, the French have shown little interest in the idea, although there have been veiled hints that the decision to take France out of NATO, which the General announced in March 1966, would never have been made if the *directoire* proposal had been accepted.

Third Tactic — The Exclusive Possession of a National Nuclear Force as a Ticket to the Great Power Club

General de Gaulle did not make the decision to build the *force de frappe*. That decision had been made by Prime Minister Felix Gaillard two months before de Gaulle came to power. M. Gaillard has been a friend of mine since the days we worked together in the French Supply Council in Washington immediately after the war. I visited him in his office in the Hotel Matignon at the time he was making the decision to undertake the construction of a French nuclear force. While obviously concerned with France's power position, Felix Gaillard seemed almost more interested in the technological benefit that France would derive from a large-scale nuclear program. But whatever the reason for Gaillard's decision I think it likely that General de Gaulle had already foreseen the political leverage implicit in the possession of a nuclear capability. In any event, he quickly decided to go forward with the nuclear program, apparently indifferent to the fact that it would impose an enormous charge on the French budget. (Since 1958 it has cost the French people over $15 billion.)

It is, however, an academic question as to whether or not the General had fully thought through the rationale of the bomb at the time he made the critical decision; what is perfectly clear is that he has, in subsequent years, employed it for three purposes.

First and most important has been its utility as a political lever, with which he has tried to force his way into the club of global powers. To support this effort, the strategists in the Elysée have constructed a full-blown doctrine, often associated with General Pierre Gallois, which holds that the possession of even a relatively small national nuclear force nullifies the advantages of superior manpower and material resources among states. Thus, so the doctrine runs, a nuclear force can give a medium-sized state the same world prestige and political authority, the same right to a seat in world councils, as the nations organized on a continent-wide basis, because such a state can exert leverage over the actions of the superpowers by being able to precipitate great power conflict through the use or threatened use of its own weapons.

I shall examine this thesis in some detail in chapter XI; I need only note here that, in my view, it is both wrong and mischievous. No one informed about nuclear strategy could possibly believe that France would ever use the bomb against another nuclear power except as part of a general war in which our nuclear weapons had already been fired. Nevertheless, the French government has come more and more to rest its claim to world power status on the ground that it has a nuclear capability — a point made explicitly clear in General de Gaulle's speech at Phnom Penh Stadium on September 1, 1966, when he spoke of the special responsibilities of "the five great powers." The figure five is significant, for the nuclear club has value as a badge of prestige and first-power status only if the membership is kept extremely small. This General de Gaulle has fully understood, and for that reason he has repeatedly moved to protect the exclusive quality of the French national deterrent in continental Western Europe.

I think it likely — although I cannot prove it — that this was one of the reasons why he vetoed Britain's entry into the Common Market in 1963. If Britain, as a nuclear power in her own right, were to become part of Europe, the exclusive quality, and hence much of value of the *force de frappe*, would be destroyed. Yet Great Britain's cooperation in the development of the *force de frappe* would have meant an enormous saving in resources for France, and had that been offered, it is possible that the General might have been prepared to let Britain into the Common Market even at the cost of France's ceasing to be the sole nuclear member of the European Community. By working with the British, France might at least have hoped to achieve nuclear parity with her.

But Nassau destroyed that possibility, since the Polaris submarines provided under the Nassau arrangement gave Britain not only a whole generation of additional nuclear life but also a modern weapons system which France could not hope to duplicate for at least ten years. Moreover, the Nassau arrangements meant a further extension of Anglo-American nuclear cooperation which, because we had refused the same assistance to France, had understandably become a thorn in the French side.

There is strong evidence, therefore, that in order to establish France's claim to first-power status the General has felt it essential to maintain his position as the only nuclear power in continental Western Europe. Not only is this consistent with his veto of Britain's Common Market bid, but it also explains his vigorous attack on our own proposal for a multilateral nuclear force, which, as I shall explain in chapter XI, would have offered other European nations, including West Germany, a role in nuclear management.

Yet even this may not be the whole reason why the General has deemed it necessary to burden the French budget and economy with vast expenditures for a nuclear force of dubious military value. He has also regarded the *force de frappe* as a means of providing a *raison d'être* for the French military, thus restoring their self-respect and keeping them out of political mischief, since for a quarter-century the French army has become increasingly detached from French national life. Discredited under Weygand's and Pétain's leadership in 1940, the officer corps was expatriated by colonial wars in the 1940's and 1950's. Indochina and Algeria wiped out successive classes as fast as Saint Cyr could graduate them, while those left behind nourished resentment at the squalid and impuissant politics of the Fourth Republic — resentment that ultimately brought General de Gaulle to power in mid-1958. Acutely sensitive to the agonies of his brother officers, but at the same time constructed of different stuff, de Gaulle recalled similar conflicts between army and state in the 1930's. In 1933 he had written (*Complete War Memoirs*, p. 14), "in the hard toil which is needed to rejuvenate France, her Army will serve her as standby and ferment. For the sword is the axis of the world, and greatness is not divisible."

In his first postwar years of power he had to put down three serious attempts at military coups d'état and he faced numerous assassination plots directed by disgruntled ex-officers. Profoundly committed to reintegrating the army — the highest embodiment of the nation — into national life, General de Gaulle has noted the relation between psychology and the modernity of equipment. Defeatism in the 1930's, he believed, was produced by inadequate preparation for tank and air warfare. Thus it was reasonable to conclude that by providing the most modern weapons he could buy back the army's self-respect, while at the same time justifying a reduction in its numerical strength by half — from over one million at the height of the Algerian war to five hundred thousand today.

These, I suspect, are the principal reasons why the French government has gone forward — at great cost — with the *force de frappe*. Yet there is perhaps another reason never mentioned officially which subconsciously enters into the calculations of many Frenchmen. It is the meaning of the weapon against the nightmare possibility of another German attack. In international diplomacy many serious problems are unspoken, or smothered under a Béarnaise sauce of platitude. But the lingering French fear of a Germany superior in population and in military resources is a fact — a reality that lies only a little way beneath the surface of any discussion about the shape and future of Europe. In the 1930's it was this fear that led France to embark on the construction of the Maginot line — an expensive piece of military folly built on an obsolescent conception of warfare. Throughout a sorry decade de Gaulle, in a steady outpouring of books, tracts and "inspired" newspaper articles and in arguments with the High Command, fought against that "reassuring panacea" and in favor of a mobile tactic of airpower and motorized armies. Today Germany possesses an army of twelve divisions equipped with the most modern American weapons, while the French army, though reduced to about the same numerical size, is less elegantly equipped. Under these circumstances, the *force de frappe* inevitably has a special meaning for France — particularly as long as Germany can be kept away from any participation in the control or the management of nuclear weapons.

Fourth Tactic — The Attempt by France to Make Other European Powers Ancillary to French Policy

Since General de Gaulle's all-absorbing interest is to advance France to her historic position as the leading power of Western Europe, he quite logically opposes any arrangement that would diminish the sovereignty of the French nation-state. Thus, as the General said in his press conference of April 19, 1963, France has "no desire to be dissolved" in a common Europe. "Any system that would consist of handing over our sovereignty to august international assemblies would be incompatible with the rights and duties of the French Republic." There is no ambiguity about President de Gaulle's reasoning in support of this thesis. As he sees it, only the states "are valid, legitimate and capable of achievement"; hence, it is necessary to think in terms of a "Europe of states," not a "Europe of the peoples." An "integrated" Europe would, in the Gaullist view, lack the vitality and validity of nationalism and hence would be easy prey to direction from outside — that is, from America. This last point is important, since the General's *cauchemar* is a vision of France "dissolved in a federation called 'European' which would actually be 'Atlantic.'"

A "Europe of the States" or of "the fatherlands" has ample historical precedents, but it has little to do with the kind of "united Europe" that Monnet and Schuman and De Gasperi and Adenauer began to build in 1950 as the culmination of a long historic process. The Gaullist design would not mean an end to European rivalries; by providing a framework for the expression of French superiority, it might well encourage them. It would not bring about the creation of common foreign and defense policies or the common mobilization of resources in support of such policies, and thus permit the European people to play a role of power and responsibility around the world. It would not provide a larger framework within which the German people could channel their energies and talents to constructive ends;

nor would it provide the kind of dilution that could make it possible for the German people to play a role of full equality without engendering the fear in Europe of domination by a powerful and resurgent Germany.

Yet, so far as the General is concerned, this marks the outer limits of permissible unity. Certainly, as he made clear in a press conference on September 9, 1965, he is implacably opposed to a Europe that might in any sense water down the purity of the French state:

> Now, we know — heaven knows that we know — that there is a different concept of a European federation in which, according to the dreams of those who conceived it, the countries would lose their national personalities, and in which, furthermore, for want of a federator — such as, in the West, Caesar and his successors, Charlemagne, Otto I, Charles V, Napoleon and Hitler tried to be, each in his fashion, and such as, in the East, Stalin tried to be — would be ruled by some technocratic, stateless and irresponsible Areopagus. We know also that France is opposing this project, which contradicts all reality, with a plan for organized cooperation among the States, evolving, doubtless, toward a confederation.

Although opposing the political unity of Europe, General de Gaulle has, for tactical purposes, not hesitated to speak in the name of Europe, and this is the key to much of the confusion, for the resulting semantic muddle has led many to believe that the General was saying one thing when he was saying quite the opposite. Like the *colons* who heard him utter Delphically at the Algiers Forum in 1958, "I have understood you," many Europeans are befuddled by his adoption of the European vocabulary. What did he mean, for example, when he offered "to contribute to building Western Europe into a political, economic, cultural and human group, organized for action, progress and defense"? (Beloff, *The General Says No*, p. 26). It was unimportant whether the General made the dialogue deliberately equivocal or borrowed the vocabulary of the "good Europeans" out of disdain for their concepts. The result has been substantially misunderstanding on both sides of the Atlantic as to the nature and purpose of present French policy.

The French language has a deserved reputation for precision, but French education pays high deference to abstractions. General de Gaulle has repeatedly said that, while France is a reality, "Europe" is a mystique, and it is in that sense that he speaks of a "United Europe." He does not mean a European state or a federation with common institutions, but a congeries of independent nations, consulting together on matters of common interest. Such a "Europe" would, in other words, resemble one or another of the shifting alliances that appeared and reappeared for three hundred years from the League of Augsburg to the Triple Entente. Implicit, of course, in the General's thinking is the assumption that France would provide the leadership for the nations of such a "Europe"; it would, at least, be *primus inter pares*.

In pursuit of what, I suspect, is a self-conscious intention to capitalize on the yearning of Europeans for unity, the General has, from time to time, appeared to lead the procession. On February 5, 1962, he announced, ". . . we are proposing to our partners an overall organization for cooperation between the States, without which there cannot be a united Europe, except in dreams, parades and stories." This "organization for cooperation" was the heart of the "Fouchet Plan," a preemptive French initiative designed to give the impression that the French government favored European unity while forestalling attempts to build a Europe of common institutions. The plan called simply for a series of regular meetings among national heads of government and their ministers. The distant goal: confederal arrangements in which the rule of unanimity applied. In short, it was exactly the kind of arrangement that had long permitted President de Gaulle to assert a negative "leadership-by-veto" for France.

The General's desire to achieve the dominant role for France, while at the same time fiercely protecting all prerogatives of the French state, has marked not only his European policy but also his policy toward a Germany that is today industrially strong but politically weak. As late as 1963, the General quite clearly hoped that, by building a "special relationship" with Germany, he might gain German support for the advancement of French objectives. In this endeavor, he had an eager partner in Chancellor Adenauer, who deeply believed — because he trusted no one and certainly not either the French or the Germans — that there would be hope for a stable peace only when France and Germany reached a full reconciliation. This feeling was, of course, shared by other Europeans as well as Americans, and no one who has looked carefully at European history can doubt its validity. But I have long been convinced that a lasting reconciliation is impossible on a bilateral basis. Only within the framework of a larger Europe could the two peoples establish and maintain a durable understanding — and that means a Europe in which Great Britain is playing a full role.

It seems to me that events of the past few years have borne this out, for the Franco-German Treaty of 1963 never had much meaning. Certainly during the period of Ludwig Erhard's government it was no more than a token document, and I doubt that the Kiesinger government will be able to make more out of it, no matter how great their desire to do so. The evidence, in fact, seems clearly to suggest that, once Adenauer was no longer in command, the General gave up the effort to invest the treaty with substantive meaning, since he apparently concluded that the Franco-German gambit had outlived its usefulness. How else can one explain the inflections of Poincaré that crept increasingly into his interviews with almost everyone? The German ploy had not checkmated the king, and the time had apparently come for France to make the final move described in General de Gaulle's *Memoirs:* to seek full freedom of diplomatic and political maneuver and thus get herself in position to play off one great hegemony against the other.

Fifth and Sixth Tactics — Freedom of Maneuver Between the Two Giants; Europe to the Urals

Viewed in this light it seems clear that the celebrated handwritten notes the General sent in March 1966 to his NATO allies, demanding that foreign forces be withdrawn from French soil and announcing his decision to withdraw French forces from the NATO command, were not a last-minute change of policy but the execution of a long-range alternative tactic, the underlying assumptions of which were, I think, clear enough. In President de Gaulle's mind there was little doubt that the cold war had reached a point where the danger of Soviet aggression could be largely discounted. In any event, we Americans, whether we wanted to or not, would have to use the Strategic Air Command to defend Europe — and, because of geography, this meant we must defend France. The General was thus in the happy position where he could quite safely order American forces from French soil without fear that we would leave France undefended and he quite clearly enjoyed this abrupt assertion of French sovereignty. I do not believe, however, that he was motivated primarily by a desire to pay off old scores for any real or fancied slights he may have suffered from President Roosevelt or other Americans during the war. Such an explanation gives less than proper credit to the consistency of his purpose and his fidelity to an ideal. In spite of a widespread but ill-informed American assumption to the contrary, the General acts far more from design than from pique, and the controlling fact was that for his purposes anything serving to diminish American prestige or influence in Europe would tend to enhance the relative position of France.

In any event the tactic was decided upon long before the March 1966 letters. The General had made no secret of his intentions. He had told me of his plans, both with regard to the expulsion of American troop units from France and the withdrawal of his own forces from NATO, when I talked with him for an hour and a half in August of the previous year. The General was carrying out his long-range strategic plan with no attempt at concealment, in order to gain freedom to deal on his own with the two great hegemonies; for General de Gaulle, like many Frenchmen, has never forgotten the politics of 1919–1939 and the model of the "Little Entente."

This then is the essence of the General's sixth move, which flows from and overlaps with his fifth: to talk of European unity in terms generalized enough to include the people on both sides of the Iron Curtain, thus confounding and confusing his opposition by capitalizing on the airy tendency, both in Europe and America, to make a mystique of détente. With this in mind he has pithily outfitted French aspirations in the verbal costume of "Europe from the Atlantic to the Urals." It is a figure of speech with interesting antecedents, partly a statement of geographic definition and partly the evocation of a disparate assembly of competing nationalisms transformed as it were by an Invisible Hand into a Force for Good, but relating at the same time to the settlement of the division of Europe. Yet, in the General's model of the universe, it would be a Europe in the old pattern, broken politically into nation-states, no one of which (except the Soviet Union) would be organized on a modern scale. The vision is not a new one; like almost all other Gaullist inventions the original formula appears in the *Memoirs* (p. 721) and has been repeated at the famous ex cathedra press conferences ever since:

> Europe could find equilibrium and peace only by an association among Slavs, Germans, Gauls and Latins. Doubtless she must take into account what was momentarily tyrannical and aggrandizing in the Russian regime. Utilizing the procedures of totalitarian oppression and invoking the solidarity of the Central and Eastern European peoples against the German peril, Communism was apparently trying to gain control of the Vistula, the Danube and the Balkans. But once Germany ceased to be a threat, this subjection, for lack of a *raison d'être* would sooner or later appear unacceptable to the vassal states, while the Russians themselves would lose all desire to exceed their boundaries. . . . After which the unity of Europe could be established in the form of an association including its peoples from Iceland to Istanbul, from Gibraltar to the Urals.

Europe from the Atlantic to the Urals is, as the General intends it, a Europe in which France and the Soviet Union could keep Germany in a position of disability and restraint, while at the same time checking the extension of United States power elsewhere around the world. But while Germany must be kept in check, the General has, I suspect, not abandoned the hope that German power and resources may still be used to serve the objectives of France. He still seems to hope that, by adroit diplomacy, France can achieve a position of political superiority on the Continent which the "verdict" of population, economic resources and geography would in the normal course of events award to her eastern neighbor. To achieve this he has given out hints that France will be Germany's spokesman and champion

with the East — receiving German "gratitude" and nuclear renunciation. But this does not excuse his acting at the same time
the role of "Big Brother" and protector to the Eastern states vis-
à-vis Germany, as in 1919–1939.

I think the General is thus tempted to believe that he might
play on the fears of a continent, yet also win some concessions in
the East for the Germans, on the understanding that a "strong
France" is in charge in Western Europe and has Germany under
its control. It is a maneuver requiring considerable diplomatic
subtlety and maneuver, just the kind he most enjoys; and as a
French nationalist — or patriot, if you will — in the tradition of
Richelieu, the Napoleons and Poincaré, he must be tempted to
believe that fate has prepared the terrain for him by placing
Germany under two inhibitions, both inherited from the Second
World War. The first springs from the fact that Germany is partitioned into Eastern and Western portions — and so long as she is
partitioned will remain both politically weak and dependent on
friends to help end the partition. The second is that, so long as
the memory of Hitlerism lives, Germany is feared and friendless
in those Eastern countries whose consent is necessary before
Germany can begin to realize her overriding national goal of becoming whole again. Playing on these two inhibitions in 1968 de
Gaulle may hope to achieve — with diplomatic skill — the preeminence for France that he was unable to win by territorial
concessions in 1945. Yet I think this is a vain hope. It seems highly
unlikely that France can get many dividends from her investment
in rapprochement with the Soviet Union. French and Russian
nationalists have only one substantial common interest — that
of preventing Germany from becoming a major force in Europe;
and again the disparity in size creates an awkwardness between
them, since the realities of medium-sized population and resources make it all but impossible for de Gaulle to play effective
big-power politics.

I have no doubt that the Russians see some obvious
value in a Western leader who stirs up the West's "ferments of
dispersal" and thus discourages a strong, single-willed and democratic "Europe" from emerging on their Western flank. But, with
a keen sense of the power realities, they know that their chief

negotiating partner in any future European or German settlement can only be the United States, the sole nation with continent-based power comparable to their own — or a unified Western Europe. Thus, under the conditions of today, any negotiation between Moscow and Paris is a footnote, a digression from the central text of diplomacy that can have little effect beyond reducing slightly the tensions between the Soviet Union and parts of Europe at some cost to the solidarity of the Western democracies; for neither nuclear illusions nor requests for a seat at the High Table can win for France a lasting power position greater than that to which her resources entitle her.

Unhappily, when a nation aspires, by and for itself, to exercise power beyond the scope and reach of its resources, it can act only destructively. It can tear down structures like NATO. It can weaken institutions such as those of the European Community at Brussels. It can break the common front of Western solidarity in dealing with the Soviet Union. But it can build very little. It does not have the means to serve the cause of stability and peace around the world. Unhappily also, when a brilliant and powerful leader hopes to fix the shape of future policy in the compass of past and present achievement, his single-minded purpose cannot be effectively carried out by the lesser men who follow. The case of Bismarck shows something, Henry Kissinger suggests, that is just as true of de Gaulle: "A structure which can be preserved only if there is a great man in each generation is inherently unstable" (*The Necessity for Choice*, p. 64).

What then of France's future? De Gaulle is himself fond of pointing out that France had one hundred and two governments between 1875 and 1940, while Britain had twenty and the United States fifteen in the same period. From the fall of the Bastille to the present day France has had, as he remarks in his *Memoirs* (p. 939), "fifteen regimes . . . each in turn installed by revolution or *coup d'état*, none succeeding in insuring equilibrium, all swept away by catastrophies and leaving ineffaceable divisions behind them."

Today France has a government controlled by a remarkable leader, but how does one read the horoscope for tomorrow when swings of the pendulum from weak democracy to authoritarian rule have been a cyclical feature of French political life for almost two hundred years? Such a phenomenon cannot be ignored nor can it be easily explained. Its origins are unquestionably complex and to try to account for it by a single glib generalization would distort history. Yet there is no doubt some validity in the hypothesis that France is a nation with an unassimilated revolution. The British royal family and the Lords long ago accepted the verdict of Cromwell and the Reform Bill of 1832, but the French people have never become fully resigned to the meaning of 1789 and that has contributed to instability in the life of the French nation. Whether or not the French people can ever fully reconcile the divisive forces in French life so long as they live in the confining framework of a medium-sized nation-state is, I think, an open question. But they have not done so yet, and the resulting rhythmic periods of discontent have produced a political *mal de mer*; oscillation decade in and decade out from the weak Directory to the dictatorship of Napoleon, from the bourgeois monarchy of Louis Phillipe to the bogus *grandeur* of the Second Empire, from the weak parliamentary democracy of the Third Republic to the strong "Administrative State" of Pétain, from the impotence of the Fourth Republic to the effective one-man plebiscitary rule of de Gaulle.

Yet General de Gaulle has not solved the problem; he has merely laid the groundwork for its appearance at a later time.

"After de Gaulle, who?" is a question that rightly concerns the whole West, because France has lived with instability since an amiable but inept Bourbon king was delivered up to the mob in 1792, and the succession problem remains a concealed time bomb in French political life. Nor does anyone know how well the Constitution of the Fifth Republic will work under a less commanding leader than the General.

Certainly the war against the parties did not solve anything, as I pointed out in a memorandum I gave President Kennedy toward the end of June 1963, on the eve of his visit to the European capitals. In the course of my memorandum I made the point that, in mounting an offensive against the whole structure of parties, General de Gaulle had decimated all but the Communist party ("which was not so much a political organization as a church"); he had weakened the institutional means for resisting Communism, thus leaving it to Thorez and his friends to offer the opponents of Gaullism the only functioning center of effective organized strength. This, I felt, might open the way for a new *front populaire* to be established in a post–de Gaulle France (since the UNR, the Gaullist party, "was not so much a political organization as a personality cult"); and I pointed with some alarm to the flirtation of the Socialists and other elements of the non-Communist left with the Communist party. This comment — only one brief paragraph in the course of my long memorandum — disturbed President Kennedy more than I had intended; and during his trip he more than once expressed caution to the Europeans that the adoption of a popular front government would mean riding a tiger.

In the light of everything that has transpired since then, I think my alarm was probably overstated. To be sure, the new French Federation of the Left has made electoral deals with the Communists; and, if I may dare to make a political prediction when the timing is so uncertain, I think it possible that the first post–de Gaulle government may well be left of center and elected with Communist support. This does not necessarily mean a *front populaire* government — I doubt that there will be Communists in ministerial posts — although continued Communist support may be necessary for the government's survival. Ultimately, I would expect a new equilibrium to be found with the evolution of a new cluster of moderate parties around a new center.

Meanwhile, it is at least possible that a united non-Communist left might gradually peel away the less fanatical part of the Communist electorate. Something like this has occurred in Italy through the "opening to the left" (a quite different process), and the French Communist Party is not so impressive or formidable an institution as it might seem. Throughout the postwar period it has been clear that the electoral strength of the party greatly overstated the number of its hard-core doctrinal adherents, since many Frenchmen have voted Communist merely out of discontent and a mindless faith in the old bromide that there is no enemy on the left. Today a new mobility, both physical and social, is working as a powerful solvent. Ancient regional allegiances are breaking down, while the prosperity of the Gaullist years has tended to make the class struggle far more shadowy and remote than even a decade ago. More and more Frenchmen have traded bicycles for *deux chevaux* Citroëns, and in a variety of ways have acquired a larger stake in the status quo.

Yet no one can say that the reentry of the traditionally disaffected as an active force in French political life could be quick or easy. It would obviously create prickly problems, scaring many in the West. Yet sooner or later something of the kind must occur if there is to be a healthy democracy in France; for it has not made much sense, throughout the whole of the postwar period, to have almost one out of every four voters effectively disenfranchised by adherence to a party that has been unable to make any positive contribution to French political life.

All of this, of course, is speculation with little direct bearing on the events of today and tomorrow, since General de Gaulle is still very much the President of France and, so long as he is in power, few new leaders are likely to stand out sharply from the edges of his shadow. Today he seems less predictable than in the past, for what we have recently seen has been a confusing series of moves that appear as improvisations not adumbrated in his battle plan. Certainly this is true of his repudiation of Israel during her war with the Arabs last June (after French factories had filled Israeli arsenals), as well as his curiously puckish intervention in the politics of the *Québecoises.* Such incidents seem unrelated to his larger purpose as though he had finally run off the edges of his grand strategy and fallen back on *pour épater le bourgeois* as a national policy.

Yet it is not hard to foresee some possible remaining moves foreshadowed in words and actions already familiar. It may well be, for example, that the French government will give notice some time before June 1968 that France is formally withdrawing from the obligations of the North Atlantic Treaty. The excitement caused by such a decision in Western chancelleries would be unlikely to last long. The impact on public opinion — the shock effect of the realization that France was no longer even in literal terms a member of the mystical lodge of "Western allies" — would be a nine-day wonder, since the General has, by taking

French troops from the integrated command and reinterpreting the Treaty, already destroyed France's automatic involvement in any new war.

Possibly also the General may announce another political veto of Britain's application to join the Rome Treaty but I doubt that this would have serious long-term consequences. Not only the Wilson government but both opposition parties have made up their minds that Britain shall enter Europe, and whether she does so now or a little later is hardly crucial.

At the beginning of this chapter I mentioned some of the achievements of General de Gaulle that are great and unchallengeable. I suggested, however, that, on balance, his European policies had been bad for the West, and I then undertook to analyze the course of his European strategy from the battle plans he himself had drawn. Such an approach has advantages of clarity but, since the evidence cited was selected to document a pre-announced thesis, the total impression of the General's works may seem to overemphasize the negative. If so, this was not deliberate, and I would like to make clear for the record that, in spite of the fact that during the last ten years President de Gaulle has obstructed many common Western decisions — and, from the point of view of a weary Washington, the word "non" has often seemed to be a French translation of "nyet" — the General's government has still done much that was useful. In addition to liquidating the Algerian crisis, restoring national confidence and serenity, and reintegrating the army into French life — enormous achievements by themselves — the Fifth Republic has put through the Currency Reform of 1958 and laid the basis for a solid expansion of the French economy.

Moreover, sometimes against the thrust of French policy and sometimes with its help, the institutions of the European Community have made substantial progress toward the eventual integration of the economies of the Six. By June of 1968, goods will move across national borders to serve a market of two hundred million people free from tariff interference. At long last a Common Agricultural Policy has been hammered out, which, although it is much too protectionist for my taste, could — given the pressures of entrenched farm lobbies — hardly have been otherwise.

Although it has caused headaches in America, it is still a major achievement since it was an essential building block in the construction of an effective common market.

In the larger arena of international economic cooperation progress has also been made. The Kennedy Round of trade negotiations has been completed, marking a giant stride toward a world of freer trade, while, after anguishing efforts, monetary reforms have been agreed on, creating a mechanism to assure adequate liquidity for the international payments system.

Finally, the General must be given credit for helping to create a climate with Eastern Europe that has made it easier for the Kiesinger government to begin, slowly and tentatively, to improve relations with its neighbors and to ease the lot of the people of East Germany.

To be sure, many of the General's actions have been explicitly or implicitly aimed at diminishing the influence of the United States in Europe and elsewhere in the world, which was bound to cause resentment in America. Yet this is not the principal ground for my objection to current French policy. As I have made clear so far in this book, I think that as Europe develops it is only healthy that it should begin to express its own views and prejudices, which will not always fully coincide with those of the United States. Yet we should look forward to such an expression of independence not as a cause for concern but a sign of developing confidence.

The gravamen of my complaint against the General is not, therefore, that he has acted at variance with American policies — or even to frustrate them — it is rather that he has acted for parochial French interests and not in support of a Europe whose name he takes so easily. His actions have too often resulted in weakening Atlantic relationships without a commensurate strengthening of European unity, and thus have contributed to fragmentation rather than the building of a modern political structure.

One could easily forgive General de Gaulle if he were a man of small talents, but it is the sweep and magnitude of his abilities that make his nostalgic, anachronistic approach to the structure of Europe a twentieth-century drama of high poignancy.

Of course, he has not played his role in an empty theater and much of the audience has been with him. But an accomplished actor need not give hostages to the transient mood of the house; by skill and patience he can shape the temper of the audience just as a strong leader can capture and direct the conflicting forces and pressures at work in the larger arena of world politics.

I am not, therefore, much impressed when apologists argue that, because nationalism is a powerful force easy to arouse, it is the wave of the future. Nationalism is a habit, a conditioned reflex, that lies just below the surface of consciousness of modern men, ready to break out at any moment; and, without doubt, given the rapid progress Europe was making toward unity at the outset of 1963, a nationalist counterattack was overdue.

But it is a great pity that General de Gaulle should have led that attack, that he should have put his extraordinary skills at the service of an outworn cause. For he — as no other man — had the charisma and authority and the iron will to lead Europe firmly and steadily toward unity.

Even from today's short perspective it is clear that, had the General applied his bold leadership to bring it about, the past five years might have seen Europe's coming of age. And, while speculation as to history's lost chances is a sterile exercise, one can still say regretfully that he could well have been the first President of some early form of European state.

What a difference that would have made for Europe, for the world, and for peace!

I X

Germany — The Heart of the Problem

WHILE Englishmen sought a new role and Frenchmen sublimated the memory of 1940 in the re-
membrance of *grandeur* past, Germans were beginning, haltingly, to recover a lost national identity. The German
state was completely smashed in 1945. The German nation, it
seemed at the time, might disappear forever. The centralized
Reich had had a life span of only seventy-five years.

I recall Germany in 1945 as a study in disarray — a blasted
surrealist landscape reminiscent in its macabre confusion of
Faust's Walpurgisnacht on the Blocksberg. Streets and rubble
were all the same thing. Railroad marshaling yards looked like
children's playrooms the day after Christmas. The industrial
barons of the Ruhr presided over a twisted mess of bricks and
mortar; for the moment they were junk merchants.

In due course all this changed. Professional activities kept me
traveling back and forth from America to Europe in the late
1940's and the fifties — one hundred or more round trips — and
I witnessed the shifting scene at first hand. Smoke began to belch
again from Ruhr chimneys, and the haunting image of 1945
retreated in the mind's eye. Industry recovered, but the political
and social fabric mended more slowly. Foreign observers saw in
postwar Germany an economy rather than a state, an administration rather than a government. In time West Germany began to reveal a personality, but it was a personality fashioned

by the memory of the war and its obscenities — docile, tentative, amorphous, and gray in color. "The secret path to chaos" that Nietzsche foresaw one hundred years before had been the road to shame and disillusion, and so Germany spent two decades in what the Japanese refer to as the "low posture," expressing whatever *élan vital* was left by hard work at home and reticence in world councils.

This was a mood for a generation — but not beyond. Like the ill-fitting cast-off Wehrmacht jackets of 1945, such a state of mind could not long stay in fashion, as events have already shown. Without question something new is beginning to appear but no one can be quite sure what it is. Yet how could it be otherwise, when more than twenty-five million young men and women, or 45 percent of the population, were born after 1937 and have no sentient memory of Hitler? Today they are beginning to ask questions. That is healthy. Already they are fixing the contours of a new German literature and politics. What they build and how they build it is of the greatest concern to all of us, since Germany, even without the Eastern provinces, is the mightiest industrial power in Western Europe, and geography has placed the German people at the center of danger.

Of course, Americans and Europeans suffer from no shortage of printed matter about the "German problem." A whole school of popular literature addresses and assesses the "state of the German psyche," whatever that means. (In an age when Woodrow Wilson is laid out posthumously on Freud's couch, I suppose this is hardly surprising.) But the mind of the German people will never be accurately assayed — as much of current literature seeks to do — by chance conversations with students in the beer halls of Munich or dowagers on the trams of Frankfurt or Ruhr Barons in the *Nachtlokale* of Dusseldorf. The Hitler period may fascinate the armchair psychologist and it properly will continue to engage the civilized conscience. But psychoanalysis written in the literary genre of "what I saw last summer on the Reeperbahn" is a bogus guide to the future, and if we wish to avoid another ghastly cataclysm, that is not the way to go about it. We should stop bemusing ourselves with the subjective peculiarities of a hypothetical Teutonic psyche and look critically and thoughtfully at the objective conditions of Germany's actual position and power and political goals in the middle of Europe.

For the future of Germany after two wars is a riddle we must solve with care. It lies at the heart of the relations between East and West. It is in many ways the most intractable and quite likely the most important problem we face.

The significance of the German problem results from many factors: her geography, her size, her military might, her history and political conditioning, her present state of dismemberment, and her effect on other nations.

Her Geography

Germany lies at the heart of world industrial power, between the Soviet Union on the one side, and Western Europe and North America on the other. In this exposed central position she has common frontiers with nine different countries. In all the world only three other nations have so many neighbors: the Soviet Union, China, and the Congo. "The nightmare of hostile coalitions," in Bismarck's phrase, has always plagued German leaders and is responsible for what some have called a geographical neurosis. Yet it has been German aggressiveness that has provoked others to unite against her in self-defense, with the inevitable result that, like Poland in 1939, Germany was crushed and partitioned by an East-West coalition in 1945.

Her Size

Unlike Poland, however, Germany is still a potentially powerful force in the world. Even a truncated West Germany has a greater population and industrial power than any other state in Western Europe; and, over the past decade and a half, population in West Germany has increased and production has expanded faster than in France or the United Kingdom. During that period, her gross national product has multiplied seven times, until today her per capita income is the highest in Europe. West Germany's foreign trade now rivals that of the United States. Her exports of $2.1 billion in 1950 had risen to $18.2 billion by 1965.

The contrast is all the sharper since Germany was at the point of practical economic paralysis in 1945 and her remarkable growth has proceeded from an abysmally low point. To be sure she had some good things running for her. When I was a Director of the United States Strategic Bombing Survey at the end of the war, we discovered, for example, that German industry's supply of general purpose tools in 1943 was almost three times that of Great Britain and more than four times that of France. Haunted by memories of the 1923 inflation, German industrialists had invested their earnings in production goods that would remain, whatever happened to the Mark. Machine tools are hard to destroy by bombing except by a direct hit, and the Survey estimated that during 1944, the year when the greatest tonnage of bombs was dropped on industrial targets, the proportion of machine-hours lost as a result of air raid damage did not exceed two to two and a half percent.

What this meant was that, when the rubble was cleared away and the railroads were running again, the Ruhr barons found they still had most of their basic industrial equipment. And they also had men to run the equipment, a labor force that would work hard and complain little; for the western migration of skilled manpower from the Eastern zone kept the trade unions off balance while providing a replenishing stream of highly industrious workers. All this, of course, does not detract from Germany's extraordinary economic recovery, but calling it a "miracle" was scarcely tactful, since it evoked bitterness in neighboring countries. It was galling for the victorious Western allies, weakened by the excision of their colonial empires, to watch the defeated Germans increasing production at a record pace.

Her Military Might

Not only is Germany today industrially strong but her industrial power is reflected in a modern and powerful conventional military force — including one of the largest and best equipped conventional armies in Europe. Measured in manpower the armed forces of the major countries now have the following strengths:

USSR	2,960,000
US	3,100,000
China	2,450,000

West Germany	450,000
France	510,000
Britain	440,000

Her History and Political Conditioning

It is not, however, the current statistics of the German military establishment that revive old nightmares among her Western neighbors; it is a deep suspicion of German intentions. This is a field outside history or politics, and I am not writing this book to identify the wellsprings of German aggressiveness; in fact, there has been altogether too much superficial discussion of that subject already. Yet one or two points seem to me both obvious and valid. That the Germans came to power only late in the nineteenth century after a long history of internal weakness and fragmentation has no doubt contributed to their drive for world recognition. That they live in the center of the map of Europe has no doubt contributed to a sense of claustrophobia. While these two points should not be overstated, neither can they be totally ignored.

It is equally relevant that the German people have had only tentative and intermittent experience with democracy. Yet that experience — brief as it is in total — has not been nearly as discouraging as is often suggested, for the Weimar Republic deserves a better name than history has given it. Suffering from what Winston Churchill called the "malignant and silly" reparations clauses of the Versailles Treaty, the Weimar democrats did not have an easy time. Yet, after Poincaré fell, the situation temporarily improved. The Western allies began, at Locarno, to treat Weimar less like a pariah, German democracy gained strength, and the economy slowly recovered from the disastrous inflation of 1923. In the 1928 elections the anti-democratic parties dropped eleven percentage points to only twenty-seven percent of the total vote (Nationalists 14.2, Communists 10.6 and Nazis a mere 2.6 percent). George Kennan, stationed at the American Embassy at Berlin, saw in the Weimar experiment "much that was enormously hopeful and exciting."

I shall not attempt in these pages to record the tragic history of the Weimar Republic or to retrace its ghastly denouement.

Hitler's rise reflected a grievous fault in German society, but the road to Auschwitz and Stalingrad was paved by shortsighted politics and bad economics. In the early 1920's it was a juggernaut inflation — causally related to the unrealistic reparations imposed by Versailles — that impoverished and almost destroyed the German middle class. A decade later it was the specter of four out of ten German workers thrown out of work by the Great Depression that terrified both labor and the middle class and set Hitler on the road to power.

Every industrialized nation tends to look back on the Great Depression as a national calamity and we are no exception. During the New Deal days we thought about little but our domestic economy. Speak to any American over fifty of the depression and he will tell you about breadlines in Chicago and soup kitchens in Kansas City and the terrible hardships of a shocked and anxious people. Yet frightful as was its effect in America, the depression's most evil result was far afield; it was not what it did to the American people but the Satanic forces it unleashed by tearing to bits the social and political fabric of Germany and preparing the way for dictatorship and war.

For we should never forget that Hitler was a creature of the depression, a sinister product of disaster. It was at the depth of the depression in July 1932 that his party reached its electoral high point, winning 13.7 million votes, just one percentage point less than the combined total of the democratic parties, 14.1 million, while Communists and right-wing nationalists held the balance. Six months later Hitler came to power by legal means through the inept intrigue of the Nationalist party, the senility of Hindenburg, the divisions among democrats and the cynicism of Communists. But the real villain was the economic crisis that demoralized the middle class, obsessed by the nightmare of another 1923. Although mobs of brown-shirts were in the streets, Hitler's party still had less than a majority and it might still have been stopped, when, in sudden panic, the Reichstag granted him full powers.

The German people bear an awesome burden of blame for Hitler, since they were his more or less willing pawns. They accepted his leadership, cooperated in turning the economy into a war machine, and expressed their fears and frustrations in a virulent racist nationalism. But the Western democracies committed sins of omission as well. Brooding over the senseless slaughter of the First World War, morally confused and politically debilitated, no Western nation raised a sword to stop Hitler's first aggressions. His march into the Rhineland in 1936 was a calculated risk that worked for one reason only: the will to crush him did not exist.

The harsh truth is that, because Europeans had ceased to believe in themselves, Europe was morally sick. The prevailing mood of Britain and France was a compound of cynicism and fatalism and fatigue. In Paris, the watchword of the day was *"il faut en finir"* — reflecting the sinking sense of a world poised before chaos. In Britain, in that tense August of 1939, a harassed Prime Minister Neville Chamberlain remarked wearily to a friend, "Every time Hitler occupies a country, he sends me another message." In America the expatriate poet W. H. Auden looked out on the end of "the dreary hopes of a low, dishonest decade" and expressed the prevailing mood of his fellow Europeans whom he described as:

> *Lost in a haunted wood*
> *Children afraid of the night*
> *Who have never been happy or good.*

Nor did we Americans show any more sense. The mood on our side of the Atlantic was one of sheer escapism. Pretending to be asleep under the bedclothes, we turned our faces to the wall. We rejected the obligations of great power until the Japanese military made up our minds for us by attacking Pearl Harbor. Yet even that classic imbecility might not have saved us from a destructive period of division and debate, if Hitler had not resolved our doubts by declaring war. In 1945 one of my colleagues on the United States Strategic Bombing Survey asked ex-Foreign Minister von Ribbentrop why Hitler had committed such a *bêtise*. Didn't he understand that if Berlin had not declared war, a strong faction in the United States would have pressed us to stay out of Europe and concentrate on America's only enemy, the Japanese? Opinion, after all, was by no means of one mind and if, under these circumstances, Roosevelt had committed us in Europe, he would have taken a divided America into the war. How then could Hitler have been so stupid as to unite America unnecessarily?

Von Ribbentrop's reply was a classic of fatuity. "The Führer and I knew nothing about Pearl Harbor," he said, "and, of course, we were dismayed by it, but what could we do? We did the only thing possible for us; we turned a smiling face toward the world and declared war on the United States."

Although Hitler, by any normal standards, was a mad dog, a psychotic prone to epic mistakes, he, like Napoleon before him, had his brief hour of mastery of the old Continent. At the height of his Satanic power, the darkest to defile the Western world for centuries, he ruled two hundred and fifty million people. Yet it does no good to call him a lunatic; that excuses neither the flatulence of the Western democracies nor the callousness and placidity of most of the German people.

Hitler left Germany with a sinister heritage: the political fact of her role in world catastrophe — a mark of Cain that will endure for a long time. It makes her neighbors sensitive to her growing power, and imposes special inhibitions on her freedom of action. Yet the doctrine of original sin has no place in world politics, and those who would erect it into something structural and permanent are themselves guilty of a sin against experience and common sense. A new generation is rising in Germany that will not willingly accept special restraints. Sooner or later the new Germans will react against inequality or discrimination; for no people so proud and competent will play the sedulous hostage to history and we would be stupid indeed if we thought otherwise.

Her Effect on Other Nations

But, for the time being, the political fact is still dominant, and translated into practical terms it means that Germany frightens people. Because of her size and power and history and psychology, there are latent fears in Europe on both sides of the Iron Curtain that her resurgent power may once more disturb the peace of the world. These fears are not felt with anything like the same intensity in America, because we are bigger than Germany and separated by an ocean. Since we never suffered the direct impact of her military aggression, it has been relatively easy for us to accept the Federal Republic as a close ally, and for almost two decades our troops and our nuclear power have formed the central core of her defense.

During that period we have gnawed away at the problem of German reunification but with no conviction that it could be settled for many years to come. This has not been a happy experience for us, since it is one of the better-founded clichés that Americans do not feel at ease with insoluble problems; thus over time we have developed a special kind of ennui with regard to Germany — ennui that contains a large component of self-deception. One hears more and more that the German problem is, after all, no longer of paramount importance; that we have for too long been a slave to German neuroses and anxieties, and that we should no longer pay so much attention to Teutonic sensitivities. The Germans have "learned their lesson," and, since they are now a fat and happy *gemütliche bourgeoisie*, wouldn't we do well to stop paying so much attention to the German government and the German people and concentrate instead on reaching a bilateral understanding with Moscow that satisfies the interests of the United States and the Soviet Union?

This view of the German problem as a harmless but irritating footnote to East-West relations has won considerable acceptance in recent years. In variant form it is expressed strongly by the Soviet Union and at times with equal vehemence in Western countries. Its starting premise is that Germany represents a "special situation" and is not to be treated in the same way as other nations; because of their history the German people must accept constraints not required of other people. When and if reunification finally occurs — though there are many even in the West who do not want to hurry the process, since they fear a reunited Germany — the Germans must pay for it by permanent self-denying ordinances. In other words, they must be prepared to accept in solemn commitments the hegemony of other states.

This approach to the German problem is not new. It was tried at Versailles in 1919 with disastrous results. It is a solution calculated to produce instability, demagoguery and frustration at the dangerous center of Europe. Both Europe and Germany deserve something more hopeful than the repetition of a discreditable past. Yet, deceptive and mischievous as I believe it to be, this argument is heard with increasing frequency from otherwise sensible people, some of them in influential places. It encourages false hopes and offers easy-sounding solutions, but it is not a thesis that can stand close scrutiny. It grossly misconceives the character of both Germany and the Germans. It conjures up a delusively simplistic model of how peace and stability can be secured. I am firmly convinced that there is no possibility for a long-range and stable European settlement unless we can find a solution that takes account of the interests of the German people, that permits them to play a role of substantial equality in Europe — a role both self-respecting and satisfying — and that enables them to direct their energies and talents to constructive ends.

It is hard to see how this can be achieved except by the creation of a modern European political structure. Within such a structure the preponderant weight of the German population and of its industrial and military power would be more than offset by the combined weight of other member peoples (including the people of the United Kingdom). Under those conditions Western Europeans could exorcise the specter of a resurgent Germany, while the reunion of the German people could be regarded as an asset in the common interest rather than as a danger to be avoided. With German power diluted through solidarity with other European peoples, even the Soviet Union might ultimately overcome its phobia about German revanchism.

This is the optimistic and, I think, the realistic model of a future European settlement. But if the path to European unity is blocked, compromising the goal of reunification, Germans in frustration may be led to seek reunification in a more dangerous way. A future German government might be tempted to emulate Bismarck's policy of trying to achieve unification by a conspiratorial playing off of West against East. Or, what is not impossible, such a government might break completely with the West and turn eastward to bargain bilaterally with the Soviet Union.

These were the underlying fears and assumptions of Schuman and Adenauer and De Gasperi twenty years ago. The Germans, they perceived, could achieve equality and reunion only within a larger European framework. This was a sustaining hope — a chance for a new generation of Germans to play a role of self-respect, an attractive outlet for the idealism of German youth in the challenging concept of "Europe." And for a time it worked. In Germany five or six years ago, I frequently asked adolescents what was their nationality. More often than not they would respond: "I am a European" — words spoken with hope and pride. To the new Germans the building of a united Europe offered a broad and handsome avenue of escape from a confining and disastrous past, an *"unbewältigte Vergangenheit."* Within the new edifice of Europe they could find ample scope for their efforts and energies for it would be a house of many mansions.

But the hard-won progress of fifteen years, Adenauer's thesis in tying his country to the rest of Western Europe, was suddenly threatened in the backwash of Paris. Assertive French nationalism coincided with new Soviet maledictions and even a wall in Berlin, drawing greater public attention to the frustrations of a divided country. Thus it was not surprising that General de Gaulle's frontal assault on the unity of Europe at the beginning of 1963 had larger consequences for Germany than for other states.

Within a week after the General's press conference of January 14 came the announcement of the Franco-German treaty of cooperation. It seems clear from information that has since come to light that the treaty — an initiative of Chancellor Adenauer — was in process of negotiation long before General de Gaulle's press conference, but the curious juxtaposition of the two events made it look otherwise. I recall responding to the French Ambassador's greeting a few days after the treaty was announced with the comment: "We Anglo-Saxons are getting on very well, thank you. How are you Gaulo-Teutons?"

To the Kennedy Administration, still shaken by the Olympian vituperation of the General's press conference, the percussive impact of these two closely spaced events raised a series of disturbing questions. Did the treaty mean, for example, that the German government was endorsing the anti–Anglo-Saxon and nationalistic overtones of the General's statement? Was this in effect a ratification by Chancellor Adenauer of de Gaulle's exclusion of Britain from Europe? We asked the government of the Federal Republic for clarification, and in response State Secretary Karl Carstens, a forthright and able man who was then my opposite number in the Foreign Ministry, was sent to Washington in the first week of February to explain the background of the treaty and the intentions of his government. Dr. Carstens allayed our anxieties about a new Bonn-Paris axis directed against other nations while promising that steps would be taken to avoid further public misunderstanding. As a result of the Carstens mission and of the popular reaction in the United States, in other European countries, and in Germany itself, the Bundestag, in ratifying the treaty, added a preamble reaffirming German support for "the unification of Europe . . . through the establishment of the European Communities, including the accession of Great Britain." It also expressed support for the "consolidation of the integration of the free people and, in particular, close partnership between Europe and the United States of America . . . and integration of the armed forces of the member states of [the] alliance."

I cite this history because of the curious myth, which has gained currency in some circles on both sides of the Atlantic, that the American government sought to force the government in Bonn to "choose" between the United States and France. Nothing could be more absurd. The United States certainly had no objection to the Franco-German treaty, although its announcement immediately after President de Gaulle's nationalistic pronunciamento was, from the German point of view, a monumental *gaffe* in timing, since it tended to associate the German government with policies antipathetic to its own larger objectives. We had made it clear again and again that a Franco-German rapprochement was a fundamental condition to stability in Europe; this has been and, I am sure, will remain, a fundamental tenet in the foreign policy of any American adminstration.

Yet to say this does not mean that we expected much from the treaty. I told my German friends that I doubted it could have more than symbolic value — and, of course, it has not had — since it ignored the conditions, indispensable to the development of a close Franco-German relationship. It had long seemed clear to me, as to most observers of the European scene, that France and Germany could never achieve a lasting understanding on a bilateral basis but only within the framework of a larger Europe, because they carried a burden of history too heavy to be supported by a fragile structure mounted on only two pillars. France could — to change the figure — never merge her fate with Germany's within the narrow confines of a bilateral arrangement without the abiding fear of being overwhelmed as German preponderance increased over the years.

Whatever the shifting nuances of the Franco-German relationship, I find this analysis as true today as it was in 1963, for the treaty has not brought France and Germany closer together in any tangible sense. So long as Adenauer was the German Chancellor, Bonn was prepared to accept a position of relative subordination and France might hope that German power could be used in furthering her own policies. But this could never be the wave of the future, and General de Gaulle's nationalistic manifesto stirred up forces in Germany that have already made the long-term acceptance of such a subordinate role impossible. From 1964 through 1966, the effect of this hardening German position on an increasingly self-centered French policy was disturbing to watch. When German leaders failed to interpret and apply the treaty in a way that would make them auxiliaries of French policy, they triggered an angry reaction in Paris, and in succeeding months the voices from the Elysée have more and more recalled Poincaré's fear and dislike of Germany.

Meanwhile in the Federal Republic, home-grown "Gaullists" began to appear on the German domestic scene, arguing for close Paris-Bonn ties on the unstated assumption that one day Germany, not France, would be the senior partner and nationalistic beneficiary of the relationship. Herr Franz-Josef Strauss, leader of the Bavarian affiliate of the governing Christian Democratic Union, argued for German financial contributions to the *force de frappe* in return for an enhancement of Germany's national position. Others like his colleague Freiherr zu Guttenberg declared that Germans must pay greater attention to their own purely national interests — especially reunification — rather than to schemes for a wider European unity. Bismarck, it was argued, had achieved national unification against great odds. Could not the same thing be done a hundred years later through the pursuit of a more "national" policy?

Nationalistic views of this kind still find resonance in German politics, but no longer do politicians seek identification with Gaullism; for, as the full import of French policy has been more widely understood, opinion has shifted away from the General. On one public opinion poll, for example, General de Gaulle's popularity in Germany sank from a sixty-one percent "favorable response" in October 1962 to a low of fifteen percent "favorable" in early 1966.

Yet the widening gulf between Germany and France did not reflect itself in a changed German attitude toward other European nations or the United States. The German government continued to play a loyal role in Europe and the Atlantic Alliance. The defeat and moral discredit of 1945, still in people's memories, put an active German foreign policy out of the question; while fear of the Soviet Union, coupled with reliance on the American defense of Germany, made Bonn dependent on Western ties.

But as the 1960's draw toward a close, both of these factors are having a decreasing relevance and impact. Memories of the war are receding as are memories of Stalinist expansionism, and the new generation growing up in Germany today will not be content with the humble and complaisant attitudes of the past; what we are beginning to perceive are the first stirrings of an affirmative and independent foreign policy — a policy that reflects an absence of guilt and a growing self-confidence. This, by itself, is not a bad thing; it is in any event inevitable, a development predicted and awaited in Western chancelleries for several years, but it will require us to think more — not less — deeply about a Germany that is showing the first signs of flexibility.

The coalition government of Chancellor Kurt-Georg Kiesinger and Vice Chancellor Willy Brandt — uniting the two major parties of Christian Democrats and Socialists in a single regime for the first time — has begun to tear down the twelve-year-old Hallstein Doctrine and reestablish relations with East European countries. It is starting to seek — more actively than ever before — a series of bilateral rapprochements with countries like Poland and Czechoslovakia whose memories are long, for they felt Nazi bestiality most horribly. Rumanian Foreign Minister Manescu and his Bulgarian colleague Budinoff have visited Bonn for the first time since the war, while German emissaries negotiate in Budapest and Belgrade and Prague. In trying to win friends and influence Communists, the Bonn government has exchanged "peace notes" with Moscow in a continuing effort — probably doomed to be unrequited for some time to come — to produce some "give" in the rigid Soviet support for Ulbricht's rump regime and opposition to reunification.

At the same time the West Germans remain abnormally sensitive to the vaguest rumors of a possible United States–Soviet deal, made without their participation, that might fail to take their interests into full account. They see, for example, in the push for a nonproliferation treaty, a cause for concern; in fact, discussion of such a treaty has given right-wing Germans, as well as others across the political spectrum, a means of expressing suspicions about the United States while at the same time displaying an independent "European" posture. Axel Springer, Germany's Lord Beaverbrook, whose tabloids and magazines and newspapers reach ten million Germans a week, has campaigned against the "discrimination" implicit in a nonproliferation treaty. He has been joined by nationalist members of the cabinet like Franz-Josef Strauss, while the Chancellor himself has professed to see "a form of atomic complicity" dangerous to Europe between Moscow and Washington.

Honest dialogue and criticism across the Atlantic are a healthy thing. To the extent that the rearticulation of German interests in recent years is a sign of growing democratic maturity and self-confidence, it is to be welcomed; but let us not be Pollyannas, since there may also be lurking dangers — domestically and in foreign policy — behind the more assertive thrust of German leadership. There are some politicians on the German scene —

to be sure not in dominant positions today — who would favor giving German policy an easterly exposure, moving from European integration to splendid isolation, doing a bilateral deal with the East to buy reunification at a high price; in short, recreating uncertainty and instability at the heart of Europe with an end no man can foresee. If a mood of national self-assertion is rising, there are those who will seek to exploit it in all parties in German domestic politics.

Throughout the history of German politics there have always been two distinct schools of thought in foreign policy; one favoring Eastern ties and the other Western. The "Easterners" — partly for good reasons and partly due to the continued neglect and suspicion of Germany by the West — have generally won these intramural debates. From General Yorck's Convention of Tauroggen in 1812 to the *Drei-Kaiser-Bund* to the Chicherin-Rathenau agreement at Rapallo and the Molotov-Ribbentrop Pact of 1939, German foreign policy has faced eastward for security and "compensation." When I have made this point to many Americans they have looked at me in disbelief, forgetting that Adenauer's policy of "the Western link" was a radical break in the continuity of German diplomacy, that it was not the norm but something quite new in the world. Today the key to the lock of reunification lies in the East, which exerts a strong pull on many Germans to point policy in a more traditional direction, repudiating the historical novelty of Adenauer's heresy. And there is an additional factor — perhaps a sentimental triviality but nonetheless a force of some minimal attraction even to Ruhr magnates — a romanticism about "the East" shared by liberals and conservatives, poets and industrialists throughout modern German history.

Meanwhile the French government, in its new policy of seeking "détente, entente and cooperation" with the Soviet Union, is attempting to curry relations with a power that shares its determination to keep Germany under a special regime. One can see in these new Franco-Soviet conversations the reflex of the old French policy of playing both sides against the middle to enhance her own power and keep Germany in her place. The old, old music of the Entente Cordiale and the showy but ineffectual

Franco-Soviet Pacts of 1935 and 1944 is being piped again — though this time all in the treble clef.

Unhappily both the audience and the performers have short memories; otherwise they would call for a new tune with a happier ending. The Western allies attempted after the First World War to impose special restrictions and inhibitions on Germany and succeeded only in breeding disaffection and providing ammunition for a demagogue; and I think it quite naïve to assume that a new generation of Germans would be long content with anything less than an equal position in Europe. To be sure, a future German government might, as part of the price of reunification, provisionally assent to some special restrictions with regard to armament or even disengagement; but the acceptance of such conditions as the price for achieving German unity would sooner or later be regarded as an action taken under duress; and all history testifies that it would build up trouble for the future, if the inhibitions were strict and not subject to revision.

Thus unless, primarily through a British initiative, new momentum can be achieved toward the building of a united Europe, the generation of Germans now coming into their majority is likely to feel frustrated indeed. Already there are clear and disturbing signs that German youths in the universities are disenchanted with the policies pursued by their fathers over the past twenty years; and if the dream and possibility of European unity are permitted to fade and nationalism again becomes the dominant idea of the day, the new generation will have no option but to concentrate on reunification as the single obsessive goal of German politics. And let us never forget that, at the end of the road, it is the Soviet Union, not the West, that can bestow reunification as part of a global bargain.

The new generation of Germans is, therefore, well worth watching and cultivating. They are citizens of a democracy that lacks deep historic roots and traditions and suffers from the discontinuous "blackout" of twelve recent years of Nazism. To their elders they are a problem, yet no less incomprehensible than present-day adolescents in other lands. A gifted, materially ambitious, and, on the whole, rather cosmopolitan generation, they appear, at the same time, politically passive and not too well informed. They feel no personal responsibility for Hitlerism (and they should not); but what is disturbing is that many are beginning to doubt that the Hitler era was as bad as reported.

They are understandably resistant to having the sins of their fathers visited on their heads, and they disdain the efforts of their fathers who for two decades have deliberately and systematically worked on the closest terms with the West. What, they ask, has been gained by it, since Germany seems no nearer reunification today than she did twenty years ago? The question is heard with increasing persistence, and, since the answers do not satisfy, the resultant cynicism and discontent should not be discounted; for, if hope for a united Europe is throttled, and the "Western orientation" continues to appear as a dead end, a new German generation may well feel compelled to reverse the thrust of German policy. One of my friends, a professor at a leading German university, described the state of opinion among his students in rather startling terms: "What we are witnessing," he remarks, "is a plot between generations that could bode ill for the future — a conspiracy of the sons with the grandfathers against the fathers."

I do not mean to suggest that at the end of the road we will find a resurgence of militarism or even a surreptitious effort on the part of the Germans to obtain nuclear weapons, as they obtained conventional weapons in the 1920's. But what may be possible some years in the future is a German effort to make a bilateral deal with the Soviet Union leading to the rejoining of the severed body of the old Reich. Though Moscow may not be ready to envisage German reunification today, this rigid attitude could well erode over time. A process of shifts and changes is under way on both sides of the Iron Curtain, and the possibility of some future Soviet overture to Bonn cannot be overlooked. Immanuel Birnbaum, the foreign political editor of the influential *Sueddeutsche Zeitung*, who has spent much of his life as a correspondent in Eastern Europe, expresses a view widely held in West Germany today. "Since reunification cannot be forced," he writes in *The Politics of Postwar Germany* (p.

457), "it must one day be bought. Today, the partners for such a transaction, the rulers of the Soviet Union, are not ready to negotiate. But once that was different, and it can again be different one day in the future."

There is no imminent danger of any German diplomatic adventure with Moscow; the realities of nuclear dependence are too well known for that. But we must think in a longer time span. The geometry of power relationships is rapidly changing; events set in train today can shape the conditions of tomorrow; and in those changed conditions a Germany not tied closely and institutionally to the West could be a source of great hazard. Embittered by a deepening sense of discrimination and bedeviled by irridentism, a Germany at large could act like a loose cannon on shipboard in a high sea. This is unlikely to happen the day after tomorrow, and only an alarmist could discern so disquieting a prospect on the immediate horizon; but in diplomacy, as in architecture, one must build for the future, incorporating a tolerance in the flexibility and internal strength of one's design to allow for the unseen stresses and strains that will inevitably challenge the structure. To presume to build for the ages may be a misguided act of *hubris*, but one can at least modestly plan against a premature obsolescence.

Thus it is not enough to say that there are no immediate prospects for a bilateral deal that might be acceptable to both the Germans and the Soviets. The elements of such a deal are known and they have no doubt been thought about on both sides. Those elements would include a substantial German "payment" to Moscow, German acceptance of arrangements that would withdraw her from NATO, and self-denying ordinances that would keep her militarily weak. Such a deal would, of course, have serious consequences in shifting the balance of power, since it could succeed only if some future German government were prepared — as it might be — to pay a very high price, including the provision of large material and financial resources for the modernization and industrialization of the Soviet Union. This last idea is not as bizarre as it sounds; I heard it advocated some time ago in certain Ruhr industrial circles, and it is what Herr Birnbaum of the *Sueddeutsche Zeitung* meant when he said that reunification "must one day be bought." But the payment in political coin could be far more important — and, in the end, quite dangerous. Such a result would not be good either for the West or for world peace and stability, since a Soviet-German deal (in which a nationalistic French government might join as the enforcer on the Western side) would necessarily rest on Germany's abandonment of her claim to equal treatment and this, while the Germans might temporarily accept it, would be dead certain to build up trouble for the future.

A better, safer path, for Germans and Frenchmen and Americans and Russians, is for seventeen million East Germans to merge their destiny with two hundred and fifty million "Europeans" in a single structure open to adherence by other European peoples. For the European idea is at the same time the most constructive and the most idealistic conception to emerge since the war. It is still capable of firing the imagination of German youth, giving purpose and scope to their remarkable energies. It can make the German people — in close association with Englishmen, Frenchmen, Italians, Belgians and Dutch — a benign magnet rather than a repelling force to the peoples of Eastern Europe. It can open frontiers rather than close minds. It can create the conditions in which the unjust and unnatural division of a single people can be ended, permitting their return to active participation in the mainstream of Western civilization. For Germans and their neighbors the construction of Europe can mean refreshment at the wellsprings of a great humane tradition. It can mean a vindication of Goethe and Schiller and Heine and Kant, the proper models of human adventure for a revitalized and liberal generation of young Germans.

X

The Far East in the Equation of Global Power

WHEN I was a young student in the latter 1920's we all read a sensational book by Lothrop Stoddard, called *The Rising Tide of Color*, crying alarm at the prospect that a massive horde of Asians would ultimately overwhelm Western civilization. To undergraduates in that innocent decade the threat of invasion by a new Genghis Khan was a titillating idea. The depression of the thirties had not yet made it popular to have what was to be smugly called a Social Conscience and not until four decades later would the Supreme Court make everyone aware of racial injustice. We were as dégagé as flower children — though we did shave and wash — more preoccupied with Proust and Joyce and such now forgotten figures as James Branch Cabell than our own narcissistic identities, and we did not recognize Stoddard for what he was, a Social Darwinist with an inadequate understanding of both demography and power.

Today, no one would think of employing such a repulsive expression as "the yellow peril" but that does not mean that Americans are cured of their nightmares. In spite of the realities of power and resources, Red China's grotesque manners still keep alive a residue of Stoddard's alarm. Some Americans still twitch at each wild flailing of the dragon's tail and particularly at any fresh evidence that the dragon might some day acquire nuclear teeth. For whether we admit it or not, China is in everyone's subconscious. One cannot help but be fascinated by a country that contains one-fourth of the human race, and a remarkably gifted one-fourth at that.

Nor is China huge merely in population. Including the outlying provinces of Manchuria and Tibet, China has a larger land area than the United States even with Alaska. Her subsoil is rich in mineral resources (antimony, coal, iron, manganese and tin) and there is a vast power potential in her rushing rivers. China is statistically overwhelming and her swollen army and rudimentary nuclear arsenal have given an ominous overtone to her bellicose grumblings. Yet if, as General de Gaulle is finding out, one cannot reverse the "verdict of number" by the exercise of strong will and singleness of purpose, it is equally true that numbers, area, and potential resources are not the sole requisites for global power. No one can be categorical about it, but, given the arrested development of the arts of government, there may well be an optimum size for a nation, the exceeding of which results in weakness, not strength.

Certainly, if population were the sole criterion, not only China with its more than 750 million* but also India with its nearly 500 million people would rank among the global powers. Nations with such vast manpower have the potential of becoming great modern powers and they may one day achieve it, but they are far from it today. Both lack industrial strength and, it appears, internal stability. Neither is remotely likely to achieve global power status within the next generation, which is as long as any social prophet can decently assert his prescience.

It is even an open question whether that power will ever be achieved, for there is enough daylight reality in the Malthusian nightmare of a ravaging population to make it clear that bloated human resources can be a liability as well as an asset. Faced with

---

*It is interesting to note that China's population growth has been slower than that of the world at large. In 1851, with an estimated 432,000,000 people, China had 36.8 percent of the world's population. Today, with over 750,000,000 people, China has only 22.7 percent (Reischauer and Fairbank, *East Asia and the Great Tradition*, p. 313).

present, and potentially larger, problems of feeding their people, it may well be that India, and less probably China, will never be able to rise to major power status by the classic pattern of self-achievement. They require much help from outside — it is not clear where China can get it — and, unless they drastically turn down the demographic curve, they will need even more assistance twenty years from now to feed their people, develop industrial economies and superimpose modern organized political structures on the resistant fabric of ancient cultures.

In 1960 Raymond Aron ventured the opinion that, of the world's four most populous states, India had the least likelihood of either attaining great power status or preserving it if it were attained. India, he wrote in *Peace and War* (pp. 319-20), "suffers from the mediocrity of resources mobilizable by the state, as a result of the preponderance in the number of men over the number of machines. The population has grown faster than the productivity of labor; the relatively liberal regime does not permit this disparity to be reduced rapidly." Moreover, India more than almost any other nation hauls a crushing load of social and religious impedimenta that constantly clutters the road to progress.

Apart from the inhibitions of a "liberal regime," most of Raymond Aron's comments apply equally to China, which he assumed, quite prematurely, was on the way toward becoming a great power. Yet, in spite of China's basic weakness, it has become fashionable within the past few years to view her as the menace of the future. The specter-haunted dream of the twenties has been revived by Peking's egregious international manners and made lurid by her rude threats. When Lin Piao, Mao's lieutenant, set forth didactically the Communist concept of "Wars of National Liberation," many otherwise sensible people concluded that a work so boring must be of major importance.

But China's nuclear capability, large armies and mass-labor methods are no substitute for the advanced technology, the high level of industrialization and gross national product, that alone give a nation the means to feed its people and menace the world. For the "troublemaker" as Raymond Aron points out in *Peace and War* (p. 316),

. . . must possess superior resources. Spain, in the period when the king of Spain was the emperor in Germany and the sovereign in South America, was also the most prosperous nation in Europe. The France of the seventeenth and eighteenth centuries was the most densely populated and most vigorously administered nation. The Germany of Wilhelm II had the foremost industry on the Continent. In each period the conditions of force were combined in favor of the state with hegemonic pretensions.

Abstractly defined, these conditions are always the same: potential of resources and degree of mobilization.

China's capacity to be the "spoiler" is not very impressive. To be sure the Chinese army shells Quemoy every other month, as part of a pre-announced program to show that hostilities between the mainland and the Nationalists are still in progress. But from comments last year in the Peking press some members of the Chinese Liberation Army apparently feel that antiquated armaments and well-indoctrinated troops are no substitute for the destructive capacity of the two superpowers. Nor is there much prospect that China's relative position will improve. The longer the arms race continues, the harder it will be for her to keep up with each generation of new weapons. The defense budgets of the superpowers are expanding in absolute terms faster than is China's total economy, and the United States alone is spending each year on its military establishment more than China's entire Gross National Product.* Meanwhile, the Chinese are still working on some kind of missile delivery system for weapons now under development.

The current exaggeration of China's capacity for mischief derives in large part from the failure to measure "power" in relation to specific coordinates of time and place. "Power" in the abstract is meaningless, as we are finding out in Southeast Asia; when a contest is waged in jungles and rice paddies, even the vast military apparatus of the United States is only marginally more effective than the conscript troops of a primitive country. Similarly, although China almost certainly has the will and power to defend

---

*China's GNP is $74 billion; one-tenth that of the United States. The per capita daily wage, therefore, is twenty-five cents.

the Middle Kingdom against a land attack or an encroachment too close to her boundaries (as she demonstrated in the Korean conflict), her ability to send her armies on aggressive adventures into neighboring countries (except against a defenseless Tibet) is probably not of a high order — and, in spite of the bellicose noises that she makes, her will to do so has not been demonstrated. To be sure, she did reach over the mountain barriers to attack India in 1962, but she made no attempt to hold most of the ground she had gained even against indifferently trained and badly armed Indian forces.

China's capacity as a "spoiler" must rest, therefore, largely on the danger that her neighbors will be intimidated by her capability to fire nuclear weapons and her threats to use them. This, however, shifts the problem of "containment" to a totally different focus. We cannot put to rest Asian fears of a Chinese nuclear attack by the deployment of land armies in tropical terrain but only by establishing that, if China uses her nuclear weapons against her nonnuclear neighbors, we will use ours against her.

China may properly, therefore, be considered as lacking the resources to be a dangerous spoiler, and she has compounded her weakness by the incredible clubfootedness of her diplomacy. The late Evelyn Waugh could have shaped an uproarious comedy out of Chinese attempts to infiltrate the new African states, whose peoples caught on quickly to the fact that the Middle Kingdom was as racially arrogant as Governor Wallace. The Chinese have done no better in South America, and in Indonesia — the prize of Asia — their adherents were wiped out on a scale exceeded in modern times only by Hitler's slaying of the Jews and the communal killings in the Subcontinent in 1947. The real danger posed by China today does not, therefore, result from her power or her adroitness but her potential for unpredictable actions. Chinese officials on several occasions have stated that they are prepared to sacrifice their countrymen in a nuclear war — and this carries a sickening flicker of plausibility in a spectacularly overpopulated country.

Only once in modern history have we had a truly "irresponsible" dictator of a great state — one who was willing to see his people destroyed for his own lunatic objectives. No leader before or since

Hitler has carried egomania to its ultimate terrible logic at the expense of the nation. None has been prepared to argue, as he did in his last gruesome days, that "if the war is to be lost, the nation also will perish . . . . There is no need to consider the basis of even the most primitive existence any longer." Up to the present time, the Chinese leaders, like most troublemakers past and present, have known where to stop — indeed they have acquired a tentative reputation for caution. But the mentality of Peking is opaque and confused and — however remote may be the possibility — no one can categorically rule out the possibility that Chairman Mao might try some day to provoke a fight between the two superpowers in the mistaken belief that China would still exist after the ensuing nuclear holocaust.

In relation to the global powers China, in spite of her masses, is still no more than a light heavyweight, and, while American diplomacy may have to exploit this weakness in the short run, in the years ahead it should increasingly seek to bring China out of her isolation into the light of day. I would concur in the assessment of Professor Edwin Reischauer, who has shown a surer perception of the play of forces in Asia than any other man I know. Commenting to the Senate Foreign Relations Committee on January 21, 1967, ex-Ambassador Reischauer said: "We have tended to overestimate its [China's] strength and its immediate menace to our interests and to its neighbors. The events of recent months have helped show how backward and troubled this country really is. Its economic progress will probably continue to be very slow for the foreseeable future. Thus our concern should be focused less on its immediate threat and more on its long-range development."

China's belligerence makes it exceedingly difficult to have diplomatic relations with her. But if the danger of Chinese irresponsibility is to be lessened, we shall have to find a new way of thinking about China and avoid thinking too obsessively about her. Our relations with China — by which I mean that vast nation on the mainland, whatever its government — have passed through a variety of phases. We have, at different times, regarded China as a rich market, a vast population to be brought to Christ, a source of danger from the "yellow peril," a valiant ally fighting shoulder to shoulder with us against a common enemy, and finally — the cycle having come round again — a vast expansionist horde threatening not only the Far East but, through nuclear weapons, our own homeland as well. China is the elephant described by blind men; it is different things to different people at different times.

For a number of years our policies toward China have consisted of little more than an attempt to keep her in isolation by blocking her admission to the United Nations and discouraging her recognition by other countries. At the same time, and particularly since the Korean War, we have sought, by a series of military alliances, to contain the specter — if not the reality — of Chinese expansionism. We have enforced these policies at great cost and effort but with quite dubious results. In fact, over the long term, our deliberate policy of isolating China may well encourage and intensify those very traits of the Chinese character that could prevent the building of a stable Asia. For its most likely result will be to sustain and increase the arrogance and introspection which spring from her historic isolation.

That isolation has left an enduring mark, since, in spite of the tremendous length of her land and sea frontiers, Chinese civilization matured without much contact with the rest of the world. For long periods of history the peaks, deserts and vast plains of the north and west were inhabited by aggressive tribesmen. To the south lay mountains and jungles. To the east was the sea; which did not serve as an avenue of commerce with the outer world as in the case of Europe, but was dreaded and ignored by successive Chinese governments.

Encysted by these natural barriers China first had contact with peoples like the Koreans and Japanese, who copied from her cultural models; then, beginning in the seventh century, with Arab and South Asian traders; and, from the sixteenth century on, with Europeans. Nonetheless, to the Chinese the "Middle Kingdom" was, and remained, the center of the world. Immune from any compulsion to compete with rival cultures, they developed an inbred disdain for the rest of the world, treating other nations as vassals and entering gifts from foreign sovereigns on their rolls as "tribute." Until 1793 they were still refusing to receive other nations' ambassadors on a basis of equality.

With this background of thought and habit it was only natural that the Western victories in the nineteenth century should have profoundly shocked Chinese sensibilities. They exposed the inadequacies of Chinese values. The military authorities in Peking suddenly felt the need for a fleet and new armaments, and civil servants found that their training in Chinese literature was poor preparation for dealing with the problems of a greatly changed world. Representatives of the West compounded the Chinese humiliation by behaving with an arrogance matching that of the Chinese themselves. They took charge of the customs service in order to circumvent corruption and, in moving over the face of China, did not bother to conceal their sense of moral, cultural and racial superiority, thus contributing strongly but unconsciously to China's almost pathological xenophobia. Yet that xenophobia had no special focus; the Chinese showed a fine impartiality in their hatred, directing it indiscriminately at all foreigners — not merely Westerners but the Japanese as well — until the Korean War. Since then they have tended to concentrate their animosity on the United States and more recently on the Soviet Union.

Yet this xenophobia, unparalleled in human history, does not fully explain China's erratic foreign policy; it is more complex than that. Nor does it at all explain the controlled chaos that has recently seized China — a kind of political Saint Vitus's dance, frantic, noisy, bizarre by our standards, but dimly attributable to history and religion. To history, for the events of the past two decades, culminating in the convulsion of today, have at least a superficial parallel in the dynastic cycles that have repeated themselves ever since 200 B.C., for the life stories of all the dynasties have been strangely similar.

The fall of each dynasty has been followed by an interval of anarchy. Then, during its first phase, the succeeding dynasty has restored order and a measure of prosperity to the peasants, resulting in an expansion of land under cultivation and the beginning of an increase in the peasant population that had been static or declining during the interval of anarchy. In the next phase the pressure of an expanding population, coupled with increasing government inefficiency and corruption, has reduced revenues and encouraged factionalism, until finally, with the ruler's entourage and the bureaucracy at war among themselves and the consequent decline in the central authority of the state, the generals have intervened and the dynasty has collapsed under the impact of foreign invasion or domestic *coups d'état* — thus reinstating the anarchy that has marked the end of each cycle.

As in the past, China's present agonies are touched by the influence of Confucian thought, which strangely foreshadows Communism with its strong emphasis on authority, loyalty, morality and self-criticism. This is the code of the bureaucrat par excellence. Historically its success depended on a strong and effective ruler, but, once his authority began to decline, problems could not be effectively resolved. As Professors Reischauer and Fairbank have pointed out:

> Unlike the party system in British or American democracy, factionalism in the Chinese type of bureaucratic state was seriously disruptive, because there was no mechanism for reconciling policy differences if the throne failed to settle them through strong leadership. Because of the Confucian emphasis on ethics as the basis of good government, opposing policies could not be accepted as the product of honest differences of opinion but were commonly regarded as signs of the depravity of one's opponents. Moreover, with good government considered to be the natural product of sound ethical standards, majority decisions would not suffice; unanimity was necessary. The democratic balance of our own partisan politics would have been unthinkable. Any opposition represented a disloyalty tantamount to both treason and moral turpitude. Such an attitude helps to account for the ferocity of the factional struggles, which led to numerous executions and the purging of hundreds of officials at a time. (*East Asia and the Great Tradition*, pp. 437-438)

It may also account for many of the features of the current power struggle now raging in China.

These then are Chinese neuroses which a sensitive American policy should aim at treating and not inflaming. Our long-range goal should be to release China from her isolation, bring her into the world community, and heal the resentments created by Western imperiousness. But successive United States governments have been disabled from pursuing such a sensible policy by domestic political pressures and our unrealistic relations with the Chinese Nationalists in Taiwan; for, in formal diplomatic terms, when an American official speaks of the Chinese government today, he still refers to the Nationalist government — or, in other words, to the government of Generalissimo Chiang Kai-shek, which regards itself as the government of the whole of China.

Today the Nationalist government is like something from *Alice in Wonderland.** Its National Assembly purports to be the legislative body for the whole of China. It elects the President and has the power to change the Constitution. Yet it was itself last elected in 1947, and, since ninety-eight percent of the total Chinese population lives on the mainland, new elections have been postponed until such time as the Nationalists can make a comeback. The Assembly, thus, is unique of its kind, a progressively aging body that suffers constant attrition as more and more of its members die. It is, in a sense, the only tontine parliament in the world, but what prize awaits the last surviving member is not very clear.

Yet, if the government is cut off from the vast territory it pretends to serve, its relations with the Taiwanese whom it does in fact govern are strained and unnatural. The island of Taiwan was for fifty years under the control of Japan. We captured it in 1945 and handed it over to the Nationalist government, which treated it juridically as a province of China. This was not the choice of the Taiwanese and in 1947 they revolted against their new masters, inciting the governor to brutal and repressive measures. The number of Taiwanese killed will never be known with precision but it probably totaled at least ten thousand out of a population of about eight million. Many thousands were thrown into jail, where some still remain.

---

*The Generalissimo's unenviable position on Taiwan is not without precedent in Chinese history. In 1664, the adherents of the overthrown Ming dynasty under Koxinga sailed over from Amoy and took possession of Taiwan. As the new Manchu government had no fleet, the refugees were able to harass the coast of China with impunity until 1683. Then the Dutch, annoyed by Formosan pirates, forced the Chinese on the island to submit to the imperial authority.

Within recent years the Generalissimo's government — largely in response to pressure from the United States — has made effective efforts to improve the situation of the local population. The island has moved at a commendable pace toward industrialization and economic modernity. Taiwanese have been permitted participation in political affairs and Taiwan is run with much less emphasis on terror and police state methods. Yet, since there have been no elections to the parliament for twenty years, the Taiwanese are not represented in that body in proportion to their numbers. The government in Taiwan is thus anything but an example of a virile and militant democracy, since the Taiwanese have little more voice in shaping their own destinies than the citizens of the District of Columbia.

The Generalissimo still remains a hero to the American Right Wing, yet our relations with his government were not always so friendly. In early 1949, many Americans had become disgusted with the knavery, inefficiency and general demoralization prevailing in the Nationalist ranks. Unsavory rumors filtered back to Washington that members of the decamping regime were even selling recently received American arms to the Communists — stories confirmed during the Korean War when those weapons were employed against our troops. Under such circumstances, further aid to the Kuomintang forces was discontinued in August 1949, and President Truman ignored strong pressures to send the Seventh Fleet or fresh equipment to Taiwan.

But time passed and memories of Nationalist corruption were obscured by long overdue military and social reforms. By 1953, attitudes had changed. The public sought scapegoats for the "loss" of China (as though we had ever owned it), and two and a half years of fighting Peking in Korea, followed by Communist activism in the straits of Formosa, persuaded Secretary Dulles that we should surround China with a ring of military alliances. As a result, we dug ourselves into a series of hard and fast commitments that deprived us of all flexibility in our dealings with the vast Chinese mainland.

There is a legal maxim, *rebus sic stantibus*, which Mr. Dulles was particularly fond of quoting. It means that commitments are binding only so long as the relevant facts and circumstances remain basically the same, and it was tailor-made to release us from the bondage of our Chinese fixation. Certainly the relevant facts and circumstances regarding the Taiwanese regime have unquestionably changed in the last thirteen years. The myth has grown so threadbare as to be embarrassing. No one any longer believes that the Generalissimo and his Taiwanese army will ever return to the mainland, or that they would be wildly welcomed by the Chinese people if they did; yet our refusal to put aside this myth paralyzes any initiatives that might bring about a more realistic position toward Peking.

The tragedy is that we were twice moving to a less artificial position toward Red China when events intervened.

Ever since the days of Woodrow Wilson, the United States — alone of Western nations — has, from time to time, inserted an element of moral assessment into its formula for recognition,* and most Americans regarded Mao's government as not fit for our diplomats to associate with. Nevertheless, while the record is not totally clear, there are indications that we were moving toward the normalization of relations with Red China in October 1949, when the Chinese arrested our Consul and his staff in Mukden. This caused a severe strain between Washington and Peking for about two months, and after that, on June 24, 1950, the Korean War broke out.

Three years of fighting in Korea and the dragging out of the recognition question did much to harden hostile attitudes. Peking might have learned to accept the conversion of a small but rich island province into another nation, but it could hardly be expected to tolerate a rival regime that masqueraded as the legitimate Chinese government and used its offshore island bases as jumping-off points for raiding parties. Nor could it be expected to like the patron and protector of that regime and the apologist for its mythology — which has been our role for almost two decades.

History sometimes repeats itself in curious ways, and again in 1961 we seemed on the verge of moving toward a more normal

*On January 6, 1950, the British government recognized the government of Mao Tse-tung as the government of China in the belief that the Communists had substantially satisfied the requirement of control of territory by taking command of most of the Chinese land area.

relationship with Red China when troubles in Laos and Vietnam intervened. I recall, during the summer of that year, a meeting with President Kennedy in which he expressed himself frankly and sadly about the irrationality of our position toward Red China. He wanted as much as any of us to disengage from a frozen line of policy that was embarrassing us around the world and impairing American prestige in the Far East. But at that time he lived under the brooding consciousness of a very narrow election victory, and, while he recognized that the voice of the China lobby had been reduced to little more than an occasional frog croak and that the "China-firsters" no longer carried much weight in Congress, he still thought it better to wait until 1962 before tackling such a sensitive subject.

He decided, therefore, that we should continue to oppose Red Chinese membership when the General Assembly met in September 1961, but that in the following spring (1962) we would take a long, fresh look at matters to see how we could inject some new mobility into the American position — perhaps by moving toward the support of a "two-China policy." But again we were thwarted by events; for, early in 1961, the troubles in Laos boiled up, and, beginning in the fall, our attention was concentrated more and more on the increasing threat of a Viet Cong takeover in South Vietnam.

From the point of view of an easy political climate there has, therefore, never been a good time to move our China policy off dead center; yet the longer we remain in our present grotesque position the greater the damage. Our present immobility limits our ability to lead others and to achieve our own national objectives, but it has been less costly than would have been the case if the Red Chinese had not gone out of their way to be obnoxious to the whole civilized world, thus tending to deflect attention from the irrationality of a China policy that gets in the way of our larger interests and is shared with no other nation.

Today, in defiance of the flow of history, we remain committed to the fanciful proposition that the Nationalist government of China is in fact the government of the seven hundred and fifty million people of that ancient land. But our fidelity is undiminished. We have gone to great pains to maintain the position of

Nationalist China not only as a member of the United Nations, but as the occupant of one of the five permanent seats on the Security Council — a seat established under the United Nations Charter on the assumption, now palpably incorrect, that China was one of the five great world powers and, hence, capable of joining with the other four in enforcing world peace.*

It is, I think, undignified for the United States, holding as it does a unique position of prestige and responsibility, to employ its political muscle to perpetuate a myth in which no other nation believes, and we have paid in hard political coin for our sponsorship of the Nationalist regime. We have made concessions in foreign aid and less tangible media to governments that did not merit them, simply to gain their vote in the General Assembly, and we have brought pressure on our friends in a manner embarrassing both to them and to us. In short, our position of lonely champion for an unpopular cause has given our Far Eastern policy a slightly crankish appearance. Tied to a myth that has lost whatever romantic flavor it might once have had, we have — at least until lately — been the main enemy of the Red Chinese government in Peking. In addition to opposing its membership in the United Nations we have obdurately refused to accord it official recognition and have maintained an iron embargo on all trade with the mainland, at high cost to our balance of payments. Our refusal to permit our farmers to sell wheat to Red China has denied us the opportunity to earn hundreds of millions of dollars in foreign exchange without in any way diminishing China's ability to buy the wheat elsewhere. Our efforts to enforce the embargo extraterritorially through subsidiaries of American companies doing business abroad have brought us into abrasive collision with friendly governments.

I should like, therefore, to see the United States adopt an intellectually defensible position that does credit to our maturity and leadership. I have no illusions that that would make the Red Chinese love us or even moderate their abuse. But it would certainly improve our reputation for realism and good sense and we would clearly be better off if we could stop having to play the

---

*In terms of the reality of power, the only Asian nation with the resources to justify a permanent seat on the Security Council is Japan.

mendicant to small nations to obtain their votes for the perpetuation of what the whole world recognizes as an outworn fiction.

Thus, apart from balance of payments considerations, I would not have cared very much whether or not the Chinese chose to buy our wheat; what concerned me was the absurdity of our futile gesture of refusing to sell it. Nor do I believe that Red China would accept a "two-China" policy if we were to favor one any more than it has permitted our reporters into China since we relaxed our own restrictions. It is as much myth-bound as we, obdurately insisting that Formosa is properly a part of the mainland just as we assert that the regime in Taiwan is the government of China. But the fact that it leads a fantasy life does not mean that America should. If anyone is to be petty or bloody-minded or unrealistic let it be the Chinese.

Meanwhile, we do continue to have periodic exchanges with Red China through their Ambassador in Warsaw. So far we have gained little information from these talks, but they have enabled us to make our own position clear, and this is important. I recall the advice given by an experienced British diplomat to young men about to serve in the Far East, as reported by Sir Harold Nicolson (in *Diplomacy,* p. 11):

> "Do not waste your time trying to discover what is at the back of the Oriental's mind; there may, for all you know, be nothing at the back; concentrate all your attention upon making quite certain that he is left in no doubt whatsoever in regard to what is at the back of your mind."

Yet, if we cannot immediately solve the Chinese puzzle, we must not let China's bellicosity or internal writhings distract our attention from the fundamental issue that preoccupies our age. To avoid world catastrophe we must keep our eyes firmly fixed on the greatest source of danger — the problems and tensions of the major nations; and, outside the Soviet Union and the West, Japan is the only large modern industrial nation. That is why any serious discussion of power in Asia must concentrate heavily on Japan.

By the rules of classic economic theory, Japan has no business having a strong industry. Like the United Kingdom, she is an island nation that lives by transforming other people's raw materials. But while the United Kingdom led the Western world into the industrial revolution because, as somebody once said, she was founded on coal and surrounded by fish, Japan has fewer natural resources than Britain — an inadequate amount of bituminous coal, some iron pyrites, limestone, and sulfur. She has only a small amount of water power, no coking coal, meager non-ferrous metals and oil, no natural gas, and only sixteen percent of her land surface is arable. Yet today Japan is a leading world industrial power and is pressing toward top ranking by increasing her production faster than any other power in the free world.

What Japan has accomplished is, at the same time, both an inspiration and an irritant to other Eastern countries. Although her population is just below one hundred million, as against the three-quarters of a billion of Red China, her gross national product is considerably higher than that of China, with *per capita* income about ten times as high and the lead growing. The disparity between Japan's production and that of other nations of the Far East is, in fact, so great as to be one of kind rather than degree. Ninety to ninety-five percent of all steel production in Asia is Japanese, and Japan has sixty to seventy percent of Asia's installed electricity capacity. One Japanese daily newspaper has a larger circulation than all other newspapers in the whole of Asia. If one compares Japan to Asian countries of similar population, the contrast is even more striking. Indonesia with one hundred and six million and Pakistan with one hundred and five million are spectacularly poor, while India, four times as populous, has only half the gross national product of Japan.

Compared with this island nation's progress the German "economic miracle" appears as apprentice magic. When the attack was launched against Pearl Harbor, Japan was producing only seven million tons of steel a year. Although her industry was smashed as badly as the Ruhr's — or worse — she was by 1965 producing forty-one million tons of steel and holding third rank in world production behind the United States and the Soviet Union. In that same year she led the world as a steel exporter (ten million tons), was fourth in electric power output and the production of motor vehicles, had a greater foreign trade (in value) than the Soviet Union, and was among the major donors of economic aid to developing countries. Even if she should fail to sustain a growth rate that has averaged over ten percent a year ever since 1950, but should slow down to a seven percent level, she is likely, in a few years, to replace West Germany as the third industrial power behind the United States and the Soviet Union.

In terms of living standards, of course, Japan is still far from the top group. With her population of one hundred million (as compared with sixty million for West Germany), she ranks only about twenty-first in per capita gross national product, behind Ireland and Greece. But she has the great advantage over other nations in that she can approach the problems of demography without being hamstrung by social and religious taboos. Through the application of a conscious government policy, she has stabilized her population at an average annual growth of under one percent — approaching the zero level that would completely flatten the demographic curve. As a result, the absolute growth of her gross national product means a commensurate growth in living standards — a situation that does not prevail to anything like the same degree in other countries.

How does one account for the phenomenon of Japan and why has she pressed ahead at such breathtaking speed, while other Asian nations have, for the most part, moved at a laggard's pace? The answer, I suspect, lies largely in the character of the people and the structure of the society they have created. Japan is a tight little island — or, more accurately, a group of tight little islands — with an intricately knit social and economic structure that has survived the dislocations of war. The cohesion of its people springs, in part, from the fact that the term "Japanese" is racially and not geographically defined. Chinese or Korean families become Japanese only very slowly, since the Japanese are clannish beyond most other people. Although the homerun king is a Taiwanese, and Nagashima, the great third baseman of the Yomiuri Giants, a Korean, Japan is emphatically not a melting pot but a homogeneous group society that operates largely by consensus. Paternalism is found in every sector of national life. One does not break another's rice bowl. When a young Japanese joins a business or industrial firm, he expects to stay there all his life, climbing gradually upwards within a complex but well-defined system.

Business is characterized by oligopoly, although perhaps not a great deal more than in several Western European countries. Organized through elaborate trade associations, the bureaucracies of big business coexist comfortably with the bureaucracies of the state. Relations between business and government are, in fact, quite different from anything we are used to in the West. The Ministry of International Trade and Industry (MITI), for example, is a sprawling organization that lives on intimate terms with Japanese industry. Like the other government agencies with which United States businessmen come in contact (principally the Ministry of Finance and the Bank of Japan) it operates not so much through the sanctions of law and regulations, as do United States regulatory agencies, as through what is known as "informal administrative guidance."

The structure of institutions and the national character interact on, and reflect, one another, for in a very real sense the Japanese invented the Organization Man. They are a talented people, educable and broadly educated, with a literacy rate higher than that of the United States. They work long hours, do not fight the system, and move doggedly but more or less contentedly within the comforting but constraining arms of paternalism. A frugal people, they save a substantial part of their earnings, faithfully feeding it into the investment stream.

Article 9 of their Constitution, which was written under United States direction, contains an extraordinary provision: "The Japanese people forever renounce war as a sovereign right of the nation and the threat or use of force as means of settling international disputes." It declares also that "land, sea, and air forces, as well as other war potential, will never be maintained." If these clauses were strictly interpreted by the Japanese government — and they are not today — there would be no basis for even the small "self-defense force" which is projected to rise to a 250,000-man military establishment by 1971. But even so, Japanese dependence on the United States for their security has contributed to their rapid economic advance, since they spend only 1.2 percent of their national revenue on defense, the smallest percentage of any major state.

The Japanese economy, as it has evolved, is an odd mixture of capitalist enterprise and governmental direction. It is built on a thin capital base with debt-equity ratios for most enterprises that would give American entrepreneurs sleepless nights. Yet the debt structure is not all that it appears, for the great combines find it advantageous to siphon off profits of their industrial divisions by interest payments to the banks that form part of the combine. This has the effect of making the reported net returns of much Japanese business seem low by United States standards, but it saves taxes.

Delicately balanced as it is, the Japanese economic structure has survived periodic crises by its extraordinary responsiveness to governmental direction, as was shown in 1964 and 1965 when governmental fiscal policies reversed a slow-down caused by the excessive accumulation of inventories. The system is finely tuned and reacts quickly to threatened breakdowns. When a big Japanese firm gets into trouble, rescue operations are rapidly set in train by combined operations of government and industry.

Since the Japanese system reflects a psychology quite different from that of American business, it is not an environment in which United States corporate managers find themselves easily at home. Nor are the Japanese fully at ease with Americans, for, in spite of their phenomenal economic progress, they continue to regard the great American industrial firms as overgrown dragons that would eat up Japanese industry if permitted to do so. Even sensational success in third markets — or, for that matter, in the American market — against unrestricted competition from United States enterprises has not greatly increased their confidence, and this lack of confidence, if it continues, can prove a serious deterrent to easy commercial relations between our two countries. It manifests itself most irksomely in the reluctance to permit United States companies to make direct investments in Japan except under restrictive conditions with regard to control that vary from one industrial sector to another. Various explanations have been put forward to explain Japanese obduracy on this issue but in its simplest terms it appears to reflect two anxieties: one is that a board of directors in New York or Kalamazoo may not be sufficiently responsive to "informal administrative guidance" to permit the delicately balanced economy to be kept under firm central direction; the other is nothing more than the familiar nationalistic desire to reserve the Japanese market for Japanese enterprise.

Under persistent pressure from the United States government, the Japanese have, over the past few years, taken hesitant steps toward liberalizing their restrictions against foreign investment but they have not gone nearly far enough. There is still a great deal of mythology prevalent in Japan as to the dangers of economic domination by huge American companies and wild stories circulate as to the extent of the United States capture of European industry.

Yet I am sure that the tide of opinion is turning in the most influential industrial circles, as the point becomes more widely understood that restrictions on United States firms seeking to do business in Japan necessarily stimulate retaliation against Japanese products in the United States.

While it is likely that part of the pressure for liberalization has come from Japan's need for technological know-how, I have been struck by the fact that the Japanese do not feel the same sense of frustration over the so-called "technological gap" as do European industrialists. Perhaps it is because they have been living with a technological gap from the very beginning. Japan was the last of the great manufacturing powers to experience the industrial revolution; she became industrially of age only in this century and has had a long way to go to catch up. Thus I find the Japanese relatively relaxed about their technological disabilities. When they need technology they buy it in a straightforward manner, and the question only now beginning to trouble them is whether they will be able to continue to buy it on their own terms or have to meet steadily tougher conditions that American business is beginning to exact.

But the problems encountered by American firms in Japan are only one aspect of Japan's relations with the West over the coming years. Those relations are important to the United States economically since Japan is our biggest agricultural market, and, next to Canada, our largest total export market. The private consumption sector of Japan is growing at an increasingly rapid rate and its potential as a market for Western goods is almost unlimited. Yet economically important as Japan is to the West, her political importance is far greater, since as the only large modern nation in Asia she must be closely tied to the West if we are to maintain the power balance in the Far East and the world. Such ties will not be easy to secure and maintain. Relations are complex and, in some areas, fragile, and strains and tensions could develop so easily that we would be making a tragic mistake if we were to continue — as we are often tempted to do — to take Japan for granted. For the Japanese are not firmly fixed in a secure framework of culture and power as are many other nations; indeed their most striking quality is a political and social rootlessness that is hard for us to plumb in depth and scope, since we cannot fully comprehend the effect of the war on the Japanese. If the Western European nations suffered a shattering of their societies by World War II, war with its aftermath worked far greater havoc in Japan. It snapped the Japanese ties with much of their past and set a whole society adrift; and, since that time, the Japanese have — for once to use a cliché where it has real meaning — been a nation in search of an identity.

This is a search they have pursued before, since Japanese history has been marked by shifting influences and attitudes. Following a period of three hundred years from the seventh to the ninth or tenth centuries when Japan's importation of Chinese artistic and literary forms reached its height under the patronage of the Fujiwaras, the Japanese created an eclectic but distinctive civilization of their own, until, by 1600, they were almost abreast of the rising Western European nations. Then came isolation; for two hundred and fifty years, after the closing off of foreign trade by the Tokugawa, Japan was hermetically sealed from the world. Not until 1854 did Admiral Perry induce the Japanese to open their doors once again, but only a narrow crack. Western ideas and technology began to filter in during the last days of the Shogunate, then were increasingly embraced after 1868 by the victorious Imperial entourage. The shattering consequences of the Second World War — military defeat, American occupation and the Communist seizure of the mainland — had a dual effect: they imposed a barrier between Japan and China, while greatly intensifying the impact of Western culture and ideas. Today, as an industrial nation, Japan turns her eyes toward the West; yet even now the atavistic pull of the mainland remains strong. Japan's trade with Communist China is increasing, and there is a constant temptation to improve her position in China by political concessions.

At home the spiritual turmoil, particularly among the young, is a source of worry and debate. Under the impact of Western ideas the Emperor is no longer regarded as a God-King, and Shintoism, the old state religion, has gone into eclipse. The authoritarian and puritanical Soka Gokkai branch of Buddhism has become a political power with fifteen seats in the Imperial Diet. The erosion of the old faith, with its emphasis on ancestor worship, has undermined the Confucian authority of the family, while the Japanese have yet to work out a synthesis of their Asian and Western heritage that can restore the lost stability.

It will not be easy to incorporate Japan solidly in a world power system, but it is essential to stability in Asia. It is a task we must approach with sensitivity and with more patience than we customarily muster. What are the basic elements in an effective relationship and what is there upon which we can build? Up to now the ties we have had with Japan have depended largely on common military and economic interests. We have underwritten Japanese security. We have recognized her extraordinary industrial achievements and are bringing her more and more into full membership in the exclusive club of Western industrialized powers. Finally — and probably most important — we have provided her with enormous commercial opportunities. It is in these areas that we must continue to concentrate, while in the meantime working at the construction of a deeper political and cultural understanding. But this will take a great deal of time, for our tradition is new and alien to the political ideas of Japan, and her civilization derives more from the mainland than the Occident.

Thus, while we encourage the flowering of a native democracy in Japan, we must recognize that seven hundred years of military administration cannot be erased overnight. We lack a common history, a common literature or a common body of philosophical ideas; while the difference in our languages is so great as to reflect disparate habits not merely of expression but of thought. Yet the cultural gulf may not be so great as many suppose; in many ways the Japanese are more at home with us than we are with them. They know a great deal about our philosophy and literature, are probably more familiar with our music than with their own, and in the visual arts a synthesis should be relatively easy, for Japanese painting and architecture, landscape design and motion pictures have already left a deep imprint on the West.

Moreover, though our societies are differently organized and structured, the life and social structure of Japan are rapidly becoming far closer to ours than to the Japan of a generation or two ago or to the rest of Asia. Travel and movies, and ultimately perhaps common television over communication satellites, can all be counted on to help bridge the difference in topical interests, and, with the passage of time, the greatest industrial power of the East will think and live more and more like the industrial nations of the West. I do not mean to suggest by this that over the next few years we can avoid all abrasions and difficulties, but they should not create insuperable problems. Pressure is growing in the United States for Japan to assume a heavier burden of military responsibility in the East — an idea that comes awkwardly from us, since it was we who insisted that Japan give up militarism. And, for our part, we are going to have to face the fact — and face it soon — that we shall have to give Okinawa and the other Ryukyus back to Japan.

It is in the economic area that our relations should be easiest if we are only sensible about it and do not let a retrograde protectionism get out of hand. The inclusion of Japan in the select club of the industrialized nations should not require much imagination or generosity, since the Japanese have earned it. When I was in the Department of State, I personally took the lead to persuade our European partners to accept Japan as a full member of the Organization for Economic Cooperation and Development, hoping that it would involve the Japanese in systematic discussions with the other industrialized powers. To an extent this has occurred but not enough; the importance of the move has so far been more symbolic than real, since the OECD has not yet become a very effective international organization.

In the long run, the problem will never be fully solved until the Western nations are prepared to treat Japan on a basis of equality in their trading relations, to eliminate discrimination, and to trade with Japan as they trade with one another. This is central to the development of close relations, since it is not only the acid test of full club membership but it bears also on the question of adequate commercial opportunities. We need, therefore, to take a fresh look at Japan as a market and as a highly competent competitor, and it is time to jettison some of the old and smug clichés. It is not enough to pass off Japan's industrial achievement as merely the product of a low-wage labor force and to argue that her exports should be kept under a special restrictive regime to preserve the standard of living of the American worker. That Japanese wage rates were historically low in relation to those in the West is undoubtedly true, but wages have for some time been rising at a rate of at least ten percent a year and are destined to continue to rise. Already Japan is losing certain types of industry to other Asian nations such as Korea, where wage rates are no more than twenty percent of the Japanese level. Of course, Japanese wage rates, even with an elaborate system of fringe benefits, are clearly lower than those in the West, but the disparity, while important, is not so great as often assumed.

The Japanese, while formidable traders, are pragmatic beyond most other peoples, and they have shown an unusual flexibility in accommodating to Western fears and pressures. The result has been a series of extra-legal arrangements, known as "voluntary agreements," whereby the Japanese have undertaken to limit exports of particular articles to the United States within a certain specified range. Today there are twenty-four "voluntary agreements" of this kind covering cotton textiles, ceramic ware, transistor radios, sewing machines, frozen and canned tuna, stainless steel flatware, baseball gloves, silk fabrics, clinical thermometers and many more products. They affect between ten and thirty percent of Japan's exports to the United States. Thorstein Veblen

once explained the difference between taxes and tariffs by ob-
serving that through taxes the government robs the citizen but
through tariffs it holds the citizen so industry can rob him.
Veblen never heard of "voluntary agreements," but he could have
fitted them into his aphorism without much change in language;
for the word "voluntary" is used in an Oriental sense,* since the
agreements have, in fact, been made under duress with threats of
mandatory quotas or prohibitive duties if the Japanese do not
agree. They have been possible for two reasons: first, being pragmatic, Japanese industrialists have been prepared to exercise restraint in the American market as the alternative to possible
exclusion; and, second, possessing a tight structural organization
and an extraordinarily close working relation with the government, Japanese industry has possessed the necessary machinery
to control exports within a narrow range.

On any objective appraisal the "voluntary agreements" have
been both a convenience and a danger. Though they have helped
to quiet the outrage of protectionist lobbies they have had a demoralizing effect on both our government and industry, since,
being too easy to work out, they have tempted hardpressed government officials to yield to industry pressure. But they are manifestly short-term expedients, crutches for a transitional period,
not a fair or efficient or honest long-range solution to the problems
of commercial competition.

Over and above the economic consequence of trade is the
West's political stake in a healthy Japanese economy. We should
have learned that lesson long ago; for just as the depression of
the early 1930's paved the way for Hitler, so also did it create the
conditions that led the Japanese to seek domination of the Far
East — thus leading to Pearl Harbor and the bomb on Hiroshima.
The logic of the Japanese position, as it evolved in those dark
days, was clear though mistaken: if Japan were to be economically secure against new depressions she must get political control of her own raw material sources. This was the genesis of the

*The Japanese capacity to describe disagreeable phenomena in euphe-
mistic terms is an old story. In 1297 the decrees repudiating various public
and private debts were called *Tokusei* or acts of "Virtuous Administration."

"Greater East Asia Co-prosperity Sphere," which in turn provided the rationale for the expansionist Japanese military drive of the 1930's. Since 1945 the Japanese have pursued a wholly different policy, and with much more success. They have made far greater gains through efficient industry than was ever possible through military might. They have plowed their savings back into improved capital and plant at an unparalleled rate. To be sure this has meant some self-denial, although the standard of living has been rising at least five percent a year in terms of real per capita income. But now it is inevitable that the Japanese people should begin to ask for a greater tangible sharing of prosperity, with the result that the production of consumer goods is beginning to mount at a more rapid pace than capital goods. Nor does this new emphasis on the individual — on greater "political and economic democracy" — stop with the private sector; it expresses itself also in a long overdue drive to improve Japanese life by greater expenditures for highways and schools, hospitals, sewers and, most important of all, adequate housing, since Japan illustrates in exaggerated form the deficiencies of Professor Galbraith's "affluent society." The quality of Japanese life must be improved. The government knows this and is beginning to do something about it.

But while Japan moves to improve her society at home, we in the West should move to get rid of the "voluntary agreements." They have already outlived their usefulness, and today they demoralize both government and industry. It was a familiar experience for me, as Under Secretary of State, to receive delegations of American businessmen bewailing the increasing imports from Japan of the particular articles they manufactured — let us call them "widgets." It was, as they saw it, irrelevant that the American widget industry was at the time enjoying an unparalleled prosperity or that it was working at full capacity. The fact that imports were rising settled the matter. Obviously, they argued, we could not permit such a condition to persist, or the American widget industry would, they told me, "be driven out of business." What was needed was a voluntary agreement cutting back Japanese imports and it was up to the United States government to get it from Japan. After all, if there were agreements for cotton textiles and radios, thermometers and baseball gloves, why not for widgets as well? Besides, widgets were essential to the national security, weren't they?

So far as I was concerned, this last comment was stupid advocacy; it invariably put my back up. In six years in the State Department, I rarely met a manufacturer of anything who was not prepared to tell me, in a fervor of patriotic virtue, that his particular product was absolutely vital to America's national security — with the strong implication that the only reason he reluctantly produced the stuff was to help his country. I remember one epic day when I received a delegation in the morning complaining loudly that imports of a certain article must be stopped or the national security would be imperiled, and another delegation in the afternoon insisting that exports of the same article must be promptly halted or we would all be in deadly peril. Why their lawyers let them use such silly arguments, I could never understand.

Trade discrimination is not only bad economics but politically disastrous, particularly when practiced against another race, and it is essential that we gradually phase out voluntary arrangements and all other forms of discriminatory treatment against Japanese goods. If the Japanese are to wear the club tie they should have the Old Boys' privileges, which means that we and the Western Europeans will have to accord them the same rights of entry for their goods that we accord one another. We should not go on deceiving ourselves that the current arrangements are sound or permanent. The fact that the Japanese may agree under pressure to accept certain forms of discrimination does not mean that they like it or that this singling out of their merchandise will not have corrosive consequences. Just as political equality is necessary if Germany is to be tied securely to the West, commercial equality is essential in our relations with Japan.

I have emphasized Japan's role because, in the long run, Asian progress and security will heavily depend on the well-being and political direction of the one large modern nation in Asia. But today there are other Asian countries that are beginning to show a new confidence and vitality. South Korea, for example, with approximately one-third the population of Japan, holds the promise of becoming, in time, a vigorous industrial nation. With nearly ninety percent of her population literate and an extraordinarily high proportion of her young men in the universities, she possesses a built-in resource of knowledge, skill and competence that can be put fully to work as the economy gathers momentum. Thailand, too, is beginning to move, as is Malaysia. Most important of all, the vast archipelago nation of Indonesia has shaken free from the flamboyant but tragic antics of the Sukarno period and is setting about, under General Suharto's government, to put its affairs in order. Given luck and patience and the continuance of political stability, Indonesia should, over the next few years, begin to approach the wealth and power that her position as the sixth largest nation in the world justifies.

I do not, therefore, feel apprehensive about Asia, which at long last is beginning to move into the twentieth century. This means that new centers of leadership can emerge that should in the course of time make it possible for us to share responsibilities with the key nations of the area, of which Japan should certainly be in the forefront. For the time being Japan remains under special inhibitions but, over the next few years, she should be able to live down the nightmare of the past, assume a progressively greater burden of economic help to the nations farther behind in the race, and become an increasingly constructive political influence. This will require sensitivity and tact and generosity, since there is a considerable residue of fear of Japanese economic domination persisting in Asia just as fear of a resurgent German nation persists in Europe, and the fact that this is an understandable result of history and the disparity in industrial power between Japan and the other nations of the area does not make it any less of an impediment.

Meanwhile, through a legacy of the Dulles era, we Americans are deeply committed in the Far East. We have security responsibilities not only for Japan but for South Korea, Taiwan, the Philippines, Australia, New Zealand and the Asian members and protocol states of SEATO. Yet this does not mean that we need permanently maintain our presence in the Far East at anything like the present level. It is sound policy to encourage the Asian people to form regional groupings and to learn to work together for their common economic good. The Japanese are already beginning to raise a larger army and participate in promising but still nascent structures such as the ASPAC (a cooperative bloc of free East Asian states *without* United States or other Western participation). Japan's dilemma — building a new politics at home and finding a new national role, consistent with deep traditions and industrial strength and the newly discovered political ideals of the West — is a microcosm of the dilemma of all non-Western countries. Her democratic evolution since the war is a hopeful beacon of modernity to others, but, if her experiment is to succeed and her example to be widely relevant, we must treat Japan as a full equal of our West European allies and tie her closely to the political traditions of a West that are old for us but so very new to her.

Out of all this, if we are patient and not too gauche and clumsy, some of the distortions in the present sharing of responsibilities can gradually be worn away, and, when we finally find the means of egress from the dismal swamp of Vietnam, we should be able to reduce our commitments in the area. This will not be accomplished overnight. Whether we like it or not we shall be compelled for a number of years to maintain a substantial presence in Asia, but we must not let it become a fixed feature of the world landscape, as unchallengeable as a mountain. For in the long run the only rational solution is to construct not an American hegemony of the Far East but a new set of relationships that will recognize the primacy of interest of the leading nations in the area and encourage them to take serious responsibilities of leadership.

X I

The Unfinished Business of Nuclear Management

FIVE nations have atomic bombs today. Ten others, according to Mr. Alistair Buchan of the Institute of Strategic Studies, are technologically able to become nuclear powers: India, Canada, West Germany, Japan, Sweden, Italy, Belgium, Czechoslovakia, the Netherlands and Israel. Other lay experts have, with lesser credibility, from time to time added nine additional countries to this explosive fellowship: Australia, Brazil, East Germany, Indonesia, Mexico, Pakistan, South Africa, the United Arab Republic and Argentina.

India, we know, could explode a nuclear device twelve to eighteen months after making the political decision to do so. Japan, Professor Kei Wakaizumi assures us in *A World of Nuclear Powers?* (p. 84), is not likely to build a bomb unless there appears "a political leader committed to some form of extreme nationalism, a Japanese De Gaulle." Any one of these countries could, by setting off an atomic explosion, become the sixth nuclear power, thus helping to set in motion a chain reaction of national emulation that might in a short time increase the number of nuclear states from six to sixteen.

Like Rousseau examining the limits on human freedom, man can say of the liberation of nuclear force in the world: The great question is not how it came about, but how we can make it legitimate, how we can put it under rational, human control.

That task, though a cardinal requirement of peace — indeed, perhaps, of survival — seems no closer to solution now than twenty years ago. Perhaps not even as close, since atomic weapons are getting cheaper and easier to make and more and more countries are achieving the capacity to produce them, if they should decide to do so.

I share the conviction, which represents the conventional wisdom for almost everyone but the French government, that any further spread of national nuclear arsenals will make the ultimate problem of rational control even more prickly and hazardous. The proliferation of national nuclear capabilities will increase the danger of the lethal pollution of the atmosphere, which is a common resource and a common source of sustenance for all mankind. It will increase the mathematical probability that at some point in the future — in spite of the precautions each nation may take — a nuclear bomb may be accidentally discharged in such a way as to trigger a nuclear war — marking the point when, in the words of Mr. Robert Ardrey (*The Territorial Imperative*, p. 316), "The wheel stops and the ball falls on the double zero, when the house wins and all customers lose, and total accident or total cynicism at last finds us out." Finally, it will increase the possibility that a bomb may pass into the hands of an irresponsible ruler — and one does not need an exceptional imagination to consider what would probably have happened to the world if Hitler had commanded atomic weapons during the *Götterdämmerung* days of April 1945.

It is, therefore, urgent business that we get the atom under control, and this means stopping the further development of national nuclear capabilities. There is nothing new about this; we have been working at the problem for a long time, because we have always recognized our unique moral responsibility with regard to the atom. We tested the first bomb at Alamagordo, and at Hiroshima and Nagasaki we dropped the only two bombs that were ever exploded in anger. During four years we had a monopoly of the absolute weapon, and in those years, we put forward a brave and far-reaching proposal which, in the light of subsequent experience, seems to have been decades ahead of its time.

The Baruch-Acheson-Hancock plan combined great imagination and eminent common sense — but it failed. It would have taken nuclear weapons forever out of the hands of national governments, vesting both ownership and control in an International Commission of Fissionable Materials for the Production of Atomic Energy, and there would have been an international inspection system to prevent covert manufacture of nuclear weapons. The United States made clear its willingness to dispose of its stockpile once these controls were in effect, and the United Nations Committee on Atomic Energy adopted its broad lines of approach, but the Soviet Union vetoed it in the Security Council. Since then, although we have been gnawing at the problem incessantly, meager progress has been made toward controlling or reducing stockpiles of weapons or turning down the nuclear arms race in other ways.

So long as we alone possessed atomic weapons, we, as a nation, felt reasonably secure, but our years of innocence lasted only until the Soviet Union also ate the fruit of the tree of science. In 1949, by exploding a nuclear device it converted our exclusive control into a duopoly — and since then the world has been quite a different place.

Frightening as it was to most of the world, however, the duopoly had a certain reassuring logic. It created a stalemate between the opposing camps and the world would have been more stable had the possession of nuclear weapons remained limited in that fashion. But, since neither we nor the Soviet Union were wise enough to let the situation alone, we both must bear responsibility for the present unstable distribution of nuclear power. I have recounted in chapter VII how we helped the United Kingdom "stay nuclear" by affirmative action on several occasions — and we are still doing it — while the Russians assisted Red China to "go nuclear." Moreover, it was our discriminatory assistance to Great Britain that provided a special stimulus for the French nuclear effort.

Like so much else in the politics of the Fourth Republic, the French decision to join the nuclear club was a slow organic growth. Successive French governments in the early 1950's appropriated funds for nuclear research at a fairly leisurely pace, but they left it open for some future regime to take the final decision as to whether to make a bomb; and at least one Prime Minister told the National Assembly that France should not have a military nuclear program. Finally, as I have pointed out earlier, France did decide to go ahead on April 11, 1958. While the motives for the decision were complex, it seems no mere coincidence that the initiation of the French program immediately followed President Eisenhower's decision to seek legislation that had two effects — both bad. It made it possible for us to help the British stay in the nuclear club and, at the same time, it offered other nations an incentive to develop nuclear systems of their own.

Apologists for the Dulles era can point out, of course, that we did not aid the British until after the Soviet Union had already begun providing nuclear help to Red China. In 1955 Moscow provided the Chinese with an experimental reactor and cyclotron, initially operated by Soviet scientists and technicians; aided China in building the vitally important gaseous diffusion plant in Lanchow which produced fissile material; provided crucial technical data; and trained nearly one thousand Chinese students at the Dubna Nuclear Research Center. Meanwhile China was also receiving unforeseen assistance from the West in the form of a remarkable brain-drain. The head of her missile research program today, Dr. Chien Hsueh-shen, had been Professor of Jet Propulsion at Caltech until 1955, while his colleague Wei Chung-hua was an ex-MIT man.

As ecclesiastical disputes flared over the precise definition of the terms "paper tiger" and "dialectical materialism" and the old national antipathies reasserted themselves, the malevolent partnership broke up. Soviet technicians decamped for home, their fraternal Asian brothers departed Dubna in high dudgeon, and Peking accused Moscow of abrogating the 1957 nuclear cooperation agreement by refusing to give China "a sample of an atom bomb and technical data concerning its manufacture." But Russia had already given her enough. To the huzzas of her ruling Maoist Mandarins, Red China exploded her first nuclear device near Lake Lap Nor in Sinkiang on October 16, 1964, and before the end of 1966 there were three more Chinese tests, with a hydrogen bomb in June 1967.

I have no doubt that the Soviet leaders now regret the decision to help the development of a Chinese bomb and that they would be unlikely to repeat the same mistake, but history is indifferent to *ex post facto* repentance. For our part, we have not yet learned the elementary lesson; we are still assisting Great Britain to stay in the atomic weapons race, and France will no doubt try to maintain a nuclear capability so long as her resources permit. One can argue with a good deal of logic that since Britain and France are unlikely ever to use atomic weapons except as a part of a general Western nuclear defense their possession of such weapons does not significantly affect the military balance. But this ignores the fact that there are serious political consequences in a distribution of atomic power that is inherently unstable.

So long as the United States and the Soviet Union were the only two nations with nuclear weapons, there was a congruence between the possession of atomic might and the other resources required for a world power role. Neither of those two nations had to base its claim to world power status solely, or even principally, on its command of nuclear weapons. The status of each was universally taken for granted because it could mobilize the material and manpower resources of an entire continent and could, and did, deploy those resources to all corners of the globe.

But with the development of nuclear systems by Britain, France and Red China, the congruence between nuclear and other forms of power no longer exists. Although it is not the case today and not certain for the future, Red China — with almost a quarter of the population of the globe — may one day become a superpower. A politically united Western Europe would clearly merit that description, but that is not true of either Britain or France as independent states. It does not in any way diminish their importance to point out that neither alone has even the potential resources to put it in that class. In spite of her valiant efforts to maintain her responsibilities around the world, Britain today is no longer the center of an empire but a nation of something over fifty million highly gifted people, while France's active overseas responsibilities are now largely confined to a handful of West African states.

The problems created by a nuclear distribution that does not reflect a congruence of atomic weapons and other elements of power become clear when one examines the two kinds of pressures that lead nations to join the nuclear club. First, nations quite naturally wish to be secure against attack by neighboring nuclear powers. Second, they seek the prestige and status associated with the possession of a national nuclear system.

Of these two pressures the concern for security is most acutely felt by the peoples and governments of countries lying on or near the borders of a bellicose and unpredictable Red China — and, no doubt, their anxiety has been intensified by China's recent demonstration that she is on the way toward being able to deliver weapons by guided missiles. In Western Europe, however, the play of pressures is quite different. There, in spite of Gaullist efforts to undermine confidence in American intentions, a widespread belief exists that the deterrent provided by our nuclear umbrella is fully effective so that the security issue is not one of priority. What does concern several of the Western European nations, however, is the problem of prestige, of world status implied by the possession of nuclear weapons. This is a quite understandable preoccupation of nations that have until recently played leading roles on the world's stage, but the issue has been blown up beyond life size by the thesis of the French government I have mentioned earlier, that the possession of a national nuclear force, however small, can give a medium-sized state the same world prestige and political authority, the same right to a seat in world councils, as nations organized on a continent-wide basis, because such a state can exert leverage over the actions of the superpowers by the threat to precipitate great power conflict through the use of its own weapons.

For a definitive statement of this contention one can turn to the authoritative apologist for the French nuclear program, General Gallois, who has written: "The atom neutralizes the armed multitudes, equalizes the size of populations, shrivels geographical distances, levels mountains, reduces the advantage which the 'giants' derived only yesterday from the vast dimension of their territories . . ." (Kulski, *De Gaulle and the World*, p. 98). As I have pointed out earlier, this argument is both wrongheaded and quite dangerous in its potential influence on other nations. It is wrongheaded because it is based on false assumptions. Can one imagine any French government firing its *force de frappe* except as part of a larger conflict in which United States nuclear power was already engaged? Certainly to fire it at the Soviet Union would assure the almost instantaneous incineration of the whole French nation by the hundreds of medium-range ballistic missiles targeted against Western Europe — and that would be the end of the story, since France has no second-strike capability. Nor can anyone seriously believe that a President of the United States would let our country be blackmailed into using nuclear weapons where he did not feel the situation justified it?

That, of course, is the answer in logic, but I am not sure it is politically persuasive. In fact, I have come to the reluctant conclusion that no matter how emphatically we may reject the French thesis, some peoples and governments are likely to be impressed by it, especially because, outside of a few capitals of the world where men have been compelled to think responsibly about the problem, there is little but myth and nonsense about what it means to command atomic weapons. The thesis can thus prove highly disturbing unless the force of the argument is blunted by the creation of an adequate sense of nuclear participation on the part of others, and it will certainly accentuate the pressures and instabilities inherent in a nuclear distribution that ignores the congruence of power. What over the years will be the effect on the industrially superior Germans — the only people so far to take a self-denying ordinance with regard to nuclear weapons — if the French government continues to go forward toward the development of a greater and greater nuclear capability, insisting at every stage that it is therefore entitled to some special political status? And what will be the reaction of the Italians, who have a respectable industrial base and a greater population than France?

Nor will the effects be limited to Europe if Britain and France — each a nation of roughly fifty million people — appear to gain substantial political advantages from the possession of nuclear weapons. Why should not India with its half billion people spend the additional margin of resources and join the club? Or why should Japan hold back when it has a population twice that of either France or Britain, an advanced industrial economy, and a gross national product approaching that of France?

In its specific consequences this is an extremely troublesome problem, since once one departs from the principle of the congruence of power, there is no logical place to stop. In its larger implications it reflects the dilemma of structure which is the central theme of this book, for, as political systems are now organized, the nation-state is a poor vessel to contain a force as great as that of nuclear weapons. We can hope that the nations of Europe, where the problem is most acute, will move in time toward some kind of effective political union that can control some form of European nuclear capability. But there is no united Europe now, and, even on the most sanguine assumption, it will be a long time before unity has proceeded to the point where a central government can make the life-and-death decisions involved in the use of atomic weapons.

It was for this reason that our government attempted, beginning with the Eisenhower Administration in 1960, to finesse the problem created by the inadequate structure of nations by proposing a collective approach to the management of nuclear power. Toward this end, Secretary of State Herter, at the ministerial meeting in December 1960, offered to make available to NATO five Polaris submarines as the foundation of a multilaterally owned, financed, controlled and manned nuclear force. In early 1961 the newly installed Kennedy Administration reviewed this proposal and found merit in it. We saw in the multilateral nuclear force proposal not a final — and certainly not a fully satisfactory — solution to the nuclear problem in the West, but rather a pragmatic first step.

Our reasoning was simple in the extreme. The national nuclear forces of Britain and France were not credible deterrents and were not destined to be; they were costly political baubles which wasted valuable British and French resources and had a potentially divisive and dangerous effect on the unity of Europe. Like other products of modern technology, nuclear weapons challenged and overleaped the old, cramped limits of the European nation-state; no single European country could have an effective force, yet all contributing together within a single political framework could create a deterrent. Thus sometime in the future, when a united Europe would be built, it might be possible to put existing capabilities into a common pool, making them the practical nucleus of either an evolving transatlantic or a strictly European nuclear force.

Meanwhile, for NATO countries other than Britain and France, participation in the beginnings of a transitional multilateral force could provide an educational opportunity, preparing Germans and Italians and Belgians and Dutchmen and Greeks for the future nuclear responsibilities of a common Europe. As a transitional device it could reduce the growing frictions and suspicions and the sense of nuclear irresponsibility, while at the same time lessening the pressures for proliferation, since, through giving the Germans and Italians a sense of participation in the management of atomic weapons, there would be less compulsion for them to embark on a costly and foolish quest for a nuclear Prester John. The multilateral force was thus conceived as an educational instrument and a healing ointment to relieve the pressures for proliferation; it was also — and this was perhaps the crucial consideration in most of our minds — a means of strengthening Western cohesion in a testing time for our common civilization and political purpose.

The multilateral force offered a chance for America to share some of its advanced technology with Europe and retain — at least for the time being — a veto on the use of multilaterally owned weapons. Cumbersome and operationally difficult as it might be, until Europe was politically united, control over the common force would have to be exercised by a number of different governments. Certainly this was no ideal solution, but one had to start somewhere, and this seemed a feasible place to begin in a practical spirit. To fail to seize the initiative, we thought, might mortgage the future.

President Kennedy reiterated the Herter proposal in a manner designed to solicit European reactions in a speech at Ottawa on May 17, 1961. He declared:

> To make clear our own intentions and commitments to the defense of Western Europe, the United States will commit to

the NATO command five — and subsequently still more — Polaris atomic-missile submarines, which are defensive weapons, subject to any agreed NATO guidelines on their control and use and responsive to the needs of all members but still credible in an emergency. Beyond this we look to the possibility of eventually establishing a NATO seaborne force, which would be truly multilateral in ownership and control, if this should be desired and found feasible by our allies, once NATO's nonnuclear goals have been achieved.

A number of governments expressed interest, and the political and technical possibilities were canvassed in NATO and bilaterally, in discussions understandably slow and tentative in view of the high importance and esoteric nature of the subject. Technical studies of feasibility, it was decided, must precede political negotiations.

I have already mentioned my talk with Adenauer on January 14, 1963, which was followed by Bonn's acceptance in principle of the multilateral force. Initially France stood aloof but this surprised no one. Western statesmen had already grown wearily accustomed to the egocentricity of the Fifth Republic and thus took for granted that it would react like Pavlov's dog to any Western initiative, displaying a conditioned reflex, first of aloofness, then opposition if and when the initiative appeared to be prospering. By the fall of 1963 eight governments were sufficiently interested to participate in a working group to plan the multilateral force, open to all fifteen NATO members and shunned only by the Scandinavian members, Portugal, Luxembourg, Canada — and, of course, France.

In the end the multilateral force did not succeed, but that was our fault; it was largely because our own government failed to take a sufficiently decisive position during 1961 and 1962. Students of political science should, I think, regard this brave but ill-starred initiative as a case study of how a great government should *not* present an important proposal. The core of the difficulty was that President Kennedy never made up his mind that the multilateral force was a good thing. He never finally convinced himself that it might prevent the building up of conflicts and feelings of inequality and irresponsibility that flow from impotence among the Europeans; so, as a result, the United States pursued a course of action which no great nation should ever follow: it was tentative rather than firm — or, as one of my friends put it, "cautiously passive."

Because the President was continually having second thoughts about the idea, he declined to treat it as something we had put forward because we thought it was a good thing; in his mind it was rather a Halloween apple we dangled before the Europeans in case they wished to bite it. As a result, events unfolded very slowly, in a kind of introspective minuet — one step forward, two steps back, then three sideways. The result was confusion followed by suspicion. European governments were baffled by the change in American style; they had been accustomed to our strong leadership ever since the war, and they could only conclude from our extraordinary behavior that the United States, tongue in cheek, was serving up a proposal of dubious merit for a dubious purpose. If we thought it was a good thing — and they had learned to respect our opinion — then why didn't we say so?

It was my feeling at the time, and has been confirmed by subsequent events, that the Western European nations were quite incapable of agreeing on any nuclear proposal of their own; they were not in the habit of doing so, and their interests were too diverse. To compare the presentational tactic of the multilateral force with that of the Marshall Plan is quite absurd. All that we asked in 1948 was that Western European governments accept the kind of assistance that was desperately needed and advise us on how they could most effectively use it. Nobody doubted that Europe needed help — they were making that clear every day; the only questions were how much and in what form. Even so — and in spite of repeated efforts by the United States to persuade them to do so — the Western powers were never able to agree among themselves on the distribution of Marshall Plan funds.

I feel quite certain that the multilateral force could have been made a reality if the Kennedy Administration had been willing to press it through with vigor, nor do I have any doubt that our Atlantic arrangements would be healthier today had that occurred. But because of the President's hesitancy, we were precluded from presenting the plan to Congress and the natural enemies of the scheme were left in full command of the field. The result of this inaction was to leave the field open for an intellectually squalid treatment of an important subject. In view of President Kennedy's dubiety, proponents of the measure suffered under an injunction not to debate it publicly, while the President's known doubts and concerns were reflected in an increasingly noisy dissent inside the Administration. Through 1963 American newspapers printed stories attributed to "Washington sources," alleging that the top command of the United States government had no enthusiasm for its own brainchild, which inevitably persuaded Europeans that it was not a serious initiative but a tactic designed to confuse and deflect European nuclear ambitions.

What happened was in some measure a repetition of the history of the European Defense Community, which ultimately failed for the same reason as the multilateral force: the tentativeness and lack of conviction of the government that had originally proposed the idea. In opposing the multilateral force the government of the Fifth Republic pursued its customary diplomacy by ambush; having originally shown an Olympian lack of interest in the proposal, it launched a virulent propaganda attack once it appeared on the way to success.

Gaullists and Communists who had together opposed the European Defense Community (the European army) again joined hands to frustrate another common effort by playing once more on Europe's fears. Because Bonn was the most unequivocal supporter of the multilateral force, the specter of a "nuclear Germany" was raised with predictable effect throughout Europe, just as the specter of a resurgent *Wehrmacht* had been conjured up to defeat the EDC. And again, just as in the case of the EDC, Chairman Khrushchev reinforced the Gaullist assault with the vitriolic hyperbole that had become a Kremlin trademark. He filled the air with irrelevance, stating that "Federal Germany would burn down in flames like a candle in the first hours of . . . war," while Gaullist Senator Alexandre Sanguinetti saw "a probable 'casus belli' for the Russians" in German participation in the multilateral force. In a scarcely veiled threat de Gaulle told Chancellor Erhard in January 1965 that the goal of reunification was incompatible with any German participation in nuclear schemes.

The fact that the multilateral force, regardless of its political complexities, would have been a substantially larger and more "credible" deterrent military power than the *force de frappe* was not lost on the Elysée Palace. Since the multilateral force would have put an end to the French nuclear monopoly on the western end of the Continent, it must, therefore, be defeated as an "American" device with overtones of supranationality. Warnings went out from Paris of a Washington-Bonn axis diabolically designed to isolate France. Gaullist innuendo and Soviet bluster convinced many Europeans that there was something sinister and dangerous about the multilateral force.

This, however, was not the only source of opposition. A more serious and plausible attack on the project was launched by some American critics who regarded it as politically utopian and unfeasible. How could five or six or seven governments, they argued, produce anything but paralysis and confusion in running a common enterprise so sensitive and dependent on expeditious decision as the firing of nuclear missiles? This was a difficulty inherent in any collective scheme, and no one could deny or avoid it. The scheme could be made manageable, however, by human and technical ingenuity; and if accepted in good faith as a starting point, the multilateral force could have led by pragmatic stages to a European force directed by a single executive that would make the question irrelevant. For like the great European initiatives of the fifties — the Coal and Steel Community, the European Army and the Common Market — the multilateral force was conceived as an organic experiment in cooperation, not as a mathematical solution of the problem, and its more literal-minded critics missed the point when they sought to judge it not on its own terms and in its own time frame, but rather in absolute terms of a final perfection its adherents never claimed or supposed. It is, I suspect, no coincidence that certain of its harshest opponents — by no means all — were the same men who now regard France and Britain and China as "great powers" just because they know how to make a bomb with a big, attention-getting bang.

It was easy to ridicule the multilateral force, but to this day none of its critics has come up with a satisfactory answer to what remains a critical problem. To say that there is no clear evidence of interest in atomic weapons in West Germany or in other Western European nations is the quintessential logic of a Colonel Blimp. The problem was never one of immediate pressure, but of the need to build an enduring structure by eliminating in advance the conditions that would be likely to breed disaffection and disenchantment in the future.

I cannot regard it as anything but self-delusion to believe that if the United Kingdom and France continue to go forward to develop national nuclear capabilities, and if France continues to brandish the *force de frappe* as a badge of superiority and a *laissez-passer* to great power status, the other major Western European nations will be happily content with their second-class status. Nor can I think of anything that could contribute more to Germany's latent feeling of claustrophobia and her capacity for self-pity and a sense of grievance than the knowledge that her ancient rivals, Britain, France and the Soviet Union, were all nuclear powers claiming a special and exclusive prestige and recognition in world councils.

It is possible, of course, that the NATO Special Committee, under Secretary McNamara's careful guidance, will evolve to the point where nonnuclear powers will be playing a role with respect to atomic weaponry supporting the Alliance sufficient to satisfy their requirements for both security and prestige. I hope so. For, while the multilateral force may be a dead issue, the problem it was designed to meet is still very much alive, and some solution must be found if we are not to pile up major troubles for the future.

Ultimately the best solution is for the nations of Western Europe either to phase out their national deterrent systems or to achieve that high degree of political unity that will enable them to create an effective European force. At the moment neither of these possibilities seems imminent, but the goal of a united Western Europe is still the only political idea that offers a reasonable chance for Europe to avoid the destructive national rivalries of the past. Meanwhile, men are searching for other useful ways to try to get the atom under control. Within the past year their efforts have been largely concentrated on trying to obtain a nuclear non-proliferation treaty under which nonnuclear powers would undertake not to make or acquire nuclear weapons.

Drafts of nonproliferation treaties now under discussion divide nations into two separate classes, nuclear and nonnuclear. Each class would undertake its own set of commitments. The commitment of the nuclear powers would be limited to an undertaking not to make available bombs or essential technology to nonnuclear powers — although they would continue to share them with one another. They would bind themselves to submit to international inspection to the same extent as would the nonnuclear powers. As a practical matter we can expect this commitment to be undertaken by no more than three out of the present five nuclear nations. China will not sign any such treaty, nor will France. Not only does the present French government reject any limitation, however theoretical, on its freedom of action, but, although it purports to regard proliferation as inevitable, it does not consider it a serious danger to the peace.

The critical provisions of the treaty are not, therefore, to be found in the obligations assumed by the nuclear powers, but in the other set of commitments — the undertaking by the nonnuclear powers not to produce or acquire nuclear weapons. This undertaking is what the treaty is all about, and the willingness of nonnuclear powers to accept it as a continuing restraint on their freedom of national action will determine its success or failure. We can, I am certain, assume that a number of nonnuclear powers will be reluctant to give such a commitment, particularly those powers that now have — or have a reasonable hope of developing — the ability to produce nuclear weapons within a reasonable time. Such a self-denying ordinance committing a nation, for an indeterminate period, not to build or acquire particular types of weapons is a national decision of critical importance, and no responsible government is going to sign on the dotted line without a cold hard look to see, as the lawyers say, what consideration it receives under the contract.

Part of the consideration can be attributed to intangibles. Such an agreement would tend to soothe the world's nerves by indicating another area in which the two antagonistic superpowers had been able to find a common interest. But, as a matter of fact, the existence of a common interest is more apparent than real. What such an agreement would reflect is the coming together of two quite separate interests in such a way as to make an agreement desirable to both sides. Thus, the Soviet Union's interest in a nonproliferation treaty is dictated almost exclusively by its desire to obtain international sanction for keeping Germany away from nuclear weapons, while the interest of our own government in such a treaty is heavily influenced by our desire to deflect such Asian nations as India and Japan from becoming nuclear powers. Nonetheless it seems clear that the troubles in the Middle East may have provided a stimulant toward agreement, since both we and the Soviet Union wish to prevent the possible transfer of nuclear weapons from Red China to the United Arab Republic (which has been vaguely threatened), while at the same time discouraging the Israeli government from going forward with the construction of a nuclear weapons system.

Happy though the nonnuclear powers might be with fresh evidence that the Soviet Union and the United States could sometimes make common cause, this would not in any way eliminate the basic defect in the treaty, which is the asymmetry in its commitments. Unless this asymmetry is corrected the treaty will not achieve any useful purpose. Many nonnuclear powers will refuse to sign or, if they sign, will not continue long to abide by its engagements. For what the treaty requires is that the nonnuclear nations accept serious restraints on their future conduct without imposing any significant limitations on the actions of the nuclear powers.

To be sure, the treaty, if widely adhered to, would assure a nonnuclear power that its nonnuclear neighbors were accepting parallel restraints, and in a number of instances this might prove reassuring — as, for example, in the case of India and Pakistan or of Israel and Egypt, where there are long outstanding local quarrels and rivalries. But I doubt that this would be regarded by most nonnuclear powers as enough of a benefit to overcome their resentment that the treaty gives the nuclear powers largely a free ride. Under existing treaty drafts the nuclear powers would not be required to restrict themselves in any way likely to have a practical effect on their decisions or actions, since the chance seems slight that any nuclear power (other than Red China, which will not sign anyway) will ever again decide to create another nuclear power.

This asymmetry in the proposed treaty has — as was inevitable — already been recognized by the nonnuclear nations, and we can be confident that, as a condition to signature, some of them will press the nuclear powers for undertakings that would, in turn, impose some restraint on their total freedom of action. If that occurs so much the better. Our country should certainly not be afraid of restraint. We have long sought to turn down the nuclear competition by offering, for example, to join in limiting the further production of fissionable materials and to freeze present stockpiles of delivery vehicles. It has been the Soviet Union that has always held back.

Thus, if the effort to gain signatures for the proposed treaty has the effect of generating pressure from nonnuclear nations for commitments that would give the agreement greater mutuality, this could be a good thing. I doubt that it will happen, but there is perhaps an outside chance that it might add just that incremental leverage needed to persuade the Soviet Union to join with us in constructive actions that we have for a long time earnestly sought. It is here that I foresee the only glimmer of hope for the treaty's success; for if in the course of the negotiations that will take place with nations in all parts of the world, the nuclear powers cannot agree to make some self-denying commitments on their own part, they will clearly not be able to enlist the signatures of certain of the nonnuclear nations.

Many governments will regard the arrangement in its present one-sided form as too redolent of cartelism — a commitment by the rest of the world not to compete with the small group of nations that have agreed among themselves to do nothing to jeopardize their own atomic monopoly. Redolent also of colonialism, since, with the exception of Red China — which will not join anyway — the nuclear powers are all white Western nations, while the nonnuclear powers include all the new states that have risen from the ashes of the old colonial systems.

The other condition essential to the success of the treaty is that it include, or be accompanied by, measures to deal with the underlying causes that lead nations to acquire national nuclear arsenals. If we do not attack those causes but merely rely on written promises, we may well find ourselves repeating the futile experience of the Kellogg-Briand Pact.

The story of that Pact is one that should never be far from our minds. Under its terms — it was concluded in 1928 — the signatory powers renounced aggressive war. The treaty was signed with elaborate ceremony. It was widely hailed as a major step toward peace, but in fact it had no effect whatever on the conduct of nations, because it did not come to grips with first causes; it did not deal with the pressures that lead peoples and governments to take dangerous or destructive actions. Nations continued to arm, to disagree, to mistrust each other, and to pursue narrow goals of national advantage — and ten years later the West very nearly committed suicide for the second time.

The fundamental sources of pressure on nations to acquire nuclear weapons are, as I have pointed out earlier, the need for security and the desire for prestige. Neither can be dealt with easily. To feel secure nations must have confidence not only that they will be defended in the event of nuclear attack but that such attacks will be deterred. Lying next door to a Red China that violated her borders as recently as five years ago, India is a case in point. Inevitably she will feel mounting concern as Peking gives increasing evidence that the Chinese will soon be technically able to drop atomic weapons on India's teeming cities. But how can India be reassured? Because of her widely advertised commitment to neutrality she would presumably be reluctant to accept a guarantee solely from the West, yet I doubt that the Soviet Union would be prepared for the reversal of alliances involved in guaranteeing India against attack from a China with whom Moscow has long had a mutual security pact. Possibly some more generalized great power assurances could be worked out through simultaneous declarations in the United Nations or through a Security Council resolution, but whether or not such unilateral expressions of intention would satisfy India's fears seems to me highly doubtful.

In any event it is clear that for the Soviet Union and the United States and Great Britain to sign a nonproliferation treaty would not be the end of a negotiation, but rather the beginning of a series of discussions with a large number of nonnuclear nations involving arrangements designed to put their security concerns at rest. Such arrangements could not be a generalized expression of piety; they would no doubt have to be tailored to the particular anxieties of particular countries or groups of countries. Nor do I possibly see how we could provide such assurances without substantially extending our security commitments and — what might prove even more burdensome — tangibly demonstrating not only our will but our ability to fulfill those commitments by maintaining nuclear forces in threatened areas or in nearby waters.

The price for securing the adherence of certain nonnuclear powers to a nonproliferation treaty is likely, therefore, to be high, since governments of nations having the potential capability to build atomic bombs will not be likely to renounce that capability without firm and substantial evidence that they need never fear nuclear attack. Satisfying anxieties about security is likely, therefore, to prove very sticky, but so also will be the question of prestige, since, so long as some nations claim special privileges by virtue of being nuclear powers, the pressure of other nations to join the club will be hard to satisfy.

There are, so far as I can see, three possible methods of alleviating such pressures. One would be for the nuclear powers to accept some significant limitation on their own freedom of action as part of the inducement to nonnuclear nations to sign the nonproliferation treaty, but, as I have suggested earlier, there is as yet no clear evidence that the Soviet Union would be prepared to join in any self-denying restrictions.

A second approach would be to create some kind of collective arrangement that would make it possible for nonnuclear nations to play a serious role in nuclear management. But, with the failure of the multilateral force, I see little prospect of anyone putting such a measure forward in the foreseeable future.

The third possibility of blunting the edge of the prestige issue is by reducing membership in the club in the direction of a more logical distribution of nuclear power.

It was with this consideration in mind that on May 3, 1967, at Johns Hopkins I included in a long speech on the proposed non-proliferation treaty the suggestion that the British could, by carrying out proposals heard within Labour party circles, use their nuclear capability in a positive act of statesmanship for which the whole world would be grateful. Britain could, I argued, by renouncing her need for a national nuclear system, achieve more than could be accomplished through any treaty to reverse the present ominous trends. In fact, I suggested, such an act might well be the one measure needed to make a nonproliferation arrangement possible and permanent. For the decision, by a power of Britain's standing and importance, to opt out of nuclear weaponry would enormously ease the problem of obtaining world agreement to a nonproliferation treaty and would substantially increase the durability of any treaty that might be signed.

I put forward this idea with considerable diffidence, noting as I have done earlier in this book that, because the unleashing of the atom was a joint Anglo-American achievement, Britain had an honorable claim to her nuclear capability. I observed, moreover, that it would be presumptuous for any American to suggest that Britain abandon her nuclear role, had not that idea already been urged in the United Kingdom by many loyal British subjects and had it not been an implied, if not explicit, part of the program of the Labour party when it succeeded to power in 1964.

I am confident that, had my full speech been made available in England, many of my British friends would have agreed with my conclusions, recognizing that this was only one of several suggestions within the context of a reasoned argument. But, as is so often the case, the press in reporting this proposal omitted the logic that gave it meaning. Thus the negative reaction that followed was quite to be expected, including what seemed to me as the rather ironic accusation that my proposal was intended to increase British dependence on the United States and thus enhance Washington's influence on British policy, which, as I have tried to make clear in this book, is the exact opposite of the objective I in fact advocate.

This initial misunderstanding of my modest suggestion created only a passing flurry. It evoked a few indignant leaders in respected British journals and a droll cartoon in the *Daily Telegraph,* but it did not result in serious attention to what I am persuaded is an important issue. I feel reasonably certain, as I have suggested in chapter VII, that Britain will, sooner or later, be compelled to reconsider her policy of trying to stay in the nuclear club — particularly as the superpowers seem to be going forward with at least a thin ABM deployment — and it would be a shame if she did not employ her retirement for a statesmanlike purpose.

The problem for the British government is to make an admittedly difficult decision; once that decision is made, a plan for gradually withdrawing from the nuclear club could be easily worked out. Britain's V-bomber force will soon be obsolete, and the F-111's and F-4's she is buying from the United States are dual-purpose planes that can carry conventional warheads. Her plans for a nuclear capability continuing into the 1970's rest, therefore, primarily on the Polaris submarines agreed on at Nassau — and which, under the Nassau understanding, are to be assigned to NATO.

She is presently building four of those submarines, but they will be obsolete against ABM defenses if she does not arm them with Poseidon missiles, which the Prime Minister has stated he does not intend to buy. Yet even without the added foreign exchange cost of Poseidon missiles, they represent a substantial long-term burden on her already greatly strained balance of payments. (In fact, she has even found it necessary to buy in dollars some steel for the hulls from United States producers.) At a time when a shortage of foreign exchange is threatening to compel Britain to scale down her overseas military effort, the United States might be well advised to take over the contracts for those submarines where the work has gone too far to justify scrapping or conversion into hunter-killers.

My suggestion would, of course, be quite out of place if Britain needed the Polarises for her security, but quite clearly her nuclear defense depends, at the end of the day, almost entirely on the guided missiles and planes of the United States Strategic Air Command just as our defense during the nineteenth century depended largely on the British fleet. Turnabout, after all, is fair play, and I am sure that, had my argument been fully presented, few Englishmen would have contended that Britain would ever have the occasion or desire to fire her Polaris missiles except to supplement (in a small way) nuclear weapons already being fired by the United States.

Thus, it seems to me, there is no serious argument for a British national nuclear system on security grounds, but is it not still needed for nuclear status? Here again, as I see it, Britain has nothing to gain from keeping her deterrent and much to gain from abandoning it. The high respect in which she is held around the world does not depend on her possession of nuclear weapons but on her continued recognition of her responsibilities, her relations with the Commonwealth, her close working partnership with the United States, and her potential role of leadership in Europe. Yet, for the very reason that there is widespread acceptance of Britain's secure position in world councils, her renunciation of a national nuclear role would go far to ease the strains and tensions involved in any effort to freeze the status quo through a nonproliferation treaty. It would lessen the danger of a developing disaffection and discontent among a new generation of Germans if they were no longer made to feel that all of the other major nations of Europe were claiming special status as nuclear powers while insisting that Germany remain permanently in a second-class position. It would be far easier for India to stay out of the nuclear club if her former colonial masters demonstrated that they did not regard a nuclear capacity as a necessary and effective *laissez-passer* to world importance. And the pressures would surely be relaxed on Japan which, over the next few years, will inevitably ask that her remarkable industrial achievements be translated into greater political recognition.

A British act of nuclear renunciation would, in brief, dramatically disclose the fatuity of the argument that nuclear bombs are a key to world status. It would return the distribution to nuclear power in the direction of an acceptable logic and thus create an inherently more stable pattern.

Yet if, as I have tried to demonstrate, Britain is in a unique position to reverse the trend toward proliferation and dampen the pressures on other governments, this should not relieve the

United States from doing her part. We should not, for example, concentrate so narrowly on the pending proposals for a nonproliferation treaty that we overlook other useful initiatives. The Western powers could negotiate tomorrow a nonproliferation and nonacquisition agreement among themselves without waiting for Soviet approval. And we could and should continue to pursue other lines of approach to achieve the same result — and achieve it perhaps on a sounder basis. The most promising approach is still through the negotiation of a comprehensive test ban. Efforts to achieve such an agreement have thus far foundered because we have insisted on a high measure of infallibility in detection arrangements while the Soviet Union has shown that allergy toward inspection that afflicts every closed society. But, if we persevere, it should at some point be possible — given some increased flexibility on both sides and continued improvement in the technology of detection — to narrow the gap to the point where a mutually acceptable agreement can be developed.

Such an agreement would have substantial advantages over a nonproliferation treaty in the form now contemplated. It would be very much easier for nonnuclear nations to accept, since it would not require a government to make the critical decision to renounce in explicit terms the opportunity for the nation ever to become a nuclear power — with the very real risk that squarely faced with the issue it would decide it the wrong way, compelled by domestic pressures, by concern for security and prestige, to join the nuclear club before the doors swung closed.

But by far the greatest virtue of a comprehensive test ban agreement is that it would reflect a sense of equity. It would not appear as solely for the benefit of a handful of specially privileged nations, but would impose significant restraints evenhandedly on nuclear and nonnuclear powers alike. Such a symmetry of commitments should go far toward assuring some measure of stability in the distribution of the control of nuclear armaments; it should at least buy us time to try to bring a little rationality into the present lunatic nuclear arms race.

XII

The Shape of North-South Relationships

FIVE years ago, in a speech of rare illumination, Lord Franks pointed out that the world is split not into two segments but three. Not only is there the familiar horizontal division between East and West, which has been the constant preoccupation of governments for the last two decades; there is also a vertical division based on "the relationship of the industrialized nations of the North to the underdeveloped and developing countries that lie to the South of them, whether in Central or South America, in Africa or the Middle East, in South Asia or in the great island Archipelagoes of the Pacific." For some time now, there has been more talking and writing about the second division than the first, and it has been fashionable to consider East-West — or cold war — relations as a somewhat *démodé* problem of less intensity and danger than relations between the North and South — the rich and poor.

In *The Reds and the Blacks,* former Ambassador William Attwood, a distinguished journalist and effective diplomat, has stated the central thesis of this school of opinion in quite categorical terms (p. 297):

> . . . we must face the fact that the Number 1 problem of our planet in the years ahead will no longer be the cold war but the war on poverty; our world *could* live in peace half-slave and half-free, but it cannot live in peace, not in this age of mass communications, one-third rich and two-thirds poor.

Mr. Attwood speaks out of deep compassion, displaying a sensitive understanding of the craving for equality and self-respect expressed in anticolonialist idioms and emblazoned on nationalist banners. He is a man of thought and experience and the warning he utters is not to be taken lightly. Yet to my mind he overstates his thesis. The world has, in fact, lived one-third rich and two-thirds poor for thousands of years; in fact the disparity in the ratios has historically been much wider; and, while mass communications may exacerbate resentments and encourage violence, the ultimate arbiter remains what it has been since the beginning of time, the possession of power. The power of the poor countries is definitely limited; they can create local situations of violence or instability and can appeal to the conscience or cupidity of the industrialized nations, but they do not, by themselves, have the ability to precipitate great power conflict or — at least until the Chinese make further nuclear progress — to involve the world in atomic war.

I do not, therefore, concede to Mr. Attwood or to anyone else who has expressed similar sentiments that the division of the world into rich and poor nations is our number one danger and hence our number one problem. Priorities have not been changed by improved communications or even a more active social conscience; our first need is to maintain an effective balance between East and West while at the same time encouraging those winds and currents that can bring about fundamental changes in attitudes and policies of the Communist countries so as to improve the prospects for long-term peace. This means, as I have tried to point out, that we must give close and continuing attention to the organization of Western power primarily by encouraging the modernization of the structure of Western Europe. But at the same time, as I shall make clear in this chapter, there are also problems of structure in the relations between North and South that relate directly to our ability to improve the standard of living of the Southern nations.

I state the objective in terms of improving standards of living of the South rather than removing, or even narrowing, the gap, since — in spite of the hyperbole of political speeches — we are not going to reduce the disparity in wealth between North and

South. In the face of all our foreign aid efforts, that disparity has been growing and it will continue to grow. Technology multiplies the rate of advance of the industrialized nations at a faster absolute pace than that at which the poor nations can possibly advance. With luck the poor will get richer, but the rich will, in absolute terms, get richer much faster. To provide even a small amount of absolute growth for the developing countries as a whole we shall have to transfer a far greater volume of external resources than we have been doing, while at the same time coming to grips far more forthrightly and even brutally with a frightening and implacable demography.

During the last decade or so we have talked incessantly about the problems of the less fortunate part of the world's population, living in what we have variously called the "underdeveloped," "less-developed," or the "developing" nations, progressively sacrificing terminological precision to a schoolgirlish fondness for euphemism. The shock of recognition of the North-South problem coincided with the falling apart of the great colonial systems, which gave us a feeling of responsibility for the plight of peoples walking the shaky bridge from colonialism to independence. Juridical independence, we quite rightly perceived, was the wine without the bread, and it could turn sour in the mouth if economic progress did not occur in the new and heady atmosphere of freedom. Yet the needs of all the new countries were enormous and some were quite impossible of fulfillment; for how were we, a nation with no proconsular tradition, to find an effective substitute for the skilled administrators, the medical and educational facilities, and the capital assistance that had been provided all too meagerly by the metropolitan powers?

Meanwhile, of course, the former colonial nations were doing all right for themselves; they were getting rich and no longer needed our financial help, so that we could, with good conscience, turn our full attention toward the distress of their former dependencies. We began modestly enough; President Truman's initial Point Four Proposal in 1949 called for only technical assistance; but within a reasonably short time the problem of economic development began to attract the attention of professors and students and experts in many fields who saw it as an

exciting and relatively unexplored area. As more and more economists and sociologists and specialists in fertilizer and house-
building and chicken diseases began to acquire experience in
strange lands, the flow of books from the academic assembly
lines swelled to a spring freshet. Economic development became
more than a natural process to be pragmatically stimulated; it
evolved as an esoteric cult with a few high priests, who talked a
strange sacerdotal language interlarded with terms having a
quaintly Madison Avenue ring, such as "takeoff," the "big push,"
the "great ascent," etc.

Interest in the subject continued to grow throughout the Eisenhower Administration as more and more Americans became
aware of, and involved in, the problem. At the same time, the
emphasis shifted from technical assistance toward "economic
development," on the quite sensible assumption that the new
nations would never be able to gain the bright goal of "self-
sustaining growth" merely by learning skills. They would, at
least, need substantial external capital resources to build dams,
roads, communications and other public works included under
the Marxist rubric of "economic infrastructure."

Many of the high command of the Eisenhower Administration,
drawn heavily from business and industry, became infected with
the fascination of foreign assistance — except, of course, Mr.
Dulles, who subscribed to an earlier diplomacy. He did not see
development as an end in itself; to him it appeared as another
tool for saving the emerging countries from the contamination of
Communism, a useful instrument for subsidizing his alliance system. Thus he gave preferred treatment to those nations, such as
Pakistan and Thailand, that took the pledge to abjure neutralism
and signed up for the crusade.

But this emphasis marked only a temporary phase of American
policy; it shifted — in words if not fully in practice — when in
1961 the Kennedy Administration came to power, effervescent
with youth and drive and idealism and teeming with scholars
and experts, who promptly set about redefining the meaning and
purpose of foreign aid. President Kennedy was in basic sympathy
with a new, and undoubtedly more sophisticated, approach. He
saw the prime objective of policy in terms not of a legally neat

alliance system — which had been Dulles's obsessive contribution — but the creation of conditions that would make it possible for nations to achieve self-sustaining growth even though they remained politically neutral. The Kennedy doctrine, as it evolved, did not threaten penalties for nations that accepted assistance from the Communists so long as they maintained even the fiction of nonalignment.

This was, I think, a basically useful change of emphasis, but it did not last long nor prove a very feasible guide to governmental practice. Any rapid change in doctrine was bound to create anxieties on the part of nations that had been profiting from earlier policies, while, at the same time, the divorcement of aid from the alliance system, by destroying a guideline that had helped to limit the beneficiaries of our largesse, had the effect of pressing us toward a universalist approach to aid. Once we accepted the obligation to help poor nations toward self-sustaining growth without regard to political intimacy or the potential for growth, we would have to install aid missions in every dusty capital.

The rationale for thus widening our circle of clients was clear enough. Our interest — so the doctrine ran — was not to have friends but to help nations build sound economic and political structures; for were not poverty and instability the real enemies that created the breeding ground for Communism and threatened the peace? This was the theory but it was not unqualified, since, in applying the new concept of aid, we were not wholly indifferent to broad considerations of world strategy. We drew as many geopolitical maps as any predecessor administration, indulged in majestic speculation, and — as Mr. James Reston said of one of my colleagues — "flung continents around" to justify what most of us regarded as a good thing to do.

In such an atmosphere answers came glibly. If, for example, we concentrated the bulk of our assistance on India which was not an ally and self-righteously scolded us in international fora, how could anyone argue that the course of policy followed by a half billion people would not have an indifferent effect on the balance of power? Yet, if a strategic justification could be supplied for the aid effort in India, that was not true of many other countries, and some of us were bothered by the fact that, in the absence of any explicit standard, it proved difficult to draw rational lines. It was hard to help some less-developed countries without helping all; no one knew how to discriminate without being arbitrary; and, as a result, American recognition of a newly created country almost automatically entitled that country to some kind of an aid program. Any American ambassador to a less-developed country who could not offer aid of some sort felt naked and helpless, and that he might better have stayed home.

At the beginning of the Kennedy Administration in 1961, I had inherited the overall direction of the aid program as part of my duties in the State Department. Prior to President Kennedy's inauguration, a task force under my chairmanship had recommmended the consolidation of the various operational agencies that were then administering the program on a fragmented basis. Soon after the Administration came to power, the President asked me to head a committee to draw up a plan for putting these recommendations into effect, by creating an aid agency outside the State Department but with the administrator subject to the policy direction of the Secretary of State. The result was the establishment of the Agency for International Development, which, under a series of able administrators — Fowler Hamilton, David Bell and William Gaud — has brought a high level of common sense and professionalism to the administration of foreign assistance. This has been anything but easy, since the tasks have been new, and the arts unknown, and we have had to learn largely by trial and error how to help other countries. In the process even the experts have developed a more realistic appreciation of what we can and cannot hope to achieve, scaling down sharply the euphoric expectations of 1961.

Since that date we have seen only a few nations move toward "takeoff," and those have been ones with high literacy and reasonable birth rates; — while certain others, in unstable flight, have taken a nose dive. As a result of much trial and considerable error, we have come to place far greater emphasis on "self-help," recognizing the hard but unpleasant fact that no nation can increase its standard of living and move into the age of industrialization unless its government is prepared to make the essential but difficult decisions that will permit aid to be used productively. Since insecure governments necessarily find such decisions hard to make, and most governments of less-developed countries are insecure, effective self-help is not automatic; it involves the adoption of adequate fiscal and monetary policies, accepting battle with entrenched feudal privileges through land reform, and providing for a better distribution of the wealth and limiting nonessential government spending. It means for most countries a frontal assault on special interest structures under which they have lived for hundreds of years. Yet if these steps are not taken, any outside resources are likely to be largely wasted, with the result that we pile up disappointments for the people, and resentment against ourselves for having failed to meet their ebullient expectations.

We have learned other hard lessons in our unprecedented efforts to lift new nations out of poverty. We have learned a lesson of structure — that few of the more than sixty new states that have been admitted to the United Nations since 1954 are of sufficient size to support efficient industry. In South America and Africa, the Orient and the Middle East, national boundaries reflect little regard for economic realities, while communications between nations on the same continents are frequently primitive or nonexistent. Thus, if efficient industrialization is to be achieved, those nations must follow the lead of Europe in the postwar years, consolidating their economies by regional cooperation and the creation of free trade areas. Only by such a regional approach can industrial development be rationalized, enabling the establishment of factories of economic size to serve the needs of all the nations in a defined area. The consolidation of economies is urgent in Latin America, where many nations are struggling with industrialization; much less so in Africa where most of the countries are preindustrial. For this reason the United States recently has put great emphasis on a regional approach in the Alliance for Progress, since it is clear that the building of industries to serve nations of five to ten million people could result only in high-cost, uneconomic production, sheltered and made profitable for a privileged few by strangling protectionism.

While seeking to encourage the creation of conditions in which efficient industrialization can go forward, we have also put new emphasis on the development of local agriculture. During several years, our country pursued domestic agricultural policies that built up substantial food surpluses, and, by distributing a part of those surpluses on soft terms to less-developed nations, we not only fed hungry people but relieved the pressure of over-hanging foodstocks on our domestic price structure. Within the last two years, however, President Johnson has initiated a full reexamination of foreign food aid programs. This reexamination is made necessary not only by our domestic situation — for we are no longer accumulating food surpluses — but also by what we have been doing to others, since, by making American food too easily available, we have tended to make many foreign countries excessively dependent on the continuance of an American food dole.

In 1966, for example, one out of every five United States wheat farmers worked solely to feed the people of India, while, for a long period of time, we fed almost half of the people of Algeria through our so-called PL-480 programs. It is not easy to persuade the governments of less-developed countries to attack the resistant problem of agricultural self-sufficiency, when the people are far more beglamored by steel mills than by efficient farming. Yet our new emphasis is starting to show results. The new nations are beginning to build more chemical fertilizer plants, particularly in those areas where the basic raw materials are available; and — slowly and reluctantly — they are tackling the improvement of tragically inadequate methods of distribution. In India, for example, roughly one-third of the domestic wheat crop is lost through inadequate transport and storage between the farmer and the consumer. What the rot overlooks, the rats devour. The building of an adequate distribution system is a task of urgent priority.

These then are some of the lessons we have learned from our experience with the world poverty program we call foreign aid, but I have left the most important to the last. For finally, and at the eleventh hour, we are facing a moment of truth. We are beginning, with blushes and hesitations, to come to grips with the reality we have tried for so long to ignore — that we will

never improve the standard of living of peoples merely by eliminating disease, balancing diets and increasing the life span, unless at the same time we can do something effective to limit the
pressure of population that these otherwise commendable steps
intensify. There is nothing more grotesquely futile than the
effort to chase a vaulting demographic curve with a rising economic growth rate, and, at long last, we are beginning to face
that fact and to overcome the medieval taboos that have excluded it from the political dialogue. But we have not gone half
far enough; we are still much too tentative, too genteel (in a
Victorian sense), and too delicate about it in our discussions with
the underdeveloped countries.

Demography can make a nightmare of the future. Today it
hangs like a suffocating cloud over Latin America and other
nations where custom and religion and superstition have impeded effective measures to cope with it. The current population of Latin America is already larger than ours — about two
hundred million — but, if present trends continue, it will be
three hundred million in the 1970's and by the end of the century
somewhere between six and seven hundred million. Yet even
now almost two-thirds of the inhabitants of that vast continent
exist on a woefully inadequate level. Average per capita income
is only about $250 a year and the literacy rate is not over thirty-
five percent. In spite of a very high percentage of abortions,
which may in many areas exceed fifty percent of the live births,
annual population growth of three percent is running well ahead
of the two percent growth in food production. These are average
figures for Latin America as a whole. In particular countries,
such as Costa Rica and the Dominican Republic, the statistics are
even more shocking.

Nonetheless few Latin American politicians will face the problem, and little if anything is being done about it in the countries
most affected. Prejudice and ignorance and superstition and
resentment and downright cussedness are still the prevailing
reaction, and we hear the most appalling nonsense from even
some educated and otherwise sensible Latin Americans. The
United States' purpose in even timorously recommending that
population growth be restricted is, they say accusatorially, to

prevent Latin America from challenging our power and position by building a larger population.

This is the kind of noxious stupidity that sends serious men to psychiatrists, for one can show a positive correlation between power and population only in industrial societies that possess substantial unexploited resources, that are already enjoying full employment and a high standard of living and achieving a rapidly rising growth curve. In other societies the correlation is necessarily negative, particularly in areas such as most Latin American countries, where the population lives largely on a subsistence basis on the land and where there is heavy urban unemployment and a low literacy rate. For such countries every additional mouth to feed is a drag on progress, and if people are permitted and even encouraged for cheap political purposes to go on heedlessly multiplying as they are now doing, those countries will be condemned to galloping poverty and debilitating weakness — like a man with progressive obesity who gradually becomes so fat and feeble that he cannot stand on his own feet at all.

Within the last few years, science has achieved breakthroughs in the control of conception, including not merely the pill — which continues to be expensive for use among the world's poor — but also the extremely cheap intra-uterine coil. Even more promising may be drugs now being tested that require injections only every three months, and can thus be administered on the regular visits of circuit-riding nurses. These devices provide the physical basis for a solution to the problem, but unless something effective can be done to transform social thinking, modify religious taboos and educate not merely governments but the peoples to a sharp realization of the tragedy toward which they are heading, the resources we have provided as foreign assistance will be only a cruel joke. We will have helped to upset the balance of nature, producing the Malthusian nightmare.

In an article "Counterrevolutionary America," Mr. Robert Heilbroner has described our dilemma in vivid words:

> Like an immense river in flood, the number of human beings rises each year to wash away the levees of the preceding year's labors and to pose future requirements of monstrous propor-

tions. To provide shelter for the three billion human beings who
will arrive on earth in the next forty years will require as many
dwellings as have been constructed since recorded history began. To feed them will take double the world's present output
of food. To cope with the mass exodus from the overcrowded
countryside will necessitate cities of grotesque size. Calcutta,
now a cesspool of three to five millions, threatens us by the year
2000 with a prospective population of from thirty to sixty millions.

Against such a surging mass of new humanity all the foreign
aid we could provide, even were we to double or triple our effort,
would scarcely enable India and many other underdeveloped
countries to do little more than hold their own. Yet Sisyphus has
never been an American folk hero, and, as a people, we take no
masochistic delight in futility. Hence we must and will, as we are
now beginning to do, concentrate with growing intensity on the
implications of demography, until the time comes when an effective program of population restraint on the part of a recipient
country is made a condition precedent to every aid program.

For a whole complex of reasons — ranging from conviction to
legislative expediency — we have tended to view assistance to
the less-developed nations primarily in the context of our competition with the Communist world. But I am not sure that we have
always seen clearly the proper measure of America's real interest.
Most of the time we have considered it essential to exclude Communists from even the most remote and least important areas of
the world, whether or not it was clear that their presence would
do the Western cause very much harm.

During the years I was in the State Department, I was awakened once or twice a month by a telephone call in the middle of
the night announcing a *coup d'état* in some distant capital with
a name like a typographical error. Almost invariably there were
sinister overtones of a Communist takeover. Or frequently I
found among the morning telegrams alarmist dispatches from
one or the other of our embassies announcing that a Chinese
mission had just arrived in the capital or that the government
in question was threatening some move toward the East.

The very drama and clamor of these reports — which reflected the turbulence and instability of much of the less-developed world — tended to put the situation out of focus. And, when an African nation was concerned, there was an added element, because our response was at least subconsciously influenced by the play of domestic politics in America. This is, of course, quite understandable. As our own people move to redress a long chronicle of injustice and to make the American Negro a full and equal citizen, there is a natural tendency to relate the domestic struggle to the struggle of new African nations for modernity and progress. After all, twenty million Americans are of African descent, and some of the rhetoric of the civil rights leaders shares the idiom of the revolutionary leadership in the new African states.

But this obscures the point. Americans, who in the current cliché are reputed to believe that all problems can be definitively settled, find it frustrating to concede that the staggering problems of the emerging nations cannot possibly be "solved" in a decade or a generation — or perhaps in an eternity. They are problems of human poverty and want on a colossal scale that boggle the Western imagination, and they are problems of how political ideas and economic techniques that originated in Europe two hundred years ago can be applied to, and amalgamated with, ancient, indigenous traditions that have different values from those of the Occident.

Admittedly this generalization, while broadly true of Africa, the Middle East and Asia, does not apply to Latin America, which is a special situation. The Latin Americans are very much a part of the traditions of the West, but they have on the whole been isolated from, and denied, some of its last crucial components: the industrial revolution, effective and broadly based democratic governments, and the social transformations that follow from the interaction of these two phenomena.

Yet when we speak about the peculiar problems of what our French friends have quaintly referred to as the "Third World," I am not sure that we always get them in the right conceptual perspective. We are attracted, agitated, excited by their noise and color, but we sometimes fail to capture their meaning except by platitude and by easy and mistaken analogy to familiar domestic problems. We consequently miss the hard, but quite obvious, reality: the fact that the loud and insistent problems of the Third World are in a real sense a hostage to what we accomplish in the industrialized nations — to how we Americans and Europeans and Russians and Japanese order and structure our own relations. And we frequently forget that, while shifts in the industrialized world can deeply affect the power balance that preserves a fragile armed peace short of general, nuclear havoc, political changes in the less-developed areas are likely to have only a marginal influence.

Thus, I believe that because Americans, like nature, abhor vacuums we have sometimes intervened more than has been strictly necessary in local conflicts in less-developed countries. This is part of a process that I well understand. It is an aspect of the American character: for we quite properly have been sending around the world, as our diplomatic and foreign assistance representatives, dedicated men and women who see their assignments in activist terms. To them the very fact that they are assigned to a country attests to its "vital importance" to American interests.

I applaud and encourage this attitude, since no American who believed that the capital to which he was posted was unimportant could possibly do a good job. Yet it was my responsibility and that of the other officials of the State Department to put the excitement of our local missions into perspective and to recognize that not all countries were of the same size or significance to our interests. This was not always an easy point to make. I once incurred the rebuke of some of my colleagues when, informed in anguished terms of the threatened ascendancy in a tiny state of a leader who was supposed to be under the sway of Red China, I responded to a recommendation for active intervention with a memorandum noting that "God watches every sparrow that may fall, but I do not see why we need to compete in that league."

For I have long doubted that the masters of the Kremlin had great interest in preindustrial societies or that they would have much better luck in establishing strong areas of influence in Africa than we have had. Nor have I felt that the Africans were anxious to acquire a new set of white colonial rulers in exchange for those they have only recently got rid of. And if, as I believe, the Russians have little interest in Africa other than as a lagoon of troubled waters in which they can fish with limited liability and thus make life difficult for the West, the Chinese have shown an almost comical inability to establish beachheads in the new African nations. Quite naturally the African peoples have resented the arrogant conviction of the Chinese that they are racially superior to the whole world, blacks and whites alike, while Indian and Chinese merchants in East Africa, by their unforgivable qualities of greed and competence, have tended to make themselves *personae non gratae.*

We could, I think, simplify our problems with Africa as well as with certain other areas of the less-developed world if we did not take such a proprietary interest in their development. In many ways we overdramatize the problem; since is it, after all, such a catastrophe if some of these new states do undertake experiments with Communism? So far there have been few areas in the world where Communism has proved a transplantable doctrine without being imposed by external military power, and if a state where we have only a peripheral strategic interest engages in a flirtation with Karl Marx why should we be upset?

The argument can, in fact, be made that in many areas with resistant and reactionary political and social institutions Western democracy will be quite powerless to bring about the essential modernizing measures that are prerequisite to progress. Only a revolutionary and authoritarian drive can wipe out the existing structure, break up entrenched obstacles to development, and compel that forced savings (at temporary cost to the general welfare) which is the only way many primitive societies will ever be able to accumulate capital. Admittedly there are risks in our failure to intervene when such events threaten, but they are principally risks of temporary instability which we should be able to live with, at least in areas where our strategic interests are not critical.

Thus, would it not be better for us from time to time to adopt a more relaxed attitude, admitting quite honestly to ourselves that our vested concern with stability, together with the tolerance implicit in Western democracy, seriously disables us from sweeping away the encumbering accumulation of institutional, religious and social kitchen middens that form roadblocks to progress. How, for example, can a government based on Western democratic models ever deal with the problems of a country where, to quote Mr. Heilbroner again, "while India starves, a quarter of the world's cow population devours India's crops, exempt either from effective employment or slaughter because of sacred taboos"?

I am, of course, not proposing that we turn India over to Moscow or Peking — even assuming that we could do so if we wished — but I am suggesting that there are many areas of the world where a less anxious policy on our part would pay off. Ever since the Generalissimo fled mainland China in 1949 there has been a tendency to regard any expansion of Communist territory as a black mark on the record of an incumbent President as well as a threat to the balance of power, and this has sometimes got in the way of a rational assessment of our own interests. For the life of me, I cannot see how we would be endangered by a Communist regime in Mali or Brazzaville or Burundi; its most likely effect would be to cost Moscow or Peking some money.

I believe that the political problems of many of the new small countries are — to recall a pre-war aphorism — "hopeless but not serious," and we should not feel compelled to tour the world with a bottle of anti-Communist serum ready to provide a dose every time any small nation shows signs of infection. I do not write this from any lack of compassion but from a realistic sense of our own limitations — limitations not of resources, since we could afford to do far more than we are doing, but of wisdom and comprehension. We should not, therefore, take such a deep proprietary interest in the affairs of each small nation that we come to feel responsible for each mishap or misstep; after all, we have no obligation to look after them all, and, when we try to do so, we run the risk of spreading our attention so thin as not to be effective anywhere.

Nor should we feel deeply aggrieved when other industrialized countries fail to provide as much aid in specific areas as we would like them to do, since they have their own ideas and their own interests — quite often selfish, to be sure — and they do not welcome instruction from us. During the early years of the Kennedy Administration we spent a great deal of time and effort trying to badger our Western European friends, particularly the Germans, into joining with us in specific aid programs in which we were interested, often acting, I am afraid, as though we regarded them as a kind of supplement to the United States Treasury, a source for funds that Congress had failed to authorize.

Sometimes we found that they were already playing a role we had not known about, since, at that time, we had very imprecise information as to what other nations were doing in the area of foreign assistance. For the most part, we received only vague rumors from the capitals, and most of what we knew about the activities of France or Germany or Italy or even sometimes the United Kingdom came from unsystematic observations on the spot by our own embassies or aid representatives.

This seemed to me to be a singularly unsatisfactory situation, so I undertook in 1961 to bring about arrangements for more effective collaboration among the industrialized nations. At a meeting in Tokyo in July of that year the delegation I headed obtained agreement to transform the Development Assistance Committee of the OECD into the Development Assistance Group with a broad mandate to collect information and arrange collaboration among the nations of the West that were helping the less-developed countries. The following year we succeeded in getting the member nations to agree on a common standard of effort. Each would attempt to devote at least one percent of its gross national product for assistance to the Third World.

But foreign aid is only one aspect of the complex relationship between nations, involving political, strategic, economic and commercial interests, and the governments of the industrialized North can never efficiently work together in assisting the poor nations of the South unless they reach some common agreement as to the substance and architecture of the whole structure of North-South relations. That is a problem which, it seems to me, has been given far too little attention; but we cannot go on ignoring it forever, since pressures are building up that will require us sooner or later to face it frankly both with our European friends and with Latin America. Central to the problem is the question as to whether we should continue to cast our relations with the rest of the world in universalist terms or should deliberately move toward some tacitly or explicitly agreed allocation of responsibilities, which cannot and should not be disassociated from the whole question of spheres of influence.

At the moment there are two existing systems of North-South relations — rarely acknowledged or differentiated. One is what we might call the Open System. The other consists of a series of Closed Systems. The basic assumption of the Open System is that all industrial countries of the free world will accept responsibility for the economic, commercial, and political well-being of all developing countries without discrimination. They will, through systematic consultation, concert their efforts to achieve that objective. The Closed System, on the other hand, assumes that specific industrial countries or groups of countries in the North will maintain special relations with specific developing countries or groups of countries in the South, and will establish preferential and discriminatory arrangements to reinforce these relations. This is the situation, for example, that exists with regard to the African states of the French Community and, to a lesser extent, within the British Commonwealth.

The United States has been the leading proponent of the Open System. Outside of some vestigial preferential relations with the Philippines and our special relations with the Commonwealth of Puerto Rico and with the Virgin Islands, we have had nothing like the British Commonwealth or French Community relationships to nourish and protect. As a result we have wholeheartedly embraced the most-favored-nation principle in our commercial relations — although still foolishly denying it to the Iron Curtain countries; and, while we have participated in special regional agencies for political consultation and action, such as the Organization of American States, we have sought no privileged markets for our products and have traded with the world on a nondiscriminatory basis. Quite obviously the existence of even incomplete Closed Systems, as in Africa, has led to demands that the United States extend similar arrangements to Latin America, many of whose products compete directly with those of African nations. Up to this point we have been firmly loyal to the principle of nondiscrimination; but recently the pressure for a special trading regime with Latin America has become more clamorous, in part at least because the nations of the European Economic Community have been expanding the Closed System, in practice if not in principle.

The activities of the European Economic Community (the Common Market) in this connection are rooted in colonial arrangements. The provision of preferential access to the products of certain African countries resulted initially from the preferential regime that existed within the French Community. At the present time, of the thirty-eight independent African states, eighteen former French, Italian and Belgian territories are already associate members. Two more areas of Africa may well come in: the Maghreb countries of Algeria, Tunisia and Morocco, and (in the event that Britain enters the Common Market) the twelve African members of the British Commonwealth. After the coup in Nigeria in January 1966, the Nigerian government signed an as yet unratified agreement with the Common Market for associate membership, which would entitle Nigeria to the privileges both of the British Commonwealth preference system and the preferential system of the European Community. Talks under way with Kenya, Tanzania and Uganda broke down last year because the African states refused to grant preferences for imports of the Six in return for full access for their exports to the Common Market, but there are indications that such talks may be revived; the African states in question have had second thoughts and may now be ready to work out some reciprocal arrangements although insisting on special protection for their own industries. Since the European Community has provided its African associates with more than one and one-half billion dollars of aid over the past seven years, the African states have found associate membership profitable in addition to trade advantages; and this does not include substantial grants of aid still provided directly from Paris to the nations of the French Community and directly from Brussels to the Belgian Congo.

During 1962 and 1963 I initiated a series of talks with the French and British governments in an endeavor to persuade them to phase out their preferential systems and move toward a regime of nondiscrimination. Unhappily these talks met with lukewarm response both in London and Paris, as did subsequent discussions with members of the Common Market Commission on the dangers of extending associate membership to other African states.

The failure of this diplomatic effort, though not unexpected, led to what Mr. T. S. Eliot called some "visions and revisions." After an intense season of probing and pondering, I concluded that this issue of American policy could not be resolved on any doctrinal basis. Sooner or later, if the Common Market continued to increase the geographical scope of its preferences to Africa, we would be faced with serious problems in other parts of the world. Those problems would become even more acute if Britain should join the Common Market and the preferences now enjoyed by African members of the British Commonwealth be extended so as to give them favored access to the whole Common Market.

To my mind these trends, while undesirable, could scarcely be ignored; it seemed clear that, if they continued, we would have to accept them as political facts and shape our policies accordingly. If Europe is not prepared to accept responsibility for the Third World on a universalist basis then perhaps some regime of Closed Systems might be necessary. But in that event should we not go the full way? Should we not seek the benefits of a geographical division of responsibilities?

The question of Closed or Open Systems is, of course, worldwide. It extends beyond relations between North and South. Not only has the European Economic Community granted preferences to various African countries but it has, by offering "associate membership" to Greece and Turkey, established a preferential regime with two countries already far advanced toward the industrial age. Countries like Spain, economically far ahead of those of Africa, are now under consideration for some form of association, and if the United Kingdom joins the Common Market the question of associate membership for the neutral members of the EFTA will again be raised.

This tendency is one that the United States cannot accept with equanimity. We have from the beginning supported the European Common Market primarily because of its political values and because the Rome Treaty contemplated not merely the removal of the barriers to the free movement of goods but ultimate integration of the Western European economies. This is a very different matter from the proliferation of bilateral arrangements between the Common Market and a number of African and European countries establishing a series of specially tailored preferential regimes. Such a development would seriously erode the most-favored-nation principle and would put United States production at a disadvantage in some of our more important markets.

During my years in the State Department I tried to establish quite clearly and firmly, as a definite principle of American policy, that we would oppose all preferential treaty arrangements that did not carry with them responsibilities and obligations going beyond mere commercial convenience or advantage. I expressed my disapproval of plans for the admission of certain of the Western European countries to associate membership in the European Community on a basis that did not require them to undertake the full obligations of the Rome Treaty. From the American point of view, as I explained, such an arrangement would create discrimination against our own production without contributing to European cohesion, as would be the case with the countries that were to assume full membership and work toward not merely economic integration but, ultimately, political unity. In fact, it seemed to me that the admission of such countries on a basis where they would accept only the commercial obligations of the Treaty would gravely tend to dilute the communities' political content and impede progress toward unity. This position got me into a great deal of trouble in the capitals of several of the neutral countries, particularly Sweden and Switzerland. I continue to believe, however, that it was and is correct and I hope that our government will continue to follow this line of policy. Application of the principle to North-South relations should, as a matter of both justice and logic, preclude arrangements for commercial preference, unless those arrangements have been coupled with the assumption of substantial obligations on the part of the industrialized partner. What this obviously implies is that the

European countries would no longer try to expand or even maintain their preference systems. But that, of course, may well be only a pious hope. If the European Economic Community continues to expand its system of preferences for Africa we should, I think, make it emphatically clear that we will look to the nations of the Community to carry the burden of economic assistance and, where necessary, political tutelage for those African countries. In practice this would mean an American recognition of the primacy of the European interest in Africa — and consequently the primacy of European responsibility for the economic assistance, education, health and defense of the African people. We would, in other words, recognize that Africa was a special European responsibility just as today the European nations recognize our particular responsibility in Latin America.

This idea has already gained a certain acceptability in Europe, particularly in France, where the concept of EURAFRICA has been widely discussed. As the Council of Europe has declared:

> The extent of its [Europe's] resources ought to allow the countries of Western Europe, acting in common, to offer Africa what it needs for its development, serving at the same time the interests of the European peoples themselves. (Moreira, *Portugal's Stand in Africa*, p. 83.)

Such a division of responsibility has much to recommend it. If the European nations are to take responsibility anywhere it should be in Africa. United States investments in Africa are small in comparison with European interests, and, geographically and strategically, Africa means far more to Europe than to America.

I recognize that this proposal will be abhorrent to many Americans and Africans. Because of our own civil rights problems we feel a special sense of responsibility for Africa, and African politicians would certainly regret the termination of a rivalry for influence that has often enabled them to obtain a larger total of economic and political concessions. Yet, though we should expect anguished cries of neo-colonialism, if we are ever to try to work out a sensible allocation of responsibilities with Europe this may be the easiest place to begin it. It would, of course, be to our interest to have relations between North and South so organized that all the industrialized nations of the North assumed a generalized responsibility for the whole less-developed world of the South. But the structure of North-South relations and of relations among the industrialized states of Western Europe are intimately related, and, for all the reasons set forth earlier in this book, so long as Western Europe remains fragmented, no single nation is likely to undertake a generalized world responsibility.

There are, of course, serious disadvantages to sectioning the world as one might an apple, cutting it into slices that define the special relationships between particular Northern and Southern areas. Clearly this is not the best way to allocate responsibilities for the poorer nations of the South. It is structurally reminiscent of colonialism, and when it is based on Closed Systems of commercial relations it interferes with the most efficient use of resources.

Nonetheless, we may in the long run be forced into it, since it may prove to be the only means of defining for Europeans a manageable area in which they can concentrate their foreign aid while looking after the education, health and defense of the African people.

Any Closed System such as I have suggested is bound to create hardship and resentment even among the members and it is particularly offensive to nations that are left completely out of the regime of Closed Systems. I recognize all this and do not like it. Nonetheless, if Closed Systems continue to develop, as in the case between Africa and the European Community, we may well find it sensible to stop fighting the trend and undertake to draw up a rational scheme that takes account of it. Certainly the present situation in which the key nations of Europe belong to a Closed System while we do not is far from perfect.

Just as Africa has a special relevance to European interests so Latin America is intimately related to the interests of the United States, but that does not mean that Latin Americans fare better in the allocation of available external resources. I do not know the latest statistics but when I had the situation examined two or three years ago, the total aid on a per capita basis from European and American sources combined was greater for Africa than for Latin America. As I recall the figures, the total European and American aid to Africa amounted to six dollars per capita as against something under five dollars for Latin America.

In view of our peculiar interest in the welfare of the Latin American peoples and the maintenance of stability in that troubled continent, I would question whether this result is in accord with our interest — particularly since Latin America is a far more highly developed area and presumably has, what the economists — with their penchant for Madison Avenue terms — call a "greater absorptive capacity." I suggest, therefore, that it is time to review again with the European nations how we should design the structure of our relations between North and South. This might, I think, be the occasion for some serious discussions regarding the allocation of political and strategic responsibilities — particularly in Africa, where the Europeans do have considerable experience, large investments, and great geopolitical interests. Such talks would be addressed primarily to responsibilities for Africa north of the Limpopo River, thus excluding the so-called White Redoubt countries (Portuguese Africa, South Africa and Rhodesia) and south of the Atlas Mountains (thus excluding the Maghrebian countries, Morocco, Algeria, and Tunisia).

The area that lies between these two barriers is by no means homogeneous either in climate or in race, and there are other factors that divide the people: religion, language, and the length and degree of their contact with their former European rulers. They are united only by a common emotion: a deep and passionate conviction that the African continent belongs to them and not to the white man, that the white man has no right to a single inch of African territory, and that the White Redoubt must be destroyed.

Excessive as may be the expression of this conviction, its origins are easy to comprehend. Africa remained the Dark Continent after most other parts of the globe had long had contacts with Western civilization. It is hard for us to realize that in 1918 there was only a handful of European colonies that had developed beyond the level of slave-trading posts, and not until the 1830's did attention first begin to focus on Africa. Then, in the latter half of the nineteenth century Africa, as the last remaining vast unexplored area of the world, suddenly worked its magnetic attraction on an intrepid band of French and English eccentrics and romantics who competed to discover its exotic mysteries. The result of their disclosures was a great European land rush. Annexations and territorial claims reached a height in 1884. But vast reaches of land and desert, greedily acquired and largely unexplored, involved years of fighting and organization before they became outposts of the great colonial empires. In fact, as recently as the 1920's, punitive military expeditions were still required to establish control in several of the more isolated portions of the continent.

Because of its late and limited contact with the West, Africa missed most of the great tides and forces that laid the foundations for development in other lands. Except in the last years of colonial rule, when primary and secondary school systems were at long last inaugurated, Western education was largely left to the missionaries. Because of the oppressive heat and forbidding terrain, the virulence of tropical diseases, and the hazards of snakes and wild animals, no more than one million white people ever tried to live in Black Africa south of Sahara at any one time. Given its present population of more than two hundred million, the white men have been a lonely minority, but they made their mark and it was not always to their credit. Memories of exploitation are still vivid, and the cruelties and excesses practiced in King Leopold's Congo prior to 1908 remain a permanent blot on white colonization. We ourselves are still haunted by a sense of guilt over the slave trade, although for the most part we were only the customers and the transporters; the active slave traders in Africa were largely the Arab peoples whose descendants live in the Maghreb and the Sudan, and now stridently join in demanding the ouster of the whites.

To be sure, some of the new African states have shown avidity for the repression of their own peoples. But that misses the point that today's world finds something peculiarly detestable about exploitation and cruelty practiced by white peoples on other races. Quite likely this special odium has something to do with the strange mystique of race itself, with all the complicated psychological freight that it carries. It also derives from a feeling of intolerable unfairness that Western peoples, with their wealth and education and command of the modern tools of force, should employ those tools in an unequal contest against others who are essentially defenseless. But whatever the cause, the resentment of Black Africa at continued white control is a major political fact and it cannot be ignored; it concentrates its venom primarily against the last outposts of the Europeans and their descendants in the White Redoubt.

That area is not a monolith. Its three principal parts, Portuguese Africa, South Africa, and Rhodesia, present three different sets of problems. Rhodesia is now caught in the movement of swiftly paced history and there is little that I can usefully say about it at this time, other than to express the feeling — which I have long felt — that economic sanctions are, in the modern day, a romantic delusion — a wishful expression of man's hope to find some means, short of the use of direct military force, to compel nations and peoples to take the desired political decisions.

Medieval castles could be besieged and capitulation sometimes brought about, but few nations today are islands totally without friends. In the modern world sanctions are not likely to work even when the siege of an economy is enforced by military power. Where military power is not employed and the enforcement of an embargo depends merely on the agreement of nations — whether or not expressed in a United Nations resolution — the result will more likely be annoyance than hardship. As disappointing as it may be to admit it, the siege of an economy is never total, the options of the beleaguered party are too broad, and the psychology of the besieged is too perverse and complex to make such sanctions more than a blunt instrument.

I approach the problem of Portuguese Africa with a certain sadness. Our government has long hoped that the Portuguese government would announce a plan offering self-determination on a reasonable time schedule. We have, therefore, supported Afro-Asian initiatives in the United Nations designed to bring this about. We have discouraged American private investments in Angola and Mozambique, refused Export-Import Bank loans to that area, and prohibited the sale of arms for use in the Portuguese overseas territories. Our frequently expressed regret at the failure of the Portuguese to move toward self-determination has brought about a considerable deterioration in our relations with Portugal. It has also produced a sense of awkwardness within NATO councils, although the Portuguese government still permits the use of the Azores base for NATO purposes.

In August 1963 I flew to Lisbon, as a personal representative of President Kennedy, for a quiet visit with Prime Minister Salazar to review the problems of Portuguese Africa. We talked for two days before I had to go on to Pakistan to see President Ayub Khan, but, at the conclusion of my conversations in Rawalpindi, I returned to Lisbon, at President Salazar's request, for another day of discussion. Subsequently he and I exchanged letters, each more than twenty pages in length.

I found Dr. Salazar a man of charm and urbanity, very quick and perceptive, extremely conservative in view, but profoundly absorbed by a time dimension quite different from our own, conveying the strong yet curious impression that he and his whole country were living in more than one century, as though Prince Henry the Navigator, Vasco da Gama, and Magellan were still active agents in the shaping of Portuguese policy. Remembering something of the grand but pathetic story of Portugal I was prepared for history to intrude itself but not so vividly; yet later, mulling over what we had talked about, I found myself asking, why not?

For, after all, during the fifteenth and early sixteenth centuries, Portugal, a tiny nation of a million and a half people, had surpassed herself; Lisbon had been the center of excitement, the heart of world exploration, the capital that stirred the imagination of all civilized men. This did not last long. After only a brief flowering, a spectacular day in the sun, Portugal fell on evil days. When King Sebastian and the cream of the Portuguese nation were annihilated by the Moors in 1578 at the battle of Alcazar-Qivir, the Golden Age abruptly ended, to be followed by a sustained season of troubles. Portugal lost her independence to Spain for a long period; she saw her maritime preeminence usurped; she had her Asian possessions seized by the Dutch. Only the obdurate resistance of the settlers in Angola and Brazil saved those territories from foreign conquest, and Brazil's tie to Portugal did not endure much longer. In the early nineteenth century, an exhausting struggle against Napoleonic aggression was perversely rewarded by the revolt and independence of Brazil, a possession larger than the United States. This marked the beginning of the end of empire. Today Portugal has her back to the wall and she knows it; for although the United Kingdom could face the loss of one-quarter of the globe without ceasing to be a major nation — and perhaps even with a net economic benefit — the loss of Angola and Mozambique would be catastrophic for Portugal.

As Dr. Salazar, the professor of economics, reminded me, Portugal is the poorest nation in Western Europe, with a per capita income of only $460 and forty percent of her population illiterate. Any successful African insurgency would debouch into her crowded metropole of ten and a half million people more than a half million refugees — and this at a time when Portuguese agriculture is stagnant and her industries are undergoing painful readjustment.

The death of the Lusitanian dream in Africa would almost inevitably be the prologue to an acute and prolonged depression at home and a balance of payments crisis abroad; for in losing the colonial monopoly market for her exports Portugal would at the same time be deprived of the artificially cheap raw materials her obsolete industries need in order to compete in world markets. In our conversations, the Prime Minister was fully convinced, therefore, that if Portugal were to lose the last 800,000 square miles of her colonial empire, she would forfeit even the shadow of a claim to be a small but respected power and would sink to the level of a backward Iberian Graustark.

Dr. Salazar was determined that this would not happen and was determined to do what he could to prevent it. In spite of the limited resources of the metropole, he contended that Portugal was improving and extending education in its African provinces. Racial discrimination — as Dr. Salazar saw it — did not exist as in other parts of the White Redoubt since there were no laws against intermarriage between Portuguese and Negroes and few social bars to men and women of mixed blood. Beyond these points, which he made with great conviction, I had the feeling that Dr. Salazar strongly believed in the "civilizing" mission of Portugal in Africa. Such a conception has a long history, going back to St. Francis Xavier and the Reconquista borrowed from Spain. The great national epic poem of Portugal, *The Lusiads,* is filled with a sense of national pride mingled with Christian purpose. As Camoëns, its author, proclaimed:

> This is the story of heroes who, leaving their native Portugal behind them, opened a way to Ceylon, and further across the seas no man had ever sailed before. . . . It is the story of a line of kings who kept ever advancing the boundaries of faith and empire. . . . You [the ill-fated King Sebastian] are sprung from a royal line more dear to God than any other in the West, even though it may not be styled "Imperial" or "Most Christian": the proof is in your coat-of-arms, recalling his [Christ's] appearance on the victorious field of Ourique, when he bestowed as your country's escutchen the five wounds he suffered on the cross.

The mystique of the civilizing mission of "this small corner of Christendom" is central to an explanation of the Portuguese position. It explains both their conservatism and their profound confidence in the righteousness of their cause.

To promise self-determination would, Dr. Salazar contended, destroy Portuguese influence in Africa as well as the Portuguese presence. Experience in other countries had shown, he argued, that announced time schedules, no matter how foreshortened, were always accelerated under pressure from the more radical African politicians. And he was convinced that the peoples of Angola and Mozambique were not ready for independence. Considering all that had happened in the Congo — this was not long after the Katanga crisis — the maintenance of relative stability in Portuguese Africa was, he contended, a real contribution to peace.

As can be imagined, my conversations with Dr. Salazar resulted in no meeting of the minds between our two governments. But for the time being it did help to clear the air, and a dialogue of this kind should, I think, be kept going. Meanwhile Portugal's troubles have gotten little better but probably very little worse. Dissident groups are still engaged in guerrilla warfare both in Angola and Mozambique, and this has required the Portuguese government to maintain sixty thousand men under arms at great cost to its budget and hence its ability to advance living standards both overseas and in the metropole. Nor is this likely to change very soon. The chances are that Angola and Mozambique will remain festering sores on the face of Africa for a long time to come; for there is no denouement in sight. Given the comparative strength and efficiency of the forces available to each side, the Portuguese position would seem secure in Angola, although somewhat less so in Mozambique; while week by week the complexion of Portuguese Africa is almost imperceptibly changing as immigrants arrive from the metropole to occupy the lands abandoned by the rebels. Progress is being made in the expansion of education, although, by Western standards, at a slow pace. But then education in Lisbon is also behind the Western average.

The situation remains, therefore, basically unhealthy. Frustration is boiling up, although perhaps more within the Afro-Asian bloc in the United Nations than in Angola itself. Portugal has been excluded from certain of the United Nations agencies; but the black African nations lack the military resources to do anything effective, and the pinpricks that other Western nations are prepared to apply to the Portuguese economy are not calculated to have much persuasive effect. Thus the direction in which Portugal and its colonies are now heading seems to me a dead end, but only after the transit of a long corridor. Over the long run, Portuguese policy is likely to show its effects most conspicuously in continued disorder and disturbance, noisy disruption in the United Nations, and an embarrassing awkwardness in the Western alliance.

It is easy to call on Portugal to do the bidding of the Afro-Asian bloc by declaring immediate independence for her African territories. But this simplistic approach overlooks the fact that the leaders of the insurrectionary movement come predominantly from two tribes, each of which is an unpopular minority within its own territory; and any effort by these men to assert hegemony over the other tribes (many of which have been armed by the Portuguese) would be followed swiftly by civil war. The ensuing disorders, with their threat to international peace, would spark demands for the long-term intervention of a United Nations peace-keeping force; and, if the past is any precedent, the United States would have to pay most of the bill — to say nothing of the heavy added costs of shoring up the shell-shocked Portuguese economy. (Our activities in support of the United Nations in the Congo cost us over $400 million.)

Yet the situation today is not one that should be beyond the genius of political leaders to resolve if they would only stop making speeches and cut through the hard shell of hysteria in which the problem is embedded. The basic requirements of any possible settlement seem to me clear enough:

First, the responsible Western nations (her NATO allies) need to display toward Portugal a tough-minded but not unsympathetic understanding of her problems and responsibilities as she prepares for the day when an act of self-determination may result in the creation of either a Eur-African Lusitanian republic or two independent African nations.

Second, Portugal needs the precious element of time to reform the educational, economic and political conditions now prevailing within her territory and that of her dependencies.

And, third, Portugal needs economic assistance: capital to develop Angola's and Mozambique's human and economic resources so that future citizens can assume their new responsibilities; capital to get metropolitan Portugal's agriculture off dead center and help complete her urbanization; capital to establish new industries and to modernize those old industries that depend on special economic relations with the colonies for their profits; and finally, capital to forward the development of the Algarve, recently opened up by the completion of the Lisbon bridge.

An unwillingness on the part of Western nations to relinquish their roles of detached but self-righteous critics will leave the Portuguese with two unpalatable alternatives. Either they can surrender and face what they believe to be instant ruin and the ultimate disappearance of Portugal as a significant state, or they can continue their current policy of military repression in the hope that a relentless defense will exhaust the African nationalists.

Neither of these courses is attractive for Portugal or for anyone else. A premature Portuguese withdrawal, as we have seen, would pose many problems for all concerned. A policy of inflexible resistance, even if successful over a long period, might impede the creation of those mutually beneficial Eur-African ties suggested earlier in this chapter. The real danger, of course, is that after a long war of attrition in which her overseas territories were devastated from one end to the other, Portugal would collapse. And the longer the struggle continued, the more likely that the Soviet Union and perhaps China would try to fish in troubled waters. For reasons I have pointed out earlier in this book, I doubt that they would have great success; yet the situation, in its very nature, would not be in the best interest of the United States or its Western European allies, since Angola and Mozambique are extensive and strategically important territories, lying at the heart of Africa.

Whether Portugal's Africa territories mature in a friendly or hostile atmosphere will depend, in large part, on how the Western nations behave; and, under the circumstances, it seems to me that the major Western European nations should put forward positive initiatives to help Portugal prepare for the day when the last of her colonial children will probably leave home. The best — and certainly the most promising — way to achieve this would be to bring Portugal into the European Economic Community through a phased evolutionary process. With help from her Community partners she could thus be provided with the capital required to raise the standard of living in the metropole to the point where the overseas territories were no longer needed as dumping grounds for her landless peasants or as happy hunting grounds for her commercial interests.

Once Portugal had become a part of Europe and Angola and Mozambique were receiving economic assistance from the Community and benefiting from participation in the Community's preferential trading system, measures toward self-determination could be taken in a calm atmosphere quite unlike the frantic concern that now surrounds the question. Such a solution would be feasible within the context of the Community, but we should not delude ourselves that any solution can be found without breakage and bloodshed so long as we continue to seek it within the present narrow framework: because in that framework the

African territories are proportionately too large; they mean too much to Portugal's economic life for her to give them up. This then is a problem that calls compellingly for a common effort through the European Community.

All too often the problems of Portuguese Africa are confused with those of the other white settler areas of Africa but that is a mistake.

South Africa, like Angola and Mozambique, is a part of the so-called White Redoubt, but there the resemblance ends. South Africa is not a colony; it has been an independent nation for sixty years and the majority element in its white population, the Afrikaners, have no metropole. They are in no sense men and women who have "come out" from the Netherlands and can go back again if they grow unhappy with the prevailing situation. South Africa is their home and their only home.

Nor do the Afrikaners regard South Africa as belonging to the Negro population. They were there first; in their lexicon, they are the natives. When they first settled in South Africa in about 1630, the only inhabitants were the Hottentots and Bushmen of whom no more than fifty-five thousand now remain in the whole country. Only after the Afrikaners had made the Great Trek to the Transvaal in 1835 did they come in contact with the Bantus, who now form the principal black population in South Africa. Thus, from the Afrikaner point of view (which is tacitly accepted by a great portion of the British South Africans), the whites were the first inhabitants of South Africa, and the Bantus are foreigners allowed to live there by sufferance. To the Afrikaners the fact that the country is a part of the African land mass is an irrelevance; it should certainly not affect their title to the real estate.

No doubt such arguments of legitimacy help bolster South African self-righteousness, but they have no practical relation to the realities of the present-day world, which puts the principal emphasis on population. The aggregate of 12.5 million Bantus and 1.7 million Coloreds is now approximately four times that of the 3.5 million Afrikaners and British, and the contemporary ethic deplores a situation of minority rule, particularly when discrimination is based on race and is given sanction by physical

force. The opinion of most of articulate mankind is clear, therefore, that the practice of apartheid is evil and that it has evil
consequences. It affronts our standards of fairness and justice.
It upsets the orderly workings of the United Nations. It keeps
the Black African peoples angry and bitter at a situation which
they equate with colonialism — although that is more a figure
of speech than a description of fact. There is thus no doubt that
apartheid is abhorrent to the prevailing moral views of the West,
but abhorrence is a state of mind, not a principle of political
action and it does little good for statesmen of the West to heap
invective on the system; their problem is to help change it.

It is here that I would question the self-righteous policies pursued by most Western nations, which seem to me ill designed to
achieve this objective. On the contrary, they are more likely to
increase the bitterness and encourage excesses, as the problem
continues to poison men's minds and inflame their passions while
engendering a deep sense of frustration. Yet we should be sure of
the dimensions of the problem. Disturbing as it is, it shows no
signs of leading to war — or even revolution. If the African nations could mobilize military force the situation would be different, but they have no effective armies or aircraft or submarines
to match those of the one modern military power on the continent,
and their impotence only adds to their outrage.

Western nations, including the United States, are equally
chagrined by South African bloody-mindedness. But so far we
have been prepared to do little other than talk about it, while
imposing a political ostracism that makes South Africa uncomfortable in international society. At the same time, by a hap-
hazard assortment of actions and restrictions, we subject the
South African economy to a series of minor and quite futile
irritations which have not kept it from leaping upward with a
growth rate as high as that of any Western European country. A
land of bountiful resources (gold, diamonds, antimony, chrome,
coal, manganese and tin), with a competent and disciplined entrepreneurial class preponderantly British in origin, the South
Africans have combined their material resources with the great
reservoir of low-cost Bantu labor to build an industrial economy
that is increasingly resilient and self-sufficient. The result is an

impasse that may last for decades, with both sides becoming a little more dug in each year and with repression intensifying as unrest increases in South Africa and discontent mounts in the rest of the continent.

In view of this drab prediction, I think it is time that we faced up to the fact that we are pursuing a self-defeating strategy. I am convinced that the deliberate isolation of South Africa has not served our objectives. Instead of weakening the oppressors it has served only to draw together the British and Afrikaners — who have not historically seen eye to eye — in enforced solidarity against a hostile world that, they feel, refuses to understand them. Instead of dividing the country over a profound social issue, the isolation imposed on South Africa has frozen movement, created a climate lethal to effective dissent, and made serious opposition difficult if not impossible.

In dealing with the Communist nations, liberal opinion in the United States has adopted as its working hypothesis that social and political change can best be promoted by opening the windows and assuring maximum intercourse with the outside world. Since that seems to me a sound policy which I support, as I shall point out in some detail in the next chapter, I fail to understand the logic of some of my liberal friends, who, while passionately promoting such a policy in our dealings with the Iron Curtain countries, insist that we pursue a diametrically opposite course with respect to South Africa. How can they show that the problem in the two countries is all that different? Both South Africa and the Soviet Union remain relatively untouched by the ideas of the West, in considerable part because of their isolation, and if those ideas are to be effective instruments for change, we must break down the barriers that shut the peoples of those nations from the rest of the world.

South Africa's isolation is complex and not well understood — part geographical, part racial, part historical and ideological. As the one important nation in Africa settled and run by peoples of European origin, she lies over five thousand miles away from Europe and more than seven thousand miles from the United States. She is no longer on a main trade route but rather a detour (though a route increasingly used with the closing of the Suez Canal and the advent of the jumbo tankers), and because of her quarrel with Britain she now finds herself outside the Commonwealth. But even more important psychologically is her sense of separation from other white nations by the interposition of a great continent, inhabited by people of different color with whom the Afrikaners feel no cultural affinity.

It is this feeling of being an island of whites in a black continent that has created a national sense of loneliness and alienation, and, for the Afrikaner (though not for the South African British), detachment from the mainstream of culture has been accentuated by the dominating hold of a reactionary and rigid Calvinist church, representing the kind of primitive fundamentalism that H. L. Mencken delighted in lampooning thirty years ago. Such fundamentalism is long since dead in America, because people have learned to read, to listen to a free though vulgar radio, to watch television, and to travel. But it is still very much alive in South Africa under a fierce and unrelenting clerical authority that not only enforces a bleak and forbidding social code (even dancing is forbidden in some Afrikaner universities as the equivalent of adultery), but sanctifies an obsolete and obscene racial ethic.

The only way for intelligent men to deal with the problem of South Africa is to go to the heart of the trouble and attempt to cure her social, cultural, religious, political and ideological isolation by subjecting her as intensely as possible to the evolving social ideas of the West. We should, in other words, use all means possible to push her into the mainstream of Western culture and expose her to Harold Macmillan's "winds of change." We should stimulate, not discourage, all possible opportunities for communication, through cultural exchanges, business contacts, scientific cooperation, and expanded tourism. We should arrange increased diplomatic discussions and high level visits back and forth, serious talks in depth about South Africa's problems, and try, meanwhile, to avoid pious statements that agitate our differences without resolving them. Above all, if anything is to come of these increased contacts, we must make an honest effort to understand the South African dilemma and try seriously to develop a United States policy that takes account of the realities.

We do not have such a policy today largely because our position toward South Africa has been shaped by the tangential rather than the fundamental. It has reflected our own sense of guilt at home, our desire not to affront civil rights sentiment, and our interest in securing the approbation of the nations of Black Africa particularly by the attitudes we strike in the United Nations (since we need their votes for our China policy, among other things).

As a result we pursue a course of action that cannot be regarded as a systematic policy, since its objective is obscure and not internally consistent. We refuse to sell the South Africans weapons (which, as we define it, includes shotguns and submarines) because they might be used for repressive purposes, thus compelling the South African government to buy them elsewhere. We deny Export-Import Bank credits for sales to South Africa, which frequently means that manufacturers in South Africa must turn to suppliers in other nations for their equipment. We join in resolution after resolution in the United Nations condemning South African social policies. In response to pressure from a Washington meeting of civil rights advocates we cancel the visit of one of our naval vessels to Capetown at the last moment (after elaborate preparations have been made by both blacks and whites to entertain the officers and crew on a segregated basis), evoking indignation and angry biracial demonstrations against us for our egregious bad manners.

These are actions that do not add up to anything affirmative or hopeful, and, because they are not rationally directed at a feasible and desirable solution, they are actions without a purpose or a future. They miss the mark primarily because they do not respond to any defined American objective. For what do we wish to see at the end of the road? The official answer is a "multiracial South African society," but that is pie in the sky. The whites are too firmly in control of the levers of power (and they alone know how to use them), and the country's economy is too advanced for such a change to be brought about by revolution; nor do I see any realistic chance that it can be brought about, even over a long period, by the consent of the dominant power group. The ratio of blacks (including Coloreds) to whites is too great —

four to one — for change to occur without submerging the whites; and we should not be put off with false analogies to our own situation. Even though similar ratios occur in some Mississippi counties there is no real parallel, since in the United States a white minority can expect protection from predominantly white state and federal governments.

Nor is there any realistic chance of a solution by external force. The black African states have no armies in any modern sense; there is no serious possibility that any Western state would intervene by force; and if the Soviet Union tried to do so, the United States would have to stop her. Finally we come back to economic sanctions, but, to my mind, these are also a dead end. I see no chance that, even if the provisions of Chapter Seven of the United Nations Charter were invoked and economic sanctions were applied on a mandatory basis, they would be effective to bring about any radical change in South Africa's policies.

First, because the South African economy is strong and to a large extent self-sufficient; second, because the sanctions would not be fully effective, since, particularly in view of South Africa's gold production, there would be leakages and chiseling — enough, at least, to keep the economy going at a modest but adequate level. Unjust as it may seem, the nation that would be most seriously hurt by mandatory sanctions would be Britain rather than South Africa. Sanctions, which a British Labour government would probably feel compelled to respect, would have a catastrophic effect on sterling, since Britain has $2.8 billion in investments in South Africa, from which she receives handsome dividends, and her visible exports alone to South Africa total $560 million a year.

These are the realities of South Africa's relative power position but they do not go to the core of the problem, and it is time we asked calmly: Even if a multiracial society could be brought about by either military or economic coercion, would that be really in our interest or in the interest of anyone else?

Would we like to see the white entrepreneurial class in South Africa driven out of the country, since, if the principle of one man one vote were ever to be forced on South Africa, it is almost certain that all but the least effective whites would emigrate?

Do we wish, in other words, to destroy, in whole or in part, an economy that is now accounting for a large percentage of the total income of Africa? And let us frankly acknowledge that we would be largely destroying that economy if the reins of power in South Africa were taken over in an atmosphere of bitterness engendered by external force, leaving the economy to be operated by people who, regardless of their virtues or native intelligence, have not been trained for the tasks of managing modern industry. The result would not merely be the loss of property by the privileged whites — that might be tolerable — but a terrible depression in income for the black population who today enjoy the highest standard of living in Africa.

I see no evidence at all that the policies we are now pursuing toward South Africa are promoting beneficent change; instead, they appear to be retarding it by uniting the British and Afrikaner populations in the face of a common world opprobrium. We are creating, in other words, a siege psychology which impels people not toward liberal evolution but toward a digging in, a resolute stand-or-die attitude in the defense of entrenched positions. The time is, I think, long overdue for us to face the facts with a mature recognition of all elements of the problem. Instead of sticking mindlessly to the idyllic formula of a multiracial society (which provides us with a moral glow), we should be looking for the useful options. The South African government has given a lead by the creation of special areas (Bantustans) in which the black population is to have semi-autonomy, and, while the scheme in its present form is far too grudging and parsimonious, instead of rejecting it out of hand we should encourage the government in every way to carry out its avowed objectives by greatly enlarging the Bantustans and making them economically viable.

This is the kind of simple common sense that is supposed to be one of America's strengths and virtues. Given the realities of the South African situation, the only policy that might be peaceably carried into execution without wrecking the economy and turning South Africa into an economic slum is some form of partition. Admittedly this will be difficult in view of the importance of the native population in the labor force, but it might prove feasible over time if the South African people were encouraged to feel that the leading powers of the world had some comprehension of their problem, that the United States (whatever its views on their social policies) was not their enemy, and that they might find some small degree of understanding at least from us if they were to take the road toward a solution they could live with even though reluctantly.

For the realistic hope of ameliorating the repulsive social practices of South Africa is not by compulsion from without — the nation is too powerful for that — but by the encouragement of internal change, reflecting the impact of fresh ideas, brought about through free interplay with the outside world, resulting in the lifting of repressive measures and the creation of a climate of frank debate. We will never make that possible by treating South Africa as a pariah, any more than men cured the plague in seventeenth-century England by sealing the victims in a house and letting no one come near them. Apartheid is a plague of the mind and it can be cured only by healing ideas — and that means opening the windows, not closing them.

XIII

Dismantling the Iron Curtain

MORE than two decades have passed since Winston Churchill lamented the coming of the Cold War. "From Stettin in the Baltic to Trieste in the Adriatic," he told an American audience on March 5, 1946, "an iron curtain has descended across the continent." Behind that line lay "all the capitals of the ancient states of central and eastern Europe. Warsaw, Berlin, Prague, Vienna, Budapest, Belgrade, Bucharest and Sofia, all these famous cities and the populations around them" were in the Soviet sphere under "police governments." Churchill expressed the poignancy of disillusion when he said, "this is certainly not the liberated Europe we fought to build up. Nor is it one which contains the essentials of permanent peace." Yet, he concluded with his customary perception: "I do not believe that Soviet Russia desires war. What they desire is the fruits of war and the indefinite expansion of their power and doctrine."

Churchill's Fulton, Missouri, speech was like a wet towel slapped across the face of the West. In some quarters it was resented, in others deplored. Still conditioned to our wartime habit of regarding the Soviet Union as an ally — albeit a prickly and cantankerous one — we Americans found it hard to believe that we could not live at peace with Moscow in spite of macabre rumors out of Eastern Europe, which we tended to regard as normal aftermaths of a great and bloody conflict.

Twenty years of experience have, of course, changed our

view. Churchill in 1946 was, if anything, sounding the alarm late in the day, since already the Soviets had gained a head start on the West. Blind as we were to the realities of Soviet power and purpose and bemused by the euphoric conviction that the peace had been won, we went happily about dismantling the formidable war machine we had assemblied so frantically during the preceding years, scattering the pieces with lunatic abandon. In stealth and secrecy, and driven by quite different motives, Stalin built up rather than tore down his military might, leaving Russia, after the dust had settled, with three million more troops on European soil than all the rest of the Allies.

Looking out through the Kremlin windows, Stalin had some basis for envisaging a red sun shining far out on the western horizon. Certainly his prospects were brighter than Lenin's had been in 1918. If the prophet of the Finland Station had regarded Germany as ripe for revolution after the First World War, Stalin had far greater reason to expect to smash up the West after the second bloody conflict, because the West was lamentably off guard. Bemused by the wishful thought that we could get along with our wartime ally and driven by a reckless but understandable desire to enjoy the peace that had been so long in coming, we were in no mood to pick quarrels with a Soviet Union that should have its hands full repairing the devastation that disfigured such vast areas of its soil. To Stalin we must have seemed foolish indeed, since we wanted so much to discover in his policies the reflection of a purpose totally alien to him.

Things must have seemed to the Kremlin, therefore, to be not only rosy but red. Stalin had at his command the ideal instruments to exploit our befuddlement — the Communist party apparatus and the Red Army — and he lost no time in employing them to push outward the boundaries of Soviet dominance. During the next three years he wrote the story of Central Europe as a tale out of Kafka. Democratic leaders, such as Nikola Petkov in Bulgaria, Bela Kovacs in Hungary and Iuliu Maniu in Rumania, were murdered at Soviet instigation. Popular political figures, who would have come to power in a free society, were thrown into jail or hounded out of the country. Democrats, peasant parties, agrarian unions and most of the Polish resistance movement were liquidated by force and terror even before Mikolajczyk fled his native land in the fall of 1947. Instead of the new free republics that the people had dreamed of during the black days of the war, the face of Eastern Europe was pockmarked by Soviet-dominated puppet states.

In the end, of course, the Communists went too far. The death of Jan Masaryk and the betrayal of Czechoslovakia finally shocked the West into action, and during the next few years of constructive effort we in the West discovered that, united by a common danger, there was little we could not do. No longer able to ignore the hard realities of the cold war, America behaved with courage and maturity. That is a judgment history has already made; a time of manifest peril provided one of our finest hours. For all our occasional blunders and hesitations and muddled moralisms and literal-mindedness, we skillfully wielded our power and wealth and diplomacy to prevent a dangerous tilt in what we recognized almost too late as a bipolar balance of power. We supplied the yeast and iron with which the West grew strong.

Today, as we sprawl around our barbecue pits and swimming pools, we tend to be a little patronizing about the past, but we have no reason to be. What if the policy called "containment" was static and defensive? The specific actions flowing from that policy have kept us alive and well. Because we took a strong lead and, in our own fashion, checkmated Soviet power in Europe after the war, the problems of that beleaguered continent are more manageable today than twenty years ago, however many time bombs may lie concealed in political closets. What we did, sensibly and with reasonable calm, was to buy time, on the confident assumption that the great tides of history were on the side of the Western conception of man and not on the model of Ivan the Terrible; and there is already scattered proof that the assumption was correct. Particularly since the Cuban missile crisis in October 1962, the cold war glacier has shown some crevasses; and, as a result, particularly in Europe, there has been premature, ill-informed and often quite silly talk about a détente. Still the fact that in some Western democracies the Communists have again become respectable has not brought them additional converts, and, at a time of better distributed prosperity, there seems little market for their doctrinal merchandise.

Certainly Marxism has lost much of its economic appeal. Applied to the conditions of the present, it seems little more than a crank theory of political economy with no greater innate value than many fringe heresies that emerged during the eighteenth and nineteenth centuries. Yet it has always been more as a political force than as an economic system that Communism has made its impact, and even that would never have occurred had Karl Marx, for all his bad digestion, not been an extremely lucky fellow. He would share the minor niche of a Proudhon, Pareto, Bakunin or Sorel if his doctrines had not been seized on as a pragmatic lever to power by a most unlikely group — the little band of Russian revolutionaries around Lenin.

It was Lenin who created Marxism as a political force; Lenin who made himself Marx's chief prophet — and in the process transformed the religion. He was one of Carlyle's "great men," who appeared at an opportune time when the oppressive old regime of Russia was collapsing from corruption and decay, and it was sheer chance that the writings of a nineteenth-century dyspeptic German were ready at hand as a convenient creed and battle cry. The man, the event and the idea were all there at the same moment, and our world was rudely altered by that fortuitous juxtaposition of fifty years ago. It was neither economic determinism nor historical necessity but one of history's more outrageous coincidences that saved Marx from the intellectual scrap heap.

Lenin, a pragmatist above all, was not a captive of Marxism but its manipulator — perceiving in the teachings of the prophet a political weapon for seizing and holding power, while justifying his resort to absolutism in high moralistic terms. Several decades later Mao went one step farther. Employing the intellectual tools of Marx and the organizing tenets of Lenin to win control of a nationalist movement, he then sought to use these same tools to propel the Chinese nation from primitive agrarianism headlong into modernity. Thus it is a bitter joke that Marxism became just the opposite of what its founder hoped. As with other religions, a later generation of high priests perverted it to serve their own power ambitions, transforming it into a reactionary dogma that perpetuated Oriental despotism in Russia and China while denying the realities of the new millennium in Western Europe and America.

Marx had attacked the capitalism of industrial societies; it was in exploitive industry that he had found the evil and it was by the reconstruction of industrial societies that he envisaged the triumph of his doctrine. In 1848 he had declared, "The Communists turn their attention chiefly to Germany." Half a century later Engels still believed "the triumph of the European working class . . . can only be secured by the cooperation of, at least, England, France and Germany."

But the Communists never came to power, as predicted, in the industrialized West. The faithful have never ceased being embarrassed that they won control of the apparatus of the state in semifeudal Russia — in spite of the fact that, if one accepts the historical materialism of Marx, a proletarian revolution in the Russia of 1917 made no sense, and, for that matter, a Communist power seizure in China three decades later made even less. History has a limitless capacity for bad jokes, and those who read the master through any but red-tinted lenses cannot help but discover that Leninism and Maoism are not Marx at all but profound perversions of Marx, the fruit of a tactical opportunism that has drained the scripture of much of its meaning.

Viewed historically, Marxism has proved neither a very self-contained nor a very formidable body of thought, but like certain other badly written religions it has — when reinterpreted by later prophets — become a potent political force. As applied by Communist governments and parties, it has served as a tool of political repression justifying rule by the "enlightened" minority. This flies directly in the face of the humanist Enlightenment tradition which posits a more optimistic view of man than the concepts of Oriental despotism papered over by Marxist verbiage. Its core is the notion that political liberty is paramount and requires a number of cumbersome and elaborate procedures — elections, constitutions, courts of appeal, repre-

sentative principles, limited sovereignties, competing newspapers
— to assure a measure of individual freedom and control
over rulers by a diverse lot of men theoretically equal in their
potential rationality. Such a credo does not belong to one Western nation or party, but to each and all. It is the common possession of all free men, the hope of men not free. Its strength
and appeal derive from the fact that it need be accepted only
voluntarily; force is its self-contradictory negation.

To those of us who have grown up in this tradition, its
validity seems self-evident, and it inspires many Americans with
evangelical fervor. They advocate the gospel of the free society
as a counter to Communist proselytizing and subversion. I have
even heard proposals for a Democratic International, but, of
course, that is a grotesquerie. Democratic principles are too
subtle and various to be merchandised like cornflakes or cigarettes, and those who would "popularize" a particular form of
democracy or argue for a formalized "doctrine" or "credo" of
the West miss most of the point. It is no wonder that the most
zealous of the groups advocating campaigns of this kind never
seem to understand the concept of human liberty they allegedly
champion.

I am aware that the West has no analogue to the Moscow
International, but it needs none. Blatherings about the "world
struggle for men's minds" that would put democracy on the
same plane with Marxist-Leninist-Maoist dogma are intellectual rubbish. They misconceive the tolerant nature of Western
political theory, which simply cannot fit men into absolute
molds but which raises the protection of human diversity to
nearly an absolute value; and they dignify the opportunistic
patchwork of Marxist textual exegesis by implying that it is an
intellectually defensible alternative to freedom. For the attractions of Communism — such as they are — are not philosophic, even granting that some ideas of Marx, including his
economic critique of the industrial revolution, have contributed
to the body of Western thought, been absorbed in modern
concepts of the welfare state and of economic development,
and found reflection in the programs of reformist parties like
the European Social (and Christian) Democrats. But the real

strength of Communism as a proselytizing movement has rested in the emotional springs it touches, not its rationalism. It appeals with particular force to the disgruntled and the oppressed by naming them as History's Chosen People and by promising them a quick, sure, bloody and righteous victory.

It is thus no accident that, from the moment Lenin emerged as the manipulator of revolution, Communism has been associated with the most disgruntled and oppressed — the peoples in the precapitalist, semifeudal societies, not the advanced modern nations. This compelled the ideologues to redefine the proletarian elect, since factory workers were only a tiny minority in a population that was largely rural.

We should not wonder then that the major battlegrounds of East and West are not the great industrial cities that Marx had expected, but the less-developed countries, since the chief selling point of Marxism is not its anachronistic economics or its tortuous intellectual content, but rather its naïve historicism carrying a simple moralistic message with biblical echoes: "The Last shall be First and the First shall be Last." With the exception of the Red Army's occupation of Eastern Europe and Stalin's coup in Czechoslovakia, Communists have come to power only in backward economies and feudal societies, while in China and Vietnam and Cuba they have painted over the hammer and sickle with the bright colors of nationalism, which confuses the issue further.

The lesson from all of this is a simple one: Communism has impressive doctrinal power only with those who have grievances. People in the Southern zone of the world have a grievance against past colonial exploitation by Europe with its overlay of racial discrimination, but today that has little more relevance than the fife and drum. It is the familiar symbol of protest against the devil they know by peoples who having at long last attained juridical independence, still find themselves — in all too many cases — oppressed by incompetent leaders and feudal social structures.

This is the tragedy of disillusion, a story repeated again and again throughout the past few years: the inadequacy of the professional revolutionary for the hard, stodgy tasks of organizing a new state; the bitter truth that independence of foreign control has not meant personal freedom but merely the substitution of oppressors; and finally a dawning awareness that access to the levers of government has not enabled the people to reap the dazzling benefits of the newly comprehended potential of modernity. Communism could ask no better conditioning, no sweeter preparation of the soil. Agitators can exploit those grievances with a minimum commitment of resources and effort, and they do; and, since the Communists thrive on chaos, they enjoy the advantage — never to be underestimated — of irresponsibility.

I do not suggest, of course, that one can ignore doctrine; that is a fatuous idea, since present Communist leaders have grown up in the Leninist church. I say, rather, that doctrine is only one part of Communist strength — and, I suspect, the lesser part — because even more significant in the anatomy of the cold war is the competition of two great systems of power, the Russian and the American. From 1945 until the Cuban crisis of 1962, Soviet power sought its extension in every direction, now in Europe, now in Asia or the Middle East, in the classic pattern of Catherine the Great; while Western power, concentrated in the United States, was largely on the defensive.

We defended with will and vigor, checking each new Kremlin thrust until, five years ago, a reckless Soviet design in the Caribbean brought the world — so we felt at the time — closer to atomic war than it had ever been. That, as we are repeatedly reminded, was some kind of a climacteric (although no one is quite sure what its meaning may have been) but we should take care not to grow complacent; it is still too early to say whether the crisis of October 1962 marked the beginning of the end of an era or just another act in a continuing tragedy. From five years' distance it appears — to one who lived through the long nights and participated in the hard decisions of that tense autumn — to have marked at least a detour in the road; since, following as it did a crop failure in the Soviet Union and another blundering Berlin crisis, it served to dramatize three new facts that may, in the end, make large holes in Churchill's Iron Curtain: (1) the nuclear stalemate, (2) the fifteen-year success of American power in defending the West against Soviet thrusts, and (3) the evolution of

Russia toward an industrialized society captivated by the techno-logical instruments of modernity.

The missile crisis was the first tangible proof of the reality of the nuclear stalemate. No longer did we have to postulate its de-terrent value purely on the basis of logic or of that new scho-lasticism called "game theory." We had had a demonstration that, at least under certain circumstances, it would work. Khrushchev had climbed down when the escalator began to accelerate and the world could again breathe deeply.

Yet we were not sure at the time that he would. I was a member of the Executive Committee (the "Ex-com" as it came to be called), the group created by President Kennedy to work with him during the crisis. None of the members of our small beleaguered band, who spent those agonizing days and nights in my State Department conference room — later referred to by my irrev-erent staff as the "think tank pad where the Ex-com mob hung out" — had total faith that the standoff would prove an effec-tive deterrent. But neither, of course, did Khrushchev, else he would never have turned his ships around. And that, I suppose, is both the beauty and the weakness of the nuclear stalemate: it will work as a deterrent only if each side is not blindly cer-tain that it will.

The missile crisis was a landmark event, but, on the evidence at hand, it would be foolish — even dangerous — to base policy on the assumption that it was a definitive watershed, because physical facts have not changed. Both sides remain armed to the teeth; both nations spend heavily and wastefully on bigger and better weapons and there seems no end of it, particularly since today's outrageous costs of defense will be exponentially increased if we go forward with an all-out competition in anti-ballistic missiles. So we can hardly say that we live with the Soviet Union in a state of peace — more a state of suspended belligerency. We have not yet found a way to break the arms spiral and we should stop taking comfort from foreign words like détente — used with little sense of nicety for language or logic.

Both we and the Soviet Union have an obvious interest in scaling down weapons costs on both sides, but we have made little progress in translating that mutual interest into effective disarmament arrangements. Progress requires mutual trust and that is something we are far from achieving, because the Soviet Union trusts nobody and we find it difficult to trust a closed society that does its business in secrecy and stealth and obdurately resists adequate inspection and verification arrangements. Let us stop, therefore, being complacent. A balance of terror at a progressively higher level of cost and destructiveness is a fragile basis for security and we should never forget it.

Euphoria then is not a proper mood, but neither is pessimism, since the world is changing and not necessarily for the worse. The most significant changes are probably those in the internal politics and economics of the Soviet Union and the Communist world, and they, in turn, are closely related to the emergence of the Soviet Union as a modern industrial nation, something that has happened — almost unnoticed — during the last twenty years. After the war the Soviet national income was smaller than Britain's, but today it is three times greater, about three hundred billion dollars. In the last seventeen years national income per capita has risen sevenfold — which, of course, does not mean that the Soviet citizen is that much better off or that the national increment has all, or even in large part, been available for consumer goods.

It is a fact of history that, except for the twelve-year Nazi interlude in Germany and the traditional military rule in Japan, no modern industrial society has been ruled by a dictatorship. One can certainly argue — though there is nothing absolute about this, as Hitlerism and Stalinism show — that modern technology unleashes forces and creates conditions that, for their sustenance, require a degree of political freedom and a relatively open society. Such forces are at work in the Soviet Union today. Their net effect is to stimulate a kind of Marxism-in-reverse. A series of material changes as impersonal as Marx ever envisioned are eating away at the working assumptions of the Soviet state.

First, secrecy has become a wasting asset. Not only are the requirements of an intricate industrial society compelling a freer exchange of ideas and a greater interplay with the outside world, but, with space full of satellites and electronic detection apparatus at a high point of effectiveness, secrecy as a technical matter is becoming progressively less efficient.

Second, the Soviet citizen is beginning to show his metal as a clamorous consumer. He is asking the hard question: Are the tangible and visible benefits of fifty years of socialism to be limited to the possession of a one-room apartment in Moscow? And the Presidium in turn must face the problem of providing incentives — consumer goods that can be bought by the workers — including collective farmers; for, otherwise, why should they produce? The Soviet government has quite clearly gotten the word; there must be incentives, and so it is increasing the production of that most seductive of all incentives: the automobile. But do the Russians understand the full implications of what they are doing? For the automobile, as we Americans know better than anyone, is no ordinary item of consumer goods. It is an ideology on four wheels with a vast revolutionary potential, and once the Soviet people begin to move about on their own wheels they will never be the same again. They will insist on paved roads and borscht bars and juke boxes and filling stations and motels — and maybe, God knows, even clean restrooms — and all the other service apparatus that a motorized society requires. Obviously such things cannot be conjured up without a sharp impact on the allocation of resources, and this means increased pressure to limit the drain of the military sector.

Third, the development of a complex industrial society requires competent engineers and managers who necessarily measure success in terms of productivity and economic pragmatism and who cannot help but be impatient when Communist theology or theologians get in the way. Such men are inclined to view interference by the Party bureaucracy with as much distaste as their counterparts in the United States regard our government's infinitely more delicate intrusion into business decisions. Slowly and painfully they are making the point clear that the centralized methods of a party-directed state are quite inadequate for the management of a large industrial society. Such methods just will not work; even the most sophisticated computers and linear programming will never enable Soviet economic managers to solve the problems of the allocation and control of resources solely by central planning. And so, in order to measure performance and need, slowly and falteringly they have had to move toward a kind of socialist market mechanism with an increasingly complex pricing system to relate supply and demand.

Such accommodations to reality cannot help but undercut Marxist economic theory, while Russia's East European neighbors conduct ever more daring experiments in the avant-garde economics of the West. Yugoslavia has recently decided to restore private ownership of retail trade, which it abolished nineteen years ago. On a small scale Moscow has decided to encourage privately owned village handicraft industries to combat rural unemployment caused by an inefficient collective agriculture. The management of Soviet agriculture has now been put on a profit basis.

We, therefore, see emerging in the Soviet Union and the East a new managerial class whose thinking about the industrial economy tends inevitably to edge toward that of the American industrial managers; while at the same time, changes are occurring in our own system, as the ownership and direction of enterprises drift apart and the professional corporate manager takes over. Nor is that the whole story. As Russia travels away from Marx and toward market economics, Western economic thought has been moving also; it has long since evolved from the Manchester School, to Keynes, to the post-Keynesians. So, over the years, as the professionals on each side tackle roughly similar problems, they will find more and more to talk about.

These accommodations to modernity in the Soviet economy, which, even in isolation, have great importance, are heightened by the interplay of forces in the tangled politics of the Communist world. Russia has formidable problems within the Warsaw Pact, but her most intense preoccupation at the moment is the bellicosity of Red China and the turmoil in that huge and ancient land. She has reason to be worried because China and the Soviet Union are intimate — and historically unfriendly — neighbors; their common frontier is a thousand miles longer than our frontier with Canada and substantial parts of it are in dispute. Can one imagine our own anxiety if we lived next to three-quarters of a billion people who daily denounced the United States in strident terms and were caught up in the swirling forces of a vast internal convulsion?

These then are elements that make for change — the growing hostility of a China touched by the sun, a lessening fear of the West, the imperatives of industrial economics, the diminished efficiency of secrecy, and a swelling demand for one Fiat in every garage. Over the next few years, I hope, these elements can combine to make possible a greater East-West understanding. Certainly the leaders of the Soviet Union do not want their country blown up any more than we wish the destruction of ours. And if we are sensible and mature and sufficiently flexible, the time may come when rationality will triumph over fear and suspicion, ideological ambitions, and the lust of power.

This does not mean, however, that we need, or should, stand helplessly by while nature works out our problems by her own inscrutable processes. We are not helpless and we should not immobilize ourselves in dealing with the obsolete orthodoxy of Moscow by an almost equally rigid attachment to an obsolete orthodoxy on our own side. Slowly and with considerable hesitation we have found some areas of common interest with the Soviet Union: the Limited Test Ban Treaty of July 1963, our sale of wheat to Moscow announced in the autumn of that year, the settlement of the India-Pakistan War, and the Consular Treaty which was ratified in March of 1967.

These limited agreements or common or parallel actions are, it seems to me, sound policy. They dispose of specific problems that it is in our national interest to solve, while at the same time contributing to an atmosphere of cooperation that is basic to any enduring peace. Thus they can serve — or so we may reasonably hope — to help create the conditions that will bring the Russians and East European peoples back into a single family of nations, back toward the Western mainstream and away from a dangerous and irrelevant Eastern despotism. Equally important, they can contribute to the education of America. They can help us break away from the fundamentalism and pieties that marked the cold war and prepare us for the more intricate problems of the future.

We can use some more education. It is sad but true that fossils of the McCarthy era are still being washed up on the American beach. Many politicians in the 1950's made political capital by treating the cold war not as an unfortunate reality of a tortured world but rather as a crusade against the powers of darkness launched and supplied from the temples of absolute virtue — and they are still at it. Though some advocates of new and bigger East-West agreements exaggerate their significance as panaceas, the opponents of such measures go far to the other extreme, denouncing any and all diplomatic contact with the forces of evil as a betrayal of innocence. This attitude reflects, to my mind, a shocking lack of confidence in the strength of our free society. If we really believe that liberty is a benign but hardy bacterium, then why should we seek to protect the closed societies from its infection?

Perhaps all people who, like Russians and Americans, have a large and relatively isolated continent to themselves, are bound to develop a sense of uniqueness and native virtue that is denied to those less fortunate in their historic geography. I think it possible that when Robert Frost said "Good fences make good neighbors," he was implying that the presence of a near and always potential hostility breeds realism. At any rate, in East-West relations one impediment to improving the general climate is America's curious and highly moralistic attitude toward trade; it is an attitude I have long observed with a certain puzzlement both as a lawyer representing commercial clients and as a diplomat negotiating trade arrangements.

Absurd manifestations of this moralism are all too familiar. In a decade where pickets, petitions and protests are a part of our national therapy, embattled patriots in many hamlets and towns have formed "Committees to Warn of the Arrival of Communist Merchandise on the Local Scene." Other groups have marched fearlessly into supermarkets to paste preprinted skull-and-crossbones labels on Polish hams. The Firestone Tire and Rubber Company was bombarded by letters from self-styled "patriotic" groups warning against the conclusion of a profitable contract with Rumania, and, partly because we did not react promptly and vigorously enough in the Department of State, it succumbed to the pressure. In early October 1963, as President Kennedy patiently briefed Congressmen on his· decision to sell wheat to the Soviet Union, one unhappy member interrupted with the question: "Mr. President, aren't we at war with them?" More recently a midwestern Senator has virtuously declared, "I would not sell the Communists anything."

I think it likely that, over the postwar years, many high government officials — and I do not exclude myself — may have contributed to this nonsense by expressing our initiatives in foreign policy in universal terms, as one can see in a progression of slogans: "unconditional surrender," "roll back the Iron Curtain," "stop Communist aggression wherever it occurs," and the like. But whatever the impact of such political slogans, it is singularly inappropriate to apply them to commercial transactions. For what is trade? It is the buying and selling of commodities in a competitive market place. It is, in the abstract, morally neutral, and it can become a political weapon only when the trading relationship is unequal.

With a gross national product substantially more than twice that of the Soviet Union, the United States can hardly be hurt by a little commerce with the East — and so far it has been very little. In 1965 non-Communist countries sold six billion dollars' worth of goods to Eastern Europe and purchased a like amount, but our share in this trade was about two percent — $140 million in exports and the same figure in imports. France's total trade with the East was two and a half times as large; Britain's four times; Germany's seven times. Have any of these countries become a political tool of Moscow by expanding their trade?

Yet some Americans, even some in public life, still insecurely believe that if our businessmen bought or sold goods across the Iron Curtain, they might somehow become the dupes of Soviet commissars. That so nonsensical a view is entertained, even for a moment, is curious and, I think, somewhat pathological. A Freudian psychologist could write a lengthy treatise to explain the American sense of guilt about trade with the East and our fear of contamination through commercial dealings. Not only is our reaction out of character, but it insults the skill and integrity of our Yankee traders and contradicts the experience of our own history.

From the Colonial period down to the First World War America was heavily dependent on foreign trade and foreign capital. In 1812 our insistence on neutral trading rights brought war with England, and during our Civil War there was substantial cross-border "trading with the enemy." But the domestic market has grown so rapidly that today foreign trade accounts for hardly more than five percent of our national income. We can thus afford to be moralistic about it, as most other countries cannot. Foreign trade is vital to Europeans but only marginal to us.

This moralizing about trade is unique in the world. The Europeans do not suffer from any such aberration, and I personally have always been at a loss to explain our own odd attitude. No other country in the world seems so moonstruck. It may in part be a hangover from the days of the Nye Committee in the 1930's, when the "Merchants of Death" were held responsible for the First World War. Or perhaps it reflects the theological politics of men like Woodrow Wilson and John Foster Dulles, with their tendency to turn wars into moral contests. If Armageddon is really upon us then we are correct in wanting no truck — or trade — with the devil. But if the Apocalypse is not imminent, if we are confident in the power and ultimate success of free societies, if we care about building a future peace, then we have nothing to lose and something to gain by increased commerce with our political adversaries.

Aside from vacant platitudes and non sequiturs and the devil theories of fearful men, what are the more rational arguments against expanding trade?

Let us consider first the question of exports. I think few would disagree with the thesis that we should not sell those articles or materials to the Soviet Union and nations of Eastern Europe that are really "strategic" in that they would contribute in a direct way to building up the Soviet war machine in a manner that the USSR would otherwise not find possible.

Whether we like it or not we are engaged in an arms race in which the technology of advanced weapons can be a critical factor. On this point we have no difference of view with our North Atlantic allies, and, in fact, NATO maintains a periodically reviewed list, called COCOM, that sets forth the strategic items the member nations have all agreed not to sell to countries of the Iron Curtain. It is when we move beyond the application of this agreed list, however, that we stir up a whole series of questions, some of fact or judgment, some philosophical.

One argument used to support our stiff-necked attitude toward exports to the East rests on the mistaken belief that the Soviet Union almost always benefits when it trades with us, because, if it can buy materials or equipment from America, it is not compelled to produce them itself. This contention, however, rests on an assumption that is, I believe, quite incorrect. Two or three years ago we tried to stop all member nations of NATO from selling wide-diameter pipe to the Soviet Union, to be used in a pipeline to move petroleum products into Western Germany. By exerting substantial pressure we even induced the Bonn government to force the cancellation of some existing contracts between German steel companies and the Soviet government.

While I did not oppose the policy at the time, and therefore share blame for the outcome, I think, in retrospect, our action was thoroughly self-defeating. Not only did we put an unnecessary strain on our relations with the German government and with German industry, but we brought about exactly the opposite result from the one we might have wished. To be sure we probably somewhat slowed down the building of the pipeline. But, in doing so, we forced the Soviet government to develop facilities to make wide-diameter pipes themselves, thus bcoming more nearly self-sufficient.

Now it should be perfectly evident that to press the Soviet Union toward autarky makes no sense from the point of view of the West; instead we should encourage Moscow to become dependent on us for certain necessary products. That is the way one breaks down barriers; advantages would accrue to both sides in a better utilization of resources, and from the military point of view the Soviet Union would be less able to wage a protracted war if it had to depend on sources of supply on this side of the Iron Curtain.

All this may be true, one can say, about such items as wide-diameter pipe, but what about American technology? In certain areas the Soviets are technologically far advanced — as far or farther than the United States — but in others they are well behind. Why should we help them to catch up by selling them our most advanced plants and equipment? Mr. Krushchev said, after all, that the Russians intended to "bury us," and, even if he used that phrase in its narrow commercial sense, why should we help the Soviets to compete against us in world markets?

Certainly we should not help them to compete unfairly, and this requires proper arrangements for the protection of the "industrial property" involved, which means the safeguarding of patents and know-how. This is primarily a matter to be settled by the parties themselves through appropriate agreements and price adjustments. In addition, we should prevent the export of equipment and machines that would contribute directly to the Soviet's war-making ability, as our other NATO allies do through the administration of the COCOM list. But beyond that there is little advantage in trying to restrict our exports through the elaborate licensing machinery we have created, except for a narrow range of equipment, since the Communists can acquire from Western Europe or Japan substantially the same equipment and technology that we are in a position to supply. After all we are no longer back in the forties when America had a monopoly on new techniques and products; today technology has been broadly shared with industries in other friendly countries of the West and with Japan through joint ventures, the licensing of patents, technical assistance agreements, and a variety of other quite normal commercial arrangements, while at the same time industries in all of those countries have expanded their own research and development along similar lines.

In most cases, therefore, the question at issue in the granting of an export license is whether the United States should refuse to

permit the sale of machinery or equipment to a Communist country even though a negative decision will not prevent that country
from obtaining the advanced technology it is seeking. One would
suppose that the answer to this question would be obvious. If
our government cannot prevent the Communists from acquiring
the equipment elsewhere, then it seems to me errant folly to keep
our own manufacturers from doing a profitable piece of business;
but, surprisingly enough, that is not the answer sometimes given.
During my tenure in the government I was fascinated to find
some people in the Executive Departments and many in Congress
who thought we should deny licenses for exports even though the
Soviet Union could buy substantially the same machines or equipment from others. I used to speculate on the primal causes of this
curious attitude, which clearly did not reflect any stratagem of
economic warfare. The only explanation I could imagine was that
it rested on the belief that we could win moral Brownie points by
resisting the temptings of the devil and denying ourselves a
profit.

This attitude always struck me as having rather odd Marxist
overtones. I could never bring myself to believe that American
businessmen were so greedy that they would be corrupted by
selling goods across the Iron Curtain and, once corrupted, would
subvert the government and weaken its resistance to Communism. What utter nonsense! Such a view (which might be in-
ferred from much of the argument of the Congressional "hard
liners") seemed to me quite as softheaded as the opposing position of the extreme "soft liners," that if we would only treat
the Communists nicely all questions of ideology and competing
interests would somehow go away. Certainly to turn down good
business deals under circumstances where the Soviet Union could
buy substantially the same equipment elsewhere seemed not so
much the carrying out of a rational foreign policy as self-flagella-
tion on a national scale.

Some of this asceticism found its way into the argument over
our sale of wheat to the Soviet Union in the fall of 1963. The
Soviet interest in purchasing our wheat first became known in
August. For several years there had been poor harvests on the
steppes of Russia and the experiment of the New Lands had

been disastrous. Quite clearly the government and the Party had not yet succeeded in mastering agricultural production through Communist methods, and they were faced with a heavy shortfall of grain. During the preceding months the government had, therefore, bought a substantial amount of wheat from Canada and Australia. We had several hundred million bushels of surplus wheat in storage and there seemed to me no reason why we should not make a profitable deal with the Soviet Union.

In normal commercial sales of wheat the purchaser can arrange shipping as he sees fit. But, feeling the pressure of shipowners and maritime unions, the President stipulated that, while we would sell wheat to the Russians at world prices, we would require that it be lifted in American bottoms. In the first exchange the Soviet Union apparently misunderstood this stipulation, which resulted in considerable confusion on both sides, but, in due course, a Soviet mission arrived and President Kennedy asked me to head the negotiations. Thereafter, over a period of days, I talked long and hard with the Soviet representative, Mr. Borisov, the Deputy Minister of Trade, a pleasant and able man who has since died.

During the course of the negotiations it became apparent that the first informal contacts had produced no meeting of the minds. The Soviet government would not agree to limit themselves to the use of our ships, and with quite good reason, since, because our shipping costs and rates are probably the highest in the world, the requirement we were imposing made it substantially more expensive to buy wheat from the United States than from other countries. Ultimately, a deal was made to sell only about half as much wheat as we had hoped, and then only after we had compromised by permitting the Soviet Union to lift fifty percent of the wheat in foreign flagships. But instead of easing relations between ourselves and the Russians, the negotiations left scars, while at the same time disclosing baffling problems of communication and understanding between the two sides of the Iron Curtain.

The representatives of the Soviet Union were understandably annoyed that we would not treat the USSR like any other customer. To them our insistence on the use of American ships appeared to be merely another manifestation of capitalistic greed and discrimination against a Communist country. When I pointed out that our longshoremen unions would very likely walk off the job if Soviet ships put into American ports to lift the wheat, they thought this only a bargaining ploy. After all, they argued, they had unions in the USSR but theirs were patriotic; they did what the government wanted them to do. Mr. Borisov was remarkably unimpressed by my lecture on the independence of the free labor movement.

I felt at the time — and still do — that the position we took was unworthy of a great nation. How could one explain to the Soviets that our shipowners and maritime unions felt it deeply immoral for us to sell wheat to the Soviet Union and would, therefore, regard it as their patriotic duty to oppose such a sale, yet be prepared to rise heroically above their patriotism if the wheat were carried in American ships? This was the kind of pocketbook morality that, in the view of the Soviet representatives, confirmed their doctrinal teachings. Failing to understand the play of forces within American domestic politics, they interpreted our whole position as motivated by some mean and sinister purpose.

I think it clear in retrospect that we should have treated the Soviet wheat deal like any other transaction and offered the same terms and conditions to the Soviet Union as would be offered to any other buyer. But foreign policy is all too often a captive of domestic politics, and I have no doubt that President Kennedy faced quite real political problems. Congress would certainly have been prickly if the President had not gone at least part way to appease the maritime unions and the ship operators. Moreover, our relations with the Soviet Union would have been embarrassingly aggravated if, when Soviet ships arrived to load wheat, they had been struck by American longshoremen and left to sit idly in port.

The wheat incident did, however, provide insight as to certain emotional sectors of American opinion. The Soviet Union needed wheat and, to a considerable extent, other world sources of supply had already been tapped. The Canadians still had wheat available but their ports were clogged with the grain they had already sold. Still this did not mean that the Russian people faced starvation. There was nothing to prevent the Soviet government, if she were prepared to bear higher costs in foreign exchange, from buying flour in France made from American wheat, as it finally did in limited quantity.

What fascinated me most was the stiff-necked puritan attitude of certain members of Congress who were quite prepared on humanitarian grounds to have us *give* wheat to the Soviet Union, but still felt that its *sale* was immoral. I frankly could not understand the logic of this argument, for to me the transaction appeared in quite a different light. By refusing to sell wheat to the Soviet Union or even by attaching discriminatory conditions, we appeared in the eyes of the world as churlish and inhumane. Why, after all, should a great nation refuse to sell food to anyone with whom she was not engaged in a shooting war? Our position made no discernible sense, since it was certainly not in our interest — or that of the free world — to bring about food shortages in Russia.

What would have been the result of bread riots, assuming that such riots might have occurred? They would almost certainly have led Moscow to return to the brutal measures of the past, and that was something we could hardly regard with pleasure. For do any of us want the Soviet Union to move backward toward the dark, repressive Stalinist years? To be sure, I do not share the wishful thinking of some of the British Labour party that a fat Bolshevik becomes automatically a happy bourgeois, but I think it perfectly obvious that a prosperous Russia, with an increasingly contented body of citizens — or comrades — would be a far more stable and less explosive element in the world mix than a Russia dominated by a Stalinist police state.

So much for our exports to the Soviet Union and Eastern Europe; the agitation on the hysterical right extends to imports as well. It takes such bizarre forms, for example, as an organized campaign to boycott cigarettes in which the manufacturer mixes a small amount of Yugoslav tobacco. In that particular case, to be sure, the Department of State and other agencies of the government took a strong public position against the boycott and the American cigarette companies were sufficiently sturdy and statesmanlike to stand up to the threats of the fringe groups involved. But opposition to imports is not limited to the embattled right wing. Recently the Soviet Union proposed to bid on some turbines that were, as I recall, to be part of a publicly owned hydroelectric facility. As I learned from the newspaper, the Russians were finally excluded from the bidding with that most shopworn of all excuses that the installation of the Soviet equipment might "jeopardize security." (Bureaucratic imagination should certainly have done better than that!) What particularly fascinated me was the statement of one American official, who was quoted in the newspaper as saying, with a sense of outrage, that the Soviet request had to be rejected since it would cast a shadow on American technology if the Soviet Union built highly sophisticated turbines for a major American power installation.

But how gullible can one expect the American people to be? What is the logic of our refusing to sell equipment to the Soviet Union for fear we may thus give them technology that is better than any they have, while, on our part, we refuse to buy equipment from the Soviet Union for fear their equipment may be better than ours? When protectionism shows its face frankly it is ugly but honest, but when it wraps the flag around its head, I find it insufferable. If we have confidence in our own technology and really believe in the "free enterprise system" we constantly boast about, then what do we have to fear? Why shouldn't we risk free competition? And why should we go on doing the Russians the honor of regarding them as better mousetrap-makers or more skillful traders than ourselves?

Today we protect our trade against Iron Curtain competition with absurd measures. Some years ago Congress tied the hands of the President by preventing him from extending most-favored-nation treatment to the Soviet Union and to most of the Iron Curtain countries. The result was that Iron Curtain imports became subject to the Smoot-Hawley Tariff of 1930 — the highest in our history. This has been a deep source of annoyance to the Soviet Union for quite good reason. Since its imports and exports are part of a state trading system, its own tariffs are not significant in determining the volume of trade, because trade is normally arranged under bilateral agreements.

I hope this foolishness will be corrected in the East-West

Trade Bill now before the Congress. That bill would restore the discretionary power to extend most-favored-nation treatment to the Iron Curtain countries whenever the President found it in the interests of the United States.

The arguments for this legislation seem to me to be so compelling that I need not develop them here. But even if the legislation passes we should not expect any dramatic and quick expansion of trade, since there is not much we want to buy from Eastern Europe and thus little opportunity for the Eastern European countries to earn foreign exchange to pay for our exports. As a result, unless the Soviet Union were willing to spend her limited supplies of foreign exchange and gold (which is highly doubtful) or unless the United States were prepared to grant substantial credits on a long-term basis (which it is not), the Iron Curtain countries could not increase their American purchases by very much.

Yet, though the lifting of the discriminatory barriers would not result in any substantial increase in trade — one or two percent of American imports and exports at the most — the action would have important symbolic consequences. It would make one more crack in the wall that surrounds the closed societies, letting in fresh warm winds — trade winds — which are winds of change in Eastern Europe. Moreover, beyond the commercial benefit American businessmen and consumers receive from trade, beyond even the political and economic net gain for the West in opening the shutters on the Eastern windows, there is a psychological reason for dropping discriminatory tariffs; because the USSR, although it is — or perhaps because it is — a Communist country, is extremely sensitive to commercial discrimination. Soviet officials see no reason why the Communist countries should be singled out for worse treatment in trading with the United States than other nations, since they pay their bills and, in commercial deals, behave with careful correctness. Thus by removing this clumsy inequity and treating the Soviet Union as we treat other trading nations, we would remove a significant element of friction and tension; and we would at the same time take one small step toward eliminating that truculent sense of inferiority which is one of the sources of Soviet belligerency toward America.

To an extent the Russian desire for good trading relations stems from their misconception of our own system. It is a central tenet of Marxist doctrine that capitalist countries are dominated by a handful of greedy exploiters, and anyone who has dealt with the Soviets soon becomes aware of their unshakable conviction that Washington is run from Wall Street and that American big industry calls the political tune. From this they conclude that if they could only involve the American capitalist class in trade they would be able to moderate American policy toward the Soviet Union. Khrushchev reflected this belief during his visit to the United States when he continually made efforts to meet and talk with businessmen and Wall Street financiers. To him — and to his successors — big business is the soft underbelly of the American system; and the best way to achieve a more friendly response from the United States is to soften up the capitalist class through trade. However absurd this belief, it can be exploited by the West, and possibly in the process the Communists will receive education in the economic workings of free societies.

But today we insist on suffering from the worst of both worlds. Our rigid policies toward East-West trade are not only an impediment to the improvement of relations with Russia but a source of constant friction to our allies, especially when we try to browbeat them into pursuing policies as restrictive as our own. They regard our attitude toward these matters as an American aberration, and they resent having their arms twisted for courses of action they consider irrational and injurious to their economies. We exacerbate the problem beyond tolerance when we try to exert extraterritorial control over American subsidiaries and licensees located abroad. Compelling American subsidiaries doing business in foreign lands to follow restrictive American trading policies, even though those subsidiaries may represent substantial foreign ownership and be competing with foreign companies under no such inhibitions, is bad politics and we should stop doing it. It is a silly policy which I have opposed in and out of government, but it still has backing among the trade moralists.

I have perhaps dwelt longer on the question of trade between the East and West than its importance justifies, but I feel strongly that we must at long last grow up and get over our insecurity and confusion about the meaning of trade. We should stop conjuring up the bête noire of "helping the enemy." We should make a quiet bonfire of all the tired old arguments and not drag them out every time an American business firm decides to sell rubber tires or paper clips or sealing wax to Eastern Europe. It is surely time to lay these ghosts to rest.

I say this with emphasis, since any American with a grain of either experience or perception knows that our country trades out of strength and not out of weakness, for national gain not for charity. The American people can appreciate the merits of a good business deal, and if the issue is fairly presented — shorn of cold war harangues and moralistic claptrap — they can understand that selling rubber plants to Rumania and buying hams from Poland are not acts of foreign aid. They bring commercial and consumer benefits to Americans; they increase Eastern dependence on Western markets and sources of supply; they expand contact with the West; and they point toward easier relations.

Liberalizing trade, then, is one simple step Americans could take that would help put holes in the Iron Curtain and moderate East-West relations. This is not to say that it would "win" or "end" the cold war or lead to sweet peace and reasonableness all around. It is only a beginning step and, if I seem to magnify its importance, it is because our professional hysterics pay it so much attention and issue such dire alarms. In and of itself, freer trade cannot bring an enduring peace or solve our gravest problems; but it can contribute to a process that will have its principal meaning in a distant future when Russians and Europeans and Americans find more and more areas of common interest and can reach basic political decisions.

The road ahead is long and will no doubt be marked by detours and disappointments but, even so, it may not be too early to sketch the outlines of a future settlement. Any such settlement must take full account of the German problem, the progress toward European unity, and the differences in outlook and philosophy between East and West: these are the essential points. Divergent purposes with regard to Africa and Asia are more easily surmountable because each side can afford to give elbow room to the other outside of Europe; and, in the long run — if one takes the optimistic view — East-West collaboration in some multilateral framework might even result in the sharing of some responsibilities for the economic development of parts of the Southern Zone.

So we return to Europe, where our inquiry began. And we pose the question, "What would a rational policy toward the Soviet Union dictate in the 1980's?" Such a hypothetical question is, of course, dependent on all of the imponderables of an unpredictable next decade. But if present trends continue, it seems to me quite clear that a settlement of the legacy of 1945 is at least conceivable. I can think of four different patterns.

One is the Gaullist notion of a Europe "from the Atlantic to the Urals," which, as I have suggested earlier, is more a mystique than a policy. This pattern implies a Europe of scattered nationalisms, where no other state in the constellation is able to balance the power of the Soviet Union. In such a framework the German problem must be ignored and left to fester; I do not see how it can be settled. When someone suggests that this is too gloomy a view and that reunification could slowly come by stages as East and West draw together, I feel I am listening either to ignorance or hypocrisy. If we are honest with ourselves we must recognize that none of Germany's neighbors, East or West, is prepared to accept the emergence in the heart of Europe of an overshadowing nation of eighty million — at least without hedging the Germans about with such humiliating restrictions and discriminatory commitments as to assure trouble in the future. This pattern is then vague, contradictory, and more an arresting figure of speech than a potential policy capable of attracting much support outside of Gaullist France.

A second pattern would be a future bilateral German-Soviet settlement of the kind discussed in chapter IX. Such an accord, unlikely and improbable as it now seems, might tempt future Soviet and German governments if their eyes were on the short term. But it would breed instability and danger at the center of Europe.

A third pattern, which has some support these days, particularly among the young and impatient, contemplates a purely bilateral Soviet-American agreement, negotiated over the heads of the Europeans. Such an agreement could do little more than freeze the status quo, leaving the German question inflamed and unresolved, while creating resentment and instability throughout Europe at the insufferable arrogance of a European settlement "dictated" by non-Europeans. It would be dangerous to the West because it would divide the West — and that would be a tragic blunder. Let us never forget that we Americans and Europeans share, after all, a common core of humane political values that have only superficially penetrated the Czarist and Communist lands, and that we could not cut Western Europe adrift by a bilateral Washington-Moscow policy of "détente, entente and cooperation" without doing violence to the values of our history and our politics and building a fertile breeding ground for disenchantment and violence.

In the end, a fourth pattern emerges as the best model, to my mind, for the distant *Pax Europa*. That pattern would involve Americans, united West Europeans, and Russians as equal negotiators. It would require, on the part of the USSR, the recognition that in this age of nuclear peril the Soviet Union does, when all is said and done, have an interest in European stability and that such stability is the indispensable element in any enduring peace. For Americans it would require the conviction gained from thought and experience that Western European unity is a good in itself, not a tool of the cold war. For all of the negotiating partners it would require considerable progress beyond the theories of Lenin, John Foster Dulles, Lord Beaverbrook or Charles de Gaulle.

I am arguing, in short, that the kind of West European political unity described in earlier chapters is an essential prerequisite to a settlement of the Second World War that includes the reuniting of the German people within a larger Europe and the dismantling of the Iron Curtain. I do not mean by this to criticize today's "bridge building" policy, which strives quite usefully to lay the groundwork for easier conversation between East and West but it cannot do more than that. To the extent that building bridges implies simply improved communications and acceptance of the status quo, it attempts to put a fence around the German problem; yet that is not a problem that can be fenced in or quietly forgotten, if what we are seeking at the end of the road is a stable world.

No matter how many bridges are built, I see no chance that the Soviet Union would ever agree to reunification until there was a fundamental change in the structure of Europe. To accept reunification under today's conditions would mean that Moscow must relinquish control over its principal satellite and thus precipitate the dissolution of the Warsaw Pact system. It would mean also the reestablishment of a German nation-state in which the West Germans (who outnumber the East Germans seven to two) would clearly dominate.

Moreover, the nations of Western Europe — even though their statesmen will not say so publicly — would be frightened to death by the reappearance of a German nation-state of eighty million people. Like the Soviet Union, they could accept it only if the Germans agreed to galling conditions and restrictions. As history has made clear, that is not the way to a stable peace. It is the road to chaos.

We Americans are in a different position from Europeans and have a different mental attitude. We would not react in such an emotional way to a reunified Germany. We are bigger and farther away, and, most of all, we have never been startled from sleep by the screaming bombs of the *Luftwaffe* or the rumbling guns and clanking tanks of the *Wehrmacht.* Yet even we must be aware that a reunified Germany, achieved under arrangements designed to consign the German people to permanent second-class citizenship, would be a house built on sand — or, more accurately, on nitroglycerine.

Schuman and Adenauer and Monnet recognized this profound political reality. They, together with those who worked with them during the days of the Marshall Plan and the golden years of the great European initiatives, perceived something that present-day Soviet leaders have not yet acknowledged: that the stability and progress which flow from a united Europe are as important to the security and aspirations of the Soviet people as they are consistent with the interests of Europe and America. This is the fact on which we should focus, because it holds the key to the solution of an otherwise intractable problem.

What are the conditions that must be satisfied if the Soviet Union is ever to agree to loosen its grip on East Germany and permit the reuniting of the German people? The most important condition is that the Soviet Union be relieved of the fear that it will ever again be faced by a resurgent Germany of eighty million people, determined, so Moscow's mythology has it — and the myth of *revanchism* is deeply imbedded in the Russian soul — on another bloody adventure against the East. The instinctive Soviet response to this specter is either to keep Germany divided or, if it should ever agree to reunification, to require extremely harsh and far-reaching commitments of self-denial from the government of the Federal Republic, reenforced by firm promises by the Western nations to help keep Germany a second-class power.

As I have indicated, this would be regarded by the German people as a humiliation but that does not mean that such a proposal could not be bullied through. My fear is that the Germans might reluctantly accept it as the short-term cost for the achievement of a central objective, but with deep reservations about the future, and that in succeeding years future generations of Germans would come more and more to regard such an arrangement with abhorrence, while demagogues would certainly exploit it as the ganging up of East and West against the German people. If we have learned anything from history it is the danger of creating situations that contain built-in discrimination, inequalities and resentment.

The far more healthy way of providing the necessary assurances to the Soviet Union would be, as I have persistently argued, to avoid the creation of another German Reich and bring the German people together in a united Western Europe. In that event, German energies could find a new outlet in an area with larger horizons, while the outward thrust of German nationalism would be submerged and sublimated. To accept such a formula, however, the Soviet leadership would have to be satisfied that a politically united Western Europe was not merely an appendage of American power. Thus, as a part of the *quid pro quo* for agreeing to the reunion of the German people, we should, I think, be prepared to leave Europe in full control of her own destiny. In broad terms, of course, what I am suggesting is a variant of the principle of mutual withdrawal, involving the removal, or at least the thinning down, of the military forces in the two halves of Germany. This is not something I foresee in the immediate future, since the underlying precondition of the solution I outline is the building of a unified Western Europe.

I recognize that this proposal will be regarded with extreme distaste by a few of my friends on both sides of the Atlantic and some may think that it undercuts the concept of an Atlantic partnership. But, if and when Western Europe is unified, its people will inevitably insist that we recognize their maturity and independence, so we shall be led, whether we like it or not, to put more stress on the first rather than the second word of the phrase "equal partnership." Quite frankly such a prospect does not disturb me, because it seems obvious that, if the partnership is to mean anything, it must represent the expression of a common way of looking at the world that is possible only when each side is equally secure in its own status, equally proud of its own achievements and equally confident of its own abilities.

Thus a true partnership will not be achieved by dreaming up additional transatlantic institutions but by the creation of the conditions that lead to a mutuality of interests; and the interests of the United States and Europe around the world will converge only when Europe has organized itself on a scale large enough to permit it to think as a superpower and to face responsibilities of world scope. When and if that day comes, we shall not have to worry about the nature of Atlantic relations. A united Europe can be our mature good friend, giving us from time to time sound advice, bringing to world councils its own insights, agreeing or disagreeing as the case may be, but acting always from the same larger purposes that it shares with us, while — to borrow a favorite word of General de Gaulle's — expressing its own special "personality."

As we move slowly toward this kind of Western world, thus laying the basis for a stable European and German settlement, we can hope that history will be simultaneously moving to reduce the conflicts of interest and outlook between Communists and Westerners. It is not, I think, too fanciful to suppose that if we can keep the peace — and everything depends on that hypothesis — we may, before the end of this century, evolve to the point where those of us now separated by an Iron Curtain can regard each other very much as Protestants and Catholics now view one another four hundred years after the Reformation and its bloody doctrinal conflicts.

To bring about the settlement of Europe on this basis is, then, in everybody's interest. It challenges the genius of the West and expresses the reality of our common civilization. It is not divisive but cohesive, since the unity of Western Europe is not directed against the East; it is open-ended and tolerant of diversity; it seeks, at the end of a long road, the eventual voluntary accession of the Russians in a single community of powers. It provides not just a pragmatic solution to present-day divisions and dangers like the German problem, but rather an extension of the best traditions of civilized life as we have learned it since Greece was the school of Rome and Italy the tutor of modern Europe. These values — this Western frame of mind we share, at once questing and confident and tolerant and humane — will inevitably infect the maturing Eastern societies, and in the end we may perhaps all agree with the words of a distinguished student of modern nationalism, Hans Kohn, who has written:

> There is no validity to the chosen people idea inherited from the Hebrews nor to the Hegelian concept that in each age one leading nation represents the spirit of the age. History is too complex for any monistic or dualistic interpretation. The world is enriched by intellectual and cultural diversity. . . . Neither American world leadership, nor the concept of a bi-polarized world with America leading one camp, is in the long run desirable or possible; . . . (*American Nationalism*, p. 228)

An ultimate settlement of European troubles and East-West conflicts that is based on the deep strengths of civilized men is, to me, an exciting and a positive concept, a concept in accord with the modern realities of power that summons our best efforts. It offers an optimistic goal, since it postulates peace not as a sterile armed truce but rather as the beginning of a human adventure like that of the great Western Age of Discovery in the sixteenth century. It leads, in other words, to a renascence of the common civilization. This concept and this approach to ending the barriers of Europe may not be new or original. To some it may appear visionary, and to the young and impatient it probably looks old and outworn, because twenty years of Western policy have still not cut through the basic conflicts of East and West. My reply to such criticism would echo that of the eminent British historian of Eastern Europe, Hugh Seton-Watson, who writes in *From Lenin to Khrushchev* (pp. v–vi):

> It may be unoriginal to argue that the West can only "be patient and strong," handle its own social and national problems on their merits, watch for every opportunity of influencing the Communist regimes in the direction of freedom, deal fairly with the uncommitted nations, and keep an open mind. If there are ready-made "solutions" which are better than this, then I shall be happy, and so will the whole human race, to learn what they are. But if such panaceas do not exist, denunciations for unoriginality do not seem to be very helpful.

XIV

From Versailles to Vietnam

SOME years ago an aphoristic European remarked to me, "America is a nation with a sense of mission but no sense of history." My friend is a man who would rather be startling than profound, and I told him quite flatly that he had missed the point. We Americans, I said, did have a sense of history, but, I added — with perhaps more self-righteousness than the facts justified — we were not imprisoned by it as were many Europeans. I did not believe that the proof of a sense of history was a compulsion to repeat all the old mistakes. Over the years we had been conscious of our history and its larger meaning, and in my country, as elsewhere in the world, the past colored the present.

It was our sense of history that had led us until a quarter of a century ago to turn our backs on Europe. We had looked hard and long at the monotonous pattern of intrigue and maneuver in the annals of European diplomacy, a story punctuated by calamity on every page. The Founding Fathers had studied the pattern and had rejected it. And it was our sense of mission that had led to the universalism which has guided much of our policy in the postwar years.

These two phenomena are, of course, not unrelated. Mr. Walter Lippmann long ago pointed out that Wilsonian universalism was the expression of isolationism in different terms. The First World War had taught us that a great nation could not stand aloof when

293

there was conflict at the heart of world power, yet Woodrow Wilson still hoped to avoid what he regarded as the noxious business of balance of power politics. To make the world safe for democracy it was necessary, he concluded, not that we organize a new Concert of Europe on an Atlantic basis but that we create a League of Nations to settle international disputes under a system of principles expressing the essence of American democracy. As a Southerner brought up to revere the doctrines of secession and states' rights, Wilson naturally insisted that people were entitled to select their own sovereigns — even though his own version of self-determination meant a fragmented and unstable Europe. But American public opinion had not been prepared for such a venturesome initiative as the League of Nations, and Wilson handled the prima donnas in the Congress with arrogance and tactical ineptitude.

Yet it would be wrong to conclude that because Wilson's grand design was rejected by the United States Senate, universalism was inherently unacceptable to America. On the contrary — as later events made clear — it was a congenial policy for a people who had conquered a frontier. We had never been isolationist out of weakness or lack of courage; we had simply been preoccupied with taming a continent and we had disdained the futility of dynastic politics. Our sense of mission, translated in universalist terms, derived from the confidence that we were right. If the United States was as good as we thought it was, there was no reason why, with our help, the rest of the world should not be made over in our image.

Thus, it was a voluble isolationist, an undertaker turned statesman from Nebraska, Senator Kenneth Wherry, who told a cheering audience in 1940, "With God's help, we will lift Shanghai up and up, ever up, until it is just like Kansas City" (Goldman, *The Crucial Decade — and After,* p. 116).

In this more self-conscious age, the Senator's apocalyptic preview of the New Jerusalem may seem a little too simple-minded to be taken at face value. Yet the fact that he expressed it is worth pondering. Because of a protected geography that made possible more than two hundred years of relative insulation and peace, we are probably even more inclined than most other large modern nations to project our own narcissistic image on the outside world.

Long borders, wide spaces, and the absence of those periodic invasions that have always been a fact of life in Europe, have helped shape some of our national peculiarities and outlook. These things have also meant that, compared to the great powers of the past half-millennium, the United States came of age untutored in the discipline of living in fear next to powerful neighbors — and inexperienced also in the manipulation of alliances and the practices of power politics first invented by crowded Europeans in the fourteenth century for their own protection.

This innocence has not served us badly. It has given us a saving flexibility. If we Americans have learned a great deal from our own history, it is to our credit that over the years we have, unlike the Bourbons, forgotten some of it. In that sense Senator Wherry's patronizing idealism simply disclosed a cultural lag. He was expressing the exuberant egocentricity of a people, separated by geography from Europe and absorbed in their own affairs, who had, in consequence, become more than usually fascinated with, and thrown back upon, themselves to the exclusion of much foreign contact. It was quite natural for him to superimpose familiar Kansas City on exotic Shanghai to make it all comprehensible.

Vestiges of this feeling persist today. We still boast a lot, although not as much as we used to, for the twentieth century has abruptly altered the chemistry of our *amour-propre*. It has brought shocks and novel involvements to the American people. But even now shadows of the old pattern remain in dim corners of the mind of each of us. For the success of the American republic is in large part due to the fact that we had a chance to work out our own destiny without interference, and the rhetoric of our politics is shot through with a sense of uniqueness and mission, the notion of America as the anti-Europe.

It was thus from the beginning. John Winthrop saw the Plymouth Plantation as "the city set high on a hill," a shining example to the distant and depraved Old World that he had left behind. Jefferson and Tom Paine, Lincoln and McKinley shared very much the same faith. Woodrow Wilson elevated America's geographic and political uniqueness a perceptible notch higher, though he was only paraphrasing Jefferson. American principles, he declared, were "not the principles of a province or of a single continent. We have known and boasted all along that they were the principles of a liberated mankind" (Boorstin, *America and the Image of Europe*, p. 21). This national expression of faith and mission is so pervasive that it has been a common article of belief among recent political figures as diverse as Franklin Roosevelt and John Foster Dulles, Adlai Stevenson and Joe McCarthy.

Nowadays it is fashionable to call this faith "Wilsonianism," but the study of American history tells us it is just as accurate to start at the beginning and call it "John Winthropism" or "Roger Williamism." Although it is clear that a stern Protestant ethic has something to do with the contour of the American world view, I would suggest that factors of pure politics, terrain and demography have been at least as influential in defining our outlook. Physical isolation and a self-imposed identity as the fugitive outpost of European civilization amid a seemingly limitless and untamed natural environment overshadowed ecclesiastical doctrine.

To recall our youth and adolescence as a nation is to anticipate the confusion that even today surrounds us Americans when we try to puzzle out our role in the world. How does one reconcile a contrary history with a new requirement for what seems an almost total involvement in the whole world's business? We have been a superpower for hardly more than twenty years and there are always traumatic dangers in growing up too quickly. Yet, given the shock of abrupt maturity, I do not think we have done too badly since the war — whatever our mistakes — which does not at all excuse us for not doing better in the future. The beginning of wisdom is to realize that we are physically a great power but psychologically somewhere in transit — after twenty turbulent years — between an insistent traditional role that is not good enough for the present and an evolving new part in a drama that is not yet terribly clear. Does a successful diplomacy require that we forget the maxims of a rich national folklore and the advice of that handful of famous Americans who have been our most serious political thinkers? This is a vexing question, but by now I think the answer is evident to most of us.

Here again we can give thanks for flexibility which permits us to transcend the limits of our history, remembering that it is not enough to discard an irrelevant tradition of universalism; we must, at the same time, develop a substitute framework, a new way of looking at the world, which quite obviously is not easy. We know the broad outlines of what we want; it is the litany of every politician's speech on foreign policy — peace, freedom, justice and an increased standard of living for everybody, and so forth. But, self-confident as we may be, we cannot achieve those ends solely by our own efforts, and thus we are brought back to the same hard questions. How should we use our vast but finite power, and where? With whom should we work, and how? What is our national interest anyway?

Earlier in history, we would have found these questions easier to answer since the beginning and the end of policy were the protection and extension of empire. The defense of territory, as a new school of ethology now contends, is perhaps the most compelling of all human instincts and a policy defined by that objective seemed both obvious and right. Thus Americans in the mid-nineteenth century could be ardent advocates of "Manifest Destiny," our doctrinal justification for assuming control over Canada, Mexico, Central America and Cuba. The imperialism of the 1890's found its expression in Kipling's invention of "the white man's burden" — a phrase that appealed to many Americans as we extended our dominion over Hawaii, the Philippines and Puerto Rico. By the early 1900's blatant aggression had become unfashionable, but Teddy Roosevelt could still boast about "taking" Panama, while Taft intervened in Latin America to protect our investments, thus practicing what later became scornfully referred to as "dollar diplomacy." Even Wilson, for all his moralism, found it not too difficult to reconcile a Calvinist conscience with intervention in Mexico and the continued occupation of several Caribbean countries in the schoolmasterly cause of "preserving order." The captious pointed out that intervention of this sort was often hard to distinguish from territorial aggrandizement, but it remained for Franklin D. Roosevelt to repudiate these practices in the name of the Good Neighbor policy.

We live in an age of paradoxes. We are frank in matters of sex but euphemistic in our diplomacy — particularly in dealing with developing countries. Nations shy away from talking of territorial interests, and they almost invariably justify their exercise of power in remote places by a nobler terminology. Yet one can say without nostalgia that the frank admission of territorial interests was a convenience, since it gave a coherent definition to the employment of power; and it is part of the American predicament today that there is no such coherent definition. We face a problem of fitting our behavior on the world scene to a rather vague body of abstractions. It is a difficulty that nations in an earlier age did not have to face because men could still speak pridefully of empire (implying without blushing the exploitation of "lesser breeds without the law"). They could take it as a widely agreed assumption that the success of a sovereign was measured by the extension of territory cloaked with such widely differing slogans as the West's "civilizing mission" or, in our own case, "manifest destiny." They could proceed with good conscience on the operational principle that trade followed the flag and that any serious challenge to trade was a *casus belli*.

It was Wilsonian universalism with its heavy overlay of moralism that first decreed such formulations unsuitable for the international dialogue, and it was Franklin Roosevelt who completed the process by securing the codification of the universalist abstractions in the United Nations Charter.

No code of moral conduct can, however, be a very precise guide to action in a given set of circumstances; that is why mankind has developed the whole immense apparatus of churches and courts and legislatures to make and interpret the laws and the scriptures. But international relations lack such an apparatus and it is thus hardly surprising that for a considerable period our foreign relations have been shaped not so much by a policy as a process. We were pushed into a practical application of universalism by the withdrawal of Europe from world responsibility — a withdrawal that was precipitate and for the most part unsystematic. We first felt the forces propelling us in that direction when we came to the defense of Greece and Turkey because Great Britain could no longer afford to assure their security. Our intervention in those threatened lands might have begun and ended at that point had we not felt compelled to justify our action in terms of a universal principle. That principle, embodied in the Truman Doctrine, by declaring our intention to support resistance to aggression in quite open-ended terms, announced our self-appointment as the world's policeman.

Since then, we have extended our military force, our assistance and our influence into the remote areas of the world vacated by the colonial powers. No doubt it was sometimes correct — as Europeans have often charged — that our fine talk about self-determination fed the pressures that precipitated their disorderly flight back to the comforting haven of the metropole. Without admitting the allegation in full, however, I think it is certainly true that when such flights occurred we felt more than ever pressed to fill the resultant power vacuum. This was not so much a matter of conscience with us as the compulsions of the cold war, since the Truman Doctrine, while implicitly conceding that we would recognize the Iron Curtain as the outermost limit of Communist power, made it quite clear that we would act to prevent Communist encroachments beyond the periphery set by the presence of effective Soviet military force.

The theory of "containment," which in the months that followed evolved as a more sophisticated formulation of the Truman Doctrine, was constructed on the assumption that we would recognize the Soviet sphere of influence that had been marked out by the power of the Red Army, thus implying that, so far as we were concerned, Moscow could deal more or less as it wished with nations behind the Iron Curtain. This has been our practical guide to policy ever since, in spite of Mr. Dulles's panegyric to "liberation" in 1952. As a campaign slogan, that may have been sweet music to certain minority groups within the electorate, but it was a fraud and a fraud quite quickly exposed. America's failure to intervene when first the Poles and then the

Hungarians revolted in 1956 revealed to the world that we would not interfere when the Soviet Union used brutal force within its sphere of influence, Eastern Europe.

In standing down while the Hungarians called for help we were not betraying our principles, merely defining them in terms that took account of the realities. There should have been no great surprise at this, since the recognition and defense of spheres of influence have — in spite of our expostulations to the contrary — been an inarticulate premise of our foreign policy for a hundred years. We made it quite clear in the Monroe Doctrine that the world was to regard Latin America as our own sphere of influence, and our intervention in the Dominican Republic was only the most recent application of that policy.

It is one of the curious hypocrisies of our time that while political leaders around the world implicitly accept the operative consequences of spheres of influence, they denounce and deny the concept. Indeed they are quite prepared to censure nations that act within the four walls of the doctrine — particularly when the occasion for great power intervention reflects a confusion of legitimacy. Thus when we launched the abortive adventure of the Bay of Pigs it was against a Castro regime that had come to power by a revolution that had accumulated popular support against a manifestly corrupt government. In the Dominican Republic the revolt that precipitated our intervention was directed against a military junta that had usurped power from a constitutionally elected government. I do not suggest that our choices were easy. Both in Cuba and the Dominican Republic all options were unattractive. If we had employed American power to destroy Castro, we would have suffered the opprobrium of a second Hungary. Because we supported an abortive and inept effort to destroy Castro at the Bay of Pigs, we reaped the humiliation of a second Suez. It was only when we moved to eliminate the Cuban missiles which directly threatened our own security that our friends applauded.

Our problems have very frequently stemmed from a lack of consistency between a perception of the limits of power that has determined our action and a sonorous universalist dogma that has infected our elocution. We have been guilty, throughout the whole postwar period, of talking one way and acting another. We have used the vocabulary and syntax of Wilsonian universalism, while actively practicing the politics of alliances and spheres of influence and balance of power; and it is now time that we stopped confusing ourselves with our political hyperbole and frankly faced the hard realities of the postwar world. For while we have invented some new, high-flying abstractions — containment, liberation, halting of aggression, and so forth, — these terms only blur and distort the ultimate purpose of the United States, which is to try to build peace not only by protecting our own interests but by recognizing the interests and the power of other peoples.

What we have learned — or have known instinctively — is that international politics is both more and less than the art of the possible; it is the art of the practical. The reason why the Soviet Union recognizes South America as our sphere of influence just as we recognize East Europe as theirs has nothing to do with cultural affinities or common traditions — most Americans are culturally more at home with Czechs or Poles than *Latinos*; it is the fact that in each case the staking out of interests has been legitimatized by a preponderance of military power. Latin America is easily accessible to the United States and it would be folly for the Soviet Union to undertake any direct military action in that continent. Hungary, on the other hand, lay wide open to the Red Army and geography precluded us from giving effective support to the Hungarian revolutionary regime without initiating a war with the Soviets.

Where military preponderance is clear, recognition of spheres of influence is thus natural and easy. But beyond that the problem grows more complex. For just as Secretary Dulles recognized the Communist sphere of influence by his actions while denying it by his words, there is reason to think that he saw the whole non-Communist world as an American sphere of influence, which he sought to protect by a chain of alliances girdling the circumference of Communist power. The result was an enormous extension of our security commitments without an appreciable increment to our security, since, unlike NATO, the alliances formed with the Middle East and Asian nations could not, in realistic terms, secure the mobilization of much effective local force against Communist encroachments. With few exceptions, local military power was more token than real, quite inadequate to stop the Red Army without massive United States intervention.

To be fair to Mr. Dulles it should be noted that he was simply making explicit the implicit commitments we had given in defending South Korea against Communist invasion in 1950, since what we did there was to fight to maintain the containment of Communist power within the borders fixed by the factual situation as it had developed during the postwar period. Although ingeniously legitimatized by a United Nations umbrella, the most logical explanation of our action in Korea was the same we later seized on to justify our action in Vietnam: to prevent the extension of Communist power beyond the lines that had been fixed by events. To say this is not, however, to suggest that the two situations were by any means identical. We were not confronted in Korea by a befuddling ambiguity as to the nature and origins of the conflict; it was from the beginning a clear case of an external force on the move rather than an internal revolt reinforced from outside. But, laying aside the factual controversy, the basis for action was the same: the conviction that it would be dangerous to permit a breeching of pragmatically established lines since that might, either by itself or by triggering further action, disturb the power balance we had so precariously established.

Our cold war policy can thus be briefly summed up as (1) an insistence on the lines fixed by events prior to 1950 as defining the outer limits of Communist power; (2) the implicit recognition that the land area contained within those lines is a Communist sphere of influence with which we will not interfere even though the Communists submit the peoples within that sphere to brutal and repressive measures (e.g., East Germany in 1953, Hungary and Poland in 1956); (3) an insistence that the areas outside those lines are a non-Communist or free world sphere of influence which the United States (in company with whatever allies we can muster) will protect against Communist encroachment by force or subversion (e.g., Korea in 1950; the Formosan offshore islands in 1955; Lebanon and Jordan in 1958; the Dominican Republic in 1965).

While a policy of holding a line may to some seem unattractive and static, it is not without support from history, since great religious and military movements have shown a tendency to alter and disintegrate, once their expansion was effectively checked by a sufficiently powerful counterforce. Within twenty-four years after the defeat at Tours (A.D. 732), the Moslems of Spain broke away from the Caliph at Baghdad, and an internal power struggle developed that extended the process of fragmentation. Provincial governors asserted the primacy of local interests against the central authorities, and by 900 the Christians were once again on the offensive, driving their enemies from lands that had seemed lost forever. A similar fate overtook the Mongol Empire in the mid-thirteenth century. Defeated at Damascus and checked in Japan and Southeast Asia, it was effectively contained. Within a century the empire broke up into four hostile, but still aggressive, parts and, while the Russians, Syrians, Chinese and Southeast Asians suffered repeatedly from fresh assaults, stubborn defense wore down even the new power centers. By 1368 the Mongols were expelled from China, the Il-Khanate of Persia had collapsed, and the Russian Golden Horde was in decay. One can derive a principle from these examples: once a revolutionary movement is contained, forces of change and disintegration set in. Internal corruption and the competition between local interests and centralism may then complete the process.

Containment, as conceived in the late 1940's, was an intellectually respectable doctrine, and few who have attacked it have put forward anything very useful by way of substitute. Mr. Walter Lippmann is an exception. He opposed containment in Europe from the beginning, since he felt it was a mistake to align West Germany as a source of power for the Western side. In his approach to the use of American strength around the world, he has long advocated a frame of action based on his own concept of not two but several spheres of influence, founded in turn on his reading of geopolitics. The United States, he contends, is a fish and a bird but not an elephant. It can with its massive sea and air power extend American security protection to the Pacific islands and continents, such as Japan and Indonesia; but, as he sees it, the Asian mainland, including Northeast and Southeast Asia, are within a natural Chinese sphere of influence, and thus we should not attempt to maintain an American military presence in that area. The lesson drawn from his analysis is that we are fighting a costly but futile battle in Vietnam, because Chinese influence will, sooner or later, prevail, since the advantage is clearly on the Chinese side.

Mr. Lippmann feels deeply — and has argued persistently over the years — that we need a tighter, better definition of the American national interest, that our foreign policy since the war has too often consisted in *ad hoc* improvisations not related to a coherent scheme, and that the open-ended and reactive nature of the Truman Doctrine of "containment" is not wise. I substantially agree with the need for structure, although I would not suggest the kind of structure that Lippmann often favors. He regards European unity not as vital, but merely as desirable. He assesses the purpose of General de Gaulle in quite different fashion from the way I have done it in chapter VIII. He thinks it at least possible that the reemergence of several separate middle-sized European states each competing in the pattern of 1918–1939 would not be a danger to everyone's future. And, while he may not have written it explicitly, I believe that, for the rest of the world, he would favor recognition of a "sphere of influence" concept whereby the industrialized nations, including the Russians, would divide specific geographical responsibilities among themselves for the security and tutelage of a developing Southern Zone.

While I am certainly not in full accord with Mr. Lippmann, his central thesis should not be cavalierly dismissed. We do need better structures in the world if, in the end, men are to invent something more hopeful and less dangerously fragile than a nuclear balance of terror on the one hand or, on the other, a potential Hobbesian "war of all against all" in the Southern lands frustrated by poverty. But I believe Mr. Lippmann would agree with me that a classic model of spheres of influence tacitly arranged among the great powers is just not feasible in today's world. Even if some day Washington and Moscow are sufficiently relaxed in their relations to agree to divide the world between them — as Spain and Portugal ran a dividing line through the New World in 1494 — the result would not stick. It would be like attempting to restore the system of Metternich after the revolutions of 1848. The force of modern nationalism is such that no self-respecting nation wants to be openly and explicitly in anybody's sphere of influence. Wherever the lines were drawn, they would be unenforceable and even provocative of trouble.

Even so, had Mr. Lippmann's Far Eastern thesis been a part of United States policy seventeen or eighteen years ago it is possible that the small states of Northeast and Southeast Asia would have found their accommodation with China as they have done over the centuries. America might have avoided involvement in Korea and South Vietnam. What, under those circumstances, would have happened to Taiwan or Indonesia is anybody's guess. Presumably, under Mr. Lippmann's formula, we might have defended both of those areas as not forming an integral part of the Asian land mass, but the political effect of Communist advances into South Korea and Southeast Asia, particularly on the delicately balanced politics of Indonesia — which in terms of population is the sixth largest nation in the world — is hard to appraise, particularly after the fact.

All this, however, is not very useful speculation. Politics must always be directed at the situation as it exists and not at what might have been; and any explicit adoption of Mr. Lippmann's geopolitical theory at this point in time would, as I suspect he would agree, be quite impracticable. There is a school of history that contends that the North Korean march against the South on June 25, 1950, was encouraged by the comments of General MacArthur and a Press Club speech of Secretary Acheson drawing an American defense perimeter that left "the initial reliance" in case of aggression, as Secretary Acheson put it, "on the people attacked to resist it" and "upon the commitments of the entire civilized world under the Charter of the United Nations." Mr. Dulles later treated this as the horrible example of how foreign policy should not be conducted, advancing as his favorite thesis the need to make clear to the other side that we are unambiguously determined to defend whatever they might be prepared to attack. He saw it as the best part of wisdom to make America's determination explicit and notorious by giving wide and public security commitments, with the result that we tied our hands against evolving situations in a wide arc around the world.

These commitments, once made, impose some restraint on our freedom of action. No one has yet devised a graceful means by which a great nation can formally disengage from assurances it has given without undermining other assurances it would like to maintain, although in practice, as I shall point out, there is normally some wiggle room for interpretation. Thus, no matter how workable Mr. Lippmann's thesis might have been had we consistently applied it since the war, it is hard to see how we could now adopt it without substantial breakage. The lines enclosing Communist power were determined pragmatically by the play of force and counterforce, but now they have been sanctified by a whole series of security assurances of varying degrees of dignity. Certainly to announce that we were planning to remove our presence from the Asian mainland and to phase out our security assurances to the nations in Northeast and Southeast Asia would be demoralizing for them and an open invitation to the Chinese to extend their dominion. Thus it is difficult to see how — except cautiously and by unavowed action over a long period of time, we could revise our Pacific policy so as to recognize Chinese spheres of influence even if we thought it prudent to do so.

Nor would I favor such a policy even if we were fully free to adopt it. No one has made a persuasive case for conceding to Peking a suzerainty over the rich lands of Southeast Asia. Except for brief intervals in history China has never been able to assert effective control in Southeast Asia outside Tonkin and there are other Asian nations with large populations and racial, cultural and economic interests in the area which, as events evolve, could someday pose a counterweight.

This does not, of course, answer the question as to whether, and to what extent, we should have involved ourselves in the troubled morass of Vietnam. That question, it has always seemed to me, should have been answered in terms of a tactical judgment. One does not need to accept the thesis made publicly by Lippmann or suggested privately to me by General de Gaulle that the Asian Mainland is within the Chinese sphere of influence to conclude that we should gravely have limited our commitments in South Vietnam.

At least two other questions have seemed to me more pertinent. The first is: Did the Viet Cong efforts to take over South Vietnam presage the extension of Chinese suzerainty or were they primarily a drive to acquire the rich rice areas of the South on the part of a Tonkinese Communist regime that — chiefly by playing Moscow off against Peking — would maintain an uneasy independence of Red China? The second and most relevant was whether this was the best place to make a stand. One decision the United States must always face is where to base its defense — and this requires a calculation of terrain, both physical and political.

To be sure we have, over a long period of years, made many bombastic promises, but always implicitly conditioned by necessary action on the part of the South Vietnamese. More important perhaps, we were signatories to the Southeast Asia Collective Defense Treaty of September 8, 1954, which is the basis for SEATO. But that treaty was drafted by careful men, who, as professional diplomats, knew the malleability of abstractions, as a careful reading of the language makes quite clear.

The key provisions of that treaty are contained in paragraphs 1 and 2 of Article Four. Paragraph 2 is designed to deal with subversion. It provides that if "in the opinion of any of the Parties" the "territory or the sovereignty or political independence" of any of the states to which the guarantees of the treaty extend is "threatened in any way *other than by armed attack* or is affected or threatened by any fact or situation which might endanger the peace of the area" the "Parties shall consult immediately in order to agree on the measures which should be taken for the common defense." The meaning of this language is clear enough. On the finding that territory guaranteed by the treaty is threatened by subversion all that the Parties are required to do is to consult. No Party need take action unless it agrees on some action with its Treaty partners in the course of consultation.

Thus prior to the early months of 1964 the SEATO Treaty gave little comfort or guidance to United States policy. But from then on, as main force units of the North Vietnamese army began to appear in South Vietnam another provision of the treaty, paragraph 1 of Article Four, became the principal support for the American position. Under that paragraph "each Party recognizes that aggression by means of armed attack" against any of the protocol states (which includes South Vietnam), "would endanger its own peace and security, and agrees that it will in that event act to meet the common danger in accordance with its constitutional process."

Our government has determined under this paragraph that, first, North Vietnam has committed "aggression by means of armed attack" in sending troops into South Vietnam, which under the language of the treaty must necessarily be regarded as endangering "our own peace and safety." But having made that finding what are we required to do about it? Only to take such action as we see fit "to meet the common danger in accordance with [our] constitutional processes." What should that action be? The President has interpreted this provision as authorizing — indeed requiring — that we send troops to fight alongside the forces of South Vietnam, since it is apparent that the Vietnamese forces by themselves will not prevail and no substantial power will be forthcoming from any other quarter. He has also decided that in order to assist South Vietnam to defend itself we should bomb North Vietnam to slow down the aggression and, we hope, to persuade North Vietnam to stop it.

All this is entirely consistent with the language of the treaty and I know that the actions we are now taking were decided by the President only after the most searching and prayerful study of all the alternatives. But the point I am making is that, while his decisions were consistent with the treaty, they were not dictated by its language; they represented the exercise of a judgment that he was entitled, and indeed obligated, to make. Other men confronted by the same set of facts and the same treaty language might have come to different conclusions.

South Vietnam is a hard case, and hard cases, as every law student is taught, make bad law. Korea, on its facts, was not nearly such a hard case. Had we had the same treaty commitment toward South Korea when it was first in trouble as we had later toward South Vietnam, President Truman would have had an easier decision, since Korea, unlike Vietnam, presented a case of overt aggression unmistakable even to the sceptical eye. In the classic manner of invaders since the beginning of history the North Korean army launched an attack across a well-defined demarcation line. There was no talk of a "war of national liberation" or even of a fight against Western colonialism; in fact, the North Koreans made little attempt to justify their actions other than to fall back on the shoddiest of all pretenses that they were counterattacking to repel an attempt at invasion by the South Korean forces — a transparent fraud, as the Seven Nation Commission on Korea subsequently made clear.

By contrast, the Vietnamese affair did not begin in a classic manner, and, if "wars of national liberation" are indeed the pattern of the future, then we may never again see many classic wars. The phrase "war of national liberation" has an intentionally seductive sound. The Communist ideologues who invented it have provided the concept with a special vocabulary and surrounded it with an elaborate doctrinal mystique. When the Communists capture a nationalist movement, they steal the terminology, investing the war that follows with a latent ambiguity which the Communists exploit. Once this process has taken place, the war is no longer easy to describe or classify. It reflects a confusion of motives and purposes, because it is neither one thing nor the other — neither purely an indigenous revolt nor an external aggression. This enormously complicates problems of decision and action for Western nations.

In the case of Vietnam the situation was particularly complex and confused, although many of us have forgotten its origins. Unlike the invasion of South Korea, the war in Vietnam is merely another chapter of a fight that began more than two decades ago as a nationalist struggle against a colonial power, and North Vietnamese propaganda has counted heavily on persuading the world that Viet Cong aspirations are primarily nationalist. That this proposition has gained some credence in Asia and Western Europe, and even in the United States, is not surprising in view of the fact that the North Vietnamese leaders are largely the same men who led the Vietminh in their long fight against the French.

The difference in the origins of the two struggles is one point of differentiation between the problems of Korea and Vietnam. Another distinction relates to the strategic significance of the areas. The defense of Korea was intimately connected with the defense of Japan, as Douglas MacArthur graphically pointed out when he said that it was a pistol pointed at Japan. But our justification for fighting in Vietnam must rest on more debatable considerations: the difficulty of defending Thailand and Laos if the Communists overran South Vietnam, and the effect on Indonesia, which was the real prize. Yet we never actually made the decision to send armed forces into the area in those terms.

After the North Vietnamese had exhausted their reservoir of native South Vietnamese, and organized units of the North Vietnamese were infiltrated to regroup in the South, the legal problems became less ambiguous, especially since paragraph 1 of Article Four of the SEATO Treaty was now clearly applicable, but by then the United States had already been involved for years in assisting the South Vietnamese; we had committed our prestige and taken casualties; we were already far down the road.

Many questions, therefore, that might have been debated quite usefully four years ago — and which some are still sterilely chewing over — are now academic. Speculation as to how strongly nationalism — or indeed idealism—may have inspired many of the Viet Cong leaders when the present systematic infiltration began five or six years ago will be a subject for intensive academic research and discussion in the years to come. But today I do not find it particularly relevant to decisions that we must now make as a nation and a people.

Whatever the situation half a decade ago, there seems little doubt that the leadership of the fighting forces has for some time been in the hands of men who take their orders from leaders in Hanoi, and any clear victory by the Viet Cong would clearly mean that the people of South Vietnam would be under the control of the Communist regime in the North. Thus, no matter what may have been the situation at an earlier time, the conflict in which we are engaged today is clearly a fight against the efforts of the North to extend its dominion. It is a struggle, moreover, in which our country has now deeply committed its prestige and in which many of our sons and brothers have been killed and wounded. These are facts that wishful thinking cannot erase nor lamentation alter, and I think it is a test of good sense whether an individual proceeds from here or retreats into fantasy.

We Americans regard ourselves as practical people. We try to deal with the hard world as we find it. Yet I do not always detect that spirit in the public discussion with regard to Vietnam. Many things said by otherwise sensible men and women reflect a refusal to look reality in the face. There is nothing practical to be achieved by bewailing the war, since it is a fact, and there are relatively few Americans who would favor our abrupt withdrawal at this late hour in the day. Yet I find, among the great body of the disenchanted, few who seem to understand the problems that we face as a nation. There is much complaint about the inhumanity of the war, but that is scarcely a new idea. Wars are by definition inhumane; they involve killing people — a kind of legalized murder — and they have from the beginning of time.

But we will not eliminate inhumanity by incantation. Someone once observed that one cannot stop earthquakes by passing resolutions against volcanoes, and we will not bring the war to a halt by carrying placards or burning draft cards. I am not suggesting that these exhibitions of mass hysteria be stopped by the police, since I revere anyone's constitutional right to make an ass of himself if he chooses to do so. But the relevant question is whether it serves any purpose. Certainly some may get a moralistic satisfaction out of the exercise, but that is a personal matter and has little bearing on the larger issue, for there is only one sensible way to stop the war and that is to create the conditions in which there can be a political solution that both sides can accept by a reasonable accommodation of their interests.

The problem that we face in seeking such an accommodation is complicated by two factors.

First, both we and the North Vietnamese have formulated our war aims in a manner that makes any compromise solution extremely difficult to design.

Second, in creating the necessary fictions to support our high purposes, we have given hostages to the South Vietnamese government that seriously restrict our freedom of action.

The beginning of comprehension of the problem, it seems to me, is to recognize that there is no possible peaceful solution to the war consistent with the stated objectives of the United States that Hanoi could regard as anything but a demand for its capitulation. Each side has painted itself into a very narrow corner. Since that day more than two decades ago when Ho Chi Minh first launched his struggle for freedom from a brutal French colonial policy, the Communists have invested so much blood and resources, human energy and fanaticism, that they could not now withdraw north of the demarcation zone, leaving the Americans in place, without conceding a disastrous defeat in a thirty years' war. At the same time, at this late hour in the day, we could not simply pull our forces out of South Vietnam without a damaging loss of respect and authority around the world.

Unfortunately, familiar mechanisms for compromise, such as the sharing of territory or power, are not available nor is it even easy to establish a cease-fire. General de Gaulle once told me that if we would only agree to a very big peace conference, including all of the interested Asian as well as European powers, the struggle between the Viet Cong and the South Vietnamese could be submerged in the larger consideration of a long-term Southeast Asian settlement. Once the conference was called, the General suggested, Ho Chi Minh "would not fire another shot."

While I could at the time (1964) see merit to a peace conference larger than even the Geneva Conference of 1954, I felt it necessary to point out that, under prevailing conditions, a cease-fire hardly appeared feasible. Some parts of South Vietnam were clearly in the hands of the Saigon government and the United States; other sections were under the control of the Viet Cong and Hanoi; by far the largest part of Vietnam was in dispute. If the Viet Cong were in control of a particular area during the night and the South Vietnamese in control during the daytime, how could one enforce a cease-fire? Would the South Vietnamese government be permitted to establish its authority over the area while the Viet Cong stood quietly by, in which case the position of the South Vietnamese government would be immeasurably strengthened? Or would the Viet Cong be permitted to move at will perfecting their political infrastructure and subverting the local population while the government elements played a purely passive role? In situations dominated by a continuing struggle for control of the local population a cease-fire seemed unrealistic, as I tried to explain to General de Gaulle.

It is the ambiguous nature of the South Vietnamese struggle — half war, half revolution — that precludes easy resort to old formulae. A settlement by further partition, for example, seems manifestly impracticable, since there is no clear territorial demarcation line. The map of South Vietnam is pockmarked; elements of the Viet Cong control this sector, elements of the South Vietnamese government control that. To try to divide territory would entail massive shifts of an unwilling population. Transfers on a large scale have been undertaken in the past not only in Vietnam in 1954 but in Greece and Turkey in 1923. But never in a situation so complicated as this. And I do not see the United States willingly sponsoring a further partition.

Nor are we likely to look with favor on any settlement based on the establishment of a coalition government by agreement. We have been burned too often. One can argue that, all things being equal, it should do no harm to give certain unimportant ministries to the Viet Cong. But in political terms all things are not equal. The disciplined and tightly-knit Communist element would so quickly undermine and dominate the politically naïve representatives of the present soggy regime in Saigon as to assure a quick and painful Communist takeover.

Another possibility is that, as the political situation evolves in Hanoi, the struggle might be moved from the battlefield to the political arena. This would require a general amnesty — extending substantially beyond the "open arms" policy now in operation — together with the expressed willingness of the Saigon government to recognize the Viet Cong as an accepted element in South Vietnamese political life.

To bring this about, however, would involve a radical change of heart and mind on both sides. Prior to the September elections such a drastic alteration of attitude was clearly not to be expected from the military clique in control of the governmental machinery in Saigon. Now that elections have been held, it is possible that the situation may gradually change. Nevertheless, there is no reason to believe that the Viet Cong would trust any Saigon government sufficiently to risk their destinies on a political process which they could not control.

Disturbed at finding the United States trapped in a situation with no visible exit, many Americans in and out of Congress have asked wistfully that the problem "be turned over to the United Nations." I can understand the political appeal of the demand but it has little practical meaning.

Those who advocate such a course apparently assume that, by a concentrated effort, the United Nations could somehow find a solution to the problem; or that, even though no solution were found, we should by this device at least share our responsibilities with the rest of the world. But such a pious hope rests on a misconception of the United Nations' operational capabilities. As an institution the United Nations cannot solve problems; the most it can do is to provide a meeting place in which the contending nations may be able to reach a solution — provided that whenever the conflict has cold war implications the solution be one both the superpowers are prepared to accept and encourage. In the case of Vietnam there is clearly no solution yet in sight that the superpowers could possibly accept. Certainly all our efforts to enlist Soviet support in a settlement have so far proved abortive.

Nor can we shed any of our own responsibilities by trying to transfer them to the United Nations. The other members of that body are both unprepared and unable to mount a serious effort at settlement, since they do not have the strength to wring unwilling concessions from either of the two superpowers. And there is a final complication: since neither Red China nor North Vietnam has been permitted membership in the United Nations, both are disdainful of its writ.

To be sure, the United Nations may at some point have a Vietnamese role to play but it will be of a different kind. Among its competencies are its ability to police agreements already achieved and to interpose a neutral force between parties who find it impossible to agree. When, therefore, a Vietnamese settlement is some day found, it will be timely to consider its possible enforcement by United Nations' machinery. Meanwhile conventional United Nations peace-keeping through the interposition of a neutral force does not seem feasible under circumstances where the forces of the contending parties are so physically intermixed as they are in South Vietnam.

The point Americans are reluctant to accept is that there is no quick and easy solution to the predicament in which we find ourselves, since doors that were once open are now closed. In fact it comes as a shock to anyone who looks at the problem carefully to discover how few options remain. There are many reasons for this of which not the least is the factitious nature of our relations with the Saigon government which are of our own making. Given the preponderance of our power and resources, and the lack of any national experience on the part of the South Vietnamese, it is obvious that any government that comes to power in Saigon — even a government selected by an improvised political process — can hold power only by our sufferance and lavish support. Yet, in a sense, we are the victim of our own fictions. We have managed over several years to prop up a series of shaky political edifices by money and rhetoric, and by pretending they were something they were not, knowing that it would deny the central assumptions of our position to treat any South Vietnamese government as a puppet. We have justified our involvement in South Vietnam on the ground that we are seeking to help the South Vietnamese people maintain their freedom from outside aggression under a government of their choosing responsive to their will and not ours. By a great deal of effort we encouraged the Vietnamese to undertake a political exercise in September which for the first time gives color of legitimacy to a Saigon government. This is an important achievement yet it does not go to the heart of the problem. Our dilemma remains what it has long been: *in order to put the Saigon regime forward as a free government and thus justify our continued intervention, we must show constant sensitivity to the views of a group of South Vietnamese leaders whose objectives — at least up to the present time — have not been fully congruent with our own.*

In a less complex and frustrating world, we might hope that, at some point, the regimes in Saigon and Hanoi would find it in their own self-interest to work out a deal in traditional Oriental fashion that would preserve the requisite face and self-interest. As an integral part of any deal each side could assert its independence of its foreign supporters; the South Vietnamese could demonstrate that they are not dependent on us by asking us to leave; the North Vietnamese could flaunt their freedom from servitude to the major Communist powers.

But I do not put high odds on this occurring very soon. The government now installed in Vietnam is still a military regime and thus presumably retains a vested interest in the war and the United States involvement. To rather simple-minded Westerners like ourselves it is not clear how any of the principal South Vietnamese personalities would fare in an atmosphere of peace with American power withdrawn. The Ky Government certainly went farther than we in promising the complete destruction of the Viet Cong and clearly General Ky could hardly be expected to have initiated any conversations on his own. But the mix of elements in the Thieu Government could lead to different results; it is too early to say.

Meanwhile the issue has been confused and confounded by a tangential argument. The naïve — or sometimes perhaps the disingenuous — pretend that the war could be ended by our undertaking to negotiate with the National Liberation Front (the political arm of the Viet Cong) on the apparent assumption that the choice of negotiating partners is merely a procedural matter. Even a first-year law student should know, however, that the issue involved is not merely one of procedure but goes to the theory of the case and is thus a substantive matter of consequence.

It requires no exceptional shrewdness for the North Vietnamese to perceive that once the United States were to acknowledge the Front as representing a significant element of the South Vietnamese population in revolt against the Saigon government, we would have compromised the juridical basis for our intervention: that we are helping the Saigon government resist an *external* aggression and not suppress an *internal* revolt.

The argument over Front representation is not, however, very relevant to the declared positions of the principal parties in interest. The contention of both the Front and the Hanoi Government is not that the Front should be among the parties at a conference but that it must be recognized as the *sole* bargaining agent for the South Vietnamese people since the Saigon government is merely an American puppet representing no one. On the other side the Saigon government has insisted that the Front be ignored as a mere creature of Hanoi.

In view of these contentions, Front representation is not a critical issue in the present state of the play — nor do I think it is likely to become one.

Our government has made repeatedly clear that — to the extent the Front might have any validity apart from its role as an instrument of the Saigon government and the Lao Dong (the North Vietnamese Communist party) — arrangements could be made, *in the course of the negotiations,* for its interests to be represented in some appropriate manner. This should be enough to meet the procedural necessities while finessing the substantive argument. One can only conclude, therefore, that the issue of Front representation is peripheral and a distraction; for the time being at least it is not worth squabbling about. Much more important to negotiations is the manner in which we are conducting the war and, specifically, our air offensive against North Vietnam.

Here we must examine the reactions of the two great Communist power centers.

Peking has necessarily regarded our bombing offensive as a potential threat to its own territory. In the eyes of the Red Chinese we remain public enemy number one, in spite of their deepening quarrel with the Soviet Union. America, after all, is the one nation that has faithfully supported Chiang Kai-shek during the long years he has proclaimed his intention to undo Mao Tse-tung and all his works. (Once in a mood of political hyperbole we even "unleashed" the Generalissimo.) Even more important, we are the most powerful nation on earth — and a Western nation to boot — and that is reason enough for the Chinese Communists to hate us.

But in addition to Peking's special antipathy to the United States there is the fact that our bombing offensive has endangered the life of a buffer state. Since the need for buffer states reflects conditioned xenophobic reflexes that have existed ever since the time of the Middle Kingdom, the possible destruction of North Vietnam must appear as a threat to China. Seeing it in the light of their own propaganda as to the inevitability of an American purpose to destroy them the Communist leaders now find in the bombing confirmatory evidence that the process may be under way.

This reaction is peculiar to China but the Soviet Union also is troubled by our bombing, because, in a climate of intense competition between the two great Communist powers for the control of the Communist party structure around the world, neither Moscow nor Peking can afford to appear less diligent than the other in helping a beleaguered Communist state.

What this all adds up to is that our bombing offensive cannot be considered solely in terms of its military utility; it adds a dangerous and confusing political element that did not exist before the bombing began. So long as the conflict remained a war of attrition confined to the South, it threatened the interests of the major Communist powers to only a limited extent. It was, as they saw it, an attempt by "American imperialists" to interfere in a civil war, a "war of national liberation" taking place in an area that had never been under Communist control. Doctrine dictated that the major Communist powers should assist the insurgents with materiel, but not that they must underwrite the success of the insurgency. In the postwar world some Communist insurgencies have succeeded; others have been frustrated — often with some help from the United States. A failure could be passed off by Moscow and Peking as merely a tactical setback.

But once we launched a bombing offensive at North Vietnam,

we started a new war, or at least greatly altered not only the ground rules but the strategic significance of the old one. We rewrote the issues between the Communist powers and ourselves. For the great Communist powers necessarily regarded the bombing as an attack by their natural antagonist, the leading "imperialist power," on a fellow Socialist Republic, which created quite a new set of pressures and problems.

The result has been to frustrate any Soviet temptation toward peacemaking. While Moscow is no doubt torn by conflicting pressures, the Kremlin would, I suspect, on balance like to see an end of the Southeast Asian struggle. But every time there has been even a suspicion of a Soviet initiative to facilitate a settlement, Peking has immediately berated the Kremlin for helping the capitalist imperialists extricate themselves from a quagmire.

And, of course, the bombing changes the issues for Hanoi. In the absence of our bombing attacks, it should not prove impossible for the North Vietnamese regime to find a face-saving formula that could permit it to withdraw its forces and support from the Viet Cong struggle in the South. But for it to offer an olive branch while under direct attack from the United States could hardly be explained as a victory by even the most outrageous Communist dialectic.

Like so many other major decisions that mark the evolution of our present Vietnamese predicament, the United States undertook the bombing offensive more for want of alternatives than for any other reason. The fact that existing measures were not succeeding seemed a sufficient justification for almost any expedient that had not already been tried. When our bombing offensive first began in February 1965, the fortunes and morale of the South Vietnamese were at a lamentably low ebb. The coup that resulted in the assassination of President Diem had been followed by a squalid succession of military cabals; the fighting was going badly and there was a desperate feeling both in Saigon and Washington that something had to be done to raise South Vietnamese morale and change the direction of the battle.

The initial decision to drop bombs was justified as retaliation — "giving tit for tat"; it was intended, in other words, as an American *riposte* to North Vietnamese terror attacks. But it is part of the crude dynamics of war that bombing offensives acquire a life of their own. Once having launched the first attack, there is compelling pressure to continue — and to escalate.

It is characteristic of bombing offensives also that they rarely reflect a single and coherent philosophy. During the Second World War, the head of the British Bomber Command, Air Marshal "Bomber" Harris, stoutly contended that the objective of the air assault on Germany should be to kill Germans — a strategy largely dictated by the limitations of his own weapons. Since Britain did not have long-range fighters necessary to escort bombers on deep penetrations in the daytime, his Wellingtons and Stirlings were restricted to night attacks; and cities were the only targets large enough to make night attacks profitable.

The United States Air Force, on the other hand, was equipped with effective escorts and better armored planes, and hence could afford a greater humanity — concentrating its efforts on so-called "precision" attacks against carefully selected systems of economic targets.

As usual the result was a compromise. Our coordinated forces bombed ball-bearing and air-frame factories and synthetic oil installations but we also mounted saturation attacks on Hamburg and Munich and Frankfurt and any number of other large cities, which caused thousands of civilian casualties.

So far in North Vietnam we have been much more selective and a searching and careful effort has been made to minimize the damage to civilians. Nonetheless we have designed our air offensive to serve more than one objective and this has necessarily resulted in a steady escalation.

Apart from raising the morale of the South Vietnamese, and of American forces in South Vietnam, support for the bombing was rested on the contentions, *first*, that it was needed to discourage the flow of supplies from the North and, *second* (and this was a dogma of which General Maxwell Taylor was the high priest), by gradually moving toward progressively more sensitive targets it was hoped that we could press the North Vietnamese toward a political decision to quit.

Quite obviously, a program designed to achieve one of these objectives was not necessarily the best type to achieve the other.

Harassment of the flow of supplies did not require the movement of the bombing line toward the North. It could be at least as well accomplished by concentrated attack on the infiltration routes in Laos and the southern sector of North Vietnam. Yet it was perfectly clear when the bombing started that it would inevitably be escalated. Each more daring penetration of North Vietnam would be regarded as in the nature of a probe and, if it produced no disastrous response, the temptation would be irresistible to move the bombing line progressively farther north, gradually shifting from military to economic targets.

In my view, it was a mistake to start the bombing, although I understood very well the considerations that prompted the decision to begin — and all the issues were exposed to the full benefits of an adversary process. The bombing has, as I see it, seriously impaired the moral authority of the United States, increased our alienation from the other free nations, exacerbated internal strains and fissures, and greatly increased the dangers of intervention by the big Communist powers.

At the same time, I doubt that it has had much effect on the war in the South. It has not critically reduced the availability of supplies, since the logistic requirements of a guerrilla army, fighting a small-arms war and largely living off the country, are almost absurdly low in the terms to which we are accustomed. Before the time of main force engagements, the requirements of the Viet Cong forces in the South were estimated, as I recall, at not much more than eight to sixteen tons a day and Secretary McNamara has testified that even now, with many battalions of North Vietnamese regular forces in the South, the quantity of "externally supplied material, other than food, required to support the Viet Cong and North Vietnamese forces in South Vietnam at about their present level of combat activity, is significantly under 100 tons per day. . . ." One coolie pushing one bicycle can transport four or five hundred pounds down a jungle trail, as the French found out in fighting the Vietminh, and the only commodity not in short supply in Southeast Asia is coolies.

In the kind of terrain where trails and even roads are concealed by the rain forest the airplane is a crude and ineffective instrument for interdiction. It is using a hammer to kill a mosquito.

Americans are conditioned to think of the supply problems of armies in very large magnitudes and therefore have trouble understanding the point, but it does tend to illustrate a principle that is becoming every day more apparent: *the sophisticated lethal instruments which are the products of advanced technology are of only marginal use in a war against primitive peoples, and if the terrain is suitable for guerrilla warfare the advantages of advanced technology are even more limited.*

This fact also has relevance to another objective of our air offensive — to force the North Vietnamese to the bargaining table by a gradual intensification of bombing with an implied threat of its extension to progressively more vital economic targets. Here again we must deal with facts foreign to our own experience. North Vietnam is an agrarian subsistence economy with a rudimentary industrial overlay. It is also a police state that has been obsessively pursuing a single objective for more than two decades. Its people have been taught a consuming hatred of the West and particularly of the United States which has from the beginning been working to thwart its objectives, and it has the support of the major Communist powers. Under these circumstances continued bombing is not likely to break the people's will in any way that can be translated into a political decision favorable to us; it is more likely to push them toward a harder position.

The principal vice of escalation is not, however, that it is ineffective but that it exposes us and the world to immeasurably grave risks of inciting direct Chinese intervention. There is a threshold which, if overpassed, can trigger a Chinese reaction. We do not know precisely what it is; we did not know in Korea until it was too late.

We do know that China is almost pathologically sensitive to Western powers on its borders and we should not necessarily assume — as many of us appear to be doing — that the civil uproar now under way in China will definitely preclude a Chinese action against our forces in Vietnam no matter what we do. Just because the dragon is sick does not mean that we can safely goad it by laying bombs on its doorstep or by destroying the economy of an ideologically affiliated buffer state. There is at least a possibility that the launching of an attack against the United States

— which is the focus of so much hatred — could be the one action capable of uniting a badly fragmented China.

But if bombing the North is not useful, if it impedes negotiations and involves high political costs and risks, why do we go on with it? Unfortunately there is a great difference between a decision not to begin bombing and a decision to stop it. The problem that faces us now relates to the consequences of halting a military operation that we have been conducting for more than two and a half years. To stop our bombing offensive implies a drastic alteration of strategy, and unless we are prepared to confess error or failure (which I would not recommend) we cannot revise our strategy without good reason.

In theory at least that reason might be found in changed conditions. As I have pointed out, we began to bomb the North because our military actions in the South did not promise to achieve our objective. But now we are doing better. Since February 1965 when we first attacked North Vietnam our deployments in the South have been multiplied by more than twenty times; we have committed our forces to active combat; and the military scorecard is highly favorable to our side. One could argue, therefore, that the air offensive had usefully served a temporary purpose and that now we should be concentrating in the South where the issue must ultimately be decided.

This argument has the merit of verisimilitude, and, since most of our friends around the world would like nothing better than for us to stop the bombing, we would lose little face with them. To be sure the Communists would claim that they had forced us to desist and that our action reflected the triumph of the American anti-war faction presaging a failure of the American will to continue the war. But that propaganda would have little permanent effect, for most of the world would applaud our decision. In their eyes we would be turning away from activities that make us seem a bully.

The fundamental problem of standing down the bombers would thus not be the effect of the decision on world opinion or American prestige; it would be the consequences on the home front. Here I would foresee great difficulties, for given the current unease of the American people with regard to the war, how would they react to a decision to stop bombing when the other side was making no equivalent concessions?

After all, we have for a long time been spending fifty billion dollars or more a year for a defense establishment and much of it for an arsenal of highly sophisticated weapons. Why then do we seem incapable of imposing our will through military means on a backward nation of only nineteen million people? The most plausible explanation is that we have been arbitrarily hobbling ourselves, but if that is the case, why should we hobble ourselves further?

These are hard questions to answer. They bring Americans face to face with the unpalatable fact that American power buttressed by American technology is of limited use in a primitive war fought in jungles and rice paddies, which, in turn, raises the central and awkward question: what are we doing in those jungles and rice paddies — and are they worth saving anyway?

Questions such as these do not create a climate in which a decision to stop bombing would be sympathetically considered. But a determined political leadership might still win public support for the decision if our military establishment did not firmly believe and loudly contend that halting the bombing would endanger the lives of our forces in South Vietnam.

Such a contention is, I think, founded on fallacy. In view of the exiguous logistic requirements of the Viet Cong and North Vietnamese, I do not believe for a minute that bombing the North will have a critical effect on their ability to sustain the war — or to kill our soldiers in the South. But the orthodox military opinion is almost unanimously to the contrary, and if we were to stop the bombing without some tangible and visible *quid pro quo* from the other side, that opinion would be angrily asserted not merely by our military leaders but in letters home from our own soldiers.

On a question posed in this way one does not need a Gallup Poll to predict the public reaction. The majority of the American people would not buy any part of it. They would believe the generals, not laymen such as myself. And they would be even more disgruntled than they are today.

That, as I see it, is the heart of the issue. It is not just a question of Presidential leadership, for I am convinced that President

Johnson would take whatever decision he thought right regardless of its effect on his own popularity. The danger is that we would destroy the residue of popular support for an already unpopular war. And that would be fatal in a democracy.

But if we must go on with the bombing there is more reason than ever to be cautious in picking target systems. Continued bombing of MIG bases could, in my judgment, create difficult problems of decision, since if successful it would almost certainly lead to the basing of the MIGs in South China, which in turn would build up heavy domestic pressure for an attack on Chinese airfields. Similarly, any effort to mine Haiphong harbor or otherwise to interrupt the entry of Soviet ships would, it seems to me, pose a direct challenge to Moscow while cutting across our own political interests. If effective it would compel the Soviet Union to turn their ships around as they did in the face of our Cuban quarantine; but would they do so without feeling the need to respond in some manner? A highly perceptive student of Soviet affairs remarked to me some time ago that, while the present government by committee in the Kremlin would probably not have made the audacious decision to put the missiles in Cuba, as the headstrong Mr. Khrushchev did, it almost certainly could not have made the decision to take them out. And a second retreat so similar in appearance would be more humiliating than the first.

Moreover, would it make political sense to interrupt Soviet sea transport and thus force the Soviet government to come to terms with Peking in order to move goods and supplies through Chinese air space or across Chinese soil? Almost certainly the severance of the umbilical tie between Hanoi and Moscow in this manner would push the Hanoi regime into an even greater dependence on Peking, which — perhaps unlike the Soviet Union — clearly desires a protracted war.

Finally, proposals for a land invasion of North Vietnam, which is no doubt militarily feasible, would, I believe, be an almost certain way of compelling a substantial Chinese response. Our bombing of North Vietnam has already created unease in China, and, based on the hard evidence of history, a land invasion of that buffer state would almost certainly compel Peking to react violently. Direct warfare with the Chinese is not to be undertaken

326 THE DISCIPLINE OF POWER

lightly. We would run grave risks of bringing about the very world war we have tried so hard to avoid, since it is unlikely, I think, that the Soviet Union could resist some form of reaction. For the past seventeen years there has been a Mutual Security Pact between China and the Soviet Union, and, in spite of the schismatic argument, there would be strong pressures within the Communist world system for the Soviet Union to intervene in some manner against the "imperialists" who were at war with a fellow socialist state.

War with China would inevitably lead to a divisive domestic argument. Many Americans would contend that we should not try to fight the vast hordes of China without employing nuclear weapons, yet nothing could be more disastrous. For us to use atomic weapons for the second time in history against Orientals would intensify racial resentment, while at the same time assuring a dangerous Soviet response; because, no matter how noisy the internecine quarrel between the two Communist powers, there is no basis for believing that the Soviet Union could sit by and let us destroy China in nuclear combat. Von Clausewitz made it a great point of emphasis that, in fighting a war, no nation should lose sight of its objective. Our objective in Vietnam is limited and precise: to secure South Vietnam against aggression and help the Vietnamese build a viable society. It is our responsibility to secure this limited objective by limited means, for it is not worth a Third World War.

But so much for the bombing. If we cannot settle the war by an offensive against the North, how can we ever get out of an intolerable predicament? We are like Brer Fox with the Tar Baby.

Some serious critics of current policy, disturbed by our deepening commitment and the dangers of intervention by the great Communist powers, have proposed that the United States fall back into a passive role, seeking to hold only those areas that are now clearly under the control of our forces and those of the South Vietnamese government and stopping "search and destroy" operations designed to destroy enemy forces and at the same time weaken their grip on sparsely populated areas they have long controlled.

On the surface such a proposal offers attractive possibilities.

Its deficiencies, however, are considerable. In the first place it would almost certainly mean giving up areas not accessible from the water. I cannot conceive that, over any extended period of time, we would, in carrying out a policy of "active defense," try to hold inland positions vulnerable to a concerted Viet Cong attack as the enemy established unchallenged control over the rest of the country. To be sure, our resources of air power are of a wholly different order from those available to the French at the time of Dien Bien Phu, but it would certainly seem dubious wisdom to try to hold enclaves deep in Viet Cong country. Yet to abandon the inland areas we now hold would require us either to carry out a mass transfer of population or leave to the untender mercies of the Viet Cong large numbers of South Vietnamese who have helped our side.

This, however, is only part of the problem. Once we concentrated our forces in beachheads on or near the sea, we would be in a state of permanent siege. Not only would we have to feed the population through imports, since we would be largely cut off from the rich rice-growing areas of the country, but we would be compelled to cope with the psychology of a people who lived without hope of reclaiming their country. Under such circumstances we could expect little help from the South Vietnamese armed forces and, as time went by, our large American garrisons would appear more and more like an occupying army until, with the passage of years, our continued presence began to recall the hated "treaty port" system in China, which to Asian eyes represented a colonialist abomination. Yet how could we help appearing in such a role when we had visibly abandoned our original justification for intervening in South Vietnam — to help the South Vietnamese resist aggression and to restore their country for independent government?

The policy would, I think, give us trouble not only abroad but at home. To maintain a large military establishment in the passive posture of "active defense" would be hard for Americans to take even if our boys were well and happy. But without question they would be subjected to a continuing campaign of terror. Experience so far has shown that it is impossible to protect even heavily guarded airfields from mortar attacks or to prevent the exploding of claymore mines in the center of Saigon. Thus, in spite of our defensive policy our forces would still suffer a certain attrition, without the macabre but compensatory satisfaction that we were killing more enemy soldiers than they were killing of ours.

Although I find considerable force in all these objections, I would still not rule out the proposal for a policy of "active defense" if I were satisfied that its central assumption was sound, that such a policy would over time lead to a negotiated solution. But I do not think it would. I see no reason why the Viet Cong and the North Vietnamese would have any inducement to negotiate. With control of the largest and richest land areas of South Vietnam and uninterrupted access to road and water transit they could clamp their administrative grip tightly over the countryside — building a Communist state at their leisure. Why then should they make any compromises with the Americans? A much more likely reaction would be for them to sit and wait, consolidating their position and enjoying the bounty of a rich land.

The best justification for our settling down in an entrenched position in South Vietnam is that it might enable us to maintain air and even nuclear rocket installations that could prove a deterrent to any overt Chinese move into Southeast Asia. In that way, we could provide reassurance to Indonesia, Thailand, Japan, the Philippines and other areas that might feel jeopardized by the developing Chinese nuclear capability. This is, however, quite a different strategic purpose from that which led us to come initially to the defense of South Vietnam, and the world would recognize it as such.

I am fully aware that it is easy to find fault with any proposal for a revised course of action in South Vietnam, and, in raising questions as to the feasibility of a posture of "active defense" (the new terminology for the "enclave" policy), I do not mean to be captious. I would like nothing better than to persuade myself that such a policy would work, but I cannot in good conscience do so. Regrettably, I have nothing better to offer, so that, obnoxious as I find the prospect, I feel we may have no serious option but to continue the course we are presently pursuing until conditions for a settlement are more propitious.

This means, as I see it, that we cannot bring the war to an acceptable end until we further wear down the enemy in South Vietnam, where the issue is joined and will be determined. Such a conclusion is not pleasant or exciting, not a prescription to make anyone toss his hat in the air; yet I think it is far safer and sounder than would be the resort to either extreme — withdrawal or major escalation.

Meanwhile there are measures we can take that may improve our international posture and the chances for negotiation. Perhaps the most important is the project for building an electronic barrier south of the so-called demilitarized zone. Proposals of this kind have been intensively studied and debated within high government circles for several years. But in the past the military have opposed any project for an electronic line or fence, ostensibly on the ground that it would consume an exorbitant amount of military manpower to make any barrier reasonably effective. They have disparaged it as reflecting a "Maginot Line psychology" and have also cited the disappointing results from the celebrated electric fence which the French built along the Algerian border in an effort to stop the FLN from using Tunisia as a sanctuary.

There is, of course, some basis for these misgivings, but I suspect that the military opposition has largely stemmed from a fear that the building of a line would be used as the justification for imposing further restraint on the employment of American air power. Since that is exactly what I favor I hope that such a fear is well founded, for the principal advantage of an electronic barrier is that it could serve as the excuse and centerpiece for a new strategy. After all, not even the most dedicated proponents of an electronic fence contend that it would wholly stop infiltration; it would have to be supplemented by other interdiction efforts. Yet, with a fence, we could advantageously employ our air power in providing just that supplement. We could conduct almost continuous bombing just to the north of it — or, for that matter, on both sides of it — to stop enemy movements. This would provide reason enough for phasing out our attacks on the sensitive Hanoi-Haiphong area. It would mean achieving at long last a single and not a diffuse bombing strategy, abandoning the self-defeating hope that increasing our threat to the economic life of the North Vietnamese would produce a decision to talk rather than to dig in, and concentrating our bombing toward the single objective of reducing infiltration.

The benefits would be multiple. We would lower the pressure on the Communist powers to intervene, and make it easier for the Soviet Union to play a useful role in promoting a settlement. We would greatly cut down civilian casualties from our bombs and improve our moral position in the eyes of our friends (and, almost more important, of ourselves). Finally, we would make it easier for the North Vietnamese to come to the bargaining table, as the continued erosion of their fighting strength in the South made it clear beyond question that they could not win against our superior force, and that we were not going to quit.

By avoiding extreme actions, including the escalation of our air attacks, and by focusing our air power on a single rather than a diffuse strategic purpose, we should, in the fullness of time, create a climate that would make negotiations feasible. Yet that leaves, of course, the need for a workable negotiating formula — and, for the reasons I have stated earlier, that is not at all easy. Certainly the peace will not be secured by diplomatic gadgetry and I doubt very much that it will be secured through the agency of volunteers who have little to offer but a gleam in their eye and the purity of their amateur standing. We have had enough experiences with adventures of this kind and they have probably done more mischief than good; for, with notable exceptions, volunteers display certain deficiencies fatal to effective diplomacy. First, in their zeal to win Nobel or Pulitzer prizes, they tend to be poor reporters, hearing what they want to hear in encounters with representatives of the other side, and reading profound meaning into manners and nuances that a case-hardened diplomat would speedily write off to the artifices of the trade. Second, they are inclined to regard themselves as the central figures in dramas of high diplomatic import and can rarely resist sharing their adventures with the general public at a time when such disclosures can cause nothing but trouble.

Our best hope lies in keeping our attention fixed firmly on the nature of the struggle into which we have injected ourselves. In spite of the implications of much of our political hyperbole, the war in South Vietnam did not result from Chinese expansion but from Tonkinese imperialism. More precisely it is another chapter in a continuing effort by a strong, largely Tonkinese Communist faction that provided the leadership and much of the manpower for the Vietminh struggle against the French which began in 1945. The settlement arrived at in 1954 gave the Communist faction its home base of Tonkin together with part of Annam, creating what we have come to call North Vietnam. Yet from the outset Ho regarded this division between Northern and Southern zones as only a transient phase in his struggle to gain control of the whole of Indochina. Since then he has tried to take over Cochin China and the balance of Annam from the Western interloper (by now America) and from that group of Vietnamese who, in the view of the Viet Cong, are continuing to serve the purposes of the West. Some of Ho's faction were Southerners who remained in the South after the settlement and all through the Diem regime and the various juntas that have followed. Others infiltrated from the North where they were sent to regroup after 1954. Within the last two years, they have been joined by increasing numbers of North Vietnamese troops who have never before lived in the South and whose participation makes this clearly a war of outside aggression.

This is not Armaggedon. It is a fight against this willful and cruel Tonkinese Communist faction for a limited objective — to keep South Vietnam from falling under its control; and we should never lose sight of that limited objective. It is, in other words, a struggle between the North and South Vietnamese for the control of South Vietnam — a struggle by the South to maintain its independence and by the North to destroy it. It is, in short, a conflict in the South for the South, and that is where the issue must be decided.

The key to a solution lies in patience and flexibility — the willingness to resist extreme action and the ability not only to accommodate our own minimum requirements for a settlement to an evolving situation but, when the time comes, the will to impress those ideas on a South Vietnamese government whose interests in the months ahead will not necessarily move closer to our own. It would be folly for us — in the frustration of the moment — to give way either to despair or impetuosity. Things are not that bad. We are beginning to win a small but nasty war of attrition, and our main obstacle to a settlement is that the other side — against the background of its experience with France in 1954 — is still confused as to our intentions and skeptical of our staying power. On this point they must be disabused. If we are to induce a settlement it will come only when the Viet Cong realizes that we have passed the point of no return and will not give up. If we are sensible about it — which means confining the use of our military power almost entirely to South Vietnam — we should find a break in the clouds somewhere down the road — although I doubt that it will occur for a year or more, and almost certainly not before the 1968 elections.

Meanwhile there are large forces that may be working in our favor, not least of which is the turbulence in China that over time may be reflected in a less rigid attitude in Hanoi. And troubled as she is by Red China — and particularly China's nuclear capability — the Soviet Union may some day decide to play a more constructive role in bringing the conflict to an end.

This is not a very joyous tune to play during the winter of our discontent and I am well aware that Americans dislike being told that they must display either restraint or perseverance. Yet, as is true of others who have lived with the problem, I am clearer about what precise things we should not do than what concrete actions we should take. That is a dilemma implicit in our situation in South Vietnam, and because it is anything but a happy situation, it would be wise, while patiently searching for a way out of Vietnam, to try to find out how we got in. Such an inquiry is a healthy exercise since it should give us a greater awareness than we have so far achieved of the special problems that we Americans face when we fight in an alien land against a confusing combination of invaders and rebels in support of a people who lack political cohesion.

For Vietnam was not the beginning and it will not be the end. Like it or not, over the coming years, we shall be faced increasingly with situations where the issues are fuzzy, yet where we can involve ourselves almost absent-mindedly by taking a series of relatively small steps over a span of time. That is what happened to us in Vietnam, and it could easily happen again if we are not fully aware of how the process works.

We were not drawn into our present trouble quickly but by a slowly accelerating process of absorption sparked by a series of critical decisions.

The first was our decision in the years immediately after the war to assist the efforts of France to regain her colonial empire from the Vietminh forces of Ho Chi Minh, which had led the fight for independence from the Japanese while the Vichy French collaborators administered the country as agents of the occupying power.

All in all, we invested more than two billion dollars in support of the French and by 1954 we were paying eighty percent of their war costs.

The result of such a heavy investment of money and prestige was to make us as much an enemy of the Vietminh as France herself. This is not to suggest that, as has been sometimes suggested, we could have moderated Ho's ambitions by cultivating his friendship. For forty years he has been proclaiming his designs on the whole of Indochina and even the Lao-related peoples in northeast Thailand.

But by subsidizing the French we clearly identified ourselves with the colonial past and that has been a burden to us ever since.

This was the first major act of involvement that led to our present predicament. The second occurred when President Eisenhower, in the wake of the Geneva Accords, pushed through the SEATO Treaty that gave a security guarantee to South Vietnam and followed this by propping up the Diem government through financial aid and military advisers. That was our first commitment of American forces and prestige in that country other than the arms and financial support we had previously given to the French.

Seven years later, in the fall of 1961, we made a third decision. Faced with heightened Viet Cong activity in South Vietnam, President Kennedy sent General Maxwell Taylor and Walt Rostow on a fact-finding mission. On their return they recommended a major increase in the level of our assistance and the deployment of a greatly increased contingent of military advisers. At the time of the Taylor-Rostow mission we had, as I recall, only about eight hundred United States military advisers with the South Viet-namese — slightly over the limit fixed by the Geneva Accords — but by the end of the year we had three thousand five hundred.

President Kennedy regarded his decision to give effect to General Taylor's recommendations as a limited measure to meet the exigencies of the immediate situation; I know he never believed that he was taking a step which would lead to a large deployment of American combat forces to fight in the swamps and jungles. Nevertheless the decision gave fresh momentum to the moving stairway. It critically changed the nature of our involvement and thus provided the basis for other decisions to be made thereafter, each, in turn, based on the hope that one more increment of effort would materially improve the situation for the South Vietnamese. When that did not turn out to be the case, additional steps were necessary — each of which inevitably tended to increase our involvement in Vietnam and to give a clearer logic to every succeeding step up the stairway toward greater commitment.

This then was how it occurred. Every individual decision to expand our effort, while seeming by itself quite a small move, tended increasingly to limit our freedom of action, as one after another of our options was painted out by the evolution of events. It is characteristic of a great nation that it cannot come to the aid of another nation half-heartedly; once it invests even a limited amount of its own prestige in the enterprise, it must make sure that it succeeds. A smaller nation, such as France, could withdraw from Indo-China without serious loss of prestige or of political authority, since it could freely admit that, given the limits of its resources, the game was not worth the candle. But the authority of the United States in world affairs depends, in considerable part, on the confidence of other nations that we can accomplish whatever we undertake.

One does not have to pass final judgment on the wisdom of our total policy in order to understand the process by which America became committed as she is today. As our freedom of choice shriveled with each decision we sank more deeply into the swamp. By the time President Kennedy was assassinated, we had more than 16,500 troops in Vietnam and, before President

Johnson could break the legislative impasse that had been building up through the previous year and turn full attention to the war, we had reached a point where we had no option, except at high costs to American prestige, but to go forward. One might argue that our prestige would suffer only a short-term setback that would not in any serious way undercut our fundamental national interests, but, as each week has gone by and our involvement has grown deeper, the potential costs of extrication have acquired increasingly long-term implications.

To understand fully why the process worked as it did one had only to participate in it. Any contention that we were building a fantastically costly and elaborate enterprise on soggy and treacherous ground and that the prudent course was to establish strategically supportable fall-back positions and cut our losses depended on a whole series of assumptions that could not be proved and that might have been right or wrong — assumptions, for example, as to the endurance of the Viet Cong, the power factors at work in Hanoi and Peking and Moscow, the effect on our world prestige and authority and the credibility of our other commitments if we achieved anything less in Vietnam than our stated objectives, and finally the impact of a carefully orchestrated United States withdrawal on Thailand and Indonesia and other neighboring nations. Nor could anyone even be sure of the facts, which disasters were perpetually confounding. For a long period under the Diem Regime and particularly before General Westmoreland took command, Washington's understanding of the actual state of affairs in Vietnam was far rosier than the facts justified.

This was the atmosphere in which President Johnson during 1965 made the fourth set of critical decisions. A decision in February of that year led to the initiation of our bombing offensive against North Vietnam and a decision in the middle of the same year committed American forces unambiguously to a combat role. These were anxious and difficult decisions, taken only after long discussion and soul-searching at a time when our military leaders were making the point loud and clear that greatly increased American intervention was necessary if the Saigon government were not to fall completely apart.

I pass no judgment as to whether or not the process of increasing engagement should have worked as it did; I merely describe it, leaving all post mortems for another time. What is important today is that we face a situation and not a theory, and a sticky situation at that. For better or worse, we have come to the help of a beleaguered small land area — or, perhaps more accurately, the beleaguered people of a small country — and, over a period of years, we have found ourselves committed to direct combat with native forces on some of the worst terrain in the world.

Unfair as it may be, when the United States undertakes a struggle of this kind, we carry a burden of special disabilities that other nations do not bear.

First — and this is true only of the leader — as we commit more and more of our prestige and resources to the destiny of a troubled area, it becomes increasingly difficult for us to accept any outcome that does not fully satisfy our stated objectives.

Second, given the preponderance of our strength, we cannot fight in a foreign land against a native population without seeming to many that we have picked up the torch of white colonialist power. This is particularly true in a so-called "war of national liberation," which, almost by definition, contains a built-in ambiguity as to the nature of the conflict. Of course, we Americans do not fight against native peoples for the same motives that animated the colonial nations, yet we should be careful not to let our superior sense of moral purpose show too flamboyantly. Although belief in the "white man's burden" or even in a Western "Christianizing mission" often served as an excuse for exploitation and selfish adventuring, yet — uncongenial as those concepts may seem to modern thinking — they frequently contained a component of idealism, albeit a condescending idealism.

Third, when the United States fully commits itself to standing firm on a terrain that is not only physically forbidding but politically and sociologically complex and confused, it necessarily assumes very long-term responsibilities. No matter how well the military struggle may go in Southeast Asia, we shall have to maintain substantial forces there for a long period of time. After seventeen years, we still have fifty thousand men in South Korea, and, even if we should achieve maximum military success in South Vietnam and bring wide-scale fighting to an end, I think it likely that we would still find it necessary to continue to deploy four or five divisions — at least one hundred thousand men — in South Vietnam and Thailand and Southeast Asia for another ten or twenty years.

This does not arise from any desire on our part to play an imperial role; on the contrary most Americans would be happy if they never heard of Vietnam again. But when the United States undertakes to help build a nation and to provide the political assistance and security to maintain that nation against what is almost certain to be a constant effort of subversion, we have signed up for the duration. No matter how definitive may be the military defeat we impose upon Hanoi, the Tonkin Communists will regard it as only a tactical phase; guerrilla warfare will continue while plans are made for a later assault by other means. It would be too much to believe that the hard-core group of determined men who have led the Communist fight for more than two decades will ever give up the hope that, through one means or another, they will ultimately achieve their objective of impressing their authority and their system on the whole of Vietnam.

Fourth, when we underwrite the security of a small country we are visited with the consequences of that nation's policies whether or not we agree with them. Thus we found to our dismay that President Diem would not take our guidance in dealing with the Buddhists, and at various times during the motley parade of generals who have subsequently held office we have been embarrassed by acts and words that we found in contradiction to our own views and purposes.

This, of course, is quite an old story, for Mr. Dulles discovered Premier Diem's obstinacy very early in the game. Under the 1954 Accords all of the Vietnamese, both in the North and South, were to express their will through an election to be held in 1956 and consultations with regard to the holding of such an election were to begin on July 20, 1955, between the authorities of North and South Vietnam. Prime Minister Diem, however, refused to participate in the consultations on the ground that his government had not signed the Accords. I think it possible that Secretary Dulles could have coerced him into doing so, but he held his hand and the consultations were never held.

This was, in my judgment, a serious mistake, and we have been embarrassed by it ever since in defending the legal position of South Vietnam. Mr. Dulles was a man of experience and astuteness and, as a well-trained lawyer, knew well the advantages of forcing the adversary to make the procedural mistakes. I find it curious, therefore, that he did not press Diem more vigorously to live up to the procedural requirements of the Accords. Because North Vietnam was a police state there were demonstrable reasons why elections were out of the question and this could have been vividly shown to the world had Diem only been persuaded to attend the consultations.

Fifth, whenever we get involved in a protracted war the ends will inevitably be discolored by the means. War is brutal and brutalizing, and when brutality is made efficient by technology the means we are compelled to employ affront the humane sensitivities not only of our own people but of the rest of the world. Nor it it a completely satisfying answer to point out that the other side is still more brutal. Even though we chafe at the unfairness of it, there is and always will be a double standard whenever the United States is concerned; for we have emblazoned our shields with the device of moral purpose and the world expects a great deal more from us than from the wretched Viet Cong.

A guerrilla war is like fighting Indians and that is no fun, as we found out a hundred years ago. Sooner or later such a conflict almost inevitably settles down to a war of attrition. There is no chance for a war of maneuver involving the conquest of territory, because, even though we can sweep substantial areas, we cannot hold much of the hostile terrain of Vietnam against the infiltration tactics of the Viet Cong. As a result we are reduced to a fight in which the kill ratio becomes the only significant way of keeping score and in which our hopes for success depend on causing so much bloodshed that we break the will of the other side. From the moral point of view this is a particularly detestable type of conflict and we suffer the odium of it. A civilized people can scarcely take much comfort from the macabre statistic of each day's body count even though our own troops have been conspicuously valiant. Nor does it raise us high in the world's respect, since in spite of our own casualties the struggle does not look even. Uncomfortable as the idea makes us, it is a bitter but inescapable fact that in fighting native peoples in foreign lands we suffer from our strength. We are bigger and stronger than any small Asian nation; in fact, individual Americans are physically bigger and stronger than most Asians as the accusing eye of the television cameras makes clear, so the other side is automatically the underdog. There is, moreover, the complication that, when we are fighting Asians or Africans, the issue of race intrudes.

Our dilemma in using force is particularly frustrating since we encounter problems whatever we do. If we show no restraint in our choice of weapons we are regarded as a bully. The fact that native peoples do not have modern arms with which to respond necessarily puts us at a disadvantage in the eyes of many, even in America. (I can still recall the abhorrence with which all of us viewed Mussolini's bombing of the Ethiopians.) And Western man is particularly sensitive to methods of killing. For curious psychological reasons perhaps connected with our theological conditioning to hellfire, we regard napalm as more inhumane than claymore mines, flame-throwers as more repulsive than mortar shells.

I have been told by European friends that we Americans use our air power too casually; they attribute this to the fact that we were never attacked and hence we do not know what it means to be bombed. I do not know about that, but to many Asians employment of even conventional air power against other Asians recalls the fact that we were the only nation ever to drop nuclear bombs in warfare; they deduce from this that we would use obnoxious weapons more freely against Orientals than against Westerners. It does not matter that these suspicions and accusations are unfounded; they exist and we must accept them as a fact of world politics.

What our experience in Vietnam has taught is that there is clearly a point of no return beyond which national options tend to fade and disappear. Once America passed beyond that point in Vietnam, her only course was to go forward; otherwise, she would have disclosed her weakness rather than demonstrated her strength — and this could have had serious political consequences all over the world. The deeper lesson, of course, is that we must be at all times aware of, and on guard against, the process of creeping involvement, by which we can, without ever making an explicit decision to do so, become inextricably involved in large-scale land warfare under circumstances where the special assets of our modern industrial and military power are only of marginal value. But what are the guidelines which our experience suggests might helpfully be followed in dealing with other situations that may arise in the future? There are, it seems to me, a few broad principles that we should consult, without regarding any one of them as determinative.

First, we should be quite certain that the area involved is of sufficient strategic importance in relation to the scale of effort that may be required to defend it. Both aspects of this appraisal are difficult to make. An assessment of strategic importance depends upon our strategy, which in turn requires a well-articulated conception as to where we wish to go in the world and how we wish to use our resources.

Second, in seeking to safeguard the power balance between ourselves and the Communist powers, we should pick our battlegrounds with special reference to our own capabilities and not try to meet the adversary at every point where a challenge is made. We should carefully examine the terrain on which we may have to fight, and by this I mean not only the physical, but also the political, social and economic terrain. We should be satisfied that the materials are at hand that can make it possible for us, within a reasonable time and without a large-scale military effort on our own part, to achieve our objective.

We should be sure that there is a well-defined country to defend, a national will to defend it, and a political structure through which that will is expressed. We should avoid where possible the support of essentially reactionary regimes against revolutionary efforts that the world may regard as at least partly nationalist in motive, otherwise we may repel the younger and brighter and more progressive elements in the country. In short, we must be certain that there is a solid political base that can support the weight of our effort, since for us to try to create a base by pushing and pulling and cajoling native politicians into building an effective government may well be beyond our means.

Third, we should be clear as to whether the area in question is peripheral or central to the interests of the great Communist powers, since this could provide a clue as to the likelihood that our intervention might provoke great power conflict.

Fourth, we should examine carefully what security commitments, if any, we may have and determine how to interpret them in order to maintain maximum freedom of decision.

Fifth, before engaging ourselves in a process that could well lead to a substantial involvement, we should be reasonably sure of the support of the major industrialized nations with whom we are allied. I regard this as of major importance. It is not that we should be guided by the lowest common denominator of opinion among our major allies, since, for reasons I have repeatedly set forth, our interests will not always be the same. But a nation with our special responsibilities of leadership should hesitate a long time before letting its policies get too far out of tune with the major repositories of free world power.

Sixth, we should be careful about inheriting other people's wars. We have suffered in Vietnam because we have appeared to many as picking up the French burden and we have thus assumed many of the disabilities of the French. At the same time we should have learned enough about the problems of warfare in that tortured land no longer to patronize the French experience. During the latter stages of the Indo-Chinese struggle many Frenchmen believed, as we believe with respect to our own current involvement in Vietnam, that they were fighting for civilization against Communist aggression. Many displayed a considerable element of idealism and of compassion for the Vietnamese people. But in the world's eyes, they were still a white nation fighting native insurrectionary forces on the mainland of Asia; in other words, they were still fighting a colonial war — and, unjust as it may seem, that is the way our own Vietnamese effort appears in many parts of the world.

We Americans are not colonialists at heart and do not wish

to be. We are a country with no imperialistic drive or proconsular tradition. Yet there is a danger, as we try to fill power vacuums in distant corners of the world under soggy and difficult conditions, that we may find ourselves carrying widely dispersed responsibilities very much in the manner of the Western European nations thirty or forty years ago, with substantial numbers of our men deployed overseas in insalubrious climates, among populations that grow progressively less hospitable, attempting with valor and dedication but diminishing effectiveness to maintain order in societies where our writ runs only incompletely.

And that is not the destiny we want for ourselves.

A Summing Up

A N erudite friend, still under the spell of reading all dozen
volumes of Toynbee's massive work on the life cycle of
nations and civilizations, once said to me: "When America
has run its course, I know what headnote will appear in the
history book. It will be 'The United States — a great world power
that died of a surfeit of pragmatism.'"

I cannot wholly disagree with my friend. It seems to me that
many of our postwar policies have mixed a vague and irrelevant
universalism with a new and transitional pragmaticism: improvised crusades and crusading improvisations. And what is bad
can get worse. As we outgrow our old missionary habits we can
easily fall into a mindless and automatic pattern of dealing with
problems always for the short term, unless, quite self-consciously,
we develop a satisfactory conceptual framework in which to fit
the jagged edges of our day-to-day decisions. Great as it is, our
power is finite, and we need a clear frame of reference to tell
us how we can use it best — or whether in given situations we
should use it at all.

These thoughts are scarcely original. I have shared many of
them with colleagues in the State Department, with Secretary
Rusk and with two Presidents. But today, freed from public
responsibility with all its burdens and restraints, I find it easier
to make categoric statements and to offer personal judgments
than in the years when I was defending an official policy in open

country that offered no cover — a fair target for the *franc tireurs* to whom any bureaucrat is a sitting duck.

Yet, in spite of the relative immunity of private life, I shall shoot no bullets or even arrows at my old colleagues, for whom I have both affection and respect. I have never regarded the ambush as a decent substitute for argument, and the life of a public official is by no means roses all the way. I know full well from my own years on the exposed steppes of diplomacy that criticism is easy, that the enunciation of a bright thought is not difficult, but that the fulfillment of a serious idea in a concrete course of action can take both patience and ingenuity; and it would unfairly disparage the intelligence and imagination of the men and women I worked with in the State Department to imply that they are not — every day — testing and questioning and innovating. For these and other reasons I have thought it best to direct my comments more to the future than to the past or present lines of our foreign policy.

A first, obvious question is what are the purposes of the American people — what are our own goals and what do we want and expect from a foreign policy? That is not a question to which one expects novel answers filled with fresh insight. When asked in the past it has evoked volumes of banality, and there is no reason to put ourselves on the analyst's couch. We want, by and large, what other advanced peoples want. We should like to be safe from attack and destruction. We should like to improve our material lot and have happy and interesting individual lives. At home we should like to see less crime, more social justice, cleaner rivers and skies and an end to racial inequality. In the lands beyond we should like to have as many friends and well-wishers as possible, but we have learned from history that a rich and powerful country like our own is more likely to be envied and feared than loved and admired.

Nonetheless, we know that we have a number of natural friends and neighbors. We share with Europeans and the Western Hemisphere countries the common cultural heritage of Greece and Rome and Bethlehem, of the Renaissance, the Enlightenment and the Industrial Revolution. The political and the economic values and institutions of the United States and of the

West are the complicated mix of these shared historical traditions. Within the past century, and even more within the last
twenty years, Asians and Africans, long isolated in their own
worlds and living in their own quite different traditions, have
begun to feel the strong impact of magnetic bits and pieces of
an alien Western heritage. They are in the throes of deciding how
to amalgamate the new Western concepts with the older indigenous ones, but to a remarkable degree they are paying at least lip
service to the political ideas of the West and the economic realities
of the industrial revolution.

All this is gratifying. It is good to be emulated if not loved,
but that is not the object of the game. Foreign policy is not merely,
or even mostly, "winning the minds of men," as the tired cliché
has it; if we are playing for more than the short term, we must
order relations between nations and peoples on a basis that has
some survival value. Because no matter how many friends or imi-
tators we may acquire around the world, that alone will not secure
our peace and security. Governments, like men, cannot cope with
their mutual affairs without some kind of rational ordering process,
some sense of priorities and a disciplined search for common interests. The material to build on is the hard gneiss of power and
interest, not just the fragile lava crust of popularity, and that requires us to arrange our affairs in some durable structure. We
cannot make do with a "stream of consciousness" foreign policy,
nor can we accomplish much by extending an endless chain of
pragmatic commitments; yet, unless we do some hard and systematic conceptual thinking, that is where we may be headed a decade
hence.

A sense of priority dictates that we regard our vital interests —
things that touch our very life and existence — as most heavily
concentrated in the world's north temperate zone. That is where
our strongest competitors and all of our most deadly enemies in
this century have been located. That is the heartland of industrial might. That is the sensitive terrain where a major political
change or military upset could tilt a fragile bipolar balance of
power and bring a war of mass death in the blink of an eye. And
that is where the Southern nations look for their models of
modernity in trying to unlock the secret of a vast strength they

envy and admire and want, both for material benefit and the satisfactions of prestige. So I think the most dangerous and most hopeful and most organically significant relationships we have in the world are with our friends and neighbors and adversaries who have assimilated the industrial revolution — that is, with Western Europe and Canada and the Soviet Union and Japan — and, for special reasons of geography and history, with Latin America. This in no way implies a lack of virtue or importance in the countries of Africa, the Middle East or the other countries of Asia; it is solely a matter of the priority of our interests. We are talking about power as seen through the most vital concerns of Americans, not about the intrinsic merit or the intellectual or moral qualities or the social problems or needs of this or that state.

I suggest as a first principle, therefore, that we should make a crucial conceptual distinction in our foreign policy between the problems of the Northern Zone, on the one hand, and the peripheral Southern areas on the other. And, if our foreign policy is to be closely tied to our deepest national interests and purposes, I believe that as a second principle we should seek a better allocation of power among industrialized countries and an improved East-West balance. I know of no one who seriously argues that the present distribution of power among the Northern industrialized peoples is ideal. There is a mighty United States and there are a number of important medium-sized states, including Britain, France, Germany and Japan, each pursuing more or less separate national policies in an outworn competitive pattern. One should be able to devise a better schema and to abstract from this old pattern and from all the experience of modern history the potential for a new power structure.

We need this power structure if we ourselves are to escape from the consequences of our own breathless universalism. For two decades now we have been going it pretty much alone around the world with little restraint or useful advice from others. It has been an exciting time and — in spite of protests to the contrary — we have thoroughly enjoyed our preeminence and the possession of what has often seemed an almost limitless ability to do what we wanted. But this is not healthy as a permanent state of affairs. We need a structure in which not only are the exertions of free men more equitably shared, but, equally important, their wisdom.

I have argued at length in this book, therefore, that the Western European nations must unite, in their own interest and in that of the whole world. One can conceive of other structures, but on balance this one seems the best and most realistic for all the nations concerned. What I am suggesting is a second Western great power, capable of sharing with the United States the burdens and decisions of the West in a way the individual European nations can never do.

Implicit in my argument is the assumption that Europeans have the desire and the will to return to the world stage and that once they begin to feel the heady sense of strength and power engendered by a growing unity they will abandon their current isolationism. This assumption is, of course, not universally accepted. Many of my more erudite friends find it fashionable to contend that, having made the happy discovery that the spectator lives an easier life than the player, they will remain disengaged from any role of leadership in world politics. Thus, they argue, even were Europe united and capable of commanding vast resources, the Europeans would still avoid responsibilities outside their borders just as we Americans did in the early years of this century. It is the European's turn to enjoy a free ride, and they no longer have any ambition to push the cart.

Plausible as this argument may seem, I do not believe it. The current isolationism of Europe is based on a sense of futility that stems from the relative meagerness of the resources of individual nations and it will disappear once they combine their efforts. I cannot prove by statistics or poll-taking or footnotes that this will happen but it is the inarticulate theme in all that I have heard from my European friends and acquaintances for two decades.

More even than that, it is affirmed by a geography that has placed the Western Europeans at the heart of power and by a history that has taught them to use it. For the moment, shocked by the new magnitudes of people and resources that leadership requires, they feel futile and impotent, but that malaise would be quickly cured by the creation of central institutions speaking with the single voice of Europe and the new sense of power that would engender.

Admittedly America a half century ago was strong yet *dégagé* but that was in a simpler and more innocent age and seems hardly relevant. With the shrinking of distances and the interdependence of today's world a united Western Europe could not — even if it wished to do so — permanently dissociate itself from the world's problems.

I do not question the motives of my countrymen who take another view, yet I sometimes wonder if much of the skepticism of European intentions does not reflect the fear that a strong Europe might, after all, become not merely an active force in world politics but a force at variance with American policy. If this is in fact their unexpressed prediction then I think they are right. Europeans, strong and united, would sometimes certainly disagree with us but, if so, *tant mieux*. Are we always right?

To me the existence of a new third superpower would add greatly to our security by breaking the bipolar balance of power that presently exists between the United States and the Soviet Union. For a long time we have been like two dogs growling at one another with no restraining leash other than each side's awareness of the frightful destruction that would follow a nuclear exchange.

It should be clear that such a fragile balancing of fear is a precarious base on which to build the brave new world. Who can say that the time will never come when an unlucky mix of events propelled by a series of small decisions could produce a situation in which even great nations might lose control of their destinies? In the heat of crisis governments and peoples sometimes act with more passion than reason. Distracted by fear or a sense of outrage great nations have done self-destructive things before and they can do them again.

So let us move away, if we can, from the bipolar balance which seems to me an inherently dangerous way to order power — and at the same time let us frankly acknowledge that it exists. Lately a number of people who should know better have blandly asserted that the United States has such a lead in technology and resources

that there is in fact only one superpower. But this is arrant nonsense — one of those transient half-thoughts that have the synthetic sparkle of a fresh idea and are repeated so many times they
begin to pass as wisdom.

For what is there on the present scene to deny bipolarity? One
has merely to examine our own relative impotence to produce a
settlement in the Middle East, the subcontinent, or in Southeast
Asia, to recognize what a small way we can go toward the dispo-
sition of ancient disputes without the agreement of both the
United States and the Soviet Union. And to reverse the coin —
once we two do agree, there are few problems that cannot be
solved. Those are the facts of life for the United Nations and for
all mankind.

Thus bipolarity does exist but it does not produce a healthy
state of affairs. In my view the world would be far safer if bipolarity were succeeded, not by American supremacy, but by the
creation of a third superpower lying at the center of power yet
sharing the history and culture of the West. Then there would
be a cushioning component; all disputed questions would not
threaten a direct confrontation between the United States and the
Soviet Union.

If one looks even a little way down the road the advantages of
such a structure shine out like a beacon. Its construction would
have a sanative and moderating influence on East-West relations,
providing a mediating and leavening element during the slow
transition of the Soviet Union to political maturity and modernity.

What this contemplates, of course, is a European superpower
that would assume a kind of collective and undifferentiated world
responsibility, but it may not work out that way. The future can
take a different turning toward some form of geographical allocation; and if it does we will not be able to stop it. If the nations of
the European Economic Community continue to extend their
preferential trading system to more and more nations of Africa,
we should insist that since privileged trade carries heavy obligations the Community should assume the prime responsibility for
that poor and exploited but by now expectant continent. This
could, of course, lead by reflex to the creation of other closed systems — as for example a preferential trading system for the West-

ern Hemisphere. I hope this will not occur, since I do not believe it would be healthy to have the world cut into sections like an apple, with resultant high costs in the less efficient use of resources, the rivalry of trading blocs, and the re-creation of relations between metropolitan and client states that might uncomfortably suggest a kind of neo-colonialism. Yet, though there are dangers and disadvantages in moving away from the nondiscriminatory world trading patterns of the past, we cannot afford to be rigidly doctrinaire if the other economically advanced nations cannot be persuaded to feel as we do.

Whatever develops with regard to Africa and South America, I do not see either the Middle East or Asia falling into any closed system. In the Middle East three separate sets of conflicting forces play upon the peoples and institutions.

First, those forces set in motion by the struggle between the Arab nations and Israel which, so far as the Arab world is concerned, have a centripetal effect. In fact, without Israel as a common enemy Arab unity would not be even cyclically resurgent.

Second, the struggle between the radical and the moderate Arab states — clearly a divisive conflict. This struggle is long and continuing but today it is focused primarily on the question of whether and to what extent the U.A.R. (which contains one-third of the population of the Arab world) will be permitted to assert leadership.

Third, the cold war, which, so far as the Middle East is concerned, echoes an earlier Russian imperialism. For several reasons the Soviet Union would clearly like a strong power position in Egypt — it is an old dream of the Czars. It is key strategic real estate sitting athwart the Canal; it is a base for subversion and disruption, to threaten the oil supplies of the West; it offers a warm-water port.

For the Western nations the Middle East also has special importance. It is an area of common strategic interest and of great, but disparate, economic interests. For Britain and the United States it is a place where they have made massive direct investments which return large annual earnings to London and New York. For Britain and Continental Western Europe it is a vital source of oil but not for America, which has other sources of oil to meet its own requirements.

With this balance of interests I do not see any closed system developing in the Middle East. Nor, for quite different reasons, do I see such a system in Asia. Certainly, the United States has no desire to create one and the European nations have largely withdrawn, leaving the problems of that troubled continent in our hands. Today when Americans think of Asia they think principally of a shooting war which tends to overshadow our other Far Eastern interests. Fortunately for us and for the world, that war is on the periphery and not at the heart of power. Although the issues involved in Vietnam are grave and substantial, they need not, if we only keep our heads, result in a collision between the great powers.

It would, of course, be otherwise if the struggle were in the middle of Europe, which illustrates a point of which we never dare lose sight — the difference between center and periphery. It is as important as it is obvious. A troubled peace was kept throughout most of the nineteenth century because the then great nations confined their armed conflicts largely to peripheral areas, and in the relation of geography to power — although not in philosophy or motive — the Vietnam conflict is not unlike a colonial war. It is conducted by a major nation at a great distance from its own shores. It involves a quarrel between native peoples on a terrain that precludes the effective use of modern weapons or the collision of mass armies. It does not directly involve the vital interests of either side except to the extent that, as the struggle has proceeded, they have engaged their prestige. One can compare Vietnam in a rough way to the Balkan conflicts that continued for decades but, since they did not take place at the heart of power, did not lead to the confrontation of major nations. That occurred only when a critical shift in the European balance was threatened because a muddled German diplomacy gave a blank check to Austria-Hungary, as the Habsburg Empire began to totter.

We can live with the Vietnam war so long as we remember that it is a peripheral contest, but we do not always act as if we thought so. Sometimes we behave as though Southeast Asia did lie at the center of power — as though, for example, Saigon were Berlin and the Seventeenth Parallel the Elbe — as though, in other words, our interests everywhere were the same size. They are not, of course, and no one of our sophisticated allies believes that they are; yet there is danger that we may become the prisoner of our own rhetoric and, by placing too high a price on the conflict, disable ourselves from accepting anything but a total achievement of eloquently stated objectives — which are, I think, quite likely unattainable or attainable only at exorbitant costs in lives and risk and effort and the deflection of our national attention from other matters.

It is this last point that is often treated too lightly. It is not that the Vietnamese war is beyond our financial resources (after all our total military expenditures, high as they are, do not exceed ten percent of our national product); but any shooting war takes a large toll in the emotions of the public and the attention of the top government leaders who are responsible for navigating the ship of state in international waters. Moreover, it tends to confuse priorities and leads to navigation by a distorted chart — like something drawn by a medieval cartographer, in which Vietnam appears as a major continent lying just off our shores and threatening our national existence. Such a figure of speech obviously presents too vivid a picture, yet it points the dilemma and the danger, because when able and determined men become deeply absorbed in a continually disappointing and frustrating problem they quite understandably concentrate all the effort they can muster on its solution, and the deflection of effort and attention from other matters is inevitable.

It is, therefore, essential to restore our national equilibrium by finding a way out of Vietnam as soon as possible; otherwise our policies will become more and more eccentric until we as a nation appear crankish in the obsessional focus of our interests and efforts. But unhappily — in contrast to the claims of others who criticize our present position — I have no pat formula for extrication.

Yet the general direction in which we must move seems clear enough, and if there is one place to start, it is by recognizing the dual nature of the combat — by frankly acknowledging that we are fighting not one war but two: a war in the South resulting from our intervention in a so-called "war of national liberation" and a war in the North that consists of our bombing offensive against a Communist nation.

So far we have been careful to state our war aims solely in terms of helping Saigon win the war in the South while being quite explicit that we did not wish to destroy North Vietnam. But it is time to look again at the assumptions under which our bombing was originally undertaken since they have been emphatically disproved by events. It is time, in other words, to end the dangerous and irrelevant Northern war.

That, at least, is the place to begin, since so long as that second war continues, we shall be unlikely to find a diplomatic solution for the war in the South that will get us out of the mire and jungle. But in all realism I must point out that, unless and until the other side offers at least a token *quid pro quo*, a decision to stop bombing would be not only unpopular but politically divisive. For what confronts us is one of the all too familar dilemmas of democracy: even though our bombing offensive has proved manifestly ineffective to achieve the purposes for which it was originally launched, the acceptance of that idea will be strongly resisted; not only does it offend a deeply held faith in the efficiency of bombing, but any costly and hazardous undertaking of this kind — in which a great number of brave and dedicated men have invested their lives — necessarily tends to create its own *raison d'être*.

However it finally turns out, the war in Vietnam will not, in my view, result in anything very conclusive in the Far East. We shall continue to be faced with the problem of finding a solid base on which some durable system of power can be erected. Japan is the obvious source of future strength since she is the only large modern state in Asia. But we have far to go to cement indissoluble ties between the Japanese and the West, and it will take patience and conscious effort. It is imperative that we bring the Japanese fully within the club of industrialized nations. We must provide them with the commercial opportunities they need and desire — and this means resisting the aberrant protectionist demands of special interest groups, no matter how much they may be wrapped up in respectability. Finally — and this will take time and patience — we must encourage Japan to take a greater and greater degree of responsibility for the defense and economic development of the Far East.

China remains the enigma for everyone and, although I suggested earlier in this book that one should make no automatic correlation between power and population and that the immediate power potential of China was often exaggerated, one can still not ignore one-fourth of the human race. Yet that is what we have been trying to do by our indulgence of a shopworn fiction, and it is time we put an end to it. This should help us not only in Asia but also elsewhere in the world. So long as we persist in trying to treat Red China as though she were only a transient inconvenience and that the ultimate end of policy was to keep her from any participation in the United Nations, we shall be giving a hostage to the Afro-Asian bloc. This is a bad thing to do. It makes the United States a mendicant, it restricts our freedom of action and maneuver. Among other things it interferes with our adopting a more realistic policy toward Africa and particularly toward the highly emotional problem that stems from the existence of the White Redoubt. If we are ever to find a solution of the white settler problem, we must expose the nations of southern Africa to the winds of change rather than trying to seal them off hermetically from all amelioratory influences.

A new conceptual approach to the kinds of "threats" posed by varieties of Communism — Soviet, Chinese, Yugoslav and the like — becomes increasingly urgent. We must sooner or later stop treating the developing nations as if they were pawns in some great world struggle, and as if their political and economic idiosyncrasies had a large and decisive impact on the world balance of power. This adjustment has been made easier for us by the breaking up of a once unitary Communism into a series of protestant sects. It is now possible to raise the question — as it was not in the world climate of the 1950's — whether it is of any great political meaning or consequence if a country such as, say, Congo-Brazzaville or Burundi "goes Communist." One can complicate the question further by wondering out loud whether such "communization" might in fact not be a net gain for the

West and a nuisance to the East. And, of course, even the term "communization" is rapidly losing any very tight descriptive meaning, especially when applied to the difficult and primitive terrain of many parts of the Southern Zone.

These questions may be a bit premature, for any man who has long served in a foreign office knows that the cutting edge of Soviet designs and hostilities is still employed in all kinds of conspiratorial hanky-panky around the world, intended to discredit and weaken the United States and gain converts to the New Faith. The Chinese are premature in their charge that the Russians are ready to work hand-in-glove with Americans — it just is not so — yet it well may be that what Peking sees as a present Soviet-Western collaboration could instead be a potential future one, because, as I suggested in chapter XII, there are a number of strong forces at work today tending to increase interdependence and create natural communities of interest among all the Northern industrialized states.

With the flux of the Communist world and the uncertain outcome of today's dangerous tests in Southeast Asia and other parts of the world, it is too early to suggest an adequate full-blown conceptual alternative to the containment doctrine — which is another name for the effort to maintain mutual spheres of influence with the Communist power. But it is not too early to start thinking about one based equally on the realities of power, since a literal application of containment is growing less relevant each year and I think its time will run out in large parts of the world. For many reasons that would be a good thing. In many of the small countries of the Southern Zone containment has seemed to require as a corollary a preemptive United States reaction to the threat of a Soviet or Bulgarian or Czech military or aid program or trade mission. It has involved us as a side effect in sometimes undignified lobbying at the United Nations. I have never thought it appropriate for a great power to be the supplicant of much smaller nations.

Meanwhile, poverty remains, and illiteracy and all the horrors they bring in train, and from these the Northern nations can no longer turn their heads. It will take a fantastic effort by all concerned if the Southern countries are ever to improve their productivity in industry and agriculture while reducing it in demography; if they are ever, by making more goods than people, to achieve the self-sustaining economic and political growth to which their elites aspire and which their masses dimly but in most countries vocally comprehend. It is unfortunate that the pressures of the cold war have intruded into the Southern Zone, for those pressures set off additional alarms and confusions that have little bearing on the implacable domestic needs of the newly independent states. They are a distraction, not the reality, since, in the long run, the problems of population and economic development will be faced, if not solved, only if the industrialized countries have the wit and character to tackle them in functional rather than merely political terms.

We come back again and again, I find, to the need for a better Western power structure, since it is the basis and beginning of a rational world. Unless and until it emerges, we Americans will probably continue to go our own pragmatic way and play a more and more lonely hand in the difficult tests of the coming years. This is the logical consequence of the disparity in strength and resources between the only global power in the West and the medium-sized nations of Europe, yet I would regard it as a major tragedy. Without the leavening renascent force of a united European people, the competition and hostility of the cold war will persist far longer than need be, while new and potent hostilities could well make a tinderbox of the Old Continent. Thus for me the goal of Europe as the world's third great power is an act of logic and optimism — almost an act of faith — that derives from an attempt to rethink in structural terms the dangers and dilemmas of modern power and its implicit threats of mass death.

The thrust of American policy on this issue seems, therefore, clear enough. We must persist in encouraging the building of a unified Western Europe as we have sought to do since the war. And, in addition, we must rigorously hew to a line from which we have frequently strayed, avoiding policies and actions that might deflect European nations from that goal. Meanwhile we should be sensitive to the difference in our interests, recognizing that only when Europe builds an adequate political structure can there be anything resembling a political partnership that fully reflects the common interests of a common civilization.

I have entitled this book *The Discipline of Power* because it seems to me that we have tended in recent years to use our power not *arrogantly* — I think that is the wrong adverb — but *exuberantly.* That exuberance has shown itself in our tendency to fill power vacuums quickly and preemptively — not always counting the cost or the profit — as well as our weakness for lecturing older metropolitan countries with just a touch of self-righteousness.

Discipline, on the other hand, implies a framework, a concept — a set of objectives by which a proposed action may be measured and its costs assessed, a set of standards by which account may be taken of other peoples' interests, and power and potential. It implies also that when we employ our power we determine whether conditions are such that we can use it effectively to achieve an objective of lasting value.

I have tried in this book to point out that, in these latter years, we Americans have become so used to the possession of our power that we have sometimes disregarded its limits, ignoring the framework of fact and policy in which it was to be used, and substituting a poorly articulated universalism for a measured employment of our finite resources.

The depressing conflict in Vietnam is the dead end of such universalism. There — in that unhappy land — we let ourselves over many years be drawn deeper and deeper into a situation where our power could not be effectively employed to achieve any objective clearly in our interests. To be sure — with any luck — we will, because we are so strong, sooner or later work our way out of the present *impasse,* but it will not have been a prudent venture on our part. For even if we do achieve what we can claim as a success, it will have been like growing orchids in Alaska; possible, no doubt, but yielding nothing with value on the marketplace comparable to the extravagant cost.

Vietnam should, therefore, be a useful lesson to us, provided we read it with care; but it could also teach a noxious heresy if, in breaking away from an unreflecting universalism, we were to swing compulsively toward an even more outworn isolationism. For our power exists and it is necessary for the world's safety that we continue to use it, provided we develop a sense of the limitations of its effectiveness. To do that we must learn a greater patience, while forming a clearer conception of the framework that we can and must create in concert with other nations if the world is to be kept on a relatively steady keel.

I would not, therefore, want us to put aside our exuberance altogether — merely to temper it with both practical and conceptual thought. For while exuberance can get us into trouble, it can also be an attractive, magnetic quality, and it would, in fact, be tragic if we Americans were suddenly to become too cautious and restrained; if we were ever wholly to lose the brash, fresh vision of *Candide* — the ability to see through sham and injustice and still build a better world — as we grow up amid stern tests and dry, hard, humorless tasks.

The years ahead are largely opaque and we shall have to steer by the stars and our innate good sense. There is no prophet to foresee clearly where science, and exploding population, and a senseless arms race may lead. But optimism is still our great national asset, and we will do well to believe that we can solve these problems as we have solved others before, surmounting the years of change and perilous grace through which we are now passing, and finally — with better structures and concepts and disciplines — finding our way to a safer and more decent world.

Bibliography

Ardrey, Robert. *The Territorial Imperative*. New York: Atheneum, 1966.

Aron, Raymond. *Peace and War*. Garden City, New York: Doubleday, 1966.

Attwood, William. *The Reds and the Blacks*. New York: Harper & Row, 1967.

Auden, W. H. *The Collected Poetry of W. H. Auden*. New York: Random House, 1945.

Beloff, Nora. *The General Says No*. London: Penguin, 1963.

Birnbaum. *The Politics of Postwar Germany*. Ed. W. Stahl. New York: Praeger, 1963.

Boorstin, Daniel J. *America and the Image of Europe*. New York: Meridian, 1960.

Bullock, Alan. *Hitler, A Study in Tyranny*. New York: Bantam, 1961.

Camoëns, Luis Vaz de. *The Lusiads*. Trans. William C. Atkinson. Middlesex: Penguin, 1952.

Cook, Don. *Floodtide in Europe*. New York: Putnam, 1965.

de Gaulle, Charles. *Call to Honor, 1940-1942*. New York: Viking, 1955.

————. *Complete War Memoirs of Charles de Gaulle*. New York: Simon and Schuster, 1964.

————. *Major Addresses, Statements and Press Conferences of General Charles de Gaulle*. New York: French Embassy, Press and Information Division, 1964.

Eden, Anthony. *Full Circle*. London: Cassell, 1960.

Engels, Friedrich. *Socialism, Utopian and Scientific*. 1st English ed. New York: International Publishers, 1935.

Freymond, Jacques. *Western Europe Since the War*. New York: Praeger, 1964.

Goldman, Eric. *The Crucial Decade and After: America, 1945-1960*. New York: Vintage, 1961.

Guedalla, Philip. *Supers and Supermen*. Garden City, N.Y.: Garden City, 1924.

Haufmann, Walter. *Nietzsche*. New York: Meridian, 1961.

Heilbroner, Robert. "Counterrevolutionary America," *Commentary*, Vol. 43, No. 4, (April, 1967).

Hook, Sidney. *The Hero in History*. New York: John Day, 1943.

Jaspers, Karl. *The Question of German Guilt*. New York: Capricorn, 1961.

Kennan, George. *Russia and the West under Lenin and Stalin*. New York: Mentor, 1962.

Kennedy, John F. *Public Papers of the Presidents: John F. Kennedy*. Washington, D.C.: Government Printing Office, 1963.

Keynes, J. M. *The Economic Consequences of the Peace*. London: Macmillan, 1919.

Kissinger, Henry A. *The Necessity for Choice*. New York: Harper, 1961.

Koen, Ross Y. *The China Lobby in American Politics*. New York: Macmillan, 1960.

Kohn, Hans. *American Nationalism*. New York: Collier, 1961.

Kulski, W. W. *De Gaulle and the World*. Syracuse, N.Y.: Syracuse University Press, 1966.

Lerner, Daniel, and Raymond Aron, eds. *France Defeats EDC*. New York: Praeger, 1957.

Lippmann, Walter. *Conversations with Walter Lippmann*. Boston: Atlantic–Little, Brown, 1965.

Macmillan, Harold. *Winds of Change*. New York: Harper & Row, 1966.

Mander, John. *Great Britain or Little England?* London: Penguin, 1963.

Marx, Karl. *The Eighteenth Brumaire of Louis Bonaparte*. New York: International Publishers, 1963.

Marx, Karl, and Friedrich Engels. *The Communist Manifesto*.

Meinecke, Friedrich. *The German Catastrophe*. Boston: Beacon, 1963.

Moreira, Adriano. *Portugal's Stand in Africa*. New York: University Publishers, 1962.

Nicolson, Harold. *Diaries and Letters, 1930-1939*. Ed. N. Nicolson. New York: Atheneum, 1967.

————. *Diplomacy*. 2d ed. London: Oxford University Press, 1950.

Pinson, Koppel S. *Modern Germany*. New York: Macmillan, 1966.

Reischauer, Edwin O., and J. K. Fairbank. *East Asia and the Great Tradition*. Boston: Houghton Mifflin, 1958.

Seton-Watson, Hugh. *From Lenin to Khrushchev*. New York: Praeger, 1960.

Stanley, Timothy W. *NATO in Transition: The Future of the Atlantic Alliance*. New York: Praeger, 1965.

Thomas, Hugh. *The Suez Affair*. London: Weidenfeld & Nicolson, 1967.

Trevor-Roper, H. R. *The Last Days of Hitler*. 3d ed. New York: Collier, 1965.

Valéry, Paul. *Oeuvres*. Vol. I. Paris: Libraire Gallimard, 1957.

Wakaizumi. *A World of Nuclear Powers?* Ed. Alastair Buchan. Englewood Cliffs, N.J.: Prentice-Hall, 1966.

Williams, Francis. *A Prime Minister Remembers*. Surrey, England: Windmill Press, 1961.